PUBLIC OPINION
AND
POPULAR
GOVERNMENT

Public Opinion and Popular Government

ROBERT WEISSBERG

*University of Illinois,
Urbana Champaign*

PRENTICE-HALL, INC. *Englewood Cliffs, New Jersey*

Library of Congress Cataloging in Publication Data

Weissberg, Robert.
  Public opinion and popular government.

  Includes bibliographical references and index.
  1. Public opinion—United States. 2. United
States—Politics and government—1945- I. Title. ₁
HN90.P8W43   301.15'43'329   76-155
ISBN   0-13-737908-0

© 1976 Prentice-Hall, Inc., Englewood Cliffs, N.J.

Printed in the United States of America

10 9 8 7 6 5 4 3 2

Prentice-Hall International, Inc., *London*
Prentice-Hall of Australia Pty. Limited, *Sydney*
Prentice-Hall of Canada, Ltd., *Toronto*
Prentice-Hall of India Private Limited, *New Delhi*
Prentice-Hall of Japan, Inc., *Tokyo*
Prentice-Hall of Southeast Asia Pte. Ltd., *Singapore*

CONTENTS

v

To Max Weissberg

PREFACE

Public Opinion and Popular Government is a book about the relationship between public opinion and public policy. We are concerned with whether mass preferences and public policy can be, in some sense, consistent; whether or not they are in agreement; and whether this agreement, if it does exist, is desirable. Though we shall examine a considerable quantity of opinion data as well as information on government policy, our goal is to stress the relationship between opinion and policy, not merely describe what Americans think and what their government does. In dealing with both mass opinion and policy in the same broad context we also hope to show that the study of public opinion involves far more than the technical skills necessary to generate and interpret opinion surveys. As we shall see, the analysis of public opinion raises some of the most important and complex questions in the entire study of politics.

We approach this relationship between opinion and policy from a variety of analytical perspectives. Insofar as we spend considerable time defining terms, making distinctions, clarifying concepts, and otherwise examining the meaning of words, much of our endeavor is akin to analytical philosophy. We engage in such exercises because much of the language commonly employed in speaking about opinion and policy is unclear and imprecise. Even the simplest assertion, e.g., the government acted in accord with public sentiment, can convey any number of different meanings and unless we make some attempt to clarify the words we use, all of our analyses of concrete facts will come to naught. For example, the statement "The public gets the policies it wants" is meaningless unless we know what terms like "the public" mean.

Like most other books on public opinion we devote a considerable part of our effort to detailing the results of innumerable polls. The empirical aspect of our approach is also manifested in the vast array of data we present on government behavior. Information as diverse as Supreme Court decisions, income tax rates, execution rates, combat casualty figures, and votes in the United Nations are presented in conjunction with polls conducted by Gallup, Harris, the Survey Research Center and other polling organizations. We do not, however, merely present these data as the unchallengeable products of scientific research. Though these empirical facts constitute the core of our analyses, we share some of the skepticism of critics of survey research and are thus quite willing to note the inadequacies of both poll data and quantitative indicators of public policy.

Finally, and very much in the older tradition of public opinion writing, we are deeply concerned with some of the normative issues raised when we consider the role of mass opinion in political decision-making. Time and time again we consider such problems as what is to be gained by having mass opinion and government actions in close agreement, who should resolve questions for which no obvious answer exists (e.g., who participates in "the public"), and so on. Such questions involve personal judgments about what is desirable and undesirable politically and are thus beyond the realm of opinion polls and other empirical data. Nevertheless, such issues are central to the study of public opinion and to avoid them merely because they do not lend themselves to scientific analysis or because they are unsolvable is to rob the study of public opinion of some of its most fascinating questions.

The relationship between mass preference and government action is a subject with both a long historical tradition and a special relevance for contemporary politics. The recent popularity of slogans like "All power to the people" or "Make government more responsive to its citizens" (and all the variants) suggests that the topic of this book is not some esoteric item of scholarship. Particularly when viewed against the backdrop of dramatic increases in public mistrust of politics, analyses of ways to bring government "closer to its citizens" could be an exceptionally timely subject. Under these conditions it would be tempting to emphasize the rise and fall of "hot" issues and the corresponding public thinking. We would, in effect, write a current history with the average citizen as the principal narrator and sometime participant, courtesy of the public opinion poll.

Instead, we have stressed political issues that have endured for relatively long periods of time. To be sure, some of these issues, e.g., American intervention in Vietnam, have at one time been "burning" issues; others, such as the amount of money to be spent on national defense, have never caused intense public debate though they have been a part of the political scene for many years. In part, this decision to focus on relatively persistent issues instead of more transient questions results from the problems inherent in selecting among the literally thousands of issues that have come and gone in the last thirty years. More important, however, our emphasis on the relationship between opinion and policy requires that we focus on the interaction between public preference and government action, and such interaction is best viewed over a period of years as both opinion and policy change.

In most booklength treatments of public opinion it is customary to devote some space to the technical details of survey research. The implicit argument is that knowledge of techniques, e.g., how to draw a sample, provides a greater "understanding" of results from survey research. On occasion we too offer some technical details of polling mechanics, but we do this because such mechanics are politically relevant, not merely statistically curious. Consider, for example, the problem of sampling error (i.e., the estimation of possible discrepency between opinions offered by a sample of citizens and opinions offered by every citizen on the same question). It is possible to treat this topic in a purely statistical fashion, but such a treatment ignores the more important political fact that so long as sampling is employed to ascertain opinion, and if government heeded every public whim, the existence of sampling error would cause violations of the public will from time to time. But because sampling is much more efficient than a complete enumeration (which is practically impossible, anyhow), such violations are thus inevitable. Put more generally, we argue that there is rarely (if ever) a purely technical issue in the study of public opinion though technical questions abound. Behind each technical issue lurks a political question though such political issues are frequently settled unthinkingly.

Public Opinion and Popular Government is also a book about institutions and formal rules of politics. The study of public opinion may begin at the individual level, but it must proceed from there if we are to speak of politics and public opinion. Prior to the advent of modern survey organizations public opinion analysts were able to spend upwards of 500 pages without recourse to a table, correlation coefficient, or methodological appendix. Contemporary treatments, on the other hand, tend to emphasize quantitative data with only passing attention to the larger political context. If institutions are considered, they are more likely to be the family, school, or some other factors influencing the holding of opinion. To the extent that we consider such topics as the organization of governmental power, methods of selecting public officials, constitutional prohibition of certain behavior, procedures for direct legislation and other "formal" (as opposed to "behavioral") factors, we place individual opinion in a richer political context. Without this context, the preferences of even 200 million people are merely interesting bits of information whose political consequence is unknown.

Before the reader turns to Chapter 1, perhaps a small warning is in order. There is almost no material in subsequent chapters requiring statistical sophistication. The most elaborate statistic we use is a correlation coefficient, and even then this is employed in only a few tables. Nevertheless, much of our analysis is complicated and may very well discourage those searching for simple, unambiguous answers. Our goal is not to settle complex issues, but to expose them. Admittedly, it is sometimes tempting to hide ambiguities, contradictory findings, and various deficiencies in data for the sake of order and consistency. Of course, lest the reader be bewildered we have simplified some things; however, wherever possible we have let complexities remain. If the reader ponders the multitude of choices we lay out, bangs his or her head against the wall seeking the correct interpretation of some data, or in some other way reaches the conclusion "there are no easy answers," one of our goals will have been satisfied.

ACKNOWLEDGMENTS

It goes without saying that Brian D. Silver read almost every word in this book and tried his best to make improvements. Ben Ginsberg also offered his usual succinct advice. Thanks are also extended to Linda Skirvin, who spent many hours hunting down facts, as well as to Mayerlene Frow who did an absolutely fantastic job typing most of this book. The Jonathan R. Meigs Fund provided invaluable financial assistance. Gertrude Fitzpatrick was her usual delightful self in providing enormous clerical assistance. Lastly, I must acknowledge many of my colleagues, too numerous to mention by name, who in their own peculiar way provided important motivation and essential comic relief.

PUBLIC OPINION
AND
POPULAR
GOVERNMENT

chapter one

INTRODUCTION

A concern for public opinion is probably as old as government itself.[1] Though David Hume may have exaggerated when he stated ". . . on opinion only that government is founded. . . ," it is undoubtedly true that virtually all political leaders—from the most despotic to the democratic—must somehow take into account the preferences of common citizens. Nor has the scholarly analysis of public opinion been a uniquely modern phenomenon. Centuries before the advent of sample survey technology and computerized data processing, writers argued over the nature and role of citizen preferences in affairs of the state. Both Plato in the *Republic* and Aristotle in his *Politics* dealt with the average person's capacity to judge political questions wisely. Machiavelli, Pascal, Hobbes, Locke, Rousseau, and many other prominent philosophers have all likewise speculated on the subject of public opinion.[2] Indeed, despite the technological aura presently surrounding discussions of mass opinion, numerous lengthy and detailed empirically oriented treatments of this topic appeared well before the advent of George Gallup or Louis Harris.[3]

[1] Several studies have even gone as far back as ancient Egyptian civilization in their discussions of public opinion. See, for example, Wilhelm A. Bauer, "Public Opinion" in *Encyclopaedia of the Social Sciences,* vol. 12 (New York: Macmillan, 1934), pp. 669-74. Bauer's analysis of 4000 years of public opinion is done without reference to a single poll result.

[2] Paul A. Palmer, "The Concept of Public Opinion in Political Theory," in *Essays in History and Political Theory* (Cambridge: Harvard University Press, 1936), especially pp. 231-239.

[3] Perhaps the most sophisticated and data-based presurvey research era treatment is A. Lawrence Lowell, *Public Opinion and Popular Government* (New York: Longmans, Green, and Co., 1913). Lowell portends "modern" analyses with statistically based appendices running almost 100 pages.

1

The deep historical roots of this concern do not, of course, imply that *Vox populi* has always been celebrated and venerated. Despite attributions of great power (and sometimes even great practical wisdom) to the *Vox populi*, it has not been until relatively recent times that people have seriously argued that mass sentiment is worthy of serious political attention. Even though Aristotle, Machiavelli, and others cautioned statesmen to seek information from common men, they also certainly rejected the idea of rule by popular plebiscite. Sir Robert Peel probably reflected the ideas of most eighteenth and nineteenth century leaders when he described public opinion as "that great compound of folly, weakness, prejudice, wrong feeling, right feeling, obstinacy, and newspaper paragraphs."[4] Particularly prior to the advent of mass literacy, the argument that the unwashed, illiterate masses, obsessed with mere survival, should actually have a say in policy making would have been dismissed as an absurdity beyond debate. As Speier in his history of public opinion observes, it took a vast increase in middle-class economic position and communications development in the nineteenth century before the idea of politically relevant nonelite opinion could be seriously considered. Even then, however, "the public" was confined to only a small portion of the entire population (i.e., the informed middle class).[5]

Though popular influence in politics can be traced back to the earliest civilizations, it is certainly true that mass preferences receive the greatest political and scholarly attention in contemporary politics. Particularly in the United States, the "voice of the people" has been frequently celebrated as a perennial source of political wisdom. As Abraham Lincoln said: "With public sentiment on its side, everything succeeds, with public sentiment against it, nothing succeeds.[6] Almost 100 years later Eisenhower paid his tribute when he asserted that "Public opinion does everything."[7] No doubt a systematic review of the statements of almost every contemporary public official would uncover similar glorifications of popular sentiment.[8] Needless to say, as the unpopularity of many Lincoln and Eisenhower actions indicates, such public pronouncements are not to be taken too literally.

[4] Quoted in James Bryce, *The American Commonwealth,* vol. II, new edition (New York: The Macmillan Company, 1910), p. 259.

[5] Hans Speier, "Historical Development of Public Opinion," *American Journal of Sociology* 55(1950): 376-88. Also see Harwood L. Childs, *Public Opinion: Nature, Formation and Role* (Princeton, N.J.: D. Van Nostrand Company, 1965), pp. 26-38.

[6] Quoted in Newton N. Minow et al., *Presidential Television* (New York: Basic Books, 1973), p.10.

[7] Quoted in Matt Shermer, *"The Sense of the People" or the Next Development in American Democracy* (New York: American Referendum Association, 1969), p. 13.

[8] Actually, American officialdom as a group seems quite adept at simultaneously glorifying and rejecting the wisdom of public opinion. Many leaders seem to be saying: In the long-run the American people cannot be wrong, but in the meantime I'll follow my own best judgment regardless of public clamor. For an excellent sampling of this ambivalency, see "Whom and What Do I Represent? Selected Quotations by U.S. Representatives and Senators Regarding the Representative Role of a Member of Congress," compiled by Mary Jane Fiske (Washington, D.C., The Library of Congress Legislative Reference Service, 1966).

The United States may lead the world in ritualistic deference to public opinion, but this concern is surely not an American monopoly. Due in part to various U.S. government agencies like the United States Information Agency, foreign subsidiaries of Gallup, and various U.S. foundations, the opinion poll has become a ubiquitous phenomenon in virtually all contemporary societies. Even members of isolated African tribes can no longer escape the pollster. Moreover, such polling is hardly limited to nations calling themselves democracies or even having pretentions that popular sentiments have some political influence. In the Soviet Union, for example, surveys on a variety of topics are regularly conducted, the results are frequently published in newspaper and other periodicals, and are sometimes openly discussed at party meetings.[9] Indeed, from the perspective of a totalitarian leadership, opinion surveys are excellent methods of monitoring and controlling popular dissatisfaction.

Concommitant with the growth in the political relevance of public opinion has been a spectacular development in polling techniques and sophisticated analysis. Straw votes and opinion questionnaires are not, of course, recent innovations. As early as the 1824 Presidential election the *Harrisburg Pennsylvanian* had conducted an opinion poll by the use of straw votes on presidential preferences. The *Raleigh Star* in Raleigh, North Carolina also conducted a presidential poll in 1824.[10] Frances Galton and Charles Darwin, the English scientists of the nineteenth century, were perhaps 75 years ahead of their time as judged by critics who complained of their endless pestering questionnaires.[11] Mention has already been made of important treatises on public opinion, e.g., Thompson's *Public Opinion and Lord Beaconsfield,* published long before the emergence of modern polling technology. Nevertheless, any bibliographic review of the subject will show that the vast bulk of material on mass opinion was written after 1930. For example, one encyclopedic treatment of social psychology published in 1935 devoted one of twenty-three chapters to mass opinion related topics; in the 1954 second edition the proportion was seven of thirty.[12] With the dissemination of polling skill and the availability of

[9] John Lear, "Opinion Polling in the USSR," *Saturday Review,* October 5, 1968. More generally, see Alex Inkeles, *Public Opinion in Soviet Russia* (Cambridge: Harvard University Press, 1950).

[10] In comparison with modern random sampling methods where 1500 respondents "represent" the entire citizenry, many of these earlier polls were spectacular endeavors. For example, the 1922 *Literary Digest* poll distributed over ten *million* ballots on prohibition (however, only a "mere" 800,000 responded). This earlier era of polling is described in George Gallup and Saul Forbes Rae, *The Pulse of Democracy* (New York: Simon & Schuster, 1940), pp. 35-40.

[11] As William James put it: "Messrs. Darwin and Galtung have set the example of circulars of questions sent out by the hundreds to those able to reply. The custom has spread, and it will be well for us in the next generation if such circulars be not ranked among the common pests of life." Quoted in Leo Bogart, *Silent Politics* (New York: Wiley-Interscience, 1972), p. 14.

[12] This comparison is between the 1935 and the 1954 *Handbook of Social Psychology,* cited in Bernard Berelson, "The Study of Public Opinion," in *The State of the Social Sciences,* ed., Leonard D. White (Chicago: University of Chicago Press, 1956), p. 302.

information processing technology, the literature has grown to where it is now virtually unmeasurable.

In view of this vast and rapid development, it is not surprising that recent studies of public opinion have been characterized by a variety of perspectives. Journalists, sociologists, anthropologists, historians, psychologists, economists and political scientists can all make some claim to expertise on the subject and each focuses on a somewhat different set of questions. Even purely technical aspects of public opinion, e.g., sampling, question wording, statistical analysis, etc., have given rise to several separate academic subspecialties. Nevertheless, despite the immense diversity of the field, two broad approaches that dominate contemporary analysis can be readily distinguished. Regardless of the particular academic label they might attach to themselves, most contemporary investigators of public opinion can be described as either "psychologically" or "sociologically" oriented towards public opinion.

Typically, psychologically oriented researchers emphasize such questions as how opinions are acquired, the reasons why particular opinions are advocated, the relationship between attitudes and personality, and the process of opinion change. In contrast, a sociologically oriented analysis would stress the association between particular opinions and such characteristics as the opinion holder's race, religion, or social class. Consider, for example, the examination of preferences for socialized medical care from these differing perspectives. The psychologically oriented researcher might investigate such questions as the relationship of this opinion on medicine to other policy preferences, (e.g., government ownership of the railroads), the personal needs satisfied by holding this preference, the stability of the opinion, and the like. The sociological perspective might instead lead to analyses of this preference in terms of its distribution within economic strata, the association between age and support for socialized medicine, or whether Democrats were more in favor than Republicans. Political scientists concerned with public opinion have made extensive use of both perspectives.

Neither one of these approaches is inherently related to the study of political phenomena. Using the psychological and sociological perspectives one could just as well examine consumer behavior or premarital sex patterns as questions of political relevance. In fact, some of the seminal work in public opinion polling was conducted by organizations developed for commercial marketing research (even today the line between political and market research is sometimes exceptionally thin).[13] In both orientations to public opinion the emphasis is on

---

[13] We are not casting aspersions on the motives or capabilities of researchers who do commercial as well as scholarly polling. With one or two exceptions, there simply is not enough money to maintain an academic polling organization without taking on an occasional commercial project. Our point is that those presently concerned with public opinion would have no problem in shifting gears from, say, toothpaste preferences to policy preferences. Not surprisingly, then, many books on public opinion *and* politics are written by people with almost no training in political science and in some ways read more like marketing reports than analyses of the political process.

what the *individual* thinks, and while many social, political and economic attributes may be associated with these thoughts, analysis rarely goes beyond describing and explaining individual opinions. Important questions such as: "Do citizen preferences influence leaders?"; "Is public opinion reflected in public policy?" are infrequently considered in either the psychological or sociological approach.[14]

These two approaches to public opinion did not always dominate the subject. As Bernard Berelson makes clear in his brief history of the field, those concerned with public opinion before the days of sample surveys and mechanical data processing were more attuned to broad historical and theoretical questions than problems of technique and statistics.[15] Bryce, Lippmann, Lowell, Tönnies, Bauer, and other early authors in the field perceived public opinion as one of many forces in political life, and were thus more concerned with the relationships between opinions and political events than with individual level analyses. Professional political scientists originally involved in public opinion—people like Gosnell, Odegard, and Herring—were not pollsters. They too conceived of public opinion as a part of the larger political process. However, beginning in the early 1930s the study of public opinion became dominated by psychologists and sociologists who emphasized quantitative techniques and the writings and theoretical perspectives of the earlier approach fell into neglect.[16] To a significant extent, the work of psychologists and sociologists like Newcomb, Cantril, Lazarsfeld, and Stouffer—perhaps due to their methodological sophistication and scientific approach—became the model for subsequent work by political scientists. As Minar put it in his 1960 criticism of the contemporary study of mass opinion: "Now public opinion has become in large part the game of the psychologists and sociologists, and we may even sense a studied avoidance of the phrase by those whose main focus is the study of politics."[17]

In contrast to the two perspectives on public opinion currently dominating the field, this book will offer an alternative orientation that can perhaps be described as the political approach. That is, rather than focus exclusively on the opinions of individuals, we ask whether opinions held by common citizens are,

[14] This is not to say that such questions are never mentioned in most treatments of public opinion. However, with one or two possible exceptions, in most public opinion texts written by political scientists, such concerns are either only vaguely alluded to or superficially considered in a concluding chapter that follows only weakly from the preceding analyses.

[15] Berelson, "The Study of Public Opinion," p. 304.

[16] Berelson, "The Study of Public Opinion," p. 313.

[17] David W. Minar, "Public Opinion in the Perspective of Political Theory," *Western Political Quarterly* 13 (1960): 31. This dependence on psychological and sociological orientations to the neglect of political considerations is also criticised by Lasswell. As he put it: "At the level of fundamental theory, nothing has been added. The basic concepts of the "public" and "opinion" were as adequate in the leading scholarly writings of the nineteenth century as they have been in the twentieth." Harold D. Lasswell, "The Impact of Public Opinion Research on our Society," *Public Opinion Quarterly* 21 (1957): 33.

in some sense, related to political decision-making. Whereas the two approaches previously described concentrate on the origins, content, and distribution of popular attitudes and values, the political approach takes such information as given and relates these data to processes and policies in the political system. Our emphasis is on the political relevance of individual opinion, not the political opinions of citizens for their own sake. Merely because citizens hold certain opinions on political subjects does not mean that such opinions have an inherent political significance. If indeed public opinion is politically relevant, this relevance must be demonstrated, not assumed or merely asserted because it would be consistent with democratic ideals.

Our choice of analytical perspective is by no means a rejection of what we have called the psychological and sociological perspectives. We certainly cannot ignore the contributions made by researchers sharing these perspectives, particularly advances in methodological sophistication. The days of discussing public opinion and its relationship to politics without recourse to concrete survey data and problems of method are not to be recaptured here. Instead, we shall build on these two other perspectives by, in effect, asking: "O.K., Gallup shows that X percent of the public thinks such and such, what does this mean?" Data on individual attitudes are essential to our purposes, so we are obviously not rejecting the work of others as "wrong." Rather, we argue that to stop at this individual level is to ignore many important political questions.

We proceed in our analysis by examining five general and interrelated aspects of the relationship between public opinion and politics. First, because many of the concepts associated with "public opinion" have had a long and frequently confused history, we shall briefly consider what we mean, for instance, when we use expressions like "government by public opinion" or "the public prefer policy Y." If such expressions are to be something more than clichés, it is essential that key terms such as "public" be defined and vague relationships be clarified. For example, does the notion of "government by public opinion" require immediate citizen approval of each policy choice before the policy is executed? Or on the other hand, would approval after the decision is made be equally consistent with "government by public opinion." Questions such as these are not mere semantic or analytical exercises; they are important political issues that not only affect who wins and who loses politically, but also are relevant to the moral and ethical judgments people make on political action.

Our second general question concerns the desirability and possibility of government in accordance with public opinion. Though many (if not most) Americans unthinkingly accept the proposition that it's a good thing for government to listen to "the voice of the people," it is not self-evident that such a state of affairs would be completely advantageous to either the government or the average citizen. Policy in accordance with public preferences is only one of many political values, and it is not obvious whether most citizens or leaders rank this value ahead of all other values as guides to political action. It is also important to consider potential costs for the political system if the influence of public opinion on policy were maximized. Moreover, even if one accepted the desirability of maximizing the role of mass opinion in public policy, it is far from obvious that this goal is possible. Many laudable political goals such as perfect equality or justice are acknowledged to be unreachable but nevertheless serve as useful standards. It is entirely possible that government by public opinion may also be the type of goal that is unachievable in the real political world.

Our third question focuses not only on opinions, but on the institutions and processes of the existing American political system. Every political system is biased in favor of some processes and biased against others. For example, the pre-World War I German system which allowed those paying one-third of the taxes to elect one third of the national legislature clearly favored the political interests of the wealthy. Though the present United States constitutional system is commonly labeled as "democratic," it is by no means clear that it promotes the impact of citizen opinion on policy-making. Historically, it is certainly not true that the writers of the Constitution attempted to maximize the impact of mass opinion on policy. In considering the suitability of the constitutional order for conveying mass opinion, we shall also evaluate various alternative arrangements for translating opinion into policy. A number of schemes have recently been proposed to bring public officials and public opinion into closer agreement, e.g., a computerized link between every citizen and government. Our analysis will consider some of the costs and benefits of such proposals.

In our fourth question we turn to the opinions of the American public and the policies enacted by government. We juxtapose one against the other to answer the question of whether citizens get the policies they want. It is important to understand that in examining the congruence between public opinion and public policy we make no claim that opinion somehow causes policy. There are many ways by which mass opinions and government actions can be in accord without the former ever causing, or even influencing, the latter. To present as rich a picture as possible of the relationship between popular preferences and government, opinion and policy data from many different points in time for a variety of issues will be presented.

Our fifth and final question follows directly from the fourth: if in fact opinion-policy congruence does exist, what accounts for this relationship between mass opinions and public policy? This question will be approached at a general level. Rather than analyze opinion and policy congruence on a case by case basis, we shall instead propose three broad explanations. The first is that the public, acting through electoral mechanisms, somehow determines public policy. A second plausible explanation views the influence process as operating the reverse way—congruence is achieved by the government manipulating public preference. The third explanation is that neither the public nor the government influences each other, but each more or less shares the preference of the other so that congruence is achieved without direct action or coercion by either the public or the government. Our analysis explores the way each of these possibilities operates either to impeded or to translate public desire into public policy.

In sum, our goal is not simply to describe or explain American public opinion but also to consider the political relevance of this opinion. This involves clarifying important concepts, asking whether existing constitutional mechanisms are sufficient for such translation, whether government policy is in fact congruent with public desire, and finally, what might account for congruity or incongruity. Unlike most previous analyses of public opinion, we make no assumptions that what the American public thinks is inherently politically relevant or related to government behavior. We attempt to consider this relevance, not assume its existence. Let us begin by coming to grips with some of the complexities and ambiguities of key concepts such as "public opinion" and "public policy."

chapter two

PUBLIC OPINION AND POPULAR GOVERNMENT

At first glance the notion of government in accordance with public opinion may appear straightforward in meaning and obviously desirable. Certainly in popular discourse there is little to suggest great complexity or hidden defects. Nevertheless, before we can say whether a connection between mass opinion and public policy presently exists in the United States or should be encouraged, it is essential that we make clear what we mean by these terms. As we shall soon see, such clarification is no mere exercise in dictionary building; much of what we can legitimately say about the link between public opinion and public policy will depend greatly on the meaning given to these concepts and relationships. We begin by considering the meaning of "public opinion."

PUBLIC OPINION

The Public

The concept "public opinion" at a minimum suggests a collection of people who hold opinions on some issue. This much is clear, but when we inquire into a more precise meaning, the situation becomes muddled. What is "the public" in public opinion? The simplest solution to this problem would be to define the public as all people living with a single political community (i.e., a people sharing a government). Though initially appealing, such a conception is rarely, if ever, taken seriously. In the first place, long historical traditions support the contention that "the public" (i.e., those people whose opinions are politically relevant) must be distinguished from the masses (i.e., those people who merely inhabit a geographical area). In ancient Athens, for example, less than a quarter of the total population were considered citizens and "public opinion" was to be found only within this group. The English philosopher Burke using the criteria of knowledge and being above menial dependence calculated that only a minority of his fellow Englishmen were considered as part of "the public."[1] The others, insofar as contributing to public debate, were irrelevant. This sentiment was echoed in 1828 by W. A. Mackinnon who said:

> Public opinion may be said to be that sentiment on any given subject which is entertained by the best informed, most intelligent, and most moral persons in the community, which is gradually spread and adopted by nearly all persons of any education or proper feeling in a civilized state.[2]

By no means was this an extreme viewed during the period.[3] It is perhaps only recently with the spread of democracy that philosophers and political commentators have used terms like "public" or "the people" to mean all individuals within a political community.

Even those who reject aristocratic divisions of the populations into citizens and masses allow for some people to be excluded from "the public." For example, children are almost never viewed as being part of the public. Of course, exactly at what age a child should be included within the public, and whether a child's opinion can be politically relevant (as in the case of educational policy) are not questions readily answered. In the same way aliens, the mentally deficient and criminals are frequently excluded from membership in the political public. Such exclusions though appearing reasonable in the abstract, can be fraught with serious problems. What if political leaders decreed that all those expressing public opposition to their policies were insane or criminals and thus barred from participating in public opinion. Leaders would thus possess an easy way of insuring that their actions would always receive overwhelming "public" support. The incarceration of dissidents in mental hospitals in the Soviet Union suggests that such redefinitions of the public to achieve political tranquility is not a far-fetched technique. And, as the American incarceration of native born Japanese during World War II shows, the public can be reconstituted by creating new aliens.

A further complication is added if we follow the suggestion of people like

---

[1] Cecil S. Emden, *The People and the Constitution*, 2nd. ed. (Oxford: The Clarendon Press, 1956), Appendix I. Also, Henry B. Mayo, *An Introduction to Democratic Theory* (New York: Oxford University Press, 1960), pp. 107-21.

[2] Quoted in William Albig, *Modern Public Opinion* (New York: McGraw-Hill Book Co., 1956), p. 7.

[3] Hans Speier, "Historical Development of Public Opinion," *American Journal of Sociology,* 55(1950): 385. Also see Paul F. Lazarsfeld, "Public Opinion and the Classical Tradition," *Public Opinion Quarterly* 21(1957): 41.

Herbert Blumer and view "the public" not as a monolithic entity, but as a collection of people sharing a common interest and interacting on the basis of this common concern.[4] In this sense we would not speak of *the* public political desire; rather, we would focus on the preferences of that proportion of the population *concerned* and involved with a particular issue. This conceptualization takes as given the very reasonable claims that not everyone is interested in every issue. Hence, unless we are to attribute political relevance to those with no interest, the "public" on any given issue would be that issue's audience. This view of what constitutes "the public" makes considerable sense when dealing with opinions on relatively esoteric subjects. Certainly to ask all adults their opinions on the spending of money to develop nuclear fusion as a source of electricity would be a pointless exercise since most citizens do not even know what nuclear fusion is. In questions such as these, it can be argued, the relevant public is the scientific community specializing in nuclear research.[5]

Like our other ways of delineating the public, this issue-specific approach is fraught with difficulties. Interest or expertise (or any other delineating criteria) are rarely distributed in a black and white pattern. Some people are very interested, others slightly less interested, and so on. Thus, on any given subject it may not be obvious where "the public" begins and ends. Equally, if not more important, however, is that this conceptualization readily leads to political manipulation. It is clear that by purposely limiting information and the scope of debate, the public's composition is controlled and one's chances of winning are increased. This type of argument has frequently been made in recent years with respect to the government claim that only a few people were really able to debate intelligently such issues as American involvement in Vietnam. Since disagreement with government policy was occasionally considered prima facie evidence of inexpert knowledge, gaining "public" support for Vietnam policy was not too difficult.

An issue analogous to treating "public" as a selective group rather than the entire population arises in connection with delineating the relevant geographical

[4] Herbert Blumer, "Public Opinion and Public Opinion Polling," *American Sociological Review* 13(1948): 543-46. The conception of "the public" as a group held together by common concerns was once more common than present usage suggests. Among others, see Kimball Young, "Comments on the Nature of 'Public' and 'Public Opinion,'" *International Journal of Opinion and Attitude Research* 2(1948): 385-92 and A. Lawrence Lowell, *Public Opinion and Popular Government* (New York: Longmans, Green and Co., 1926), pp. 8-15. Lowell presents perhaps the best argument for this position when he gives the case of a traveler robbed by two highwaymen and then asks if such robbery is consistent with the public opinion of those three men. Obviously not, answers Lowell, since the victim rejects the values of his attackers.

[5] Governments are not the only organization that will occasionally try to decide who is and who is not a member of "the public." For many years automobile manufacturers claimed that they were the relevant public when it came to mandatory antipollution controls, safety equipment, and other regulations. In effect, they asserted since these issues pertained largely to them, their opinions ought to carry the greatest weight.

political community. If our aim were to ascertain the opinions of people in a particular city on a local issue it is not a foregone conclusion that the relevant public consists of only the city's population. It is reasonable to argue that many people not legally residing, but working or spending money within the city, are an integral part of the city's public. Such reasoning could also lead us to include in the relevant public all those whose tax money helps support city policies (and this number could run to the tens of millions). Going yet another logical step, imagine that the president of the United States decided (1) to send troops abroad to protect our national interests and (2) to follow public opinion in all decisions. In this instance, whose opinions are to be counted? Only the opinions of Americans? The opinions of citizens of the nation to which the troops are being sent? The opinions of the troops themselves? The opinion of anyone who might conceivably be affected by this decision (and this might include the entire world)?[6] Obviously, there exists no precise or universally accepted way of linking a particular policy to a particular "public." Though certain customary solutions to this problem are available, they are not beyond serious contention.

Opinion

Just as there are serious problems about the concept "the public," so the term "opinion" is fraught with important, politically relevant complexities. To prevent conceptual problems from getting completely out of hand, we shall define a "public opinion" as a preference for a course of action. We exclude from this definition beliefs about political reality and political values. Thus, a preference for a progressive income tax would constitute an opinion on tax policy. A belief that such a tax would lead to a decline in work motivation is not, at least for our purposes, a public opinion. Nor is a person's high esteem for financial success considered as part of public opinion. Moreover, for the sake of convenience, we limit ourselves to verbal or written opinions.[7]

But even limiting ourselves to verbal or written opinions poses some difficulties. Consider, for example, the distinction between private opinion and a statement someone might make to a poll taker or on a recording mechanism that would be kept as a permanent, available record. Though we would expect that in most cases there would be little difference between public utterances and private feelings, we cannot assume the two to be identical or even similar. This

---

[6] In the context of recent controversies over natural resources it has even been suggested that weight be given to the preferences of unborn generations. Since most public policies will affect the lives of future citizens, the type of argument is more general than merely the conservation of natural resources. A similar reasoning is sometimes employed on the abortion issue—the preferences of those yet unborn are as relevant as those currently alive.

[7] While we might consider such behavior as rioting, draft evasion, and passive resistance as expressions of opinion, such a decision would pose very severe problems of analysis. For our purposes, an opinion is a verbal or written preference for a policy.

possibility is well illustrated by the results of an experiment conducted by Hadley Cantril in which some respondents were given a regular interview while others expressed themselves through a "secret ballot." In general, discrepancies between the two methods were greatest on controversial issues. Thus, while 56 percent of the interviewed people agreed that Jews had too much power, the figure jumped to 66 percent when responses were totally anonymous.[8] Similarly, Lindsay Rogers reports of a study which showed that many people who voted for the so-called Ham n' Egg proposition in the 1938 California election would not publicly acknowledge their feelings to pollsters because the scheme had been widely characterized as "crackpot" by newspapers.[9]

These discrepencies should come as no surprise. Psychologists have long been aware of the impact of social desirability in responding to questions, and it would be unlikely if many people publicly endorsed socially undesirable positions even if they privately thought otherwise.[10] If we were to believe only publicly stated preferences, there would be virtually no market for gambling, pornography, and other morally disreputable activities. Given the need for public appearances, no doubt many citizens frequently publicly affirm what ought to be, e.g., a desire to have world peace, while privately wanting the opposite, e.g., a desire to wage atomic warfare on one's enemies. Perhaps Will Rogers put it best when he said of prohibition in Oklahoma: "Oklahomans will vote dry so long as they can stagger to the polls."

Another conceptual problem concerns how we are to evaluate opinions created by the instrument designed to measure this opinion. As an illustration, let us suppose that the government wants to determine the public's preferences on giving full diplomatic recognition to The People's Republic of China. Let us also assume that prior to this polling most citizens have never even thought about this issue of recognition. Finally, let us assume the following distribution: BEFORE THE POLL 6 percent favored recognition, 3 percent opposed recognition, and 91 percent are oblivious; AFTER THE POLL 25 percent favored recognition, 60 percent opposed recognition, and 15 percent are not sure. On the basis of this latest information the government rejects diplomatic recognition of Communist China because of public opinion. Since it is well

[8] Hadley Cantril, *Gauging Public Opinion* (Princeton: Princeton University Press, 1944), pp. 78-79.
[9] Lindsay Rogers, *The Pollsters* (New York: Alfred A. Knopf, 1949), pp. 188-89. Rogers also relates an interesting experiment in which interviewers in a race prejudice study put away their questionnaires and conducted an intensive, informal interview under the guise of "just talking." Differences in attitudes showed up in 20-25 percent of the cases. Rogers, *The Pollsters,* p. 185.
[10] This is quite reasonable, of course, since poll takers are usually total strangers and a respondant can never be sure that information about social or political deviance will not be used against them. The entire issue of inherent problems in interviewing is discussed in Eugene J. Webb, Donald T. Campbell, Richard D. Schwartz, and Lee Sechrest, *Unobtrusive Measures: Nonreactive Measures in the Social Sciences* (Chicago: Rand McNally, 1966), Chap. 1.

known that some people will offer an opinion on anything, even if they have not given the issue the slightest thought, are all the "new" opinions to be considered a legitimate expression of the popular will or rather an artifact of the process of ascertaining public feeling?[11] In some way this problem of the very measurement of something changing the phenomenon to be measured is not unlike the examining of minute objects under a microscope—the light necessary to see these objects changes what is viewed.

How we deal with opinions that derive from an immediate stimulus becomes more complicated when we realize that people can have very real preferences, but these can remain unarticulated until a person is presented by a concrete choice. Thus, in many instances, particularly among less well educated and less articulated citizens, it is essential that an interviewer actively search out preferences and fully explain alternatives rather than hope they emerge without encouragement. Indeed, it could even be argued that without such probing and explaining, many citizens will either give incomplete, shallow responses, or more likely, be relegated to the "No Opinion" category.[12] Government by public opinion would then become government by those who could readily express their positions and quickly grasp the issues, and it is unlikely that these citizens would express the same preference held by less articulate citizens.

There is, of course, an obvious difficulty and potential danger in searching for opinions when they do not initially appear to exist. Unless considerable care is exercised, an interviewer can easily steer an unsure respondent towards a particular position by using subtle cues of reinforcement and disapproval.[13] An occasional smile, a look of heightened interest, and show of approval are all essential elements of an interviewer's repertoire of techniques of encouraging

[11] From time to time an enterprising reporter will ask people their opinion on a nonsensical issue to prove public gullability and the misleading nature of poll results. Supposedly, one California reporter conducted a survey on whether the Mann Act (which forbids the transportation of females across state lines for immoral purposes) was good or bad for organized labor. Only a small percentage of those interviewed saw the absurdity of this question. Likewise, Leo Bogart tells of a question in 1948 about a nonexistent "Metallic Metals Act." Only 30 percent offered a "No Opinion" response; 59 percent agreed that it was a good thing but should be left to the individual states and 16 percent agreed that it was all right for foreign countries, but it should not be required here. Leo Bogart, *Silent Politics* (New York: Wiley Inter-Science, 1972), p. 18.

[12] For an excellent illustration of this in-depth probing technique to ascertain the political opinions of citizens who in most polls would appear to be not very articulate or interested, see Robert E. Lane, *Political Ideology* (New York: The Free Press of Glencoe, 1962). It should be added that Lane needs over 400 pages to convey the opinion of fifteen men in a way that makes sense politically.

[13] The use of subtle interviewer responses to manipulate opinion and behavior has become very well developed in recent years as a psychological therapy technique. Operant conditioning, as this technique is called, has been found effective in dealing with a wide variety of psychological ills. This technique is described in Joseph Wolpe and Arnold A. Lazarus, *Behavior Therapy Techniques* (Oxford: Pergamon Press, 1966).

communications, but such techniques can frequently result in the interviewer consciously or unconsciously manipulating policy preference. This (sometimes) unintentional cueing of respondents is well illustrated by a 1940 Gallup experiment in which interviewers also filled out questionnaires. On a question dealing with U.S. assistance to England, 60 percent of the respondents interviewed by prointerventionist interviewers endorsed aid compared to only 44 percent of the citizens questioned by antiintervention pollsters.[14] Perhaps the most famous case of interviewers cueing is a World War II poll of Blacks which asked them if they would be better off if the Japanese conquered the U.S. When the interviewer was black there was a greater willingness to say that things would be better or would not change much.[15]

Not only can a thorough probing for answers create and influence opinion, but the very nature of such probing techniques generates an enormous quantity of data, and if such data are to be relevant to concrete policy decisions, it is crucial that information be severely condensed. Here again opportunities arise to manipulate—intentionally or unintentionally—the opinion content. The usual procedure is to condense the multitude of responses into two or three broad categories, but great care must be taken to insure that these summary positions accurately reflect the original sentiments.[16] This situation of having to use only a portion of the total generated data is not unlike the one faced by the media in presenting only a small portion of a statement and yet providing an accurate picture of the entire message. If you multiply by 1500 these difficulties in accurately reducing information, it becomes apparent that ascertaining public opinion via an in-depth, probing technique presents formidable complexities and possibilities for misinterpretations.

Another problem in measuring and counting opinions concerns opinion intensity. That some people are more firmly committed to their positions than

[14] Cantril, *Gauging Public Opinion*, p. 108

[15] Cantril, *Gauging Public Opinion,* p. 116. Even if no subtle cues are given by the interviewer, the sex, manner of dress, speech accent, and other characteristics of the interviewer can have an impact. For example, lower class men exhibit a tendency to agree to various statements when the interviewer is a middle class woman. It seems that these men see agreeing to these statements as a way of not offending the nice lady. Short of having nonpersonal ways of gathering data, there is no solution to this problem (an interviewer machine may also pose problems of unintentional influence). More recent data confirming the importance of the interviewer's race are reported in Howard Schuman and Jean M. Converse, "The Effects of Black and White Interviewers on Black Responses in 1968," *Public Opinion Quarterly* 35(1971): 44-68.

[16] The pitfalls of bad pre-coding were vividly displayed in two 1942 Gallup questions on opinions of what Russia would do if it defeated Germany. In one question two alternatives were presented, but in addition, forty respondents were interviewed at greater length with no precoded answer. Only three of these forty respondents spontaneously mentioned the two precoded responses. Cantril, *Gauging Public Opinion,* p. 11.

other individuals is well known; how these differences should be treated has been a perplexing problem perhaps as old as the idea of opinion itself.[17] Consider, for example, a situation in which position X was only casually supported by an overwhelming majority and position Y was vehemently advocated by a handful of citizens willing to die for their cause (and some citizens' intensities ranged between these extremes). Should we reject a "one man, one opinion" dictum and give special weight to intense feelings? If so, exactly how much extra consideration should be given? Even if we were to define "opinion" to exclude lightly held, frivolous preferences, this would still not eliminate the problem since variations in intensity will still remain. In the real political world this problem of differences in conviction must be dealt with continually, and political philosophers have suggested all varieties of solutions, but it is clear that there exists no obvious, agreed upon formula for combining lightly held opinion with strongly held opinion to reach an overall picture of public opinion.

Our discussion of the conceptual complexities inherent in the terms "public" and "opinion" is not designed to be an exercise in speculative analysis. These are real, not imaginary, issues and are clearly relevant if leaders were to attempt to base their decisions on "true" public opinion. Consider, for example, a policy decision on air pollution control. What is the relevant public? Pollution experts? Those with some opinion on the subject? Residents of communities in which polluting industries were located? Or all those who benefit and lose as a consequence of the pollution? Similarly, what would constitute valid opinion on the subject? Would we ask even those people who never thought about the subject? Should such opinions be considered the same as opinions derived from careful study of the issues and held with deep conviction? Support could be found for all points in this controversy and since no obviously correct solutions are known, we cannot dictate that leaders accept one method of interpreting "public opinion" over another. Thus, even if leaders were fully committed to following public opinion and could learn every citizen's opinion, it is by no means certain that leaders would agree on the exact content of public opinion. Regardless of these differences, however, each leader might in good conscience claim to act upon true public opinion.

---

[17] Among others, see Willmoore Kendall and George W. Carey, "The 'Intensity' Problem and Democratic Theory," *American Political Science Review* 62 (1968): 5-24; Douglas W. Rae and Michael Taylor, *The Analysis of Political Cleavages* (New Haven: Yale University Press, 1970), Chap. 3; Robert A. Dahl, *A Preface to Democratic Theory* (Chicago: The University of Chicago Press, 1956), pp. 48-50. The usual "solution" to measuring intensity of opinion is to include both "agree" and "strongly agree" alternatives to a statement. However, this technique does not tell us whether two people feel the same degree of intensity if they choose the "strongly agree" alternative. Though social scientists frequently speak of differences in opinion intensity, an accurate way of measuring these differences does not currently exist.

Ascertaining Public Opinion

Even if we were to agree on the rules for delineating a public and criteria for describing "true" opinion, problems remain on how to ascertain these preferences. We shall subsequently examine the ways by which public opinion can actually control public policy, but for the moment let us ask the much simpler question of how we determine public political thinking. While other means besides contacting individual citizens directly are possible, let us restrict our discussion to this method.[18] We begin by considering who determines the voice of the people.

Much of what we know about public opinion in the United States currently comes from large scale commercial or academic survey organizations. The government also conducts a large number of opinion surveys, but these are rarely concerned with determining popular policy choices. That organizations like Gallup, Harris, and Roper are private, commercial organizations is not without political importance. Other than counting on their desire to be topical, there is presently no way of forcing these organizations to include questions about pressing public issues worded in a way to provide policy guidelines. Though polling organizations frequently do succeed in being timely, many issues (particularly nonnational ones) are commonly ignored or the response alternatives given citizens are imprecise instructions to leaders. Moreover, this limiting of data collection is encouraged by the commercial nature of polling organizations. Gallup, Roper, Harris and the others derive their income from fees paid by newspapers and other media, and since only a limited quantity of data can be used by the media without saturating the public's interest, financial considerations limit the scope of data gathering.[19]

A second consequence of polls being privately conducted is a lack of public accountability in their entire operations. Conducting a public opinion poll is a process involving many steps, and at each of these steps there is always the possibility of manipulation. It has been well demonstrated that such factors as

[18] Our discussion will also sidestep the question of whether people lie to interviewers. Obviously, some people do lie, but a variety of survey techniques exist for discovering minimizing and lying. A related problem is interviewer cheating—probably every large survey consists of some responses made up by the interviewer in order to simplify data gathering. Though modern sophisticated polling organizations spend considerable effort countering both interviewer and interviewee misrepresentation, the fact that it can never be completely eliminated poses problems for ascertaining "real" public opinion (especially where divisions of opinion are very close).

[19] A further problem involves the enormous cost of training and maintaining a highly competent staff. Some polling organizations cut costs by using part-time help, telephone interviews, nonrandom samples, and other corner cutting procedures and the end result is an inaccurate reading of public sentiment. Even established organizations with excellent reputations cannot always produce high quality results since the costs would be prohibitive.

sampling procedures, question wording, characteristics of interviewers, methods of recording and coding responses, and timing all can have a measurable impact on the final results.[20] Especially where an issue is closely contested and the time of release has a bearing on events, e.g., just before or after an election, important political decisions are made by private individuals who cannot be held politically responsible. This is not to suggest that the Gallups and Ropers would abuse their position to further their own political goals. Most poll organizations are characterized by a high degree of professional integrity and competence, and any obvious attempt to use their position for political gain would undoubtedly result in severe repercussions (including financial loss). Nevertheless, right now there is no way by which polling organizations can be required to act in an unbiased way.[21] This lack of public control would pose an especially difficult problem if government were to be run strictly in accord with public preferences. If this were the case, the temptation to bias polling procedures would be considerably greater.

What about the government itself running public opinion polls? Though this alternative would eliminate the problems due to commercial limitations, other equally if not more serious problems present themselves. Perhaps the most obvious is that elected officials could influence information gathering to further their own careers. Recall that President Johnson would frequently use polls on our Vietnam involvement to bolster his position against critics. When these polls became less supportive, they were conveniently ignored. Johnson was, however, largely powerless to influence the results. This might not have been the case if the data were gathered by the executive branch. Perhaps only a few sophisticated people would have noticed and objected if, for example, Americans were asked "Do you support President Johnson's decision to protect

---

[20] Roll and Cantril claim that a number of survey organizations will purposely misrepresent their findings for a fee or other consideration. This seems particularly prevalent where a poll is conducted for a candidate for public office. See Charles W. Roll, Jr., and Albert H. Cantril, *Polls: Their Use and Misuse in Politics* (New York: Basic Books, 1972), pp. 12-13. This biasing of poll results may, however, be extremely subtle and not obvious even when all the data are presented. Arthur Kornhouser's analysis of polls on organized labor suggests a number of reasons why surveys usually find extensive antilabor sentiment. For example, of 155 questions between 1940 and 1945, 81 dealt with labor's faults compared to only 8 dealing with favorable aspects of unions. Samples were frequently drawn to under represent better educated working women who tended to be prolabor. Finally, particular statistics were reported in misleading ways. Arthur Kornhouser, "The Problem of Bias in Opinion Research," *The International Journal of Opinion and Attitude Research* 1 (1947): 1-13.

[21] From time to time a public official particularly upset about some specific poll result will implore that "there ought to be a law" regarding polls. To date, no serious discussion of legislation has occured. The only regulation that exists is the National Council on Public Polls, which is run by the leading polling firms and is mainly interested in newspapers accurately reporting poll results.

South Vietnam from Communist aggression" instead of "Do you approve of our decisions to enter the war in Vietnam?" The results of the former questions no doubt would have been more pleasing to Johnson. Polls sponsored by congressmen have frequently been good illustrations of manipulative devices as opposed to information gathering mechanisms. The following question is typical of such intent:

> Do you feel demonstrators who block U.S. troop trains, burn draft cards, and send gifts and blood plasma to North Vietnam should be fined and imprisoned when such acts would be considered treasonous if we were in a declared state of war?[22]

Another, but very different, objection to government administered polls concerns the issue of the government's right to gather vast quantities of information about its citizens. The controversy over building massive data banks containing literally tens of thousands of pieces of information on citizens has highlighted this question of potential government control of its own citizens via centralized data storage. Even if we reject the argument that increased government data gathering will eventually bring totalitarian control, there still remains the issue of government officials knowing exactly who thinks what politically. Recall that during the late 1960s as a result of the Vietnam war many government officials were not only angered over outspoken dissent but were engaged in certain types of harassment and surveillance to control this dissent. A roughly comparable situation exists in the case of black militants who have publicly taken radical positions. Given past behavior, it may be reasonable not to express one's true opinion to a pollster who also happens to be a government agent. This is especially true if one's preferences were deemed highly radical or otherwise "strange." Thus, even if government administered polls were not the first step towards a 1984 totalitarian society, intentionally or unintentionally they very well could minimize dissent and provide a convenient mechanism for ferreting out political heresy.

The possibility of public opinion data being used for repressive purposes raises some interesting questions about survey methods. It is universally assumed that the ideal is a method that truthfully records every nuance of a preference. That such penetrating accuracy might be an invasion of privacy (or even a 1984 mechanism of thought control) is of little concern given the present state of polling technique. One can always play dumb or refuse to cooperate and thus be safe. However, methods of data collection based on physical reactions such as

---

[22] Quoted in Bogart, *Silent Politics,* p. 5. Congressional polls are discussed further in Harry Alpert et. al., "Congressional Use of Polls: A Symposium," *Public Opinion Quarterly* 18 (1954): 121-42.

pulse rate, pupil dilation, perspiration, and other semiinvoluntary responses are developing and these may allow "opinion" measurement regardless of individual desire or even without people being aware they are being surveyed.[23] One can even imagine information gathering techniques becoming so effective that the differences between, say, a Gallup Poll and police interrogation could vary only by content.

Even if the question of *who* was to administer polls were settled, numerous problems of *how* polls were to be conducted remain unresolved. We have already seen in our discussion of in-depth versus more superficial questioning that many ways exist to gather opinion and each of these procedures may offer certain political advantages. Another question concerns sample size. Because it is impossible to interview all citizens, scientific sampling is absolutely essential. However, though the degree to which a sample reflects a complete enumeration can be readily calculated on the basis of probability theory,[24] what should be sampled is not self-evident. Contemporary major survey organizations use samples that approximate a cross-section of the national population (usually about 1500 people). While perfectly adequate for measuring national opinions, many important groups and interests are present in such small numbers in these national samples that it is statistically impossible to ascertain their preferences.[25] This problem is largely a technical one to be overcome by significantly increasing sample size, but the increased costs of this decision would virtually require government assistance or control.

Our review of some of the conceptual problems associated with "public

[23] These techniques are reported in an unpublished paper by John Wahlke and Milton G. Lodge. Some of these results are cited in Bogart, *Silent Politics,* p. 17. Much of this development has taken place in the field of advertising where there has been a greater emphasis on "gut" nonverbal reaction.

[24] Of course, the decision to take samples of the population, as opposed to asking everyone's opinion is not a closed issue. Even samples of very large size will not convey a perfectly accurate picture of everyone's thinking. Present national samples by Gallup and other competent organizations contain about 1500 interviews and on any given opinion distribution there may be a ± 3% error due to differences between the sample and the entire population. Thus, a figure of 50 percent may really be 53 percent or 47 percent. Increasing sample size to 4,000 would only reduce this sampling error range to ± 2 percent. Substituting interviews of an entire population for samples poses enormous difficulties. Not only would such an endeavor be very expensive and time consuming, but it is highly unlikely that all members of a population could be found and interviewed. Even the U.S. Census Bureau which makes a herculean effort to contact everyone, misses tens of thousands of people. What is significant about these omissions is that these "lost people" are probably not a cross-section of the entire population (blacks in particular are "lost" by the Census).

[25] This difficulty of sampling presupposes that certain numerically small groups are important enough so that their opinion should be accurately known. In recent times this issue has come up with respect to minorities—national polls do not include sufficient data from Indians, Chicanos, Puerto Ricans, and other minorities to ascertain their opinions on matters that very much affect them, e.g., government enforcement of antidiscrimination laws.

opinion" and certain issues relating to ascertaining public opinion brings to the fore problems that must be solved one way or another. We have suggested some solutions to these issues, but perhaps the knottiest of all questions is *who* will decide, for example, what the relevant public is in a conflict or what shall constitute a preference? An answer such as "the people themselves" gets us nowhere since this method presupposes solutions to the problem who "the people" are whose opinion counts on this question. Hence, whatever solution is in force at any given moment could be questioned, with the further result that whatever the content of "public opinion" on a policy choice, some could reject this popular message as being a product of the "wrong" methods of definition and measurement.

PUBLIC OPINION AND POPULAR GOVERNMENT

The relationship between publicly stated preferences, government action, and popular government is not easy to disentangle. A number of alternative relationships between these concepts can readily be imagined. Following the pattern of previous analysis of public opinion let us begin by examining the meaning of key concepts in this relationship.

Public Policy

What does "public policy" mean? As is the case with so many political concepts, this term can mean different things to different people. To some it could mean government intention and purpose. For example, under Lyndon Johnson the federal government embarked on a massive series of programs designed to eliminate poverty. Likewise, the Employment Act of 1946 committed the national government to a policy of abolishing unemployment. Though both of these goals have been only partially realized, an enormous effort continues to be made on behalf of them. While poverty and unemployment still persist, it is (in a sense) fair to say their elimination is existing public policy.

A narrower, but perfectly legitimate, conception would emphasize the content of *legal statutes*. This approach acknowledges that the details of legislation sometimes conflict with the publicly stated purpose of a law and that the former is more important than the latter. For instance, if a person is asked what is the public policy on air pollution, he would cite the relevant legislation and, if necessary, court interpretations of these laws.

A third meaning would take the *actual behavior of public officials* as the appropriate datum in defining public policy. This conception recognizes the frequent discrepancy between what the law says and the way it is actually enforced. One of the most common illustrations of this discrepancy is the enforcement of traffic laws—policemen who allow you a certain number of miles per hour over the legal speed limit before taking action in effect raise the legally set speed limit. One of the historically well-known instances of this transformation of law was the antiunion use of the Sherman Act which was intended to control industrial monopolies and cartels. Of course, this approach can present many practical problems in analysis since the actual behavior of officials may have their own idiosyncratic behavioral guidelines. In the case of traffic law enforcement, for instance, some police might tolerate ten miles over the limit others twelve miles and so on.

Going one step further than actual behavior of officials, we could conceptualize public policy in terms of actual *outcomes* of government decision-making. It has occasionally been argued, for example, that while much recent political rhetoric and legislation has appeared to favor disadvantaged interests, the actual outcome has proven otherwise. This can readily be seen in what has happened in the area of government subsidized medical care. Though Medicare and Medicaid have aided the poor, they have also become financial windfalls for some doctors and may have raised the price of medical care for all but the very poor. Similarly, much of the money allocated to help disadvantaged school children has been a boon to middle-class educators and manufacturers of school equipment while being of only marginal value to disadvantaged children. In both of these examples one might guess that the real purpose of public policy was to help established interests while justifying it in terms of assisting the disadvantaged.

Though some of these conceptualizations may be more commonly accepted than others, all have their respective merits and advocates. Since what might be public policy according to one definition may not be public policy according to another, demonstrating a correspondence between public opinion and public policy is no simple matter. What would our judgment be if the public demanded a particular law, the law were passed and strictly enforced, but in time it became clear that the law resulted in disastrous consequences? Would this be an example of correspondence or noncorrespondence? Obviously, no authoritative answer can be given.

The Link Between Government and Public Opinion

That the actions of government ought to bear some relationship to the preferences of the public is undoubtedly accepted by most Americans. However, if we proceed beyond generalities and ask what particular type of link ought to exist, disagreements quickly arise. There are a number of differing ways by which government action and public opinion can be considered to be in agreement, or disagreement. Let us consider four alternative criteria of government action-public opinion concordance.

The most obvious kind of concordance could be characterized as strict adherence to each and every public demand. This would be government by public opinion in the most literal sense—public officials would merely register public sentiment and have no opportunity whatever for independent action. Though conceptually simple, and not without some appeal, this formulation presents serious real-world obstacles. Most conspicuous is that no public could possibly be willing and able to instruct leaders in each and every policy area. Even in an idealized New England town meeting type of government, delegation of some authority to leaders is a practical necessity for citizen and official alike. Moreover, as we have previously suggested, even if leaders were committed to adhering to public opinion, the inherent ambiguities and complexities of the public message virtually mandate some degree of official leeway of interpretation.

A second, and perhaps more reasonable linkage between the public and government action, entails the public's preferences providing broad guidelines for government action, with officials constrained to operate within these limits. For example, the public might decide that medical care should be made cheaper and more readily available, but it would be up to leaders to decide the details. Unlike the previous linkage, this criterion does not make severe, highly constraining demands. Its principal advantage is that it clearly recognizes that the public is unable to provide crystal clear instructions to leaders and that leaders require some freedom of action. This very advantage, however, also opens up a potential Pandora's box. Specifically, in many issue areas the public mandate may be construed so broadly that it may well be nearly impossible to violate it. Consider, for example, a public demand that something be done about poverty. Any number of actions, from declaring May national antipoverty month to instituting a major redistribution of wealth, would qualify as falling within the permissible bounds of public opinion. Even if the broad guidelines were made narrower, the availability of numerous alternatives still confuses a determination of the degree of congruence.[26] And, as the guidelines become increasingly specific, we approach the problems mentioned in the first formulation, i.e., strict public control.

Yet a third reasonable way of conceiving of the linkage between opinion and policy is in terms of publicly approved leadership. That is, rather than public approval of *policy* choices being the criterion for a judgment on the degree of correspondence, correspondence is said to exist when citizens support *leader-*

---

[26] In describing this type of linkage, public opinion is sometimes likened to sturdy dikes that broadly control the flow of government activity. Such imagery, though occasionally accurate, can sometimes give a misleading picture of control over policy content. An alternative, but similar, image is that of the public being a set of beaches surrounding an ocean. For example, in the years since Franklin Roosevelt's election, substantial support for increased government support for social welfare policy has existed. During this period the government's response varied from doing almost nothing to instituting major programs such as Social Security. Obviously, since "something" is being done, one could say that the public exercises some degree of control. Interpreting this type of relationship as one of real control amounts to using a very weak criteria for determining public influence.

ship. Thus, even if public officials ignore citizen policy demands, government by public opinion occurs as long as citizens generally think officials are taking the correct action. This type of support is well illustrated by Sigel's study that found over 70 percent of a Detroit sample would approve a President's defiance of public opinion in sending U.S. troops abroad.[27] Not infrequently in American history the public has rallied to support leadership despite their unpopular actions (e.g., "I don't like Nixon's Vietnam policy but we should support our president"). In some sense, this type of linkage is not unlike the granting of power of attorney—approval of actions taken on one's behalf derives not from action by action approval, but from a general confidence in those representing your interest.

A fourth and final link between public opinion and public policy is after-the-fact approval. The public's preferences *prior* to the decision would be irrelevant and leaders would have a free hand to do whatever they deem best. Once action was taken, however, public approval would be necessary; if such approval was not forthcoming, a new policy would be tried and approval sought again. Hence, poll questions such as "Do you want government to do X?" are replaced by "Do you approve or disapprove of the government doing X?" The obvious practical advantage of conceiving of the linkage in these terms is that it absolves the public from making difficult, complex evaluations of policy impact. Consider, for example, the likely difficulties citizens would encounter if asked to choose between differing policies designed to reduce inflation. It is much simpler and more efficient to accept or reject results and leave the choice of means to experts. This after-the-fact approval in some way is similar to paying for goods only after delivery and satisfactory testing. The principal danger of this approach is that it is highly vulnerable to manipulation. Particularly in the United States where government is generally viewed as competent and well-intentioned, mere government action can generate public support for a policy.[28] Hence, the easiest way to achieve perfect opinion policy congruence would be to convince a majority that the government always did the correct thing.[29]

In sum, as we have seen in our previous analyses, issues revolving around the policy impact of public opinion have no ready, self-evident solution. It would

[27] Roberta S. Sigel, "Image of the American Presidency: Part II of an Exploration into Popular Views of Presidential Power," *Midwest Journal of Political Science* 10 (1966): 123-37.

[28] This possibility of after-the-fact creation of majority opinion support is documented by Mark V. Nadel in his analysis of opinion polls on the Vietnam War before and after President Nixon's decisions. On the issues of invading Cambodia, halting the bombing of North Vietnam and rates of troop withdrawal, the president's decision substantially increased public support for these policies. Mark V. Nadel, "Public Policy and Public Opinion," in *American Democracy: Theory and Reality,* edited by Robert Weissberg and Mark V. Nadel (New York: John Wiley 1972), p. 539.

[29] The various roots of this power of manipulation and the likelihood of its elimination is further discussed in Robert Weissberg, "Mass Communications, Political Socialization, and Political Manipulation," in *American Education in the Electric Age,* ed. Peter Kling (Englewood Cliffs, N.J.: Educational Technology, 1974), pp. 78-94.

not be unreasonable for two people to disagree about whether government adhered to public opinion and yet for both of them to be correct. Indeed, when we include the distinction between "fundamental" and "trivial" policies, strong opinion and indifferent opinion, and other problems associated with mass opinion public policy linkages, it is possible to formulate many additional conditions that would, at least to some people, constitute opinion-policy congruence. With all these alternative conceptualizations available, it is unlikely that either leaders or citizens will all agree on both the criteria for opinion-policy congruence and its actual existence.

TRANSLATING INDIVIDUAL PREFERENCES INTO PUBLIC MANDATES

Assuming that solutions to the knotty conceptual questions posed in the preceding pages could be found, the problem of aggregating individual opinions into a public mandate of some kind still remains to be decided. To simplify our analysis, let us assume that such a public mandate will exist when a preference is expressed that represents the policy choices of a majority of citizens. The formulation explicitly ignores the intensity issue discussed earlier. Though the emergence of a public opinion mandate may appear to be a rather straight-forward task, numerous complexities and difficulties can intrude. Let us begin by considering whether what is publicly desired is the sum total of what is individually desired.

Economists have long been aware that what might be desirable for each citizen might be disastrous for everyone. The classic illustration of such unintended consequences is the situation where each citizen saves a large portion of his income to better himself financially, but so much money is removed from circulation that economic depression results and everyone is worse off. Many parallel situations in political preferences can be imagined. For many years Gallup polls have shown that majorities believe that existing tax levels are too high.[30] Though it is difficult to say exactly what would happen if tax rates were lowered, one likely possibility would be a sudden increase in inflation (which is opposed by nearly everyone). What most people probably really (and frequently unconsciously) mean when giving a personal preference for a tax decrease is a tax break for themselves while keeping the same tax level for everyone else. However, this message will usually get lost when hundreds of separate opinions are aggregated, so the collective message merely states widespread opposition to existing tax levels. The implementation of this demand for lower taxes would thus not be the action required to satisfy citizens' desires.

[30] Of thirteen surveys taken between March 1948 and March 1973, only in three instances did a majority not claim that taxes were too high (and only once did those saying that tax rates were about right outnumber those saying they were too high). *The Gallup Poll: Public Opinion 1935-1971* (New York: Random House, 1972) and *Gallup Opinion Index Monthly Reports.*

Besides this discrepency between individual and collective desires, there are many poll results for which there are no universally accepted rules of interpretation. One of these difficulties concerns the number of alternatives presented to citizens. Many polls solve this problem by offering only two alternatives (e.g., agree or disagree), but in many instances this procedure is a misleading oversimplification of choices. As an illustration, let us examine Table 2-1, which presents poll data on public preferences on military involvement in Vietnam (only those with an opinion are included to simplify analysis).

Table 2.1 Public Preferences on Vietnam Policy, 1972

	Issue Positions							
	Immediate and Complete Withdrawal			In-Between		Greatly Increase Military Effort		
	1	2	3	4	5	6	7	
Percentage	21.2	9.8	13.6	24.9	12.1	6.3	12.1	100.0%
Number of Respondents	482	223	310	569	276	143	275	2278

SOURCE: Survey Research Center, University of Michigan

What does this distribution of public opinion tell leaders? It could be interpreted to mean that since no particular policy receives support from more than a quarter of the sample, the public's collective decision is fragmented and leaders are thus free to do whatever they want. If the choices were simplified by collapsing adjacent categories, we find that 44.6 percent favor at least some degree of withdrawal (categories 1, 2, 3); 24.9 percent (category 4) support a balanced policy (whatever that would mean); and 30.5 percent support increased military action of one kind or another (categories 5, 6, 7). The most obvious method for generating some opinion mandate is to add the middle category to other responses. Thus, we could say that 69.5 percent (categories 1-4) reject increasing our military commitment; or 55.3 percent (categories 4-7) reject withdrawal; or even that 50.6 percent (categories 3, 4, 5) favor a "moderate" position. Since all of these figures exceed 50.0 percent, each can, in some sense, be said to convey a public mandate. There is no set of rules, either statistical or philosophical, that tells us which of these various interpretations is the correct one.

Another problem in interpreting public opinion poll data focuses on what should be done with respondents who claim no interest or express no opinion about the subject. Consider the responses to the questions whether farmers and businessmen should be allowed to trade with Communist nations (Table 2-2).

It is clear that merely by including the "not interested" in this distribution, the "Allow Trade" preference receives only a plurality of support, not a majority. (Among those with opinions, however, this choice is preferred by 65.4

Table 2.2 Public Preferences on Allowing Farmers and Businessmen to Trade with Communists, 1972

| | *Issue Positions* | | | | |
	Allow Trade with Communists	Don't Allow Trade	Not Interested	Don't Know	
Percentage	44.6	23.6	30.4	1.3	99.9%
Number of Respondents	578	306	394	17	1295

SOURCE: Survey Research Center, University of Michigan

percent.) Can we say that less than half of the American public favors trading with the Communists? Or, do we say that those favoring such trade outnumber those opposing it by an almost two to one margin? Or, do we completely throw out these poll results as politically irrelevant. In actual practice we find that all these techniques are used on occasion though justification of one method over another is rarely explicit.

Another problem in translating opinions into an interpretable message arises when we face the possibility of ties in preferences. Though an exact tie is very unlikely in any given situation, a system of government entailing frequent opinion measurement would eventually encounter some ties, and rules must be formulated to deal with this problem. Let's suppose that the public is asked whether money should be spent to send an astronaut to Mars. Let's further suppose that opinion split 50 percent to 50 percent (a 40 percent, 40 percent, 20 percent situation and the like pose similar problems, but to simplify the issue we use only a two position response and eliminate "don't knows"). If leaders conclude that no majority exists for this program, this represents a victory for the 50 percent opposed to sending someone to Mars. It is equally reasonable, of course, to argue that since a majority does not object, the program should proceed. Perhaps the easiest and most practical solution is to conduct another survey and hope that someone has changed his mind in the interim.[31]

The last problem we shall examine is what is frequently labelled "Arrow's Paradox," after Kenneth Arrow who emphasized the significance of this problem for democratic decision-making. There are numerous variations and complexities in the Arrow Paradox, but its essential character is revealed in Table 2-3, which depicts the hypothetical first, second, and third policy preferences on the Vietnam War of three groups of roughly equal size.[32]

[31] The probability of a tie on any particular poll is very small, but because many issues will be closely contested, and sampling procedure makes small percentage differences irrelevant, ties must be reckoned with. Thus, a 51 percent vs. 49 percent distribution could be classified as a tie in view of a ± 3 percent sampling error.

[32] The original problem is stated in Kenneth Arrow, *Social Choices and Individual Values* (New York: John Wiley, 1951). Further analyses of this problem are found in William H. Riker and Peter C. Ordeshook, *An Introduction to Positive Political Theory* (Englewood Cliffs, N.J.: Prentice-Hall, 1973), Chap. 4; and Gordon Tullock, *Towards a Mathematics of Politics* (Ann Arbor: The University of Michigan Press, 1967). Chap. 3.

Table 2.3   Policy Preferences on Three Groups on the Vietnam War

	Group		
	A	B	C
First choice	withdraw troops	limited involvement	escalate war
Second choice	limited involvement	escalate war	withdraw troops
Third choice	escalate war	withdraw troops	limited involvement

Each of these groups' policy preferences are all quite reasonable in the context of public debate. For example, group A corresponds with the "dove" position, group B comprises the moderate anticommunists favoring containment without risking large scale war, while group C can perhaps best be described as the "all or nothing" position—either make a big effort or do nothing at all. By summing these preferences it can readily be seen that no issue position dominates any other. Among first choices, each position receives one first place vote; if first and second choices are added together, the results remain unchanged—no choice wins. In effect, no choice can be made that is preferred by a majority. This state of affairs can be made more complex if we introduce a fourth group consisting of a single individual who favors limited involvement, withdrawing troops, and escalating war, in that order. This addition would result in "limited involvement" receiving a plurality among first choices, yet both A and C (who together constitute a clear majority) prefer withdrawing troops to a limited involvement. Many other variations and considerations could be introduced to a situation in which different groups (or individuals) held different preferences in different orders, but the important point that individual opinion need not easily add up to a collective opinion mandate should now be clear.

PUBLIC OPINION-PUBLIC POLICY CONGRUENCE VS. OTHER VALUES

To this point we have assumed that agreement between policy opinion and public policy is desired. The various complexities and ambiguities we analyzed were considered as difficulties impeding congruency between public opinion and policy. However, it must be made clear that maximizing this congruency may entail costs as well as conflict with other political values. To simplify our analysis we shall leave aside objections based on antidemocratic ideologies, e.g., fascism, that claims that citizen influence on policy is inherently wrong. Our discussion considers only these costs incurred where congruency is taken to be desirable.

One possible cost of opinion-policy congruence is a loss in government efficiency. Regardless of whether leaders are required to consult citizens on all issues or on just the broad questions, this consultation requires time. Particularly if the issue is to be publicly debated and information conveyed to all citizens, the process of choosing can become very drawn out. If consultation were frequent, it would be as if there were a continual election. Given the fact that many decisions must be implemented immediately if they are to be effective, e.g., placing economic controls on prices, lengthy debate can undermine leadership effectiveness. Moreover, especially in the area of foreign policy, open public discussion might reveal military secrets and thus weaken our international position.

Closely related to the issue of government efficiency is the question of the role of experts. Though the list of great statesmen attributing ultimate wisdom to the voice of the people is a lengthy one, such testimony is hardly conclusive proof that the people know what is best. Indeed, given the growing complexity of modern political questions and the difficulties of communicating large quantities of technical information to citizens, it would seem more reasonable to suppose that the average citizen is unable to decide as well as experts. Hence, unless the public's role is limited to deciding relatively simple issues, government by mass opinion might very well be less than competent governance.

A third argument against maximizing the role of public opinion concerns the burdens of deciding among policy choices. Not all citizens are deeply concerned about politics and these citizens may well prefer other activities than keeping abreast of public affairs and making policy decisions. To require such involvement may thus represent a real hardship on some citizens who prefer to be apolitical. Even if citizens wanted to decide public issues, the time demands of acquiring information and discussing alternatives would certainly intrude on other valued activities (e.g., watching television). Moreover, as Rosenberg has noted, political conflict by its very nature can disrupt friendships, affect employment, and expose one to various unpleasant experiences.[33] Not wanting to make one's voice heard may be irresponsible from a democratic perspective, but such behavior may be perfectly justified on personal grounds.

CONCLUSIONS

We began by stating that the idea of government in accordance with public opinion presents many more complexities than might initially be imagined. Our discussion has shown that people may reasonably differ about what constitutes government in accordance with public opinion. It follows, then, that people will also disagree about what changes must be made to achieve opinion-policy congruence or whether the existing system can be described as one in which a close opinion-policy relationship occurs.

We have not raised all these ambiguities and complexities to discredit the idea that government should follow the wishes of its citizens. Rather, by bringing

[33] Morris Rosenberg, "Some Determinants of Political Apathy" *Public Opinion Quarterly* 18 (1954): 349-66.

these issues to the surface we hope to avoid simplistic interpretations when we consider data on opinion-policy agreement. Instead of saying something like "Gallup poll data consistently show that government ignores the American public," we should append: "This last statement is true if we define "public" as the entire American population over age eighteen, "opinion" as verbal response to a highly structured question, "lack of congruity" as a noncorrespondence between opinions and legislation (as opposed to say, actual outcomes), and 50.1 percent of all people who were asked their opinion, and so on and so on until all the various complexities were settled. It would also be reasonable to question this assertion by claiming that the Gallup organization is an inappropriate tool for assessing public opinion and that a sample survey is inherently inaccurate.

We should also emphasize a point made previously—there are not ready-made, obvious answers for these complexities. The fact that some solutions are currently accepted does not preclude change. Moreover, in many instances the decision on how terms will be defined and what decision rules are to be employed may be far more important than the resources available to the contesting parties. For example, deciding to replace an urban ghetto with office buildings would probably meet a different fate if the public were defined as (a) residents, (b) the affected business community, and (c) ghetto property owners as opposed to only the residents. The criteria for what constituted an "opinion" and the rules for deciding which opinion won would also affect the outcome. In sum, the questions we have raised are not semantic and analytical quibbles; they represent some of the key problems in analyzing the whole issue of the relationship between government and its citizens.

chapter three

THE INTELLIGIBILITY
OF PUBLIC OPINION

Given the existence of large-scale polling organizations and the willingness of most Americans to offer opinions on political issues, it does not take much to get a reading of public sentiment. However, that we can get a response from the mass public does not necessarily mean that this *vox populi* is an intelligible guide to a policy maker who wishes to heed public opinion. It is certainly not true that any citizen response, individually or collectively, to a set of Gallup type questions can be considered as an interpretable, meaningful expression of a policy preference. Just as individuals can speak nonsense, so can millions of people collectively offer nonsense. Hence, before we can examine the issue of the correspondence between public opinion and public policy, we must first consider the public's capacity for meaningful opinion. Put somewhat differently, if the public were to speak, would anything intelligible be said? After all, we cannot hold leaders responsible for adhering to public opinion if there is nothing of substance to respond to.

How are we to judge whether public opinion is a reasonably clear statement of policy preferences or merely a mumbo-jumbo of poorly expressed thoughts? We assume that more is demanded from the public than picking questionnaire alternatives if leaders are to believe that such choices represent genuine messages. If public opinion were to convey intelligible messages, the following minimal criteria must be met:

1. *Political issues must be reasonably well-understood.* If people are picking policy alternatives with little or no understanding of what these choices are, we can hardly expect leaders to be guided by such decisions.

31

2. *Policy preferences must be characterized by some degree of stability.* The opposite of this would be complete fluidity in which policy alternatives for each individual might as well be decided by one's current mood or by flipping a coin. Under such circumstances of volatile and unstable preferences, public officials would face an everchanging, and hence unmeetable, set of demands.

3. *Policy preferences on similar issues must be related in some coherent manner.* Because it is impractical to ascertain public opinion on every possible issue, it should be possible to ascertain public sentiment on a number of interrelated issues from the poll results on a single broad issue. For example, if a majority favored government reducing its regulation of railroads and trucking, we should also expect a majority favoring a similar policy with respect to airline regulation. Without such opinion coherence, polls on general policy issues would be impossible.

Let us review a variety of findings on the public's capacity to offer meaningful, intelligible messages on public policy preferences.

POLITICAL UNDERSTANDING

On a person-to-person basis we would probably experience little difficulty in deciding whether someone was politically knowledgeable. However, when we ask whether an entire citizenry is knowledgeable, this determination is much more complex. First of all, exactly how much knowledge must a public possess before we can say that its opinions are knowledgeable? Certainly, it would take little effort to devise a test that would classify virtually every citizen as politically incompetent (e.g., name ten bills currently being considered by Congress). By the same token, we could argue that since everyone more or less knows what they want in life, everyone is competent to pass judgment on important political controversies. A second issue involves the extent of an individual's political knowledge. Specifically, must everyone know about all questions or can the knowledgeable citizen be one who restricts his concerns only to those issues of greatest personal importance? For example, should we expect farmers to understand issues relating to urban crime in addition to knowing about agricultural policy? If we accept this reasoning, a survey showing 90 percent of the public uninformed on farm policy would thus not necessarily demonstrate public incompetence. On the other hand, it could be argued that since issues like agricultural policy ultimately affect all citizens, this vast ignorance does indeed constitute public incompetence. The issue of the public's knowledge becomes even more complex when we realize that as we move away from simple factual knowledge, e.g., "Who's buried in Grant's Tomb?" to more difficult questions, e.g., "Does the oil depletion allowance increase the price of gasoline?" it is not always clear what constitutes an "informed" and "uninformed" opinion (experts on both sides of the oil depletion allowance controversy accuse each other of being uninformed).

Though the above problems are important, our purpose in raising them is not to formulate solutions, but rather to stimulate awareness that determining public political understanding involves many conceptual complexities. Leaving these difficulties aside, however, let us proceed to the data on the public's understanding of politics. Our analysis will begin with assessing public knowledge of simple "textbook" types of information and advance towards more demanding types of political sophistication such as the ability to figure out and identify complex events. We should note at the beginning that one type of political knowledge that will not be considered is informal savvy about how things "really" operate (as opposed to the way things merely appear to function). Knowing, say, that international Jewish bankers really run the United States may or may not be an indication of great political wisdom, but since it is nearly impossible to verify such "inside dopester" claims, we must exclude the dimensions of knowledge from our analysis.

Knowing Elementary Facts

Though the United States has virtually eliminated illiteracy and few adults lack at least eight years of formal education, opinion polls have long demonstrated that many citizens do not possess even the most elementary political knowledge. In 1945, for example, the National Opinion Research Center found that 79 percent of a national sample did not know about the Bill of Rights or anything it said![1] Similarly, in 1954 only about a third knew that the first ten amendments to the Constitution were called the Bill of Rights.[2] More recent data do not suggest that this type of "civics knowledge" has become much more widely distributed. While 50 percent of those between eighteen and twenty years old in 1954 did not know what the three branches of government were, Merelman reports that 38 percent of the high school seniors in two California cities did not know this fact (among those 50 years and older in 1954, only 15 percent could name the three branches of government).[3] Likewise, the term "electoral college" baffled almost two-thirds of the population in 1955 and in 1970 almost 40 percent of the population was unaware that Presidential tenure was limited to two terms.[4]

Not surprisingly, given people's tendency to pay closer attention to events closer to home, knowledge of many basic facts about foreign affairs is especially poor. Consider simple factual knowledge about where various countries are

[1] National Opinion Research Center (NORC), Nov. 1945. Cited in "The Polls: Textbook knowledge," ed., Hazel Guadet Erskine *Public Opinion Quarterly* 27 (1963): 137.
[2] Ibid., p. 137.
[3] The 1954 data are from a March 1954 Gallup Poll cited in *Ibid.* p. 139; the Merelman data are reported in *Political Socialization and Educational Climate* (New York: Holt, Rinehart & Winston. 1971), p. 86.
[4] The 1955 Electoral College data are from a February 1955 Gallup Poll cited in *Ibid.,* p. 139; information as the public's knowledge of the Presidential's term is from the Survey Research Center's 1970 election study.

located. In 1955 when given a map of Europe without the countries being labeled, about two-thirds of the respondents could correctly identify England and France. Only a little more than half could identify Spain; and countries like Austria, Yugoslavia and Rumania were identified by less than a fifth of the sample (in similar tests in 1947 and 1948, the location of England was better known than that of New York State).[5] This ignorance of facts about other countries is well-illustrated by a variety of questions posed in recent years about Communist China. Consider the following data:

> In 1964, 28 percent did not know that mainland China had a communist government and about the same proportion was unaware of the other Chinese government in Formosa.
>
> When asked to guess China's population in 1965, only a fifth of the respondents' estimations were within the range of 500 million to one billion.
>
> When asked who the head of the Communist Party of China was in 1966, 58 percent correctly stated Mao Tse-tung; 19 percent answered Ho Chi Minh, and 23 percent said Chiang Kai-shek.[6]

Even on issues of foreign alliances closely involving the United States, public knowledge is limited. Thus, while about three-quarters of a national poll had read or heard of NATO in 1964, only 58 percent knew that the U.S. was a member. Thirty-eight percent believed Russia to be a NATO member even though the explicit purpose of NATO was to protect Western Europe from Soviet aggression (and 21 percent included Sweden, which is not a member.)[7]

What about knowledge of people and situations that bear more directly on one's life? One type of knowledge that has considerable political relevance is knowing the names of public officials. Though the president's name is very well-known, there is considerable ignorance about less prominent officials. In 1967 Gallup reported that 70 percent of the American public claimed to know their town mayor's name (no check on accuracy is indicated by Gallup).[8] However, knowledge of state representatives is considerably lower—only about a quarter claimed to know their state Senator or Assemblyman's name. (Again, there is no indication of an accuracy check).[9] Moving to the national level, we

[5] All these data are from various Gallup Polls reported in Ibid., pp. 136-37.

[6] Cited in Don D. Smith, "Dark Areas of Ignorance Revisited: Current Knowledge About Asian Affairs," in *Political Attitudes and Public Opinion,* eds., Don D. Nimmo and Charles M. Bonjean (New York: David McKay 1972), pp. 269-72.

[7] Lloyd A. Free and Hadley Cantril, *The Political Beliefs of Americans* (New York: Simon & Schuster, 1968), p. 199.

[8] Gallup Opinion Index, February, 1967.

[9] *Ibid.* The reader should be aware that variation in how questions such as these are asked might yield very differing results. At least some citizens might recognize the representative's name without being able to recall it. Moreover, part of the reason for such ignorance could be recent court decisions requiring extensive redistricting. Thus, both in these data and similar data, ignorance may partly be attributed to the political systems as well as the individual.

find a lack of elementary factual knowledge to be a pervasive feature of contemporary politics. In 1947 Gallup reported that 38 percent claimed to know their Congressman's name, though this figure had risen to 46 percent in 1965 and 53 percent in 1970. However, in 1965 Gallup found that 70 percent did not know when their Congressman came up for reelection despite the great simplicity of the every other year system in the United States.[10] The public's knowledge of other facts about their Congressmen is even less impressive. For example, 38 percent of the public in 1970 were not aware of their Congressman's party;[11] even during the electoral campaign, data from 1964 and 1968 indicate that most citizens were ignorant of the candidates for Congress and their partisan affiliations.[12]

It is sometimes claimed that while Americans are uninformed about the details, they know enough to "throw the rascals out" when the government performs poorly. This capacity may be found among some citizens, but even here many lack the knowledge necessary to punish leaders for their errors. Dispensing electoral punishment requires knowing which Congressional candidate was the incumbent and which party controlled Congress, but polls conducted by the Survey Research Center at the University of Michigan indicate considerable ignorance of these elementary facts. For example, in 1968 while about two-thirds of the public (64 percent) correctly identified the incumbent Congressional candidate, slightly less than half (49 percent) knew which party had a Congressional majority (and would thus be more responsible for government policy).[13] Though the size of these percentages changes somewhat from year to year, and according to when during a campaign the questions are asked, the existence of fairly substantial ignorance about Congress is quite clear.

Familiarity with Political Concepts and Personalities

If citizens are to participate intelligently in political debate they must have reasonable comprehension of the terms and personalities in this discourse. Consider such poll questions as "Do you think the police should use the 'third degree' in gathering evidence?" Or, "Which political leader do you admire the most?" Each of these questions assumes some political knowledge. In the first question, an answer is meaningless unless the respondent knows what "the third degree" is.[14] A vague understanding of this concept could very well lead

[10] Gallup Opinion Index, October 1970.
[11] *Ibid.*
[12] Survey Research Center's Presidential Election studies of 1964 and 1968. In 1964 the proportions of correct responses was 31 percent; in 1968 it was 30 percent.
[13] Survey Research Center, Presidential Election Study of 1968. In 1960 this figure concerning which party controlled Congress was 64 percent; in 1964 it was 64 percent; and in 1970 it was 49 percent; and in 1972 it rose to 69 percent.
[14] The likelihood that at least some people will misunderstand even the simplest terms is much higher than a well-educated person would probably imagine. Awareness of such problems, however, only occurs where the question results run counter to expectations.

someone to agree with this statement on the grounds that the police should not be hindered in gathering evidence. A very different answer might be offered if "the third degree" were perceived as synonomous with police brutality. Similarly, regarding the question on admired leaders, only well-known leaders might be named if citizens' scope of political knowledge were limited and it might be erroneously inferred that highly visible officials were greatly admired when, in fact, they were the only ones known.

A rough idea of the public's familiarity with many of the concepts involved in various policy debates in the last forty years can be ascertained from the following survey results:

In 1947, 80 percent of the public correctly knew what the term "veto" meant. Among this knowledgeable group 88 percent knew that Congress could override a Presidential veto; however, only 63 percent of this group knew that a two-thirds majority in Congress was needed.[15]

In 1949, Gallup found that only 54 percent had a reasonably correct understanding of what "fillibuster" meant. Nineteen years later the exact question produced an identical response—54 percent giving the correct answer.[16]

The term "wiretapping" was correctly understood by 67 percent of a Gallup sample in 1949. However, twenty years later the proportion had increased to 84 percent. (Note, though, that 10 percent of this informed group could not give even a single argument for or against wiretapping).[17]

In 1949, while there was considerable public debate over what was labelled "the welfare state," only 36 percent of the public could offer a reasonably accurate description of this concept.[18]

In 1954, a little more than half the public (54 percent) could correctly identify what was meant by "farm price support."[19]

During March 1966, when the Vietnam War was rapidly expanding, 97 percent of the population had heard of this war, but 64 percent had not heard of the terms "hawk" and "dove."[20]

This is well illustrated by a survey which asked: "Should the government control profits?" When a large number of low income Negroes answered "no" researchers were puzzled. Further interviewing indicated that these respondents had *religious* prophets in mind when answering the questions. Cited in Lindzey Rogers, *The Pollsters* (New York: Alfred Knopf, 1947), p. 110.

[15] These figures recalculated from Gallup Poll data reported in "The Polls: Textbook Knowledge," ed., Hazel Gaudet Erskine, *Public Opinion Quarterly* 27 (1963): 140.

[16] The 1949 data are reported in "The Polls: The Informed Public," ed., Hazel Gaudet Erskine, *Public Opinion Quarterly* 26 (1962): 674. The 1968 data are reported in the Gallup Poll: Public Opinion 1935-1971, vol. III (New York: Random House, 1971), p. 1870.

[17] The 1949 data are reported in "The Polls: The Informed Public," p. 675; the 1969 data are from the *Gallup Poll: Public Opinion 1935-1971*, p. 2211.

[18] Gallup Poll data cited in "The Polls: The Informed Public," p. 675.

[19] *Ibid.*, p. 675.

[20] Gallup data cited in Smith, "Dark Areas of Ignorance Revisited," p. 269.

In 1960, the Survey Research Center asked respondents to provide meaning for the terms "liberal" and "conservative." Thirty-seven percent could supply no meaning whatever (and 11 percent of those who did gave a liberal definition of conservative and a conservative definition of liberal.[21]

In 1967, when the government was debating the merits of various open housing laws, 58 percent of Gallup's respondents could not say what "open housing" meant.[22]

It should be emphasized that none of these information tests requires a detailed specialized political understanding. Concepts such as "welfare state," "liberal," or "open-housing" are not esoteric technical terms, but are part of the normal public debate of issues. We must realize, however, that not knowing terminology is not the same thing as having no preference on specific issues. No doubt many of those not having the foggiest notion of what "open housing" stood for had real preferences about blacks living near them. This suggests that great care must be exercised when viewing opinion surveys containing terms such as "hawks" and "doves." Without explaining such concepts or adding information filters to eliminate the uninformed, at least some measure of opinion would be nothing more than reactions to strange words.

We encounter a similar problem of public unfamiliarity when we look at knowledge of various political personalities and groups. Though almost every citizen can name highly prominent leaders such as the president and vice-president, knowledge falls off sharply when we inquire about lesser officials.[23] For example, in 1950 and 1966 about two-thirds of the public (66 percent) could correctly identify the name of the Secretary of State.[24] Similarly, 72 percent of the public in 1965 knew that J. Edgar Hoover was the head of the F.B.I.[25] This information fall-off is well illustrated by the data in Table 3-1 which presents public familiarity with selected leaders for various years.[26]

[21]Philip E. Converse, "The Nature of Belief Systems in Mass Publics," in *Ideology and Discontent,* ed., David E. Apter (New York: Free Press, 1964), pp. 219-27. Further evidence of the public's limited understanding of "liberal" and "conservative" is provided by a 1970 Gallup Poll that asked respondents to indicate the first thing that came to their mind when they think of someone who is liberal (or conservative). Few of the responses had any concrete political meaning and many of those that did were limited to specific issues or personalities. See *The Gallup Poll: Public Opinion 1935-1971,* Vol. III, pp. 2244-45.

[22]*The Gallup Poll: Public Opinion 1935-1971,* Vol. III, p. 205-7.

[23]However, even highly placed leaders may be unknown to significant numbers of citizens. For example, in 1952 only 69 percent of a Gallup sample could name the Vice President (Barkley). Cited in "The Polls: Exposure to Domestic Informations" ed., Hazel Gaudet Erskine, *Public Opinion Quarterly* 26 (1962): 671.

[24]Cited in Smith "Dark Areas of Ignorance Revisited," p. 271.

[25]*The Gallup Poll: Public Opinion 1935-1971,* Vol. III, 1956.

[26]Since respondents were actually given names, these data probably exaggerate political awareness. A Gallup experiment in 1939 surveyed opinions on European leaders with some respondents given lists of leaders while others had to recall names by themselves. The popularity of leaders was clearly affected by their fame. See Hadley Cantril, *Gauging Public Opinion* (Princeton: Princeton University Press, 1944), p. 38.

Table 3-1 Public Familiarity with Political Leaders in
Selected Years

	Percent Correctly Identifying and Knowing What He Does
1947	
Harry Truman	98
Douglas MacArthur	97
Dwight Eisenhower	95
Thomas Dewey	91
Robert Taft	82
Henry Wallace	75
Alben Barkley	51
Harold Stassen	50
1956	
Adlai Stevenson	88
Estes Kefaufer	83
Averell Harriman	51
Lyndon Johnson	32
Stewart Symington	31
1963	
Nelson Rockefeller	78
Barry Goldwater	45
George Romney	31
William Scranton	28
1966/67	
Robert McNamara	58
George Romney	43
Dean Rusk	65
Ronald Reagan	75
George Wallace	72
Charles Percy	71

SOURCES: 1945 and 1956 Cited in "The Polls: The
Informed Public," pp. 670 and 673; 1963 and 1966/67
data are from *The Gallup Poll: Public Opinion 1935-1971,*
Vol. III, p. 1811, 1989, 1991, 1997, 2035, 2066, 2070.

Though some of these persons and their positions may be only vaguely recalled at the present, all formerly occupied prominent positions when these questions were asked. For example, Henry Wallace may seem obscure today, but in 1947 he was a recent ex-Vice-President of the United States and still very much in the public limelight as an aspirant for the presidency. Similarly, Averell Harriman at the time of the 1956 poll was the Democratic governor for New York and was seriously mentioned as a candidate for the presidency. These data, like those on the public's familiarity with political concepts, suggest that open discussions of ideas and personalities will be characterized by substantial ignorance.

Awareness of Government Policy

A third aspect of the public's capacity to offer intelligible opinions concerns the question of whether people really know what public policy is. Such knowledge is particularly crucial if we accept "after the fact" approval of government actions as a legitimate mechanism for obtaining congruency between public opinion and public policy. Obviously, such congruency would be impossible if many citizens were oblivious to government action. Even where public preferences instruct public officials, knowledge of existing policy is crucial. Consider, for example, a typical poll question such as "Do you think the government should make a larger effort to curb air pollution?" How should we interpret "yes" responses to this question if most people have no information about what officials are doing about pollution? Perhaps current policies such as tax incentives to install industrial air pollution devices are desired by people, but because of ignorance of these policies a cry goes up for "more action" when existing policy is perfectly acceptable.

Are most citizens cognizant of what their government is up to? A variety of opinion surveys going back to the 1940s all suggest considerable public ignorance of important government programs. For example, the Wagner Act passed during the Roosevelt era is an historic piece of legislation providing considerable protection to organized labor, yet in 1947 when labor legislation was still a controversial subject only 19 percent of the public had a reasonably correct understanding of this legislation.[27] A relatively better performance was given in 1950 when about two-thirds of the public (63 percent) knew what the Marshall Plan was (recall that this was the highly publicized massive aid program to European allies).[28] One of the most extensive probes of public awareness of government policy was undertaken in 1956 by the Survey Research Center. Table 3-2 presents some of these data on citizen awareness.

Table 3-2 Public Familiarity with Selected Issues, 1956

Issue	No Opinion	Hold Opinion But Do Not Know What Gov. Is Doing	Hold Opinion and Know What Gov. Is Doing
Give aid to neutral countries	28%	19%	53%
Act tough towards Russia, China	20	11	69
Leave electricity, housing to private industry	30	19	51
Segregation of schools	12	34	54
Government guarantee of jobs	10	23	67
Racial equality in jobs and housing	14	19	67
Government aid to education	10	23	67

SOURCE: Angus Campbell et al., *The American Voter* (New York: John Wiley, 1960), p. 174.

[27] "The Polls: The Informed Public," p. 673.
[28] *Ibid.*, p. 675.

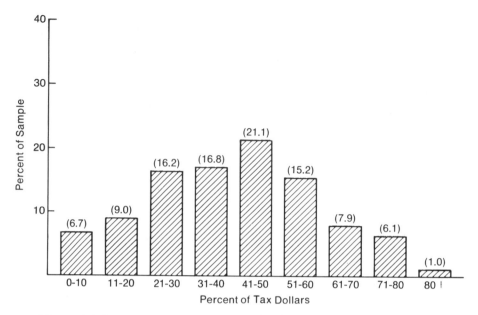

Figure 3-1 Public Estimation of How Much of Each Federal Tax Dollar Is Spent on National Defense, 1968

Correct Answer: 45%*
Percent Exactly Correct: 1.9%
Don't Know (Not Included in Calculations): 22%
*Reported in *Congress and the Nation II, 1965-1968*, p. 133

On the whole, these results do not suggest a picture of an informed citizenry avidly following the ins and outs of government policy-making. Depending on the issue, between half and a third of the public could not offer informed advice on policy changes. It is important to realize that these issues are not flash-in-the-pan current events that suddenly disappear. Issues like public ownership of utilities, segregation of schools, and aid to education had, when this poll was conducted, been part of national policy controversies for a number of years. The questions on economic policy in particular were hotly debated since the 1930s and the legislation of Roosevelt's New Deal.

In 1968 the Survey Research Center again sought to ascertain public knowledge of government policies. The method employed was to ask respondents how much of each tax dollar the national government spent for three functions—national defense, health, educational and public welfare, and foreign aid. We should emphasize that particularly the first two areas—military and social welfare spending—have been widely debated, and polls on these subjects have been taken on numerous occasions. Figures 3-1, 3-2, 3-3 display the distribution of guesses on government expenditures.

Perhaps the first thing to be noted is the relatively large proportion of people who simply answer "don't know" (the question did not require guesses in actual dollar amounts, just percentages). It is also clear that even if we make generous allowances in calculating the number of reasonably accurate guesses,

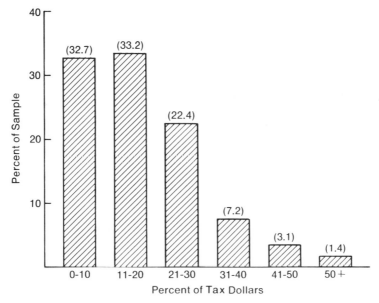

Figure 3-2 Public Estimation of How Much of Each Federal Tax Dollar Is Spent on Health, Education and Welfare Expenditures, 1968

    Correct Answer: 30.5%*
    Percent Exactly Correct: 8.8%
    Don't Know (Not Included in Calculations): 23.2%
    *Reported in *Congress and the Nation* II, 1965-1968, p. 133

the extent of misinformation is substantial. Despite the fact that military expenditures have regularly consumed about half our national budget, only about half of those giving answers guessed somewhere between 31 and 50 percent. Moreover, well over a majority seriously underestimated the 1968 commitment to social welfare activities.[29] However, if citizens underestimate social welfare, they more than make up for it in the guesses about foreign aid. The United States spent only 1.1 percent of its budget for foreign aid yet almost everyone believed that a great deal more was being spent. Given such misinformation, how could we interpret a poll that showed, say, that most people believed that the government spent too much on foreign aid? Perhaps those believing we spend thirty cents of the budget dollar on this function think it ought to be lowered to only ten cents, while those believing that ten cents per dollar was spent thought that five cents per dollar was sufficient. Both responses, however, are tabulated as "spend less for foreign aid" despite the fact that both respondents want to increase foreign aid expenditures!

    Another illustration of public unawareness of government policy can be found in popular understanding and knowledge of the United States involvement

[29] We should note, however, that ascertaining expenditures on government social welfare activities is more complex than determining military or foreign aid expenditures. For example, expenditures for veterans involving medical care, pensions, etc. are usually included under defense expenditures but could just as well be included as part of the HEW budget. Similarly, at least some programs financed by HEW are only marginally related to its welfare activities.

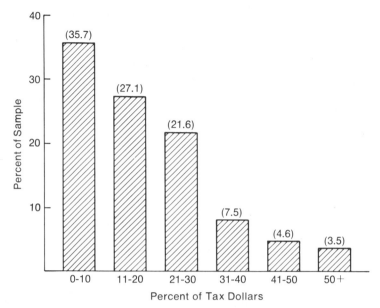

Figure 3-3 Public Estimation of How Much of Each Federal Tax Dollar Is Spent on Foreign Aid, 1968

Correct Answer: 1.1%*
Percent Exactly Correct: 1.5%
Don't Know (Not Included in Calculations): 23.8%
Reported in Congress and the Nation II, 1965-1968, p. 56

in Vietnam. The Vietnam War was sometimes called "the TV war" since it received an enormous amount of TV news exposure. Hardly a night went by for many years that TV newscasters did not report an official government proclamation on our war aims together with charts and figures on troop involvement, war deaths, bomb tonnage, *etc.* Nevertheless, surveys suggest that this involvement was poorly understood. In 1967, for instance, at the height of our commitment, Gallup reported that only 48 percent of the public claimed to know what we were fighting for in Vietnam.[30] In addition, when the number of American troops reached the 450,000 level, only 34 percent of the public knew that between 300,000 and 600,000 troops were in Vietnam (and when the number of American soliders killed was 11,600, a mere 20 percent guessed the casualty figure to be between 9,000 and 14,000).[31] Hence, for sizeable segments óf the population, Vietnam policy preferences were based on faulty information and ignorance.

Our last set of items indicating public familiarity with government actions concerns knowledge about the behavior of particular officials. In 1965, when Gallup asked Americans whether they knew how their Congressman voted in major bills this year, only 19 percent could answer yes (no check on accuracy is

[30] The Gallup Poll: *Public Opinion 1935-1971*, Vol. III, p. 2068.
[31] Cited in Smith, " 'Dark Areas of Ignorance' Revisited," p. 269.

indicated by Gallup).[32] Five years later this figure had increased to 21 percent.[33] When asked whether they could name anything their Congressman had done for their district, 86 percent could not.[34] Similarly, Gallup also found that in 1966 only 19 percent claimed to be aware of their Congressman's stand on the Vietnam War, while about one in seven said they knew his position on strikes and labor (again there is no evidence of an accuracy check).[35] To be sure, substantial evidence indicates that Congressmen who support highly unpopular policies do face electoral retribution, but outside of a few very salient issue areas, public ignorance seems to be pervasive.[36]

The Capacity for Complex Political Analysis

The fourth and last aspect of the public's political understanding we shall consider is the extent to which Americans can make sense out of complex concepts and occurrences. This capacity demands more than just knowing the facts and names. Even if all these were known, this would be no guarantee that citizens could offer intelligible opinions on policy questions. Without a minimum degree of analytical capacity, possible implications and consequences of various alternatives would remain obscure. Consider, for example, a choice on tough enforcement of antipollution laws. A reasonably astute citizen would quickly grasp that such enforcement might lead to slower economic growth, higher prices for almost everything, and unemployment in certain industries. Such drawbacks would then be systematically weighed against likely benefits. A less sophisticated citizen, however, might support such legislation without considering these disadvantages. It is entirely possible that the "real" preference of this less sophisticated citizen is for weak antipollution laws so a lack of analytical ability impedes the transmission of a "true" preference into public policy.

Measuring the American public's capacity for such analytical thinking is difficult. In the first place, what constitutes a well developed capacity for such thinking? On a more practical level, the format of most surveys prohibits all but the most superficial inquiries into a respondent's analytical capacity. As we previously discussed in Chapter 2, in-depth interviewing does have a number of costly disadvantages and can rarely be used in large-scale national samples. Our solution to this problem is to employ a number of factual questions requiring relatively sophisticated answers. In effect, these questions require the use of analytical thinking, but are not themselves direct tests of this capacity.

[32] The Gallup Poll: *Public Opinion 1935-1971*, Vol. III, p. 1969.

[33] *Gallup Opinion Index*, October 1970.

[34] The Gallup Poll: *Public Opinion 1935-1971*, Vol. III, p. 1969.

[35] Cited in Norval D. Glenn, "The Distribution of Political Knowledge in the United States," in *Political Attitude and Public Opinion*, eds., Dan D. Nimmo and Charles M. Bonjean (New York: David McKay, 1972), p. 273.

[36] This possibility is analyzed in greater detail in Donald E. Stokes and Warren E. Miller, "Party Government and the Saliency of Congress," *Public Opinion Quarterly* 26 (1962): 531-46.

Table 3-3   Perception of Which Party is More Conservative, 1960-1970

Party	Year			
	1960	1964	1968	1970
Democrats	11.0	13.5	8.8	16.3
Republican	61.2	59.3	62.8	50.8
Don't Know	27.8	27.2	28.4	32.9
N =	1811	1435	1338	1495

SOURCE: Survey Research Center, University of Michigan

One such test is the ability to associate ideological terms with political groups and policies. A straightforward measure of this ability is presented in Table 3-3, which depicts responses to the question, "Which party is more conservative?" from 1960 to 1970.

Though few would argue that every Republican is more conservative than every Democrat, the vast bulk of evidence, both scholarly and day to day events, clearly indicates the Republican party to be the more conservative of the two parties.[37] It is interesting to observe that in 1964, when the Republicans nominated Barry Goldwater, certainly one of the most conservative presidential candidates in recent times, the proportion viewing the Republicans as the conservative party was not particularly higher than in other years. All in all, though the majority of citizens "pass" this test of analytical capacity, many lack even the willingness to make a guess and a sizeable number who do guess, choose the wrong party.

A second measurement of this capacity is provided by a 1966 Gallup question on the Vietnam War. Recall from our previous discussions that in 1966 a majority had still not heard of the labels "dove" and "hawk." Even when these terms were explained, however, many citizens lacked the ability to associate correctly these concepts with well-known political leaders. For example, one-third of the self-proclaimed doves erroneously believed Ronald Reagan to share their dovish sympathies; a quarter of these doves also believed that George Wallace was a dove on the war.[38] Clearly, then, significant numbers of citizens were unable to associate important concepts with the actions of political leaders. In the light of these data, one can only speculate on what many citizens really mean if asked whether they agree with, say, Wallace's stand on Vietnam?

[37] The clearest indicator of the two parties' ideological center of gravity can be found in their collective voting records in Congress. Interest groups with clear liberal or conservative orientations, e.g., Americans for Democratic Action, have consistently rated Democratic Congressmen more liberal than Republican though exceptions exist. Some illustrative data on these ideological differences are found in *Congressional Quarterly Weekly Report,* April 16, 1971, pp. 865-67.

[38] Cited in Smith, " 'Dark Areas of Ignorance' Revisited," p. 269.

STABILITY OF POLICY PREFERENCES

Our analysis thus far has considered whether political preferences are rooted in sufficient knowledge so they can be taken seriously by political leaders. A second requirement for a preference to qualify as intelligible is that these demands are characterized by some degree of stability. Stability of a preference implies that the opinion is not a momentary, passing sentiment liable to shift with every small change in circumstances. Stability also suggests that the preference is held with some degree of conviction and is not a frivolous, inconsequential demand. In terms of actual measurement, policy preferences are considered to be stable when repeated inquiry yields similar or identical results.

The importance of this stability becomes obvious when we imagine political leaders trying to satisfy a continually shifting pattern of policy preferences. Few, if any, public policies can be adjusted on a day to day or week to week basis to keep in tune with shifting public sentiment. The net effect of any attempt to follow such opinion gyration would be political chaos. No doubt, practical considerations would require that citizen opinion be disregarded under such conditions.

To what extent are policy preferences strongly anchored, relatively enduring dispositions? An important major piece of research on this subject is the panel study conducted by the Survey Research Center in 1956, 1958 and 1960. Unlike most surveys, this one interviewed the same people at three different points in time as opposed to the usual practice of drawing separate samples for each time period. This procedure of following the same people through time is crucial, for we cannot infer stable preferences from stable percentages unless the same people are interviewed each time. Thus, if 50 percent of the public supported policy X at Time 1, and 50 percent support this policy at Time 2, one *cannot* automatically say that *individual* opinion remains constant—at least statistically it is possible that every person switched sides on the issue.[39]

Respondents in this panel study were asked a variety of questions all of which related to important government policy: whether the Federal government should guarantee each person a job; whether the Federal government should intervene if Negroes are discriminated against in their jobs; whether the United States should provide economic aid to poorer nations; whether the United States would be better off by not being involved in international politics; and whether U.S. troops should be stationed overseas to prevent Communist aggression. Partisan identification was also ascertained. It is important to emphasize that all these issues involve broad policy decisions, not highly specific choices that would be changed in the course of daily events. One might, for example, frequently

---

[39] Of course, one obvious solution to the problem of opinion instability would be to disregard individual shifts and concentrate only on the overall results. Thus, even if two successive 51 percent majorities consisted of largely different people each time, policy makers would only recognize the fact that a majority did exist. While a practical solution, such a convention would ignore the fact that opinions displaying this high turnover might be meaningless for the opinion holders.

change position on the details of foreign aid, but we would expect one's basic inclination to remain fairly constant. Moreover, these issues are hardly esoteric controversies: the Federal government's role in the economy, race relations, and international affairs are some of the major public questions of the last few decades.

Comparisons of responses across time to these questions produced some startling results. Even when those with no opinions were eliminated from consideration, the data showed considerable turnover in individual responses. The overall pattern of responses remained relatively stable, but only about thirteen of twenty respondents gave the same policy choices twice in a row (one would expect ten of twenty to remain on the same side by chance alone).[40] The actual stability of these different issue preferences between 1958 and 1960 is depicted in Figure 3-4:

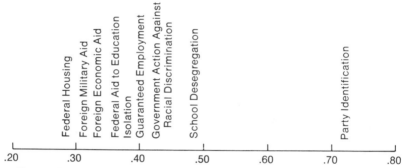

Figure 3-4 Temporal Stability of Different Belief Elements for Individuals, 1958*

SOURCE: Philip E. Converse, "The Nature of Belief Systems in Mass Publics, p. 240,
*The measure of stability is the rank order (tau-b) correlations between individuals
1958 and 1960 positions

Note that as a policy area becomes increasingly remote from one's daily existence, stability declines. Thus, issues like federal involvement in housing or economic aid to poorer nations are more likely to flip-flop than issues involving domestic race relations. The greatest degree of stability is displayed by partisan identification, an identity acquired relatively early in life and generally reinforced by family and environmental forces.

Moreover, analysis of opinion shifts over all three time periods suggests that many citizen opinions on subjects like government's role in housing and electricity fluctuate almost randomly.[41] Using methods of analysis too complex

[40] Converse, "The Nature of Belief Systems in Mass Publics," p. 239. Converse's methods have, however, been recently challenged. See John C. Pierce and Douglas D. Rose, "Nonattitudes and American Public Opinion: The Examination of a Thesis," *American Political Science Review* 68 (1974): 626-49.

[41] Converse, "The Nature of Belief Systems in Mass Publics," p. 243. This random change and its implication is also discussed in Philip E. Converse, "Attitudes and Non-Attitudes: Continuities of a Dialogue," in *The Quantitative Analysis of Social Problems,* ed., Edward R. Tufte (Reading, Mass.: Addison-Wesley, 1970), pp. 168-89.

to describe here, one researcher associated with the panel study concludes that at least as far as these issues are concerned, the public consists of two very disparate groups: a small group holding stable opinions and a much larger segment whose preferences could, for all intents and purposes, be based on a toss of a coin. The size of a third group—those who might change their preferences in a genuine, nonrandom way—is surprisingly small.[42] To be sure, evidence from these particular questions cannot be generalized to all political issues and for all time periods. Nevertheless, the flip-flop character of the public response on at least some political important issues should not be minimized.

COHERENCE OF POLICY PREFERENCES

It is obvious that even in a political system organized to respond to every public whim, it would be impossible to continually ask citizens their opinions on each item of public business. Continuous polling is not only a practical problem of considerable magnitude, but most citizens undoubtedly have better things to do than offer daily advice to their leaders. Given these considerations, it thus becomes imperative that if public desires are to determine policy, leaders must be able to infer one policy preference from another. That is, political leaders should be able to say: "We don't know public sentiment on issue A, but since a majority favors issue B which is quite similar to A, we can safely assume that a majority also exists for issue A."

To be able to infer more than one policy preference from a single response is particularly important if the public's role in policy formation is to provide a broad framework that constrains policy choices without spelling out specific details. Unless leaders can safely say what the public "really" wants on the details without actually conducting a survey, the concept of a broad mandate is meaningless. For example, let us suppose that a majority of the public endorses the broad idea of reducing differences in economic equality. Leaders should then be able to advance more specific laws like a progressive income tax, inheritence taxes, and similar measures without having to worry about offending public opinion. If the public did not favor the specifics that were "logical" correlates of the broader preference, considerable opportunity (albeit unintended) would exist for noncongruity of opinion and policy.[43]

---

[42] Converse, "The Nature of Belief Systems in Mass Publics," p. 244. We should note, however, that other researchers using different methods and samples have challenged Converse's conclusions. Among others, see Steven Brown, "Consistency and the Persistence of Ideology: Some Experimental Results," *Public Opinion Quarterly,* 34 (1970): 60-68 and Normal Luttbeg, "The Structure of Beliefs Among Leaders and the Public," *Public Opinion Quarterly* 32 (1966): 398-409; and Pierce and Rose, "Nonattitudes and American Public Opinion."

[43] As is reflected in our use of quotation marks around logical, it is certainly not true that some completely objective method exists for logically deducing one policy preference from another. Reasonable people may differ on what sorts of preferences go together logically. For example, someone desiring a strong state might logically view government ownership of banks and government censorship of the media as "logically" interconnected; on the other hand, such positions would appear to be inconsistent to many contemporary liberals favoring greater economic equality.

Table 3-4   Relationship between Opinions on Initial Vietnam Involvement and
Preference for Current Policy, 1968

Current Policy Preference	*Opinion on Initial Involvement*				
	Did Correct Thing in Getting Involved	Depends	Should Have Stayed Out	N	%
Pull out entirely	4.1	6.7	35.0	277	23.2
Keep soldiers there but try to end fighting	44.9	33.3	36.4	472	39.5
Take stronger military action if necessary	50.0	60.0	28.6	445	37.3
	100.0%	100.0%	100.0%		
N	441	15	738	1194	
	36.9%	1.3%	61.8%	100.0%	

SOURCE: Survey Research Center, University of Michigan

Though it may appear relatively simple to infer one opinion from a second, related one, this is not always the case. An interesting instance of this difficulty continually occurred in the late 1960s on public preferences on U.S. involvement in Vietnam. Some of the problems of inferring policy preferences are illustrated by the data in Table 3-4 which crosstabulates opinion on the correctness of initial entry into Vietnam with preferences for what should be done now.

These data indicate that at the time of this survey, a clear majority (61.8 percent) of those with opinions considered our involvement in Vietnam a mistake. However, contrary to which might "logically" be the case, only about a third (35.0 percent) of those believing our involvement to be a mistake advocated immediate U.S. troop withdrawal. Indeed 28.6 percent of this group criticizing our initial military commitment now pressed for a stronger military presence. No doubt leaders supplied with only the responses to the question on initial involvement would falsely conclude that most citizens also support immediate disengagement. But in truth only 23.2 percent of the public supported this dovish position.

Another area where the supposed coherence of public policy preferences has been an important issue has been civil rights. Legislation governing racial equality is multifaceted—housing, jobs, schools, public transportation, political participation, even marriage laws—and not infrequently survey results from questions on a few of these areas are taken as indicators of changes in the public mood on race relations. To the extent that people's attitudes are easily predictable, this sampling of issues to gain a broader picture is a useful, resource-saving device. However, the existence of inconsistency across all these diverse issues can result in very misleading interpretations of poll data. To test the extent of coherence on civil rights policy preferences, we present in Table

3-5 data showing the proportions of people who are either consistently liberal or conservative on different pairs of questions (only those expressing opinions are included in our analysis).[44]

From the perspective of a public official trying to ascertain a broad picture of civil rights sentiment, the above data suggest caution in going from one issue to another. Even where a relatively high degree of consistency is achieved, e.g., the government's role in enforcement of school integration and enforcing antidiscrimination laws on the job, many people who take a liberal position in one instance take the conservative (or neutral) side in another instance. If we were to calculate the proportions taking a consistent position on all five questions, this figure would undoubtedly be very small. A lack of greater coherence across issues need not be considered some defect in the quality of public thinking. Indeed, a number of reasonable arguments could be made on why being anti-civil

Table 3-5 Consistency of Opinions on Various Civil Rights Issues, 1968

	Integration/ Segregation	*Govt's Role in School Integration*	*Govt's Role in Job Discrimination*	*Housing Integration*	*Public Accommodation*
Integration/ Segregation	–	43.1%*	31.8%	49.4%	45.9%
Govt's role in school integration		–	69.1	59.8	69.0
Govt's role in job discrimination			–	55.1	64.8
Housing integration				–	74.3
Public accommodation					–

*Each percentage indicates the proportion of respondents who were either consistently pro-civil right, consistently in-between, and completely anti-civil rights for each pair of qusetions.
SOURCE: Survey Research Center, University of Michigan

[44] The actual questions are:

"Are you in favor of desegregation, strict segregation, or something in between?"

"Some people say that the government in Washington should see to it that white and Negro children are allowed to go to the same schools. Others claim that this is not the government's business. . . . Do you think the government in Washington should—"

"Some people feel that if Negroes are not getting fair treatment in jobs the government in Washington should see to it that they do. Others feel that this is not the federal government's business. . . . How do you feel? Should the government in Washington—"

"Which of these statements would you agree with: 1) White people have a right to keep Negroes out of their neighborhoods if they want to; 2) Negroes have a right to live wherever they can afford to; just like anybody else."

"As you may know, Congress passed a bill that says the Negroes should have the right to go to any hotel or restaurant they can afford, just like anyone else. Some people feel that this is something the government in Washington should support. Others feel the government should stay out of this matter. . . . Should the government support the right of Negroes—"

rights on one issue is consistent with the opposite position on a different policy (e.g., one could favor racial integration in all areas but schools on the basis that school integration, though desirable, is politically and practically impossible and thus not worth supporting). Our basic contention is merely that leaders will experience difficulty in trying to infer one opinion from another.

A third, and final analysis of policy coherence concerns an issue under enormous debate since the early 1930s–the role of the federal government in managing the economy. Even more so than civil rights, it is frequently assumed that opinions on this subject are characterized by predictable interrelationships. Some researchers have even gone so far as to claim that this broad issue area constitutes the basic ideological dimensions of politics.[45] Table 3-6 presents data on responses to four issues frequently considered central to this controversy: the growth of the national government, federal assistance to local schools, government subsidized medical care, and government guarantee of a job.

Table 3-6   Consistency of Opinion on Various Government Involvement in Economic Life Issues, 1968

	Govt. too Powerful	Govt. Aid to Education	Govt. Subsidy of Medical Care	Govt. Guarantee of Jobs
Govt. too powerful	–	62.8%	55.8%	55.3%
Govt. aid to education		–	56.9	57.9
Govt. subsidy of medical care			–	56.7
Govt. guarantee of jobs				–

SOURCE: Survey Research Center, University of Michigan[46]

[45] For example, Anthony Downs uses this state invention in the economy as the basic dimensions of political conflict. However, few scholars (including Downs) would go so far as to claim that this conflict was the only meaningful political division. See Anthony Downs, *An Economic Theory of Democracy* (New York: Harper & Row, 1957), p. 116.

[46] The actual questions are:

"Some people are afraid the government in Washington is getting too powerful for the good of the country and the individual person. Others feel that the Government in Washington is not getting too strong for the good of the country. . . .What is your feeling, do you think–"

"Some people think the government in Washington should help towns and cities provide education for grade and high school children; others think this should be bonded by the states and local communities . . . . Which are you in favor of?"

"Some say the government in Washington ought to help people get doctors and hospital care at low cost; others say the government should not get into this . . . . Should the government in Washington–"

"In general, some people feel that the government in Washington should see to it that every person has a job and a good standard of living. Others think the government should just let each person get ahead on his own . . . . Do you think the government–"

On the whole, these results closely parallel those found on the civil rights questions. People who give the liberal (or conservative) response on questions about say, federal aid to education, are also likely to offer liberal (or conservative) responses on the subject of subsidized medical care, but a sizeable minority follows a different pattern. Moreover, these data confirm a pattern first analyzed in detail by Free and Cantril—many people can desire the expansion of particular government programs like guaranteed jobs while simultaneously calling for a reduction in the size of the national government.[47] Of course, there is no inherent contradiction between these two demands provided one is also willing to reduce spending in other areas such as defense, highways, agricultural subsidies, and other noneconomic welfare policy (or to make government more "efficient" so it provides more with fewer people and less money). In any case, it is apparent that substituting a broad ideology, e.g., economic liberalism, for measures of more specific policy preferences is not the convenient simplifying instrument it might be. If preferences are to be ascertained on these issues, they must be measured one at a time, not by a single broad question.

CONCLUSIONS

The fundamental purpose of our analysis was to get a rough idea of whether the message conveyed by public opinion could provide an intelligible guide for the formation of public policy. We asserted that if mass preferences were to be such a guide they would have to meet three criteria: (1) preferences would be based on reasonable substantial amounts of *knowledge;* (2) preferences would be characterized by a moderate degree of *stability;* and (3) preferences would display sufficient *coherence* to infer one policy position from a closely related second position. Unless these criteria were satisfied, leaders would be extremely hard put to satisfy public desires regardless of their commitment to this task.

It should be clear from our review that much of the usual public opinion message does not constitute a meaningful guide to policy making. To be sure, the results of public opinion polls are usually sufficiently clear that public officials might *claim* that their behavior is consistent with the public will, but such a claim assumes qualities in this opinion not completely borne out empirically. Consider, for example, a leader's problems if confronted with a poll showing 60 percent of the public favoring a greater government effort to abolish

[47] Lloyd A. Free and Hadley Cantril, *The Political Beliefs of Americans* (New York: Simon & Schuster, 1968), pp. 36-38. Free and Cantril find that in their 1964 sample about half of those objecting to greater federal government power endorse particular programs requiring a larger, more active national government. We should also add that coherence of preferences can change over time as issues change. On this point, see Norman H. Nie and Kristi Anderson, "Mass Belief Systems Revisited: Political Change and Attitude Structure," *Journal of Politics* 36 (1974): 540-91. Nie and Anderson find increased coherence between 1956 and 1964, but coherence appears to decline betweeen 1964 and 1972.

poverty. First, the official would wonder, how many people really know what current government policy is? Perhaps if people knew how much was currently being spent, the projects that were planned, the types of people who were administering the program, and the probable long-range social consequences of economic redistribution, public enthusiasm would wane.

This hypothetical official might also wonder whether this preference was offered with any degree of conviction. At least some people, he might argue, could be on the other side of the issue if they were subsequently reinterviewed. And, since antipoverty programs are a relatively long term proposition, could he be sure that this policy mandate might not change to opposition, change back again to support, and so on? Given this prospect, this official might justifiably retreat to doing what he felt was best for the country and hope the public more or less acquiesces.

Finally, even if this public mandate were heeded, a response to a single question (or even a number of questions) might not provide sufficient guidance for a large-scale antipoverty program consistent with public opinion. Many programs might reduce poverty, but one cannot be sure that someone favoring antipoverty programs in general supports each of these more specific programs. Indeed, it is likely that at least some people endorsing a war on poverty oppose such anti-poverty programs as a housing allowance, compensatory education, free medical care, and other government "handouts." Thus, it would not be beyond the realm of possibility to find majority public opposition to the specific programs comprising a broad policy favored by a clear majority.

Despite these problems and complexities it would be a mistake to dismiss all public sentiment as meaningless mumbo-jumbo. Our evidence might disturb someone viewing Americans as ideal citizen-rulers, but the data also suggests that on many issues many citizens possess the capacity to offer meaningful political opinions. It is difficult to estimate the precise quantity of intelligible opinion on any given issue, but on questions involving close at hand choices requiring limited information, a majority of opinion would probably be classified as intelligible according to our three criteria. Thus, questions like "Would you want your child bussed to inner-city schools in order to achieve racial integration?" would undoubtedly produce an intelligible response. On the other hand, asking citizens "Should the U.S. remain a member of SEATO?" would generate little of policy-making value.

In the language of communication research, the unintelligible opinion component of mass opinion can be viewed as "noise" in the process of translating public desires into public policy. The important question is whether such noise largely prohibits the nonnoise portion of the message from getting heard. In the case of extreme distributions of opinion, e.g., 90 percent vs. 10 percent, it is likely that a leader would be correct in asserting that a majority of intelligible opinion can be found within the 90 percent. However, as the distribution approaches a 50-50 split, the disrupting impact of this non-intelligible opinion "noise" poses a greater problem. Of course, it could be argued that this "noise" is randomly scattered and thus should not affect the direction of public opinion. Hence, even if most opinions were disregarded as meaningless, the poll results would constitute an accurate guide for public officials. Unfortunately, this argument ignores the well-established fact that those with "nonopinions" tend not to be a random, cross section of the public. The poor, the less well educated, and blacks in particular are disproportionately likely to be found among those offering unintelligible opinions on most (but not all) issues. And since these groups have different interests than the well-to-do, better educated, and whites, making the assumption of a random distribution of "noise" would bias political outcomes against the disadvantaged groups.

What is to be done? The traditional reformist cry of "more education" is unlikely to change matters substantially. Considerable research on the impact of school on producing "better" citizens, i.e., more ideologically sophisticated and aware citizens, strongly suggests that greater education will produce only marginal change at best.[48] For better or worse, the public's limited capacity to offer intelligible policy prescriptions should be taken as a given at least for the foreseeable future. As for the alternative of completely disregarding mass opinion, this extreme solution is not warranted by our data: the transmission of some "noise" is not tantamount to the transmission of complete garbledness. All we can reasonably offer is the caution that not all poll results are prima facie indicators of "true," "meaningful," public opinion. Depending on the issue, such results may or may not be a mandate or meaningless noise.

[48] See, for example, Kenneth Langton and M. Kent Jennings, "Political Socialization and the High School Civics Curriculum," *American Political Science Review* 62 (1968): 852-67. Much of the literature on the impact of school on political values is reviewed in Robert Weissberg, *Political Learning, Political Choice and Democratic Citizenship* (Englewood Cliffs: Prentice-Hall, Inc., 1974), Chap. 8.

chapter four

PUBLIC OPINION AND POLITICAL INSTITUTIONS

Even if public opinion were intelligible and interpretable, and everyone agreed that mass opinion should be the basis of government policy, these conditions by themselves do not guarantee that public policy would accurately mirror public preferences. Unless we assume that leaders possess intuitive capacities for correctly knowing true public sentiment and are also sufficiently altruistic so that coercion is unnecessary, some procedural mechanisms must exist for discovering mass opinions and holding leaders responsible for obeying this opinion. Put another way, if one wanted a political system that maximized the role of popular preferences, what would such a system look like? What kind of institutions would such a system have? Moreover, is such a political system possible or even theoretically conceivable?

More specifically, our analysis will examine three questions all having to do with the institutional mechanisms for translating public opinion into public policy. First, and most important, does the existing American political system's basic structure—particularly its Constitutional form—encourage the implementation of citizen opinion into policy? Our answer to this question emphasizes the *capacity* of institutional arrangements for translating opinion into policy, not whether in fact opinion is the basis for policy (this question will be considered in Chapters 6 and 7). We assume that public preferences *could* determine policy in any form of government (including an absolute monarchy), but systems differ considerably in whether a close relationship between opinion and policy is encouraged.

Our second question focuses on the various attempts to modify the existing political system so as to encourage a closer link between opinion and policy.

Particular attention will be paid to the mechanisms of popular initiatives and referendum which were advocated as powerful means of giving "the voice of the people" a greater say in the law-making process. Our analysis will consider both the intent of such procedures as well as how they worked out in practice.

Finally, and most speculatively, we shall briefly consider some of the hypothetical political mechanisms designed to allow much closer "citizen control of government." Since the advent of high speed, interlocking communications networks connecting almost all citizens with each other, and the development of electronic computers, several schemes have been advanced that will supposedly overcome the democratic deficiencies of traditional political forms. A number of these systems will be examined with particular emphasis on (a) the likelihood of their achieving a close opinion-policy relationship and (b) their costs and benefits compared to present political arrangements. We want to know, for example, whether such schemes as giving every citizen a "yes" or "no" button connected with a central computer would foster policy that would be more responsive to popular desires while also preserving other political values. Let us begin, however, by considering the historical basis of the American political system.

THE EXISTING POLITICAL SYSTEM AND THE MAXIMIZATION OF PUBLIC OPINION

That the United States as a nation traces its origins back to what is sometimes described as a popular uprising against an unresponsive government, might imply a long standing commitment to the direct role of mass opinion in government. Nevertheless, though historians disagree sharply over whether the American Revolution was a radical or conservative event, even those who find abundant evidence of its democratic, popularistic roots do not go so far as to claim that the independence movement sought to make the voice of the people the actions of the government.[1] For example, Merrill Jensen, a leading advocate of the essentially democratic character of the Revolution, argues that the basic issue prior to 1776 was the seat of political power, not whether the colonists' desires were being carried out by the government. Thus, even if George III had somehow ascertained public sentiment and acted accordingly, such behavior would not have satisfied colonists' demands for participation in the governing process.[2]

Not unexpectedly, the immediate institutional legacy of the successful Revolution did not give great weight to popular sentiment. The Articles of

[1] For a sampling of this debate, see the various articles in George A. Billias, ed., *The American Revolution* (New York: Holt, Rinehart & Winston, 1965), especially pp. 48-117.
[2] Merrill Jensen, "Democracy and the American Revolution," *Huntington Library Quarterly* 20 (1957): 321-41.

Confederation made no provision for direct popular election of either the legislature or a national executive. The vast bulk of political power resided in the separate states, and while limited progress was made in the states in "opening up" the political process by expanding the suffrage and allowing recall of legislators, the concept of rule by popular opinion had made no advancement since the overthrow of the British.[3] Moreover, even when the opinions of "the people" were spoken of as the root of all power or a fountain of true wisdom, these "people" were taken to be free male property owners, not the adult population of the states.[4] Save perhaps for the most radical republicans the central political issues continued to revolve around the institutional sources and distribution of power, not responsiveness to popular sentiment.

The constitutional convention that convened in 1787 had many pressing issues on its agenda, but making government more responsive to popular opinion was not one of them. Indeed, a number of schools of historical thought—most notably that pioneered by Charles A. Beard, but many others as well—have maintained precisely the opposite, i.e., the founding fathers were attempting to turn back the democratic impulses generated by the revolution.[5] David G. Smith, a leading historian of this period, notes that by no stretch of the imagination did delegates to the Constitutional convention hold liberal democratic beliefs. The delegates, Smith writes, ". . . openly declared their hostility to democracy as a method of government, to popular state legislatures, and to the democratic provisions of the articles. They were concerned particularly to withdraw the power of decision from the 'grass roots' and to strengthen the less directly representative branches of government."[6]

The antipopular biases of many of the framers clearly manifest themselves in the debates over the creation of the House of Representatives, the organ of government intended to convey the "voice of the people." For example, Elbridge Gerry, a foe of direct elections, speaking of the public's capacity to govern, stated:

> The evils we experience flow from the excess of democracy. The people do not lack virtue, but are the dupes of pretended patriots. In Massachusetts it has been fully confirmed by experience that they are daily misled into

[3] David G. Smith, *The Convention and the Constitution: The Political Ideas of the Founding Fathers* (New York: St. Martin's Press, 1965), pp. 10-13 and Gorden S. Wood, *The Creation of the American Republic* (Chapel Hill: University of North Carolina Press, 1969), pp. 132-43.

[4] The actual proportion of citizens allowed to vote is an unanswered question. The situation varied greatly from area to area. Though in some states the suffrage was limited to the wealthy, recent evidence shows that this was not a universal tendency. See Chilton Williamson, *American Suffrage from Property to Democracy,* 1760-1860 (Princeton: Princeton University Press, 1960), Chap. 2. Also see Wood, *The Creation of the American Republic,* pp. 162-73.

[5] Charles A. Beard, *An Economic Interpretation of the Constitution* (New York: The Macmillan Company, 1913).

[6] Smith, *The Convention and the Constitution,* p. 25.

the most baneful measures and opinions by the false reports circulated by designing men.[7]

Similarly, Roger Sherman, a delegate from Connecticut, said:

> Elections should be by state legislature. The people immediately should have as little to do as may be about the government. They lack information and are constantly liable to be misled.[8]

Though both Gerry and Sherman were defeated in their attempts to make elections to the House indirect, the general sentiment to thwarting the opinion of average citizens prevailed. The founding fathers wanted a Republican form of government, not a democracy, and this meant government by representatives of the people not government by the people themselves. This desire is well stated by Madison in *Federalist No. 10* in defense of the Constitution. Representative government will, according to Madison:

> . . . . refine and enlarge the public views, by passing them through the medium of a chosen body of citizens, whose wisdom may best discern the true interests of their country, and whose patriotism and love of justice will be least likely to sacrifice it to temporary or partial considerations. *Under such a regulation, it may well happen that the public voice, pronounced by the representatives of the people, will be more consonant to the public good than if pronounced by the people themselves,* convened for the purpose. (Emphasis added.)[9]

It can be argued, of course, that while such intentions informed the process of Constitution-building almost 200 years ago, much has happened since then to subvert these antipopular sentiments. Certainly the suffrage has been greatly expanded to include virtually all adults, and many of the antidemocratic provisions of the Constitution, e.g., indirect election of the President and Senators, have been removed either in practice or by Constitutional amendment. Nevertheless, despite the Jacksonian revolution, various Supreme Court decisions, changes in the character of American political life, and advances in communications, the essential institutional framework and decision-making rules adopted in 1789 remain as real now as then. In a sense, the evolution of the Constitutional framework is not unlike, say, the evolution of baseball in the last seventy-five years—the game has experienced many changes, but play today is governed by essentially the same constraints as in 1890. Let us consider the

---

[7] Quoted in Jane Butzner, ed., *Constitutional Chaff* (New York: Columbia University Press, 1941), p. 8.
[8] Butzner, *Constitutional Chaff*, p. 8.
[9] *The Federalist*, ed. Edward Mead Earle (New York: The Modern Library, n.d.), p. 59.

Constitutional legacy as it relates to the effective translation of public opinion into public policy.

THE FORM AND DISTRIBUTION OF POLITICAL POWER

Perhaps nothing frightened the framers of the Constitution more than the possibility of the masses (sometimes referred to as a "majority faction") taking power into their own hands to promote (it was assumed) the cause of the poor and landless against the rich and landed. Compared to this fear, worries about the well-born tyrannizing the masses were minor. Indeed, the means necessary to control this "majority faction" while simultaneously securing the public good and private rights was one of the most perplexing problems faced by the Constitutional framers. Not content to rely on altruism, and rejecting the forced elimination of differences between groups as a solution worse than the original problem, the framers created a series of institutional arrangements to curb "majority factions" that function with considerable effectiveness even after almost 200 years of change.

One such method of constraining majority factions was simply to have a vast republic in which representatives would be chosen from large electoral districts. This would increase the number of interests (or "passions" to use the perjorative term employed by the Framers) and hence diminish the likelihood of a single majority dominating politics. As Madison put it in *Federalist No. 10:*

> Extend the sphere [of the election district] and you take in a greater variety of parties and interests; you make it less probable that a majority of the whole will have a common motive to invade the rights of the other citizens; or if such a common motive exists, it will be more difficult for all to feel it to discover their own strength, and to act in unison with each other.[10]

Of course, it could be maintained that this argument made more sense 200 years ago when difficulties of transportation and communication discouraged interactions within a large geographical area. At the same time, however, we must also realize that (a) the physical size of the republic and its population have also increased enormously; (b) the number of electoral districts in the House of Representatives have not increased with population growth so the number of citizens per official is now usually over 400,000 (and into the millions in the case of Senators); and (c) modern society has probably increased the number and diversity of "factions." Thus, while the existence of large-scale political

---

[10] James Madison, *The Federalist No. 10,* p. 61. This principle is actually challenged, however, in Robert A. Dahl, *A Preface to Democratic Theory* (Chicago: University of Chicago Press, 1956), especially pp. 29-30.

units does not inherently thwart majority sentiment, it probably continues, just as Madison hoped, to discourage the emergence of clear national majorities. Compare, for example, the problems of articulating and organizing a local majority on an issue to the difficulties of expressing a national majority on the same issue even if public sentiment were overwhelmingly in one's favor. No doubt it would take substantial effort to create such a "public will" among citizens who are physically distributed over three million plus square miles and segregated into numerous separate political jurisdictions.[11]

Even more important than a large republic for weakening majority factions, however, were the formal arrangements for the exercise of political power. Rejecting the contention that individual virtue would be sufficient to block tyranny (either majority or minority), the drafters of the Constitution incorporated a set of provisions that would greatly retard the domination of government by one sentiment. These provisions—which have collectively been referred to as checks and balances and separation of powers—are still very much intact today despite occasional attempts to modify them and vast changes in the political environment. Included here are such institutional features as a two-house legislature usually elected from different constituencies, an independent chief executive, a separate judicial system, a variety of provisions specifying interbranch cooperation (e.g., Senate confirmation of certain presidential appointments), and various mechanisms of mutual checking power (e.g., presidential vetoes, authority to impeach, legislative approval of executive budgets).[12]

Moreover, in the years following Constitutional ratification a number of institutional conventions and tendencies have emerged that while not formally part of the Constitution itself are nevertheless fully consistent with the original goal of undermining unified political control. This is particularly evident in Congress where the development of the committee system coupled with the seniority principle (and the filibuster in the Senate) has on occasion allowed a small minority to stalemate the legislative process. Likewise, the legitimization of judicial review in the *Marbury vs. Madison* decision offers yet another device through which one portion of the government can block action by another. Finally, the more recent proliferation of independent regulatory agencies and commissions, *de facto* semiautonomous bureaucracies, has no doubt added to the possibilities for stopping a "majority faction."

[11] It could be argued that modern public opinion polls enable "majority factions" to realize their own strength and thus dominate. However, as valuable as polls may be in articulating "majority factions" they are of little help for the political organization of such a faction. The problems of mobilizing vast numbers of citizens dispersed over an enormous area are reduced but only slightly by knowing that more than half endorse a particular issue position. At best, favorable poll results might encourage an effort to mobilize a "majority faction," but the mere existence of a known majority does not cause the implementation of its will.

[12] The capacity of checks and balances and separation of powers to thwart majorities is considered in greater detail in Dahl, *A Preface to Democratic Theory*, Chapter 1.

An examination of the Constitution also shows a strong proclivity for majorities far in excess of 50 percent plus one. Article V, for example, requires that a proposed Constitutional amendment be approved by two-thirds of each house and three-fourths of the states. Similarly, convictions on impeachment require a two-thirds vote of the Senate in addition to a simple House majority. Even where only a minimum majority is necessary, the very existence of a two-house legislature (not to mention the further requirement of executive approval) is biased in the direction of stalemating policy. That is, if a .5 probability of passage exists in *each* house, the probability of passage through *both* houses is only one out of four. With presidential approval added to this calculation (assuming a .5 chance that the president will approve a bill), the chance of passage is one in eight.[13]

Not content to lay only these obstacles in the path of dominating factions, the Constitution and subsequent amendments explicitly delineated what the national government could and could not do. By no means did the founding fathers wish a government to be able to do anything it or the people wanted—regardless of the popular outcry—and these restrictions are written into law and are exceptionally difficult to change.[14] Thus, for example, public clamor for such policies as limiting free speech to "safe" ideas, allowing the President to rule by decree, firing unpopular Supreme Court justices, and similar unconstitutional demands run up against serious legal obstacles. This is not to argue that unconstitutional preferences never become policy. The Constitution is amendable (though with difficulty), judges and other officials can stretch the meaning of these limitations, and legal restrictions can simply be ignored in actual practice, but constitutional constraints on government action still impede the smooth conveyance of the popular will into policy. That is, the Constitution makes a large number of policies difficult to implement, though in the long run perhaps any public sentiment could become law.

Furthermore, the fact that the Constitution distributes representation largely on a state, not citizen, basis adds yet another potential roadblock in the way of government by popular sentiment. For the sake of argument let's suppose that every Congressman (a) knew precisely what his/her constituents thought on every issue and (b) voted in strict accordance with the majority preference in their district. Would such a state of affairs lead to policy preferred by a majority of Americans? Obviously not since the present system of representation of two

---

[13] We are assuming, obviously, that at least some of the time public opinion desires change. If the public 100 percent of the time desired no change whatsoever, then those institutional obstacles to law-making would *encourage* a close relationship between opinion and policy.

[14] According to Article I, section 9, for instance, the writ of *habeus corpus* cannot be suspended except in special circumstances; no bill of attainder or *ex post facto* law shall be passed; no intra-state export taxes are permitted; and no titles of nobility are to be issued or accepted by officials. Numerous Constitutional Amendments, especially I-V, VIII, and XIV, also greatly constrain government against certain demands.

senators and at least one representative per state means that some citizens are inevitably "better" represented than others. This discrepancy between numbers of peoples and numbers of representatives is most conspicuous in the Senate where, for instance, Nevada with a population of approximately 500,000 is equally represented with California which has forty times the population. Even in the House of Representatives, which is explicitly contrived to mirror popular feelings, people in thinly populated states like Nevada, North Dakota, and Idaho receive a "bonus" due to our constitutional system.

LEADERSHIP SELECTION RULES

Originally the Constitution provided for only limited direct popular participation in the selection of national officials. Gradually, however, with such changes as the elimination of the property requirement, the enfranchisement of blacks and women, the *de facto* obsolescence of the electoral college, and the direct election of U.S. senators, the present system certainly gives the impression of being able to register accurately the choices of the people (or at least those citizens who vote). Nevertheless, even if every American voted for the candidate who precisely reflected his or her own views, the very nature of the system we employ to register these choices would significantly distort the overall picture of the public will.

Perhaps the least obvious, but clearly one of the most important, distorting factors is the geographical basis of leadership selection. That is, a popularly chosen official represents a collection of people all residing in the same general location (e.g., a state or Congressional district). In some cases, e.g., rural agricultural areas, almost all the people in a district may share similar preferences; in other areas, especially in populous states, preferences may be highly diverse and fragmented. As any politician experienced in redistricting knows, which opinions are represented and which ones lose can depend as much on how the district lines are drawn as on the actual distribution of preferences. Consider the following highly simplified political system: (1) there are five election districts of equal population each electing a single representative; (2) there are one hundred voters of which forty are farmers, forty are merchants; twenty remaining are professionals, mechanics, actors and other types; and (3) each occupation votes along occupational lines for their distinct interests. It is entirely possible that due to a variety of circumstances the actual distribution of citizens is as shown in Table 4-1.

Table 4-1 clearly shows that either by chance or conscious design the partitioning of the electorate into separate districts can lead to distortions of preferences. Observe that while farmers represent only 40 percent of the population, their physical distribution allows them to control three of five election districts, while merchants, who are equal in number to farmers, clearly

Table 4-1   Hypothetical Distribution of
             Population Within Election Districts

| | *Election District* | | | | | |
	1	2	3	4	5	Total
Farmers	11	11	11	4	3	40
Merchants	6	6	6	10	12	40
Others	3	3	3	6	5	20
Total	20	20	20	20	20	100

dominate only one district (number 5). Thus, full citizen participation coupled with strict observance of majority preferences will invariably lead to farmers winning on each issue. Of course, these hypothetical figures can be manipulated any number of ways, e.g., farmers could be given eight votes per district and hence be a minority in every district, but the point to be emphasized is that since it is extremely unlikely that *each* election district will mirror the entire population, it is almost certain that distortions of the above type will occur.[15]

Closely related to the principle of geographical division is the so-called "first-past-the-post" system of settling electoral outcomes. In other words, whoever gets the most votes wins even if this totals less than 50 percent. In the first place, unless provisions are explicitly made for run-offs whenever no candidate receives a majority, officials reflecting only a minority position could be selected (in both the 1960 and 1968 presidential elections this situation occurred). More significant, however, even if all winning candidates receive a majority of the vote, accidental (and purposeful) distributions of citizens can readily distort the total picture of public preferences. If in the hypothetical situation depicted in Table 4-1 official positions in each of the five election districts were awarded on a proportional basis instead of the "winner-take-all" system, the opinions of merchants would be more accurately reflected in government.[16] Finally, unless an election district is highly homogeneous on almost all issues, or all choices are dichotomous and coincident majorities exist

[15] Perhaps the most famous example of this distortion in American politics is the overrepresentation of senators from largely rural states. Thus, "big city" states like New York, New Jersey and Pennsylvania are equal to North Dakota, Nevada and Alaska in terms of U.S. Senate voting.

[16] The "winner-take-all" system also makes for distortions in presidential elections due to the existence of the electoral college. As is well known, a winning candidate need only win a plurality in a few key states in order to win a majority of all electoral votes and thus become President. Though only one instance of a loser receiving more popular votes than the winner has occurred in American history, it is clear that certain interests due to their geographical distribution are given greater weight by candidates in their campaigns. The biases of the "winner-take-all" system are considered in greater detail in Douglas W. Rae, *The Political Consequences of Electoral Laws* (New Haven: Yale University Press, 1967), Chap. 5.

(i.e., all majorities are comprised of the same people), it is difficult to see how a single official can accurately reflect popular sentiment. For example, if on two issues there were three positions of comparable popularity, a total of nine issue combinations would exist and a single official in this district could only represent one of these nine positions.

A third general feature of the Constitutional system of leadership selection worth noting concerns the timing of elections. The Constitution specifically lays down both the length of official tenure, e.g., six years for a Senator, and almost the exact date of election. Whether it was the founding fathers' intention or not, this rigid system of leadership selection undoubtedly insulates the government against shifts in public opinion. Thus, even if the entire American public were up in arms over some policies and sought to "throw the rascals out," this would be impossible unless by chance this sentiment occurred just prior to an election. Of course, it will be argued that fixed, calendar-determined terms of office provide the security for leaders to go about their daily business, but it is evident that part of the cost of job security is the restriction of the flow of popular influence.

It is important to realize that the particular devices for selecting leaders handed down by the Constitutional framers are hardly the only means to accomplish the same goal. Electoral systems abound, and not all of them contain the same potential for distorting popular sentiment. For example, many democratic nations employ a system of proportional representation to insure that a party or a faction receiving, say, 20 percent of the vote, receives a proportional share of the legislative seats. In Israel, not only are legislative seats distributed on a proportional basis, but the entire country is a single election district removing the misrepresentation due to accidental distributions of people. Other systems of elections, e.g., representation according to social group characteristics or lottery, conceivably could provide a more accurate reflection of popular opinion, but for a variety of reasons, these alternatives remain beyond serious consideration.

It should be clear from this brief review that if one were a delegate to a constitutional convention intent on formulating a political system to maximize the relationship between popular preferences and public policy, the existing constitution would probably be rejected as unacceptable. True, it may be an adequate set of rules for preserving liberty against tyranny, promoting the general welfare, and providing "good" government, but its potential for accurately translating opinion into policy is relatively low. The sheer size of political units, institutional devices to thwart "majority factions," and various other Constitutional features all "stack the deck" against accurate translation. To be sure, history shows that perhaps the purposes of any formal institutional arrangement can be perverted, but this does not seem to be the case with the U.S. Constitution. All in all, those desiring a closer fit between opinion and policy must labor under circumstances inherently unfavorable to their goals.

INCREASING THE ROLE OF PUBLIC OPINION:
THE INITIATIVE AND REFERENDUM

The inability of the existing constitutional system with its elaborate mechanisms for thwarting "majority faction" to convey accurately popular sentiment has not gone uncriticized. Numerous reform groups have advocated political changes to provide a closer connection between mass opinion and public policy. Of all these schemes, however, two institutional devices have enjoyed particular popularity—the initiative and the referendum. Both devices allow citizens to vote on legislation directly with the difference being that in the initiative the proposal originates among citizens while in the referendum the legislation is first formulated by elected officials. As we shall show, many proponents and opponents have seen these mechanisms of direct legislation as fundamental institutional changes in the existing political order.

Our analysis of the initiative and the referendum will proceed as follows. First, we shall consider the development of these mechanisms in the United States as well as the form they took in various states. We shall discuss such issues as the ease of employing these devices, what policies are excluded from consideration by direct legislation, and their actual popularity in practice. Second, we shall address the much more complex problem of whether the initiative and referendum represent a significant improvement in the translation of opinion into policy. Reaching an answer to this second question requires that we examine the types of issues decided by direct legislation, the quality and quantity of participation in this process, and the net policy consequences of initiative and referendum voting. Even though the initiative and referendum are currently used only on a limited basis, our analysis will show whether these mechanisms *could* subvert the antimajority intentions of the Constitutional framers.

The Development and Forms of the Initiative and Referendum

The idea of direct popular intervention in the law-making process is, of course, an old one going back to ancient Athens. The more modern institutional features of citizen consultation on laws is traceable to sixteenth century Switzerland, though only in the early nineteenth century did the Swiss formally institutionalize this practice. Similarly, the United States had a long history of direct citizen intervention prior to the modern codification of the initiative and referendum. Even as early as 1636 in the Massachusetts Bay Colony there were instances of freemen offering instructions to, and being consulted by, their representatives in the General Court. Prior to the Revolution certain town meetings made it a practice of sending "Instructions" to their representatives;

and just prior to the outbreak of war with England, the Massachusetts House called for a statewide vote on the issue of independence.[17]

The custom of putting issues to the people or soliciting suggestions for new laws continued after the Revolution, though on an *ad hoc* basis with no provisions to regularize the procedure as a legitimate channel of popular influence. This was particularly common in the case of new state constitutions. New Hampshire, New York, Maine and several other states submitted their post-Revolution constitutions to citizen approval. The location of state capitals also became in the 1850s a popular issue to submit to the general electorate (Texas originated this practice in 1850). Perhaps the closest attempt at a modern-day referendum occurred on the eve of the Civil War when Senator Crittenden offered a resolution calling for a national referendum on the slavery issue. Following a full debate, the resolution was defeated by a single vote.

The demand to routinize popular intervention and consultation was first advanced by socialist groups in the last decade of the nineteenth century. From there the demand was passed along through a variety of groups and spokesmen: the Farmers' Alliance, People's Party, Democratic Party, and the Progressive of the Republican Party at various times and places called for direct voting on legislation.[18] At times the demands for initiative and referendum were part of a large "reform" movement that also championed public ownership of utilities, the popular recall of elected officials, the commission form of urban government, an end to bossism and "good," "uncorrupted" government in general. At times, the initiative and referendum were put forth as the means to a democratic utopia. With these institutions, said Senator Jonathan Bourne, Jr.:

> ... there can be no class or community action against the general welfare of the citizens ... The individual, through realization of the impossibility of securing special legislation for himself and against the general welfare of the community, soon ceases his efforts for special privilege and contents himself with efforts for improved general welfare. Thus, the individual, class and community develop along lines of general welfare rather than along lines of selfish interest.[19]

Moreover, it was also commonly claimed that the opportunity to participate directly in the legislative process would greatly enlighten the American citizenry.

---

[17] Edwin M. Bacon and Morrill Wyman, *Direct Elections and Law-Making By Popular Vote* (Boston: Houghton Mifflin Company, 1912), pp. 1-13. The historical origins of direct legislation are also described in Ellis Paxson Oberholtzer, *The Referendum in America* (Philadelphia: University of Pennsylvania, 1893), Chaps. 2 and 3.

[18] Bacon and Wyman, *Direct Election and Law-Making by Popular Vote*, pp. 19-20.

[19] Senator Jonathan Bourne, Jr., "A Defense of Direct Legislation," in *The Initiative, Referendum and Recall*, ed. William Bennett Munro (New York: D. Appleton and Company, 1912), p. 197.

As Professor Lewis Jerome Johnson put it:

> One cannot help believing that the consequent toning up of the public standard of thought and morals would be in the long run the most important feature of the system. Direct legislation tends thus automatically to produce a highly trained and self-respecting electorate, and to lay the deepest and most promising foundation for permanent good government.[20]

Such arguments must have been convincing since beginning in 1898 with South Dakota, state after state embraced the initiative and referendum. By 1911, in addition to South Dakota, Utah, Oregon, Nevada, Montana, Missouri, Oklahoma, Maine, Arkansas, Colorado, and California had enacted full versions of these twin procedures, while Massachusetts and Michigan had incorporated them in modified form. Moreover, several of these states authorized their cities and towns to employ direct legislation; and even some states lacking state-wide voting procedures authorized localities to use direct legislation under special circumstances. Once authorized, there was no lack of enthusiasm for their use though they were more popular in some states than in others. For example, in 1904 Oregon citizens voted on two initiatives; by 1908 they were faced with nineteen measures. Indeed, in the South Dakota general election of 1910, the ballot was seven feet long and six of those feet were devoted to initiatives and referenda.[21]

The means by which citizens could place issues on the ballot or require laws to be popularly approved varied in detail across states, but most states shared certain basic features. Typically, to be put on the ballot a measure needed a number of signatures of eligible voters equal to some small percentage (commonly 5 percent) of either the whole electorate or the number of voters for some office in the previous election (e.g., Governor). In states allowing direct amendment to the state constitution, the number of required signatures was

---

[20] Lewis Jerome Johnson, "Direct Legislation as an Ally of Representative Government," in Munro, *The Initiative, Referendum and Recall,* p. 153. Such arguments are not limited to the early part of the century. Even today, reformers exist who view popular consultation on issues as a virtual cure-all for the world's ills. See, for example, Matt Shermer, *"The Sense of the People" or The Next Development in American Democracy* (New York: American Referendum Association, 1969).

[21] Bacon and Wyman, *Direct Elections and Law-Making by Popular Vote,* pp. 25-26, 47. The spread of these devices is described in greater detail in Charles H. Beard and Birl E. Shultz, *Documents on the State-Wide Initiative, Referendum and Recall* (New York: The Macmillan Company, 1912). Though direct legislation received its greatest fame in the first part of the century, the practice is very much alive today, particularly in such issues as public approval of school budgets, bond issues, and property tax levels. However, the major votes generating publicity today are local referenda on fluoridation and open housing. In recent years there have averaged about 300 state-wide referenda in even-year elections, 70 in odd-year elections. These data are reported in Hugh A. Bone, "Easier to Change," *National Civic Review,* 57 (1968): 120.

raised somewhat (usually to 8 percent). Legal and technical requirements regarding proper forms, filing fees, timing, and the like were usually straightforward and not very burdensome. Finally, both California and Oregon further encouraged citizen participation by distributing pamphlets to each voter listing the various measures and pro and con argument on all issues.[22]

Did these provisions literally give all legislative power to the people? It was usually the case that laws providing for initiative and referendum explicitly stipulated that measures approved by a citizen majority were beyond executive veto. However, the same statutes invariably placed certain types of laws beyond public review or mentioned special circumstances that would exclude the possibility of a referendum. Typical was the referendum law of South Dakota which excluded from public consideration ". . . such laws as may be necessary for the immediate preservation of the public peace, health, or safety, support of the State Government and its existing public institutions." Montana's statute excluded, among other things, laws dealing with appropriations of money.[23] It is obvious, of course, that government officials can readily subvert much of the public's involvement by declaring laws "urgent" or "necessary for the public safety" or the like. This possibility is well illustrated by what happened in California during the 1930s when two-thirds of all bills were deemed "urgent" to avoid the possibility of public rejection at the polls.

The Political Significance of the Initiative and Referenda

It is clear from the above discussion that the initiative and referendum have the *potential* to be effective transmission devices for translating public opinion into official policy. Whether or not this potential is realized in practice is, however, another matter. Though we may all differ about what would constitute an "efficient" translation mechanism, it would appear that if the initiative and referendum were to fulfill their basic purposes, the following five conditions must be met. First, voters would have at least some opportunity to decide on substantial issues framed in intelligible terms. Second, voting would be extensive and representative of all citizens, not just a small minority. Third, a fair degree of competence would be displayed by voters on each issue and all the decisions taken in the aggregate. Fourth, the availability of direct legislation would, in some sense, have a political policy impact apart from merely adding more issues to the electoral campaigns. Finally, the opportunity to participate successfully in

[22] For a sampling of some of these legal details, see Beard and Shultz, *Documents on the State-Wide Initiative, Referendum and Recall,* Chaps. 1-22. We should also note that many states either complicated the direct legislation process or, like California, allowed for various types of referenda. Since we are entirely concerned with the applicability of these mechanisms in their more or less pure forms, we shall omit discussing these variations.

[23] Bacon and Wyman, *Direct Elections and Law-Making by Popular Vote,* pp. 26, 30.

direct legislation would be reasonably available to a variety of groups and interests. If all five of these demands were satisfied, the initiative and referendum would clearly go a long way in overcoming some of the limitations of the existing constitutional system.

Regarding the requirement that voters be presented with substantial nonfrivolous issues, a review of hundreds of proposed measures suggests that at least in some states this requirement is well satisfied. Particularly in the period just prior to World War I, many questions of basic political importance were placed on the ballot. For example, Oregon citizens made decisions on the direct election of U.S. senators, the extension of suffrage to women, the recall of elected officials, the use of proportional representation, and even the creation of a "Board of People's Inspectors of Government" to oversee public officials. Other states offered choices on prohibition, the regulation of public utilities, income tax rates, creations of primaries, and other matters of obvious and widespread importance. At the same time, however, and not unexpectedly, various measures of marginal interest to the average citizens also found their way on to the ballot. For instance, while Oregonians were busy deciding major issues they also had to pass on whether to have an official state printer or whether to authorize free railway passes for elected officials. South Dakota citizens were faced in 1910 with the profound questions of whether the names of embalmers should be placed on coffins shipped within the state, while in 1934, Californians had to decide whether to license "naturopaths." On the whole, however, votes on such minutiae were relatively rare.[24]

A question closely related to the meaningfulness of direct legislative content concerns the intelligibility of proposals. In many states, especially at the beginning, no provisions existed to guarantee that measures made any legal sense or were actually feasible. Hence, it would have been possible to have measures calling for lower taxes with increased services, or the abolition of sin. Even if intentions were reasonable, sloppy and ambiguous drafting could render measures inoperable. Since it is not clear what "good" legislation looks like, a precise answer to this question is impossible, but LaPalombara and Hagan in their 1951 review of Oregon's popularly approved laws found little evidence of poorly conceived legislation. To be sure, instances of "bad" bills can be found, but the citizens' record on reasonableness and workmanship is no worse than that of the state legislature.[25] As for the charge that direct legislation will encourage "crackpot" laws, here again the proof is lacking. In California, supposedly the most fertile soil for hairbrained schemes, of the over 600 ballot propositions since 1911, only a very few (particularly the single tax and old age

[24] Bacon and Wyman, *Direct Elections and Law-Making by Popular Vote,* pp. 25-43. A sampling of measures voted on in California is given in Winston W. Crouch, *The Initiative and Referendum in California* (Los Angeles: The Haynes Foundation, 1950), pp. 44-49.
[25] Joseph G. LaPalombara and Charles B. Hagan, "Direct Legislation: An Appraisal and a Suggestion," *American Political Science Review* 45 (1951): 411.

pension measures) have been commonly deemed "crackpot." Even here, however, it is not perfectly self-evident that such proposals are inherently disastrous or unworkable.

Our second requirement concerns the amount and representative character of popular participation in direct legislation. Many studies have demonstrated that even the simple act of voting does not appeal to all citizens, and analyses of initiatives and referenda indicate that these are even less appealing than choosing among candidates. For example, in the fifteen Oregon elections between 1902 and 1930, there was on average a 10 percent difference in the turnout for the most popular legislative measure and the vote for the most popular office. In special elections called to decide important issues, the average turnout of registered voters were a mere 41.7 percent, suggesting that the opportunity to make laws is not particularly attractive to most people. It should be noted, though, that participation on important questions relevant to everyday life, such as prohibition, tends to be higher, though it again does not exceed voting for officials.[26]

The evidence from other states and different time periods reinforces the conclusions drawn from Oregon's experience. Thus, in California, which like Oregon has voted on many major political issues, turnout in direct legislation in general has exceeded 80 percent of the total vote a mere 14 percent of the time. If we exclude measures submitted by the legislature and consider only citizen initiated measures, the turnout figure is higher but it still lags behind vote for governor and other visible offices.[27] Finally, a similar pattern of lower voting rates is found in Maine, and as in Oregon, special Maine elections dealing only with legislation draws even fewer votes (turnout is commonly 20 to 30 percent of the vote for governor in previous elections). Even in those Maine elections considering important issues such as women's suffrage, turnout has been low.[28]

One result of these low participation rates is that much legislation is approved by a minority of citizens who actually show up to vote on election day. According to Schumacher's analysis of Oregon voting between 1920 and 1930, 68.2 percent of all proposals were either accepted or rejected by a minority of citizens who turned out.[29] No doubt the situation is quite similar in other states. Hence, not only can questions be raised as to whether the "people" have really spoken at the ballot box, but whether even those voting on direct legislation are representative of all those turning out to vote.

[26] Waldo Schumacher, "Thirty Years of People's Rule in Oregon: An Analysis," *Political Science Quarterly* 47 (1932): 244-47.
[27] Crouch, *The Initiative, and Referendum in California*, p. 43.
[28] Lawrence Lee Pelletier, "The Initiative and Referendum in Maine," *Bowdoin College Bulletin*, No. 300 (1951), pp. 31-34. As an indication of what is of interest to citizens of Maine, Pelletier observes that a 1936 proposal regulating hunting and fishing drew almost a quarter of a million votes, while a measure the subsequent year dealing with taxes for education and old age assistance drew less than half that turnout.
[29] Schumacher, "Thirty Years of People's Rule in Oregon," p. 249.

The frequency of laws being passed or defeated by minorities raises the important question of whether the messages conveyed by direct legislation mirror the sentiment of the people at large. To answer this question properly we would need survey data on referenda and initiative voters in order to compare their respective policy preferences to a cross-section of the general population. Unfortunately, however, despite the great frequency of initiatives and referenda, analyses of direct legislation voting have very rarely ascertained the opinions of nonparticipants, and even those studies that have are limited in scope. Nevertheless, based on what we already know about voting and nonvoting in general plus evidence from the few existing studies, we can make some informed guesses on the subject.

Specifically, given lower turnout rates on initiatives and referenda, compared to voting for officials, it is probably fair to say that voting on direct legislation requires greater motivation and interest than either voting for candidates only or abstaining completely. That initiative and referendum voters are generally more politically involved suggests a number of characteristics that differentiate them from nonparticipants. Those voting on direct legislation are probably better educated, are wealthier, more likely to be male, less likely to be black, and more likely to be middle-aged than those not voting.[30] More important, considerable research indicates that these more politically attuned, higher status citizens differ in the policies they prefer as well. In an analysis of Toledo's open housing referenda, for example, it was found that nonvoters were distinctly more favorable toward open housing than voters.[31] In general, direct legislation voters are probably more conservative on major socio-economic issues, e.g., government intervention in the economy, while more liberal on civil libertarian issues such as the rights of suspected Communists.[32] Hence, an initiative on, say, socialized medicine, would likely yield a measure of public sentiment more conservative than the polling of every citizen.

Of course, it could be argued that the nonrepresentative character of initiative and referendum decisions is not an inherent defect but something readily "cured" by increased electoral participation. Stopping short of compulsory involvement, however, the prospect for universal participation is quite dim. Even the elimination of legal obstacles such as prior registration and the placing on the

---

[30] This supposition is confirmed by Hamilton's study of open housing in Toledo, Ohio in 1967. Hamilton found that those higher in education, income, and occupation were more likely to participate. Perhaps most surprising, even though the issue of open housing directly affected blacks more than whites, blacks were more likely to be nonvoters. See Howard D. Hamilton, "Direct Legislation: Some Implications of Open Housing Referenda," *American Political Science Review* 64 (1970): 129.

[31] Hamilton, "Direct Legislation," p. 129.

[32] Essentially, we are arguing that in terms of characteristics and political preferences what distinguishes voters from nonvoters will further distinguish candidate voters from direct legislation voters. For an analysis of differences between voters and nonvoters, see Sidney Verba and Norman H. Nie, *Participation in America* (New York: Harper & Row, 1972), especially Chap. 6.

ballot of issues of great personal and political relevance are unlikely to produce 100 percent involvement. In sum, to accept direct legislation necessarily means accepting law-making by an unrepresentative segment of the public.

The third requirement that must be met to allow direct legislation to function as intended concerns voter competence. There are really two aspects of the question. The first is the soundness or "rationality" of the choice made by the individual voter. In other words, when confronted with a piece of legislation, do voters favor laws consistent with either their own or the public good (somehow defined). After all, if voters are too ignorant to select the side which they really want, then the whole process of direct legislative intervention is pointless beyond its symbolic value. Unfortunately for our analysis, however, while a vast literature on the "rationality" of choices of candidates exists, there is almost nothing comparable for initiative and referendum voting.[33]

Nevertheless, there is a second way of looking at voter competence in direct legislation and that is to consider the behavior of the electorate collectively. An opportunity for such analysis occurs since on occasion voters are presented with measures that are exact opposites of each other. To the extent that the collective policy choices are consistent we can say that at least in this limited way voters in the aggregate behave in a competent manner. Schumacher's study of Oregon voting reports on three such cases (1914, 1926, and 1930) and in each instance the electorate behaved consistently though the discrepancy ranged from 4.33 to 6.03 percent.[34] California has likewise offered voters contradictory proposals and here again the net result was consistency among choices.[35] To be sure, in many instances California and Oregon voters approved or rejected similar propositions backed by opposing groups, but such action did not result in conflicting legislation.[36] In sum, at least by this standard, American voters appear to possess the necessary competence to make use of direct legislation.

The fourth requirement deals with the actual political consequences of popular participation in the legislative process. In other words, do they make any difference? One aspect of this issue concerns the proportion of initiatives

[33] An exception to the lack of individual data in direct legislation voting is Mueller's study of California absentee ballots. Mueller found that on two antithetical measures on a state lottery, only 47 percent voted consistently. Whether this pattern is a general one is difficult to say. John E. Mueller, "Reason and Caprice: Voting on Propositions," (unpublished manuscript, 1968) cited in Hamilton, "Direct Legislation," p. 131.

[34] Schumacher, "Thirty Years of People's Rule in Oregon," p. 250. Of course the amount of individual inconsistent voting may be much greater than the net difference between totals, but our concern here is the capacity of the electorate—not individuals— to make consistent choices.

[35] Crouch, *The Initiative and Referendum in California*, pp. 20-21.

[36] For example, in 1908 rival fishing interests in Oregon put two measures on the ballot—one banning commercial fishing on the lower Columbia River, the other banning fishing on the upper part of the river. Rather than give the advantage to one group of fishermen, Oregon voters prohibited commercial fishing on the Columbia River entirely by passing both measures.

and referenda actually adopted. The evidence here suggests that the public is far less willing to dabble in law writing than might be imagined. For example, of 214 measures submitted in regular Oregon elections between 1902 and 1930, only 79 were passed.[37] The evidence from a number of states also indicates that initiatives in particular fare poorly. For instance, in California between 1912 and 1949, only 14 of 51 (27.5 percent) statutes submitted by popular initiative were adopted compared to 70.6 percent of the non-Constitutional measures submitted by the state legislature.[38] Similarly, Maine voters between 1910 and 1951 faced seven initiatives, but accepted only two of them.[39] Examination of the content of enacted direct legislation does not suggest that those statutes actually adopted are more sweeping or profound than those rejected.[40] Clearly, then, initiative and referendum are limited, supplementary law-making mechanisms in no way replacing regular legislation.

Another aspect of the consequences of direct legislation concerns what happens to laws once popularly enacted. Are such popular efforts at law-making subverted by public officials or other groups? The evidence suggests that adopted direct legislation is as valid as any other legislation. To be sure, the constitutionality of initiatives and referenda have been attacked on several fronts, but the Courts have almost always resisted such attacks.[41] At the same time, however, laws providing ways for law-makers to get around popular influence, e.g., by declaring a law an "urgent law," have likewise been judicially upheld.[42]

Our final argument concerns the popular availability of direct legislation. After all, their purpose was to place some law-making power in the hands of "the people" but if only powerful, well-off interest groups can successfully play this game, the aims of the initiative and referendum are defeated. A number of factors influence access, but the most obvious is the required number of voters' signatures to be obtained. As we have mentioned, the requirement is typically based on either votes in some previous election or the total electorate. Though the percentage—usually 5 percent—appears to be very low, the sheer size of modern electorates makes getting on the ballot very difficult. Thus, to get on the 1972 California ballot required 325,000 signatures (in practice many more signatures are required since some will always be declared invalid). One does not get 325,000 signatures by having friends and family man the local street corners! Obviously a major and expensive solicitation effort is required, and if one

---

[37] Schumacher, "Thirty Years of People's Rule in Oregon," p. 251.

[38] Crouch, The *Initiative and Referendum in California*, p. 42.

[39] Pelletier, "The Initiative and Referendum in Maine," p. 26.

[40] Also, recall our earlier discussion of statutes providing for direct legislation prohibiting certain important subjects from popular votes. Hence, even if voters accepted every proposal they saw, they could not influence many political issues.

[41] LaPalombara and Hagan, "Direct Legislation," pp. 401-4.

[42] A summary of important California cases on the subject is presented in Crouch, *The Initiative and Referendum in California*, pp. 52-53.

possesses "adequate" financial resources, organizations can be hired to get signers at a dollar or so per concerned voter.

Even if a cause successfully overcomes this hurdle, formidable obstacles remain. Though states like California and Oregon provide each voter with a pamphlet giving the pros and cons on each issue, experience demonstrates that expensive, professionally run campaigns better insure success than reliance on the peoples' wisdom. As is true of campaign finances in general, precise data on expenditures is difficult to come by (even in states having laws requiring expenditure reports), but it is more than likely that in states like California and Oregon a reasonably extensive campaign today would cost over a million dollars. Of course, it could be argued that if a measure were genuinely desired by the people, obtaining sufficient signatures and campaign resources would be simple, but at least the experience of California suggests that being monied and powerful to begin with helps considerably in taking one's case to the people.[43] This is not to suggest that direct legislation is a conduit for the influence of substantial interests, but rather if any group is likely to succeed (and recall that most do not) it is more likely to be, say, the State Real Estate Association than Friends of the Downtrodden.

All in all, does our analysis show that mechanisms to involve the average citizens in law-making substantially overcome the bias against "majority factions" built into our constitutional system? Our answer must be—only slightly. Certainly an enormous potential exists in the initiative and referendum, and certainly cases can be found exhibiting this potential, but even under conducive circumstances a considerable gap remains between what was intended and what occurs in practice. Even during their heyday use in South Dakota, Utah, California, Washington, Oregon, and other states, direct legislation never superseded elected representatives, and a serious question exists whether votes on issues were a more accurate expression of the public will than the votes of state legislators. It may be argued, of course, that in theory the initiative and referendum are fine, but the traditional mechanism to register citizens' preferences—the ballot box—was cumbersome and inefficient. What is needed, the argument continues, are modern, more effective means of registering preferences. To consider this argument, let us examine some possible computer-assisted means to modernize the initiative and referendum.

MODERN TECHNOLOGY, PUBLIC OPINION, AND PUBLIC POLICY

Though the initiative and referendum have at best only partially helped bring popular preference and policy into closer agreement, advocates of new ways to achieve closer congruence have not given up. Some schemes, e.g., the return to

---

[43] Crouch, *The Initiative and Referendum in California*, p. 17.

small units of government on an ancient Athens model, are clearly beyond serious political consideration even if they could achieve perfect opinion-policy congruence. Others, like plans to make each and every citizen into a perfectly informed activist, may be politically more acceptable, but they are probably beyond practical reach. Much more reasonable are the various plans to employ modern communications technology to the problem of allowing citizens to determine or at least to influence policy. Several such schemes have been advanced and we shall consider a number of them to see whether they are capable of overcoming the "defects" of the constitutional order or direct legislation.

Perhaps the most commonly suggested and elementary use of communications technology to amplify the "voice of the people," is to automate voting and allow each citizen to vote using his telephone or some device attached to the television set. For example, V.K. Zworykin, who helped invent television, proposes that important national questions be broadcast over the radio and citizens would then phone in their vote.[44] Such a system, according to Zworykin, would bring about a closer alignment between policy and opinion while frequent consultation could overcome feelings of political ineffectiveness and foster public responsibility.

Zworykin's proposal, though technically feasible, is open to the criticism that at-home, push button-voting may increase the volume of the public message, but by itself it does nothing for the *quality* of the message. That is, choices would still be based on considerable misinformation or faulty reasoning so leaders could very well dismiss the public's views as irrelevant. To overcome this deficiency, Robert Paul Wolff in his *In Defense of Anarchism* proposes a more elaborate version of Zworykin's idea.[45] First, all citizens would possess a television set that could transmit votes to a computer in Washington, D.C. (to avoid fraud, a thumbprint recording device could be installed). Each evening a televised debate would occur between representatives of different views and, when necessary, there woud be technical background briefings and question periods. Experts could be commissioned to gather data, make suggestions, and draft laws. A position of Public Dissenter might be instituted to guarantee that dissident points of view are given a fair hearing. Debate would go on for a week and on Friday a vote would be taken and decisions would be reached by majority rule.

Though Wolff's scheme attempts to produce an informed expression of sentiment, it nevertheless is little more than an automated mechanism for tallying votes. Indeed, except for the convenience of at-home voting, it differs hardly at all from an election campaign involving direct legislation. Perhaps the

---

[44] V. K. Zworykin, "Communications and Government" in *The World in 1984* edited by Nigel Calder (Harmondsworth, Middlesex, England: Penguin Books, 1965).
[45] Robert Paul Wolff, *In Defense of Anarchism* (New York: Harper and Row, 1970), pp. 34-35.

most conspicuous weakness of the plans discussed so far is that they make no provision for citizen interaction—communication occurs between citizens and government (or vote recorder), but discussion among citizens themselves is left to chance. If one takes ancient Athens or the classic New England town meeting as the model of meaningful citizen participation in policy-making, it is clear that a communications system must allow citizens to interact with each other prior to voting.

To overcome this lack of capacity for intercitizen communications, Amitai Etzioni and his associates have developed and partially tested a communications system named MINERVA (after the ancient Roman goddess of political wisdom).[46] By such electronic devices as cable television, radio, over-the-air television, telephones, and a satellite relay system, the MINERVA system attempts to simulate the political environment and face-to-face contacts of the Greek *polis,* New England town meeting, and the Israeli *Kibbutzim.* In effect, MINERVA would allow for a gigantic town meeting characterized by citizens addressing their immediate neighbors, people engaging in dialogues with others sharing similar interests but dispersed geographically (e.g., all black Americans), leaders ascertaining immediate feedback to their proposals, and the occasional interjection of expert information into the dialogue. Every person possessing a radio or television and who has access to a telephone—and even now this includes just about all citizens—could thus participate in the discussion and resolution of public affairs. Because people would not have to leave their homes or face anxious moments addressing large crowds, many people presently politically inactive might be encouraged towards greater involvement. Finally, the very opportunity for meaningful participation would motivate increased political concern so MINERVA would produce both a quantitative and qualitative change in citizen activism.

How is all of this accomplished? The basic building blocks of this system are small groups of citizens (up to 30 people) who can be linked via automated telephone connections into a discussion group. Though it is convenient if members of such groups live near each other, there are no geographical constraints on this primary unit. These groups are in turn part of larger communities in which interaction occurs through two-way cable TV in small communities (300 to 2,000) and over-the-air TV, plus regular telephone in larger communities. Typically, issues would first be discussed in smaller groups, then on a community-wide basis; but individuals could skip the first stage and join directly at the next highest level. Finally, at the level of a region, nation, or even world, citizens would be linked up with a broadcast carried by various devices. Of course, at this level the active participants would be limited

[46] MINERVA is described in various places. See, among others, Amitai Etzioni, "MINERVA: A Participatory Technology System," *Bulletin of Atomic Scientists* 27 (1971): 4-12 and Amitai Etzioni, "MINERVA: A Study in Participatory Technology," Working Paper I (February, 1972) New York: Center for Policy Research, Inc.

to leaders, representatives and experts, but the final decisions would rest in the hands of the viewers.

Certainly one of the foremost problems of such a system concerns rules of access to the debates. If only votes were to be conveyed, the problem is simple, but if a decision is to be reached among, say, 10,000 people and 200 at any given moment want to speak, providing for a life-like town hall meeting requires both an enormous amount of time and effort. The developers of MINERVA are yet undecided on a single solution to this problem, but have suggested several possibilities. For example, would-be participants could be selected (a) on a first-come, first-served basis; (b) randomly; (c) on the basis of some special attributes such as expertise; or (d) according to how many other citizens a person represents. MINERVA's designers have also included a capacity of conveying individuals' feelings on an issue prior to voting without the need of saying anything. It is well known that nonarticulate audience reaction to a talk, e.g., coughing, shuffling of chairs, cross-talk, etc., can be as meaningful as a speech from the floor and the MINERVA system would provide viewers with "approve" and "disapprove" buttons conveying signals which would show up on a large screen to give a speaker a "feel" for how well he was doing.

What about the technology for systems? As we have indicated, the basic elements—telephones, cable television, and so forth—are well developed and in fairly widespread use.[47] Moreover, the required modifications entail adaptations of existing technology, not new technology. For example, the smallest unit would interact via telephone with the use of a device called a conference bridge and an electronic switching system, two mechanisms currently in commercial service. There is also a problem of telephone voting since telephone lines are capable of conveying only a limited amount of information (if 25 percent of users dialed at once, the system would be made temporarily inoperable), but this problem could be overcome by holding the vote on the phone while a central computer scanned the lines at a millisecond per line. Similar problems in other communications equipment are also well within existing capacity.

Certainly the most crucial question, however, is: Will it work? There is clearly no point in offering all these communications channels if citizens do not use them or if the consequences of use are different than intended. Though the final judgment on MINERVA must be delayed until all the technical difficulties are solved and the system is fully deployed, at least some answer to this question is offered by the results of an experiment with the Tenants Association of "High Rise Village," a middle income housing project located in a very large city with

[47]MINERVA's technology is described in greater detail in Stephen H. Unger, "Technology to Facilitate Citizen Participation in Government," New York: Center for Policy Research, Inc. February 1972 and Noam Lemelstrich, "Two-Way Communication: A Design Analysis of a Home Terminal," New York: Center for Policy Research, n.d.

2308 living units.[48] Through the use of cable television, radio, and face-to-face meetings, many of the essential features of MINERVA were created, but it must be stressed that this experiment was very much a first approximation of the final system and must be judged accordingly.

The experiment was divided into two distinct parts. In the first part a film about prisoners ("Are you listening to 'Prisoners'?") was shown over cable TV a total of three times in a one month period. An extensive publicity campaign preceded the showing. Questionnaires on issues related to the film were distributed in some instances by simply placing them under peoples' doors and in other instances through the "floor captains" in each building. The purpose of this variation was to measure the impact of personal contact on mobilizing opinion. As expected, tenants who were personally contacted were twice as likely to hand in questionnaires, but what is more significant is that the total response vote was a mere 4 percent! Considering the very slight relevance of prison reform to these apartment dwellers, however, this low response is hardly surprising and confirms the well-known fact that it takes something major to get people involved in issues.

The second part of the experiment purposely selected an issue of high relevance to each tenant—building security (the housing complex was located in a high crime area). In addition, more election communications channels were introduced to allow greater mutual feedback between tenants and their association. The procedures were as follows. On Monday evening four speakers offered varying solutions to the security problem via a local FM radio broadcast. Tenants were then given opportunities to offer videotaped reactions to these broadcasts after first discussing the issues among themselves. On Wednesday these tenant reactions were shown at a meeting of the Tenants Council and then on Thursday the local cable TV stations carried both the tenant videotapes and the Council response. Finally, postcard ballots and questionnaires were also provided to ascertain reactions. Did all this effort produce an improvement over the normal system of governing by elected representative and public apathy?

In the first place, despite the salience of the security issue, all the publicity, activity, and commotion, this version of electronic democracy was not terribly successful at mobilizing the masses. A mere 35 percent voted (compared to a figure of 47 percent in the most recent general election) and about a fifth of all living units returned questionnaires. Even among those interested enough to return a questionnaire, involvement was meager. For example, of these tenants only 28 percent listened to at least a portion of the radio program and 21 percent watched any of the cable TV program. Nor was the attraction of

[48] Our entire discussion of this experiment is drawn from Robert Aussman and Nancy Castleman, "Electronic Town Hall Meetings: A Preliminary Exploration," New York: Center for Policy Research, 1973.

appearing on TV very appealing: 49 out of 4000 tenants offered a videotaped response. Finally, as is true more generally, activists were not a perfect cross section of the population—they differed in both age and length of residence in the housing complex.

What about the quality of citizen involvement? Even if the MINERVA system failed to mobilize everyone, it could perhaps be judged worthwhile if it upgraded the level of public debate. On the whole, the evidence on this point is mixed. For example, while some citizens found the radio and TV debates overly formal and stilted, others appreciated the tighter organization and absence of digressions. Compared to the regular meetings of the Tenants Association, most found the electronic version equally or somewhat more informative.[49] There was also extensive agreement that this format was highly convenient since it saved getting babysitters, going out at night, etc. (but others missed the face-to-face interaction). Moreover, as involvement increased so did claims of better understanding of the issues though even among the most active, only a little more than half claim a high degree of comprehension. One of the most interesting reactions concerns the sheer bulk of information generated by the experiment. Even with modest participation rates, viewing all the speeches was frequently a tedious, boring process, yet when videotapes were edited to provide more succinct messages, opinions about the accessibility of the system became more negative. That is, many citizens dislike the tedium *and* being "edited out" for brevity's sake. Finally, tenants were only slightly more likely to think that their views on the security issue were better represented through the MINERVA system than in the regular tenants' meetings.

The last question raised by this communications experiment is, Do citizens want these opportunities? As before, the evidence is mixed. Few participants reject the idea totally, yet very few are deeply committed to the idea. Thus, when tenants were given a choice between regular and electronic meetings, about one-third preferred one, one-third preferred the other, and one-third thought they were about the same. When asked about their participation in a weekly current events TV program soliciting popular sentiment via the telephone, involvement falls off quickly as the personal cost increases. While the idea of a "Dial-in-Your-Opinion" receives an overwhelming endorsement, fewer volunteer to participate personally in this endeavor, and very few are willing to pay $2.50 a month for this privilege. By the same token, the vast majority would not pay $2.50 a month to participate in an electronic town meeting (and this is even true among those who have previously taken part).

It should be clear from our analysis of these "electronically enhanced" democracies that the mere possession of the technology to link citizens to government is no guarantee that citizen preferences will automatically be

---

[49] It should be noted that all these data are drawn from returned questionnaires and it is likely that these tenants are more favorably disposed towards this communications project than those who did not complete questionnaires.

translated into public policy. Perhaps the most serious obstacle to this translation is not faulty technology (though problems do exist), but the political interests and capabilities of cizitens. Computerized voting, cable TV discussion, "Dial-in-Your Opinion" programs, and the like are meaningless unless citizens have something to say and want to express themselves. Of course, some future society may produce a citizenry capable of engaging in public debate that would lead to a closer relationship between opinion and policy decisions, but the very limited success of the MINERVA experiment (and direct legislation, as well) suggests that this is a difficult—perhaps impossible—task.

Less obvious, but no less important, even the most complex and sophisticated of these translation devices does not come to grips (let alone solve) many of the important theoretical issues in the whole relationship between opinion and policy. For instance, the MINERVA system allows an infinite variety of people to interact with each other prior to decision time, but no criteria are offered as to *which* public is relevant to a particular decision. Should Los Angeles blacks vote on urban development in Harlem? Likewise, the thorny question of agenda setting, question wording, number of policy alternatives, differences in intensities, nonresponses, and so forth, are no better solved electronically than by present means. If the further complexities of contradictory majorities, insoluble preference orderings, and "misinformed" mandates are thrown in for good measure, it becomes clear that electronically ascertaining the sentiment of every citizen may exacerbate, not solve, the problems of government by public opinion.

THE POLITICAL SYSTEM AND
OPINION-POLICY CONGRUENCE: CONCLUSION

In the space of a few pages our topics have ranged from the American Revolution to electronic, computer-assisted forms of citizen influence with an intermediate stopover on direct legislation. This has been a diverse selection of topics, but the basic question has remained constant: What mechanisms can bring about a close relationship between opinion and policy? It is acknowledged that policy *could* mirror opinion in any political system (if only by accident), but our concern is the means for increasing the *likelihood* of such congruence (the *actual* extent of opinion-policy congruence will be dealt with in the subsequent chapters).

It should be evident from our discussion that there is no institutional scheme guaranteed to achieve congruence. The present constitutional order incorporates several mechanisms to thwart the supposed evils of "majority factions" and while considerable political change has occurred since 1789, most of these institutional devices are nevertheless still functioning. The initiative and referendum certainly have a high potential for increasing opinion-policy congruence, but the data indicate serious deficiencies in their actual operations.

Electronic "town meetings" like MINERVA are perhaps too undeveloped to render a final judgment, but numerous problems have yet to be solved and the results of field experiments are not encouraging. This is not to say that methods of increasing congruence do not exist or cannot be invented. We have not considered numerous political formuli, e.g., parliamentary democracy, and even if nothing is presently conceivable, the matter is hardly forever closed.

What is the meaning of the fact that our analysis has been unable to come up with a sure-fire means of enhancing government by public opinion? Have we uncovered some kind of theoretical or institutional inadequacy in need of immediate remedy? Obviously not. As we have previously emphasized, a precise opinion-policy concordance in every issue is unlikely to be the highest political value held by citizens (even citizens of a democracy). Citizens may well prefer such values as stability, peace, economic prosperity, efficient management, personal freedom, leisure time, or some other condition to opinion-policy congruence. Not that congruence is not valuable; it just is not as precious as other political commodities. Viewed in this context, the existing constitutional structure, direct legislation politics, and the limited accomplishment of electronic town meetings may not be "failures" as much as expressions of the priority of other values. Hence, inadequacy for the task of translating opinion into policy does not automatically require their replacement with new and "better" political methods.

chapter five

PUBLIC OPINION AND PUBLIC POLICY: CONCEPTUAL AND MEASUREMENT PROBLEMS

As we saw in our previous discussions of "public opinion" and "public policy," even when these terms are clearly defined, the relationship between them remains complex. This is true even if we ignore the most difficult problem in this relationship—determining whether public opinion *causes* public policy. In Chapters 6 and 7 we shall concentrate on whether public policy is *consistent* with public opinion but the knotty question of causality is temporarily put aside. That is, we ask whether the government does what the public wants, not whether the latter has any *influence* over the former. Even though this procedure represents a considerable simplification, several complications still exist. While we cannot completely solve all these, it is important that we first consider some of the important problems before examining opinion and policy data, lest our conclusions be based on an overly simplistic interpretation. Our procedure shall be to first consider some of the broader conceptual problems of opinion-policy congruence and then to examine difficulties related to measurement and data collection.

CONCEPTUAL PROBLEMS IN DETERMINING OPINION-POLICY CONGRUENCE

What do we mean when we say, "Leaders follow public opinion?" We could mean that at any given moment leaders' actions are in accord in a *majority* of public sentiment. This is a perfectly reasonable interpretation, but it presents a highly static picture of what is really a dynamic process. Assuming that mass opinion and government policy were almost *perfectly unrelated,* it might

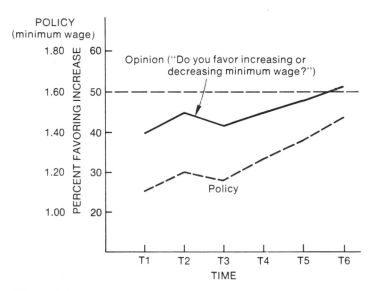

Figure 5-1 Public Opinion and the Minimum Wage (Hypothetical)

nevertheless be true that on at least some occasions leaders and followers would be pretty much in agreement. Moreover, if leaders did attempt to follow public opinion there would inevitably be a time lag between publicly expressed preferences and leaders' reactions, so a single measure of agreement at one point in time might not reveal a close relationship. Obviously, the need to eliminate one-shot "accidental" agreement as well as allowing leaders sufficient time to respond to the public (or vice versa) requires conceptualizing opinion-public policy as a dynamic, over-time relationship. Merely knowing public sentiment at Time 1 and public policy at Time 1 is not enough: we must have the same data for Times 2, 3, 4, *etc.*, if we hope to determine whether opinion and policy are consistent.

One hypothetical picture of such opinion-policy consistency is presented in Figure 5-1. Public responses to questions such as "Should the government raise the minimum wage?" and the actual minimum wage might follow a pattern like the one found in Figure 5-1.

In Figure 5-1 we find that as support for a higher minimum wage increases, the actual policy changes to a higher wage shortly thereafter. The reverse is also true—a decline in public support is closely associated with a reduced minimum wage. Put in the language of statistics, the correlation between opinion change and policy change is virtually 1.0. For the sake of brevity, let us label this approach to opinion-policy congruence as the Co-variation Model.[1]

[1] The reader should be aware that attempts to draw conclusions about co-variation between policy and opinion by visually inspecting the data might be greatly influenced by the scales employed in the presentation. Hence, by using very small units of measurement, e.g., actual dollars as opposed to rounded-off figures, the impression of sizable unrelated variation can be exaggerated. Alternatively, "smoothing out" information by rounding, fewer data points, and other such techniques can result in a misleading image of similarity between policy and opinion. Obviously, there is no clear "correct" way of visually presenting various types of data.

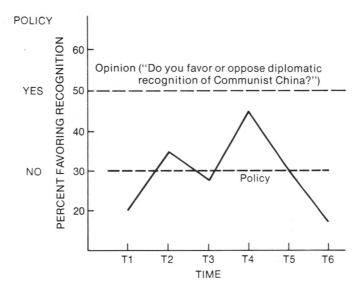

Figure 5-2 Public Opinion and Diplomatic Recognition of Communist China (Hypothetical)

Though this Co-variation approach has much to recommend it as a standard for judging opinion-policy consistency, it suffers from certain limitations. As our illustration suggests, this approach is particularly well suited to policies that can vary incrementally, e.g., expenditures, tax rates, number of troops overseas, etc. Not all public policy, however, can be treated like the minimum wage level. Consider, for example, the American decision to use nuclear weapons in World War II. This decision was an all or nothing proposition and even if small scale atomic bombs were available in 1945, the black-white character of policy would remain. Especially at the early stage of policy consideration, the choices to be made are often of the either-or type though subsequent decisions may incrementally increase or decrease previous commitment.[2]

A second drawback to this Co-variation approach is that it ignores the existence of a majority. Our interpretation of Figure 5-1 treats the percentage difference between, say 45 and 48 percent as identical to the difference between 48 and 51 percent. But if we conceive of policy-opinion consistency as existing only where a *majority* support a policy, then a shift of opinion over the 50 percent point is absolutely crucial. Indeed, in this approach a change in opinion from 51 percent to 100 percent (or 0 percent to 49 percent) would be politically inconsequential.

A hypothetical instance of opinion-policy consistency according to what might be called the Majoritarian Approach is depicted in Figure 5-2 which depicts public opinion and public policy in the diplomatic recognition of Communist China.

[2] For example, even tax policy—which can be considered almost infinitely incremental—starts with black and white decisions on what types of taxes are to be instituted. Thus, the question of "Should we have a progressive income tax" has to be decided "yes" or "no," but once initiated, the tax rates can increase or decrease.

Unlike Figure 5-1, we find that movements in popular sentiment are almost totally unrelated to government policy. Nevertheless, it is clear that a *majority* of the public agrees with public policy of nonrecognition of China at every point in time. If this Majoritarian Approach were applied to the hypothetical data in Figure 5-1, the interpretation would differ from our initial judgment. Specifically, it is not until T-5 that a majority favored increasing the minimum wage, yet for about two-thirds of the period between T-1 and T-5 the government was increasing the minimum wage. Thus, what was almost perfect opinion-policy according to the Co-variance Approach becomes a considerable lack of consistency by the criteria of the Majoritarian Approach.

Besides the Co-variations and Majoritarian notions of opinion-policy we can also distinguish a third model. This model—which we shall call the Satisfying Model—emphasizes the government's attempt to satisfy various segments of the population. Let us make the following assumptions. First, among citizens favoring a policy upon which no action has been taken, differences of opinion exist on exactly how much action should be taken. For instance, if 80 percent endorsed antipoverty spending in general, only 5 percent may support a 10 percent increase, 8 percent want a 15 percent increase, and so on until we are left with a minute proportion desiring enormous, unspecific spending increases. Second, government moves to satisfy public opinion over time by satisfying the least difficult demand first. Finally, citizens whose demands are satisfied change their preferences accordingly. This notion of congruence is depicted in Figure 5-3.[3]

The pattern depicted in Figure 5-3 is graphically very much unlike those in Figures 5-1 and 5-2, yet it too describes a responsive relationship between opinion and policy. When no policy exists, the magnitude of the public demand for antipoverty expenditures is large; when the first small expenditures are made a portion of the public is thus satisfied and no longer calls for government action. As more and more money is spent, more and more people are satisfied until a point is reached where satisfied people constitute a majority and the government no longer must respond further to public demands. Note that in the process of a majority being satisfied, the statistical association between opinion changes and government action will be negative (as one increases, the other decreases). Moreover, if we equate the establishment of a government antipoverty program with the spending of "substantial" sums, Majoritarian congruence will be achieved only after a considerable time lag (characterized by "half-hearted" solutions to an immense problem) and only when the public provides the barest of majorities.

---

[3] A further necessary assumption is that people who are satisfied by a particular level of effort are either indifferent to or are tolerant of at least some action beyond their own precise preferences. If each segment of the population were satisfied with only a particular degree of effort and rejected all others, it is clear that *no* policy would ever satisfy anyone but a small portion of citizens.

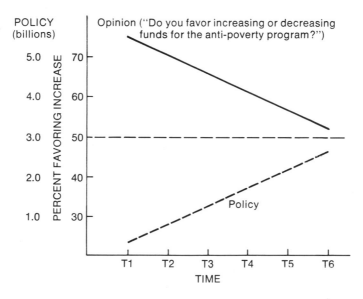

Figure 5-3   Public Opinion on Anti-Poverty Expenditures (Hypothetical)

There is, obviously, no self-evident reason for choosing one approach over the other as *the* correct model of opinion-policy consistency. If we wish to use such expressions as "government following the ebb and flow of popular sentiment," or "the growing pressure of public opinion" (both of which suggest the importance of *every* change in opinion) and we are dealing with incrementally divisible policies, the Co-variance approach is appealing. If, on the other hand, our principal concern is the majority's preference the Co-variance approach is inappropriate. On the other hand, if we think in terms of the government moving to satisfy more and more citizens, the third approach is relevant. We certainly cannot reject any of the approaches as irrelevant to the issue of opinion-policy consistency. Our own solution in dealing with these alternatives is to leave the question open—the opinion and policy data will be presented in some detail so the reader will not be forced to accept only one version of opinion-policy consistency.

Another, and very different, type of conceptual problem in establishing congruence is how we treat government failures to meet public preferences. This issue would not be a problem if political leaders were omnipotent, i.e., they could accomplish anything they desired. In such circumstances we could reasonably state that a lack of opinion-policy consistency represented a deviation from the public will. However, political leaders and governments are far from omnipotent: all sorts of forces can conspire to frustrate and destroy government policy. Failures in technology, actions of other governments, the weather, or changes in world economic conditions can all affect policy regardless of government intentions or actions. Thus, we can have circumstances where what appears to be opinion-policy incongruity really masks considerable, but unsuccessful, attempts by leaders to achieve consistency.

As an illustration of this type of situation consider government agricultural policy in recent years. Let us assume that a majority of the public favors a policy that guarantees large food supplies at cheap prices. We also know that food prices have risen substantially recently and occasional shortages have occurred. Does this mean that the government has "failed" to heed public sentiment? No doubt many an official would claim that prices would have jumped even further and shortages become even more acute had they not responded to public opinion. They would argue, and with some justification, that increased world food demand, weather conditions, and a number of other uncontrollable elements prevented government from *completely* following public demands and instead only allowed a very rough meeting of public desires. Hence, if we allow these outside factors to be considered, government action and public opinion were as consistent *as possible*.

An essentially similar situation transpired in the late 1960s over American involvement in Vietnam. A clear majority favored disengagement (though the specifics were unarticulated) and President Nixon continually emphasized his herculean efforts to bring about this disengagement despite the clear unwillingness of the North Vietnamese, Viet Cong, Chinese, and others to cooperate in this task. Though it took years between the emergence of a majority preference for disengagement and the actual complete withdrawal of U.S. troops, it is not unreasonable to conclude that the public's antiinvolvement feelings were being followed during this period. Of course, as Nixon's critics were quick to note, the claim that "I'm trying my best, but progress is slow" is always a good excuse for not doing what the people want. Indeed, at a more general level, we can readily see that by viewing public policy in terms of what is possible under given circumstances, we open a Pandora's box since leaders could always claim that precise congruence was impossible and that existing opinion-policy relationship in effect amounts to congruence.[4]

The last conceptual complexity relating to assessing opinion-policy congruence concerns not whether a particular public preference and a specific policy are in accord, but rather how we judge the overall matter of opinion-policy congruency. Certainly in examining public opinion and public policy in the United States we might want to make an overall judgment about the extent of consistency. The first and most obvious difficulty is that polling organizations like Gallup, Harris, and Roper provide surveys on only a small portion of all

---

[4] One factor in this argument that rarely receives public attention is the constitutional constraint on American officials. At least in some instances the public might demand policies and actions that are unconstitutional or otherwise illegal according to publicly supported laws. One wonders what the public reaction would be if a leader following a public mandate clearly violated the Constitution (assuming that most Americans oppose violation of the Constitution).

policy areas. Moreover, there is no reason to believe that the policy areas examined are a cross-section of all policy areas, hence any conclusions drawn from existing data could be misleading. (And recall from our discussion in Chapter 2 that increasing the number of polls would virtually require government run polls and this in turn poses serious problems.)

More difficult, however, than problems of insufficient data are questions involving the weight given to different policy areas in making a judgment of overall opinion-policy consistency. Certainly, few people would claim that all policies were of equal significance. For example, broad economic policy affecting the distribution of wealth is hardly in the same league as a proclamation making May national tavern month. Though we might all agree on the principle of giving different policy areas different weight in judging opinion-policy congruence, there are no agreed-upon criteria for making specific decisions. Would we consider government action in school integration as being equally important as overseas military involvement? Some people might; others would disagree. Moreover, judgments made at one time may be irrelevant at a subsequent date. Recall that during the 1950s, 1960s, and early 1970s, government action on energy resources was not considered of fundamental importance. However, with increased public awareness of an energy shortage this policy suddenly became salient. Does incongruity during one year of the so-called energy crisis equal years of congruence when the issue was far less salient?

We mention these conceptual problems in the analysis of opinion-policy congruence so that the reader will have a more sophisticated appreciation of the data in subsequent chapters. As we noted in our previous discussion of "public," "opinion," "policy," and so on, by emphasizing complexities, ambiguities, and unresolved issues, we are not putting roadblocks in the way of understanding. Unless the reader is aware of these issues, attempts to relate opinion data to policy decisions will be simple-minded and haphazard. Let us continue our theoretical concern for opinion-policy congruence by reviewing some more concrete problems of measurement.

MEASUREMENT PROBLEMS IN DETERMINING OPINION-POLICY CONGRUENCE

In our discussion in Chapter 2 on the goals of private polling organizations we observed that their essentially commercial character required surveys of topical, controversial issues. Few newspapers or other poll consumers would be much interested in questions about policies where the distributions of answers were self-evident, e.g., Do you favor apple pie and motherhood? Such data would be as newsworthy as features on banks not robbed, murders not committed, and so on.

At least for our purposes, this omission of polls on noncontroversial, highly consensual issues means that areas of close congruence between opinion and policy are underrepresented in our analysis. There are a large number of important political policies whose existence is accepted by the public with little disagreement. Among these are: an economic policy of growth, the support of a strong military force, a system of anticommunist foreign alliances, government regulations of professions like medicine, private ownership of banks and transportation, free public education through secondary school, a federal system of government, and many other policies that can be considered as part of the "givens" of American politics.[5] To be sure, pollsters do occasionally ask questions on details of policy choices within some of these broader areas, e.g., Should twelve years of schooling be legally required for everyone? But hardly ever is the fundamental question, e.g., the desirability of free public education, the object of analysis.

The net result of ignoring highly consensual issues is a picture of opinion-policy consistency heavily biased in the direction of incongruity. In the case of educational policy, for example, we are likely to find many discrepencies between public demands and public policy on numerous details such as decentralization and busing, yet few citizens reject the basic structures and goals of the present educational system. Hence, unless we are willing to substitute our intuitive beliefs about public support for the existing educational system for unavailable poll data, our conclusions might be that considerable opinion-policy incongruity exists in the area of education policy. At the same time, however, we must be aware that by stressing highly consensual policies we could reach the equally misleading conclusion that opinion-policy congruence is highly pervasive except for certain policy details. Obviously, then, some balance must be struck between a reliance on actual poll data which probably exaggerates incongruity and a concern for the broad consensual questions about which there is little difference of opinion.[6]

A second measurement problem, one that also involves the availability of data, concerns the accessability of policy data. Our analysis of the various meanings of "public policy" argued that everything from official intentions to actual outcomes might be construed as "public policy." No doubt a complete analysis of opinion-policy congruence would entail indicators of policy based on these differing conceptions. Thus, if we were considering air pollution policy we would examine legislative intention, the actual statutes, daily enforcement, resultant reductions in pollution, and so on, in order to get an accurate overall picture. It is clear, however, that certain kinds of policy data are more readily available than others. In particular, the day to day implementation of many policies may be beyond systematic scrutiny. Also, in some instances the true

[5] This acceptance of many features of American politics as "givens" beyond realm of daily controversy is further elaborated upon in Robert Weissberg, *Political Learning, Political Choice and Democratic Citizenship* (Englewood Cliffs, N.J.: Prentice-Hall Inc., 1974), especially Chap. 1.

[6] An interesting historical analysis of the patterns of consensus in American politics which stresses unconscious agreement on crucial issues is found in Louis Hartz, *The Liberal Tradition in America* (New York: Harcourt, Brace and World, Inc., 1955).

nature of a policy may not be understood for decades and even then, their precise character may be ambiguous. Consider, for instance, the problem in determining the "real" nature of statutes regulating the transportation industry—do agencies like the ICC (Interstate Commerce Commission) or FAA (Federal Aviation Authority) help citizens as much as they do the industries they are supposed to control? At one time it was assumed that the ICC and FAA were consumer-oriented; today the answer is less clear. Hence, if we were faced with strong public support for a policy of "public oriented regulation of airlines, trains, etc." it would be very difficult to contrast this sentiment with prevailing policy.[7]

Despite a long term concern for government policy making and policy outcomes among political scientists our data in public policy, except for a few time-bound case studies, are severely limited. In many policy areas, and for long periods of time, our knowledge consists of only the most obvious sorts of information, frequently records collected by the government itself. Take as an illustration data on government enforcement of racial integration in schools. In many instances it is virtually impossible to get accurate data on what proportion of a school district's black children are in the same classrooms as white children. Some racial integration data report only the proportion of school districts with *plans* to integrate their schools racially; other data might tell us the percentages of blacks and whites in the same school, but no mention is made of whether classes are integrated. A similar problem exists in obtaining the "real" data on federal income tax policy. Particularly in the upper income brackets, the actual tax rates are considerably lower than the official rates but such information is obviously difficult to ferret out (and methods of collecting and organizing the data also change). In both school integration and income tax policy, analysis must thus proceed with only limited, and frequently approximate policy data.

A third set of measurement problems revolves around interpreting the policy implications of imprecise words on questionnaires. Perhaps the most common culprits are words and phrases like "do more" or "make a greater commitment to." In the first place, survey respondents can differ on how much more they mean by "more" or what precisely amounts to a "greater effort." Second, as we saw in Chapter 3, citizens can differ on what they believe to be actual policy, so a demand for "more" may really mean satisfaction with the *status quo* or even a preference for "less." As an example of this problem consider the predicament of a public official aware of citizen ignorance of tax laws and faced with a public outcry for lower tax rates. Would a tax cut of 5 percent (or 10 percent or 25 percent) constitute a policy consistent with public demands? A tax *increase* might actually be consistent (in a sense) if people exaggerated existing tax rates.

---

[7] On almost every important issue some reasonable case can be made that the policy will produce results diametrically opposed to what is supposed to occur. For example, it has been maintained that steps towards disarmament will increase the chance of war, not peace; government medical insurance will generally provide worse medical care; price controls ultimately produce higher prices; and so on.

Moreover, how is an official supposed to respond to public demands for ambiguous policies? For instance, what would be the appropriate response to a public outcry for a "tougher" policy with the Communists? Some people might be satisfied with more belligerent speeches and sabre rattling; others would consider such behavior superficial and be satisfied with no less than vast increases in military expenditures or aggressive confrontations. Undoubtedly the most ambiguous opinion mandates are those responses to questions on "the most important problems facing this country" (or sometimes, "what are you most concerned about"). Implicit in responses is some type of call for government action. Needless to say, the imprecision of responses to such questions makes an analysis of opinion-policy congruence very inexact. What must frequently be done is to disregard these types of questions, even though the feelings lying behind the responses are very real and may be highly significant politically.

Though one might conclude that such problems could readily be solved in future polls by offering citizens more precise and policy relevant alternatives, this solution has its own problems. On any political issue a multitude of specific responses exist, and it is debatable whether pollsters have the right or capacity to select out the handful of choices that will define public debate. This process was well illustrated in the late 1960's when pollsters presented the public with only a sampling of numerous plans to end the Vietnam War. A second difficulty is suggested by much of the data in Chapter 3—once we move beyond generalities and diffuse feelings many citizens are unable to offer interpretable opinions to poll questions.

A fourth problem in the analysis of opinion-policy congruence also involves semantic interpretation, but here the issue is one of words changing their meaning over time. This difficulty is especially relevant for our analysis since we make extensive use of polls asking the same questions over many years. Consider, for example, a question on racial equality asked every year from 1950 to the present. In 1950 Americans probably had a different conception of what "racial equality" meant than respondents to the same question in 1975. In 1950 racial equality probably was interpreted in relatively narrow, legalistic terms, e.g., the absence of discriminatory laws. By the 1970s, however, "racial equality" connotes a vast array of policies affecting numerous aspects of social and economic life. Between these two time points the concept of "racial equality" was probably undergoing continuous change in the public mind. Though this illustration may be an extreme case, similar changes have occurred in the meaning given such terms as "isolationism," "welfare," "sexual equality," "freedom of expression," and "law and order."[8]

---

[8] This difficulty is nearly identical to the one faced by researchers doing cross-national or cross-cultural studies. Our discussion only touches on some of the obvious aspects of this problem. A more sophisticated analysis can be found in Adam Przeworski and Henry Teune, "Equivalence in Cross-National Research," *Public Opinion Quarterly* 30 (1966-67): 551-68.

The net result of such shifts in meaning is that a government policy consistent with public opinion at Time 1 may not be consistent with public opinion at Time 2 even though the government policy and the distribution of opinion both remain unchanged. Let us say that between 1950 and 1970 a majority demanded government subsidized medical care. Let us also suppose that during this period government health care expenditures increased yearly. Does this pattern constitute a growing opinion-policy consistency? It does if we assume that "government subsidized health care" meant in 1970 more or less what it meant in 1950. However, by 1970 such things as community mental health programs, sex counseling, and other medical innovations might be included implicitly in the policy demand so government actions may still lag behind public preferences. Obviously, this would not be a problem if more specific questions were asked each time, but as we have suggested before, increased precision in polling generates its own set of difficulties.

A further complexity also concerns equivalences, but of a more technical nature. Specifically, because of advances in social science methodology, polls conducted forty years ago differ from contemporary polls in terms of sampling, questionnaire design, interviewing techniques and other important aspects that can affect comparability of findings. Take, for instance, the consequences of improved sampling techniques. Modern sampling allows us to be confident that responses by 1500 randomly chosen people accurately reflect the opinions of 200 million people within certain known limits. Moreover, if we have two perfectly random samples we can compare the results with only a slight possibility that differences derive from a difference in the composition of the population being sampled. However, if one of the samples is drawn according to different rules than the other, differences attributable to these sampling decisions are more likely to arise.[9] Hence, because polls conducted in the 1930s are generally not as accurate as contemporary polls, statements about changes in opinion between the 1930s and the present can only be approximations about the real shifts. Similarly, early polls frequently did not allow for "Don't Know" or "No Opinion" responses, so comparison with more recent results are somewhat imprecise. All in all, the changes in polling technology require that when comparing early poll data with more recent data we must concentrate only on broad patterns, not minor shifts.

The final complexity of ascertaining opinion-policy congruence that we shall examine concerns the decentralized character of policy making in the United States. Though some policy decisions, e.g., diplomatic recognition of Communist China, are made only at the national level, a wide variety of policies are

---

[9] Perhaps an extreme case will make this problem clearer. Suppose that a sample of Klu Klux Klanners showed no support for racial integration of schools. Also suppose that a second sample, this one of NAACP members, showed overwhelming support for integration. Given the differences in the populations being sampled it is obviously incorrect to speak of changes in opinion between the two surveys. This problem is considered in greater detail in Norval D. Glenn, "Problems of Comparability in Trend Studies and Opinion Poll Data," *Public Opinion Quarterly* 34 (1970): 82-91.

simultaneously made at federal, state, and local levels. Particularly in such areas as education, crime, taxation, housing, and many welfare issues the actual operating policy results from decisions made at all three levels of government. For example, one's total tax bill is determined by provisions of the federal tax code, state laws, and local property taxes. Thus, to make precise statements about opinions and tax policy in general, we would need opinion surveys in each political unit and the relevant policy data.

In theory, such an analysis is possible though it would be very complex and extraordinarily expensive. In fact, such an analysis usually is impossible since with the exception of a handful of state and local polls, our opinion data indicate *national* opinion only. If, for instance, a Gallup Poll showed 60 percent favoring policy X we *cannot* say that 60 percent of the people in every state or city thus favor policy X (such a statement would require a poll of about 1500 respondents in each state and city). Even with a national figure of 60 percent, it is entirely possible that in some states and cities the nationally favored policy would receive less than a majority. Hence, where policy X was an issue at least partly determined at the state or local level, statements on opinion-policy congruence based only on national data could be highly misleading. As an illustration of what could happen, consider the hypothetical data in Table 5-1.

If states A, B, and C were the only states, a national poll would show that less than a majority (48.8 percent) favored policy X. However, people in two states (B and C) which comprised 55 percent (125/225) of the population lived where policy X was law. On this basis we might conclude that substantial incongruity existed. Nevertheless, a state by state analysis shows that perfect congruity occurs in each state. Put another way, a majority in each state got what it wanted although a national majority is satisfied to a very limited extent. When we realize that states and localities differ enormously in population (and frequently in policy preferences as well), the possibilities for misinterpretation suggested by these hypothetical data are very realistic. It is not unlikely, for example, that policies widely favored in populous states (e.g., mass transit, urban

Table 5-1   A Hypothetical Distribution of Opinion and Policy

	State			
	A	B	C	Total
Population	100	75	50	225
Number of people favoring X	45	38	26	109
Percent favoring X	45%	51%	52%	48.8%
Policy X is public policy	No	Yes	Yes	For 55% of public

development) constitute a national majority, but are rejected by majorities in most states who have no need for, say, mass transit.

CONCLUSIONS

We have seen that making statements about public opinion-policy congruence is fraught with complexities. We have stressed these difficulties not to intimidate the reader, but rather to avoid reaching conclusions based upon naive assumptions and simplistic notions of politics. It is important to realize that many of these complexities and difficulties are not easily resolved (if at all). Hence, merely to acknowledge them is not enough; issues such as the best method of establishing opinion-policy congruence, gaps in poll and policy data, changes in the meaning of political concepts over time, and other problems of meaning and method must continuously be kept in mind when we examine detailed data in subsequent chapters.

chapter six

OPINION AND
POLICY CONGRUENCE:
DOMESTIC ISSUES

The basic purpose of this chapter is to compare public opinion with public policy on a variety of domestic issues. In making these comparisons we in no way imply a cause-and-effect relationship between opinion and policies. We simply wish to examine the shape of this relationship between public policy and mass preferences over time. The analysis will pursue the same goal for foreign policy issues in the next chapter. The important and difficult question of whether opinion causes policy or policy causes opinion will be considered separately in Chapters 8-10.

In examining policy-opinion consistency we clearly face a problem of selecting a small sample of issues to examine. Since the advent of reasonably accurate opinion polling in the late 1930s, hundreds of political controversies have come and gone on which we have at least some opinion and policy data. For pragmatic reasons we must limit ourselves to only a handful of issue areas and there can be no guarantee that our analysis considers a perfectly representative sample of issues. In partial compensation for this limitation, we shall emphasize issues that have endured for relatively long periods of time as opposed to the "flash-in-the-pan" variety. Most issues examined will involve controversies that have persisted for ten years or more, occasionally surfacing as major issues of the day. Hence, we shall avoid controversies such as the appropriate government response to the urban riots of the late 1960s, the cessation of atmospheric nuclear testing of the 1950s, the Supersonic Transport (SST) debate of the early 1970s, and other such one-time questions. To be sure, these less enduring questions can be highly important politically, and the relationship between opinion and policy on a short-term basis can be very interesting, but such topics are beyond the scope of our analysis.

The domestic issues that we consider can be grouped into three categories. The first category includes issues entailing significant government impact on economic and social relationships. We shall examine opinion-policy congruence in three such areas: spending for national defense, an activity that consumes the largest share of the national budget; government involvement in medical care financing, which directly affects almost every citizen; and federal income tax policy, a subject whose personal relevance needs little justification. All three of these issues have repeatedly surfaced as salient issues and involve billions of dollars. A second class of issues involves the federal government and conflict over race relations, in particular the role of the national government in achieving racial integration in public schools. Though this issue is much more relevant for some people than others, the forced integration of schools has been among the most explosive and violence-filled questions of the last fifteen years. The last class of issues rarely involves much money and rarely directly touches most people, yet public debate over it is frequently highly passionate. Specifically, we shall examine policy and opinion in the area of capital punishment, gun control, and prayers in public school.

We proceed by considering one policy at a time. The presentation of each case will follow a similar format. The first question will be: How do we interpret the public mandate? As we have previously suggested, this is not always an easy task and we will frequently emphasize a conservative interpretation of the data; i.e., what is the most obvious demand conveyed by poll results. Second, we will briefly consider what particular policies are relevant to the opinion mandate (assuming, of course, that such a mandate is discernible). Finally, we will reach a conclusion on the degree of congruence between policy and opinion.

DEFENSE SPENDING, 1951-1973

If only because of the vast monetary sums involved, the issue of how much ought to be spent on national defense has been important during the last twenty-five years. Liberal reformers in particular have pictured the Defense Department as a bureaucratic monster consuming larger and larger amounts of money that could better be spent for more humane purposes. The dramatically increasing cost of military hardware resulting from more sophisticated technology and vast cost overruns have recently prompted even the military's traditional defenders to question the wisdom of spending ourselves broke on national defense.

In the abstract, ascertaining the public's feelings on whether military expenditures ought to be cut back is relatively simple, i.e., we would simply ask people how much they would increase or decrease expenditures. However, as we clearly saw in Chapter 3, the public exhibits considerable ignorance on military expenditures so it is possible that one person demanding a cutback might really want the same level of spending as someone desiring an increase.[1] Obtaining an intelligible mandate thus requires that peoples' erroneous beliefs be either corrected or somehow taken into account in calculating preferences. A different type of problem concerns discerning public preferences on the specifics of increases or decreases in expenditure levels. If leaders sought public guidance on what to cut or expand, it seems more than likely that preferences would be so diverse that no mandate could be discernible. Without such a mandate on specifics, even well-intentioned officials might find it difficult to follow the public's general sentiment.[2]

These and other problems of interpretation become apparent when we examine the opinion data in Table 6-1. First of all, there is no indication that Gallup's interviewer determined whether respondents possessed even a roughly accurate knowledge of defense expenditures. Nor do the data spell out what should be increased or decreased. These are important omissions, but rather than dismiss these data as completely uninformative, we shall side-step both of these problems by assuming that as far as leaders are concerned, demands of "increase," "decrease," or "keep same" are viewed as meaningful, followable expressions of public desires.[3] To be sure, a leader could disregard the messages depicted in Table 6-1 on the basis of public ignorance and lack of specificity, but without concrete data on distorting factors, these messages must be assumed to convey the same meaning. What, then, is the message in these data?

The most obvious point in Table 6-1 is that only once does a majority exist any one of the three policy options—in 1969, 52 percent favored decreasing defense expenditures. In the other six years we must infer a policy mandate without a clear majority (of course, we could create majorities in some of these

---

[1] Moreover, even if everyone had exact information on government expenditures, people might reasonably differ on what constituted "military" expenditures. For example, some of the Defense Department's money goes for educational benefits to veterans, health care for military families, and similar functions that could be considered as closer to social welfare than defense. Military expenditures also encompass much scientific research and programs with considerable benefit to nonmilitary agencies such as the space program.

[2] This situation seems likely to occur when defense cut-backs involve closing down military bases or ending contracts responsible for sizable employment. Because the impact of drastic cut-backs of this type can produce severe and extensive public dissatisfaction, implementing a mandate for expenditure reduction can undermine the mandate itself. Hence, both official action and inaction produce incongruity between policy and opinion.

[3] One simplifying assumption that could be made in handling these and similar data is that faulty knowledge is randomly distributed. Hence, even though some people who really want "decrease" due to ignorance select "increase" (and vice versa), such mistakes cancel one another out so the polls reflect "true" opinion in the aggregate. This assumption is plausible and if correct would make these data more plausible to policy makers.

Table 6-1 Public Satisfaction with Levels of Defense Spending*

Year	Increase Spending	Decrease Spending	Keep Same	No Opinion
1952	29	26	25	20
1953	22	20	45	13
1960	21	18	45	16
1969	8	52	31	9
1971	11	50	31	8
1972	9	35	40	9†
1973	13	46	30	11

*In 1952 the question was "Do you think the Government should spend more money or less money for defense purposes." In other years the questions were along the lines of whether what the Federal Government in Washington spends for national defense should be increased, kept about the same, or reduced.
†In 1972 the alternative "ended altogether" was offered and 5 percent agreed with this position.
SOURCE: Gallup Poll.

years by eliminating the "no opinion" response from our calculations). Nevertheless, if we disregard the 1952 poll where the distribution can be interpreted in almost any way, some expression of popular sentiment can be ascertained. Certainly in 1953 and 1960 the thrust of public opinion was towards maintaining existing levels of expenditures (if we did exclude "no opinion," "keep same" would constitute a majority in both polls.) However, in 1969 and 1971 there is a noticeable shift of opinion with "decrease spending" the most popular alternative. The results in 1972 and 1973, while not free from ambiguity, do show a considerable lack of enthusiasm for greater military spending. Overall, except perhaps for the 1952 results, we can characterize the public's preference during this period as alternating between decreases and maintaining the *status quo,* but certainly not preferring increases of Defense Department spending.

A number of different policy indicators might reasonably be used to ascertain opinion-policy accordance. The first type of data one might consider is the annual Defense Department budget. Though such data are readily available, they suffer from the obvious drawback that a defense dollar in 1952 was worth considerably more than one in 1973. In addition to taking inflation into account, changes in defense expenditures policy might also be viewed against the backdrop of other government expenditures or the economy in general. It is entirely possible, for example, that while more money is now spent on military matters than before, defense spending has shrunk compared with expenditures in other areas. In view of the inadequacy of a single indicator of spending for national defense, Figure 6-1 depicts trends in three different indicators: (1) the amount of money spent for defense each year (excluding veterans benefits); (2) the proportion of the entire Federal budget allocated to the military; and (3) the proportion of the Gross National Product (GNP) consumed by the military.

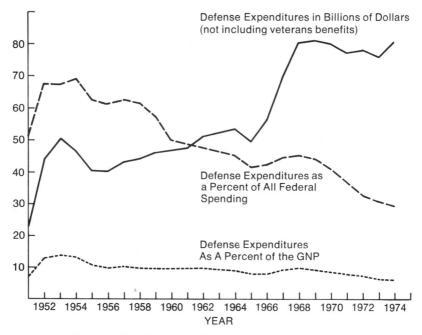

Figure 6-1   National Defense Expenditures, 1951-1974

SOURCES: 1952-1959 data are from *Statistical Abstracts of the U.S.: 1960*, p. 239.
1960-1972 data are from *Statistical Abstracts of the U.S.: 1973*, p. 248. 1973-74 data
are from *Statistical Abstracts of the U.S.: 1974*, p. 306

The juxtaposition of the public opinion data from Table 6-1 against the three measures of policy in Figure 6-1 does not produce a single statement about opinion-policy agreement. Between 1953 and 1960 the actual level of expenditures (the solid line) did remain relatively stable, which is roughly consistent with opinion during this same period. Unfortunately, we lack public opinion data for 1965-1968 when due to the Vietnam War military spending increased dramatically. We do know, however, that at least until 1968 a majority of the American public did support our military involvement in Vietnam, so it is likely that these expenditure increases were also supported. Beginning in 1969 (which was a period of growing anti-Vietnam sentiment) we find strong public support for decreases in spending (or, in the case of 1972, a plurality in favor of the same level of expenditures). Again, in a rough sense, the actual expenditure levels for this period correspond to the major thrust of public opinion.

Examination of Defense Department budgets as a proportion of all Federal expenditures and the GNP produces some interesting patterns. On the whole, the actual amount of money consumed by the military grows during the period described in Figure 6-1 (though we must realize that the massive jumps are clearly associated with the Korean and Vietnamese Wars). At the same time, however, there is a general downward trend in the "piece of the pie" taken by the military for this period. Put another way, the Defense Department may be getting more and more, but it is not doing as well in comparison to other interests. The downward trends give a certain credence to military supporters who claim that on the basis of traditional allocations of resources and overall changes in the economy, we should be spending much more for national defense.

Do the patterns displayed by these two "relative" indicators fit with public sentiment? If we were to interpret the data in Table 6-1 as saying that from 1953 to 1973 the public will, though frequently divided on whether to decrease or to maintain spending levels, clearly did not support increases, then these two comparative indicators are consistent with public opinion. Of course, one could very well argue that such opinion-policy correspondence is fortuitous and really has very little to do with military expenditure levels. That is, the United States experienced enormous economic growth during this period and long standing demands for expensive social welfare programs, e.g., antipoverty agencies, could finally be met. Thus, the military sector only appeared to shrink in comparison with other programs. Opinion-policy congruence, then, is only an accidental by-product of other policies and not the intended result of government decision-making.

Whether or not patterns of military expenditures are "really" in accord with public opinion is a question that has, obviously, not been conclusively answered. Even though we have somewhat arbitrarily put aside the intelligibility of a public preference on defense spending, the nature of the opinion distribution and divergences in trends among policy indicators allow numerous differing conclusions. Our analysis has not tried to manipulate the data in order to reach a single answer. If there is a clear conclusion, it is that in some ways opinion and policy are in accord on the issue of military expenditures but in other ways a lack of congruence exists.

GOVERNMENT ASSISTANCE FOR HEALTH CARE
1936-1972

Like the issue of how much should be spent on national defense, the Federal Government's role in providing for personal medical care has periodically surfaced as a major source of controversy. The enormous and sometimes frenzied efforts of the American Medical Association to mobilize citizens against the supposed menace of "socialized medicine" are well known. And for every AMA anti-government-intervention campaign there are perhaps dozens of defunct schemes to help citizens with the financial burden of medical care. Given both the rising cost of medical care and technology as well as growing numbers of elderly heavily dependent on medical care, the government intervention question is likely to persist.

Unlike the pattern displayed by poll data on military expenditures, the results

Table 6-2   Public Support for Government Assistance for Health Care, 1936-1972*

Date	Support Government Aid	Oppose Government Involvement	Qualified	Don't Know No Opinion
1936	74	20	–	6
1937	74	19	–	7
1938	78	18	–	4
1942	74	21	–	5
1956	54	26	8	12
1960	60	20	12	8
1964	50	28	6	16
1968	52	27	5	16
1970	39	35	13	13
1972	44	39	14	3

*The questions for 1936, 1937, and 1938 asked respondents whether the government should provide free medical care for those unable to afford it. The 1942 question asked whether more tax money should be spent for medical care for those who need it. The 1956 through 1968 questions were in the form of approving or disapproving of government helping people get doctors and hospital care at low cost. The 1970 and 1972 questions were seven point scales ranging from support for a complete government health insurance to opposition to any government intervention.

SOURCES: 1936-1942 reported in Michael E. Schiltz, *Public Attitudes Toward Social Security* (Washington, D.C.: U.S. Department of Health, Education and Welfare, 1970), p. 128. Other years from the SRC, University of Michigan. Additional opinion data on this issue are reported in "The Polls: Health Insurance," compiled by Hazel Erskine, *Public Opinion Quarterly* 39 (1975): 128-43.

of questions on health care assistance presented in Table 6-2 depict a relatively clear public disposition. Of the ten data points, only in 1970 and 1972 does support for government involvement fall below 50 percent, but even here the progovernment position constitutes the most popular sentiment. If willingness to involve government in health matters constitutes "socialism" then many Americans are indeed socialists. Of course, one could conceivably argue that these preferences do not necessarily involve doctor-patient matters, i.e., people want government interventions in medical school construction, basic research and educational programs, but not personal health care. Though such assertions cannot be positively refuted, a much more plausible interpretation of these data is that since 1936 most citizens want the government to assume at least part of the cost of medical care.

In analyzing the policy response to public sentiment our basic question is: between 1936 and 1972 has the Federal Government acted to subsidize the personal health care of citizens? In nations like Great Britain, Sweden and the Soviet Union where all health services have little or no direct cost to the user an answer to such a question is simple. However, health care financing in the United

States is very complex, involving such procedures as tax deductions for some medical expenses, government financing of medically related research and hospital construction, and a variety of public health programs to mention only a few complicating factors.[4]

Though the actual cost of medical care to the average citizen might initially appear to be the best indicator of government effort to decrease medical costs, this indicator of policy presents serious problems. First, greater affluence has increased public demand for health care so that costs, even taking inflation into account, have risen dramatically since 1936. Thus, even if the government bore an increasingly greater share of the cost of medicine, the individual financial burden may still be growing larger and larger. A related consideration is that the quality of medical care has improved since 1936 allowing consumers to buy many services previously unavailable. For example, 30 years ago people with certain types of kidney diseases would have died; today, however, technology has provided a cure, albeit an expensive one, for some of these kidney disorders. The availability of new and expensive cures makes over-time comparisons difficult since more is now being bought. (It is also possible that despite greater outlays for medicine, in terms of results the services now rendered may be cheaper than before.)[5]

Another policy consideration that deserves mention concerns how we evaluate different distributions of government medical assistance. It is not necessarily the case that greater government financial contributions to medical services result in ever larger numbers of people benefiting from good medical care. Would we consider, say, complete subsidization of 10 percent of the population as roughly equivalent to a partial contribution to everyone's health care? This complexity emerged recently over Congressional authorization of federal aid to a very small number of people completely dependent on extraordinarily expensive artificial kidney machines. Such aid could ultimately run into the billions and it was argued by some that the money would be better spent on more people. Unfortunately for our analysis, the opinion data in Table

---

[4] The issue of measuring government intervention in health care finances becomes even more complex if we include tax rates in our analysis. Except perhaps for inmates of institutions or those without work, there is no such thing as "free" medical care so long as the government taxes you to get the money to pay for medical care. Thus, one can pay dearly for "free" medical care if one's tax bills are very large. To keep matters simple, however, we will not deduct that proportion of one's total tax bill going to government medical programs from one's own medical benefits to compute net government medical subsidy.

[5] Take, for instance, the treatment of polio. Twenty years ago, polio was a very expensive illness; today the problem is solved by the Salk vaccines for a few cents per person. If we could chart some sort of "cost per cure per illness" over time we might possess a much better indicator of true medical costs, but such a measure is currently unavailable.

6-2 do not specify how the government should distribute medical benefits, so this important issue cannot be considered.

Our analysis of government action in the area of medical care will consider two types of data. First, we shall examine the legislative record to determine the nature of government involvement since 1936. This record will reveal any serious attempts to meet public demands as well as the provisions of government medical assistance programs. A second aspect of policy involves changes in the costs and benefits of medical care from 1935 to 1972. Of particular relevance is the porportion of medical costs being borne by the government. We shall also consider the role of private insurance, e.g., Blue Cross, in helping to meet the burdens of health care.

Let us begin by considering the various successful and unsuccessful attempts of the federal government to provide health care assistance. Table 6-3 presents a brief history of such governmental efforts. In light of the unambiguous opinion favoring public action during the 1930s and 1940s, it is interesting to note that the first action on the part of the national government occurred in 1950 and even then the policy change was relatively minor. To be sure, presidential efforts at providing extensive medical care assistance did occur, but these intentions amounted to little. Even Eisenhower's modest, private insurance oriented proposals fared no better than the more grandiose plans of Roosevelt and Truman.

In 1960, with the passage of the Kerr-Mills bill, the federal government undertook its first serious involvement in medical aid to citizens. However, this aid is directed only at the needy elderly, and state participation in Kerr-Mills is optional (though few, if any states can resist the lures of "free" federal money).

Table 6-3   Health Care Chronology, 1935-1972

1935-	Roosevelt, in report by President's Committee of Economic Security sent to Congress, endorsed principle of compulsory national health insurance but made no specific program recommendations.
1943-	Senators Wagner, Murray, and Dingal introduce bill calling for sweeping revisions and broadening of Social Security Act to provide compulsory national health insurance for everyone to be financed through a payroll tax. Legislation died in 1944.
1945-	Roosevelt in State of Union message alludes to right of "good medical care" but makes no specific recommendations. President Truman sends to Congress a plan for a comprehensive, pre-paid medical insurance plan covering everyone and financed by increasing Social Security tax. Plan would cover doctor, hospital, nursing, laboratory, and dental services. Coverage for needy people would be paid for by general revenue funds.
1946-	Senator Taft introduces alternative to Truman bill that would authorize $230 million in federal grants to states to provide medical care to the needy. Hearings on Truman and Taft bills held but no action taken.
1949-	Truman in State of the Union message again calls for national compulsory health insurance. Truman proposals are debated in Congress and after bitter opposition from American Medical Association and other groups, no legislative action taken.

1950-   Truman again calls for national compulsory health insurance and once more Congress does nothing. However, legislation is enacted to have federal government help states provide medical care for welfare recipients. Because of these federal funds, states increase payments to doctors and health care institutions for medical services to people on welfare.

1954-   Eisenhower calls for legislation that would help meet some medical costs for needy citizens through government reinsurance of private insurance companies. Such reinsurance would protect firms against possible heavy losses. Bill was attacked by the AMA as leading to socialization and by those favoring government action for the scheme's limited scope. House defeats Eisenhower proposal.

1956 and 1957   Eisenhower endorses plan allowing small insurance companies to pool resources to expand medical expense coverage; receives no Congressional action.

1960   Kerr-Mills bill passed and signed into law. This legislation provided for federal assistance to states for care of elderly people under the existing Old-Age Assistance Program. No limits were placed on the amount of benefits provided. However, state participation in the program was optional.

1961-   President Kennedy's proposal to provide health insurance to the elderly through Social Security is rejected by Congress. However, Kerr-Mills bill is changed somewhat to give more federal money to the state.

1962-   Senator Anderson's bill providing for extensive medical services to the elderly (but only certain doctor bills) to be financed by a payroll tax is defeated in the Senate. However, the federal contributions to state program for the blind, disabled, and elderly are increased.

1964-   Senate passes comprehensive health care plan designed to assist elderly, but plan is blocked by House.

1965-   Medicare program becomes law. This program is financed under Social Security and for the elderly it provides 90 days of hospital care, extensive nursing home care, and for a payment of 3 dollars a month, 80 percent of doctor bills and related costs are covered. Medicaid program in which the federal government contributes to state medicaid programs for the needy (regardless of age) is also enacted. In the first year of Medicaid the cost to the federal government was about one billion dollars.

1966-   Congress enacts a variety of bills providing federal funds for public health. These programs include grants to state authorities for public health services, planning health care programs, and the training of health personnel.

1967-   Partnership for Health Amendments of 1967 authorizes $589 million for fiscal 1968-70 for grants to state planning and health services.

1968-   Legislation passed to improve medical training and research facilities, implement program for the treatment of various serious diseases, and established programs for the treatment of alcoholism.

1969-   Despite considerable Congressional debate on health care and Nixon warning that a "massive crisis" in health care due to skyrocketing costs, nothing much more done.

1970-   Overriding a Presidential veto, 2.79 billion is authorized for hospital construction for 1971-73. Nixon vetoes plan to increase number of family doctors but financial support for programs in specific areas, e.g., alcoholism, drug abuse, paramedical training, and mental retardation, is approved.

1971-   A number of national health insurance plans defeated in Congress, but only actions taken were expanding government aid to medical training and cancer research.

1972-   Congress authorizes federal money for a number of programs on specific diseases, e.g., sickle cell anemia, multiple sclerosis, and arthritis. No action taken on national insurance plans debated in 1971.

Between 1960 and 1965 the government's role in medical care was expanded incrementally—more funds were authorized for existing programs and a number of new but very circumscribed health programs were created. The Medicare and Medicaid programs enacted in 1965 represent significant departures from previous policy in terms of financial commitment. Nevertheless, as in Kerr-Mills, the scope of the program is limited (covering only the elderly in the case of Medicare and the poor in the case of Medicaid). Following the Medicare and Medicaid enactments, the federal government followed a pattern similar to the one of the first half of the 1960s: medical assistance programs were enacted on a piecemeal basis, i.e., for a particular problem, with much of the money going for existing state programs.

What is conspicuous by its ommission from this chronology of government medical policy is passage of plans affecting the expenses paid by most people for their usual medical problems. Though the elderly and the poor might have the greatest need for government help, and government assistance may be most essential in expensive areas like cancer research, these efforts have little direct bearing on most peoples' run-ins with medical care. This situation stands in great contrast to English medicine where the emphasis is on government assistance for everyone and for more humdrum, but personally very important medical problems.

A different aspect of federal government medical care involvement is presented in Figure 6-2 and Table 6-4 which considers these issues in terms of overall financial efforts. The most striking feature of the date in Figure 6-2 is the enormous increase in per capita health expenditures between the 1930s and 1971/1972 (though examinations of this cost in terms of the total GNP reflects a much more modest increase in the proportions of the national income allocated to medical spending). These data also show a corresponding sharp increase in government spending during this period, particularly from 1965 onward when the Medicare and Medicaid programs were operating.[6] Neverthe-less, this sharply increased government share of the total cost burden (both in percentage and absolute terms) should not obscure the fact that the private per capita expenditures were growing consistently larger during this period. Put another way, government was making more of an effort, but the net result was not a decreasing private burden in terms of actual dollar outlays.

Additional light on the question of medical spending is shed by the data in Table 6-4, which depicts the relative share of medical costs (excluding research, hospital construction, etc.) borne by private individuals, private insurance

---

[6] Though these data on parallel increases on medical costs and government outlays might be interpreted to show government response to rising costs, the opposite interpretation is also plausible; prices rose in response to massive government intervention in direct medical care. Proponents of this second view would claim that such factors as increased demand due to government payments, more bureaucracy, fraud, and other factors, "artificially" increased medical care costs.

Table 6-4 Distributions of Personal Health Care Expenditures,* by Source of Funds, 1934-1972 (by percent)

Year	Private				Public		
	Total	Direct Payments	Insurance Benefits	Other	Total	Federal	State and Local
1935/4	85.2	82.5	–	2.7	14.8	3.4	11.3
1939/40	84.7	82.0	–	2.7	15.3	3.9	11.4
1949/50	79.8	68.3	8.5	3.0	20.2	9.4	10.8
1955/4	77.2	59.0	15.5	2.7	22.8	10.4	12.4
1959/60	78.3	55.3	20.7	2.3	21.7	9.2	12.4
1964/5	79.2	52.5	24.7	2.0	20.8	8.5	12.3
1965/6	78.2	51.5	24.7	2.0	21.8	9.2	12.5
1966/7	69.8	45.4	22.6	1.8	30.2	18.1	12.1
1967/8	65.0	40.8	22.5	1.7	35.0	22.5	12.5
1968/9	64.1	39.0	23.4	1.6	35.9	23.6	12.3
1969/70	65.2	39.3	24.4	1.5	34.8	22.7	12.1
1970/71	64.6	37.6	25.6	1.5	35.4	23.5	11.9
1971/72	62.8	34.9	26.4	1.4	37.2	24.7	12.5

*Personal health care expenditures include all expenditures for health services other than (a) expenses for pre-payment and administration, (b) government public health activities, and (c) expenditures of private voluntary agencies for other health services. *SOURCE:* Barbara S. Cooper and Nancy L. Worthington, "National Health Expenditures, 1929-1972," *Social Security Bulletin*, Vol. 36 (January 1973): 16.

companies, and various levels of government. Observe that the relative cost borne by individuals through direct payment has declined sharply over this period. By 1971/72 only about a third of all money spent on items like doctor bills, hospital stays, dentists, etc., came directly out of peoples' pockets. What clearly accounts for this drop is both the policies of the government (especially the federal government) and the rapid expansion of private health care programs such as Blue Cross (though programs like Blue Cross are not usually free to the individual). Clearly, then, Americans are getting more and more help in paying for medicine though, as the data in Figure 6-2 show, the costs of such care are rising enormously.

To return to the central question in our analysis: Do all the opinion and policy data on governmental involvement in health care show public opinion and public policy to be in accordance with each other? Certainly it is difficult to claim congruence before 1960 when public sentiment unambiguously called for a government commitment yet the response in terms of programs and expenditures was relatively slight. However, since 1965, the government's actions have changed and made amends for previous inaction though it is far from obvious that the policy response is exactly what the public has in mind. As we have seen, almost all the government programs are directed towards specific classes of citizens, e.g. the elderly, or towards well-defined problems, e.g. cancer research. The nonelderly and the nonneedy with mundane medical problems are not the great beneficiaries of the legislation of the late 1960s, though such

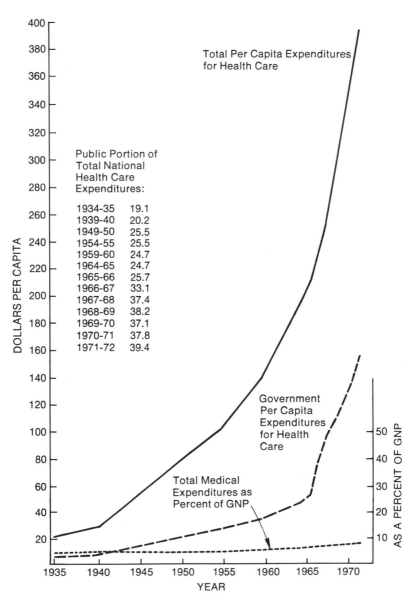

Figure 6-2 Per Capita Health Care Expenditures, 1934-1972, by Sources
of Funds

SOURCE: Barbara S. Cooper and Nancy L. Worthington, "National Health Expenditures, 1929-1972," *Social Security Bulletin*, Vol. 36 (January 1973): 16.

groups are in the majority. Similarly, as the expenditure data show, the
government has contributed mightily to medical care finances, but despite these

efforts (and the efforts of private insurance companies), the financial burden of medical care in actual dollars continues to grow.

A complicating consideration in the juxtaposition of opinion and policy is that the level of public support is by 1972 less than a clear majority though government assistance appears to be on the increase. It seems plausible, however, that as the government steps up its involvement, the proportion of people satisfied by such efforts increases, so the demand for more government action declines. Eventually, perhaps, an equilibrium point will be reached in which a majority would leave the *status quo* unchanged. More generally, these opinions and policy trends illustrate the interesting possibility that meeting public demands may result in an inverse relationship between policy and opinion—the greater the policy effort the less the public demand, as more and more people become satisfied with the response.[7]

Overall, it is probably fair to say that public opinion and government medical assistance policy are generally consistent if we were willing to discount somewhat the long time-lag between the existence of the public sentiment in the 1930s and eventual government response in the 1960s. This congruence derives in part, however, from our inability to say precisely what the public mandate requires to be satisfied. If we were to infer a demand for a policy similar to British National Health Insurance which covers all personal medical expenses, then congruence is certainly not occurring. However, if we adhere to a minimal interpretation of public preferences, i.e., "Something ought to be done by the government about the costs of medicine," then congruence becomes more apparent. Though such a minimal interpretation may avoid some important issues in the health care controversy, going beyond this interpretation may require making assumptions about public sentiment that are unwarranted in the light of our previous discussion of citizen capabilities.

INCOME TAX RATES, 1948-1973

Though the issue of federal income tax rates has rarely been a burning controversy, it is an issue that few citizens can ignore (particularly on April 15th). Of the various debates surrounding the federal income tax, the one that is probably most salient to the average person is the amount of personal income absorbed by taxes. No doubt the shock of seeing one's first paycheck decimated by federal withholding or the experience of having to come up with additional money at tax time has encouraged serious thought about the justice of the tax system.

---

[7] Recall our previous discussion of alternative models of opinion-policy congruence in Chapter 5 on the type of congruence. Though we lack the necessary data to verify the existence of a "satisfying" model, it is clear that none of these data approximate the Co-variation model.

Not unexpectedly, the Gallup Poll data presented in Table 6-5 shows considerable feeling that the income tax rates are too high. Only in 1948 did a majority believe that rates are "about right" (though in 1961 and 1962 the "too high" position was most popular only by a plurality). The public has thus been making its preferences clear during this time: reduce the amount we have to pay in income taxes. Of course, as in so many other policy areas, exactly how much of a change is demanded is left unstated. Some citizens might be satisfied with a 10 percent cut; others might wish a return to the original maximum rate of 2 percent. Moreover, since the Gallup interviewers do not confront respondents with possible losses in valued government programs, e.g., medical care subsidies, the demand for tax relief is an easy choice. Thus, it could be argued, these sentiments may be superficial ones readily shifted should people be given hard choices between, say, tax cuts or fewer government services. Nevertheless, these considerations that would make public sentiment an unintelligible mandate are only *possible* considerations, not certainties, so we can assume that a demand for lower tax rates is a meaningful, meetable request.

What would be the appropriate policy response to demands depicted in Table 6-5? One relatively easy and highly visible response would be to cut federal income tax rates. However, it is well-known that the official rates are rarely what people pay (particularly in the higher brackets), so we must go beyond official tax tables. It is also obvious that between 1948 and 1973 income levels in the United States rose sharply. This means that even if tax rates remained unchanged or lowered somewhat, most people would pay increasingly larger amounts of tax as their income moved up through the tax brackets. Such complexities require that we examine not only tax rates, but income distributions and actual tax burdens since 1948 to see whether government has responded to public opinion.

Table 6-5   Public Satisfaction* with Federal Income Tax Levels

	Too High	*About Right*	*Too Low*	*No Opinion*
1948 (March)	57	38	1	4
1949 (March)	43	52	1	4
1950 (Feb)	56	40	–	4
1951 (Feb)	52	43	1	4
1952 (Feb)	71	26	–	3
1957 (April)	61	31	–	8
1959 (March)	51	40	1	8
1961 (Feb)	46	45	1	8
1962 (Feb)	48	43	–	9
1966 (Feb)	52	39	–	9
1967 (March)	58	38	1	3
1969 (March)	69	25	–	6
1973 (March)	65	28	1	6

*"Do you consider the amount of Federal income taxes which you have to pay too high, about right or too low?"
SOURCE: Gallup Poll

Table 6-6 Federal Individual Income Tax Rates, 1948 to 1972

Taxable Income[1]	1948 -49	1952 -53	1954 -63	1964	1965 -67	1968	1969	1970	1971-72 Single	1971-72 Joint
2001-4000	19	25	22	20	19	21	21	20	19	19
4001-6000	23	29	26	24	22	24	24	23	21	22
6001-8000	26	34	30	27	25	27	28	26	24	25
8001-10,000	30	38	34	31	28	30	31	29	25	28
10,001-12,000	33	42	38	34	32	34	35	33	27	32
12,001-14,000	38	48	43	38	36	39	40	37	29	36
14,001-16,000	41	53	47	41	39	42	43	40	31	39

[1] Income after exclusions, deductions and exemptions
SOURCE: U.S. Bureau of the Census, *Statistical Abstract of the United States:* 1973, Washington, D.C., p. 391.

Turning first to the actual tax rates between 1948 and 1972 (Table 6-6) we find considerable fluctuation, but no clear trends during this period. For example, if we compare the 1948-49 rates with the most recent rates (1971-72) we find that within each income category recent rates are slightly lower. However, a number of periods subsequent to 1948-49 show increased tax rates, e.g., 1952-53 and 1969, so we certainly cannot say that income tax rates have consistently declined during this period of public dissatisfaction. Additional data on this question are presented in Table 6-7, which shows over-time shifts in peoples' income categories. These data dramatically show the rise in personal income between 1950 and the early 1970s—by 1970 almost 30 percent of the tax returns showed incomes in excess of $10,000 compared to less than 4 percent in 1950.

These various types of tax data can be interpreted in a number of different ways, but in none of these interpretations is it possible to conclude that the tax bite has been alleviated. For example, the average tax rate depicted at the bottom of Table 6-7 has varied over time, but it certainly has not become lower than the 1950 figure of 10.2 percent (note that the average income tax payment has about tripled). Alternatively, if we compare the tax rates given in Table 6-6 with the average taxable incomes in Table 6-7, the rate for the average tax payer has remained about the same or increased slightly. Thus, while in 1955 someone with the average taxable income fell into the 26 percent bracket, in 1970 the average tax payer was in the 29 percent bracket.

All in all, despite a long history of public dissatisfaction with the federal income tax bite, the government has provided no relief. Today's tax payer is not only handing over more money to the government, but a larger proportion of peoples' incomes are going to taxes. To be sure, if we were willing to include benefits derived from each tax dollar we might conclude that since federal spending has increased enormously during this time span, the average citizen is getting more per tax dollar than before. Thus, even though more is paid out to the government than before, federal taxes are a relative bargain compared to the

Table 6-7   Number of Taxable Returns by Income Category, Average
Taxable Income and Average Tax, by Selected Years 1950-1970

Taxable Individual Returns by Income Group[1] *(in percent)*	*1950*	*1955*	*1960*	*1965*	*1970*
Under 1,000	4.1	3.2	2.8	1.0	.1
1,000-1,999	15.7	11.0	8.7	8.4	2.1
2,000-2,999	22.9	14.1	10.5	8.1	6.3
3,000-4,999	37.7	33.9	25.4	19.1	14.8
5,000-9,999	16.0	32.1	41.6	42.9	36.9
10,000-14,999	1.8	3.4	7.6	14.3	23.7
15,000-24,999	1.6	1.4	3.2	5.9	2.4
25,000-49,999	1.6	.7	3.2	5.9	2.8
50,000-99,999	.2	.1	.2	.4	.6
100,000-499,999	*	*	*	.1	.1
over 500,000	*	*	*	*	*
average income per return	3416	4314	5224	6409	8552
average tax per return	349	512	651	737	1138
average tax rate	10.2	11.9	12.5	11.5	13.3

*less than .05%
[1] Adjust gross income class
SOURCE: 1950-1970 data from *Statistical Abstract of the U.S.: 1973*, p. 396

old days. Such reasoning, though ingenious, would probably not constitute a satisfactory policy response to people dissatisfied with tax rates.

RACIAL INTEGRATION OF PUBLIC SCHOOLS, 1956-1972

The issue of racially integrating public schools has been one of the most enduring and explosive policies in the 1950s, 1960s, and 1970s. When the United States Supreme Court ruled in 1954 that state-required racial segregation was unconstitutional, it set off an enormously complex set of events affecting millions of people. The battle over school segregation has over the years taken a variety of forms and raised many other issues such as school financing, curriculum content, and even the value of much of our educational system. Immediately following the Court's decision, attention was focused on the south and the attempts of leaders to either defy the law (e.g., Governor Faubus calling out the National Guard to prevent integration in Little Rock, Arkansas) or circumvent it through legal maneuvers or manipulation of school district boundaries. More recently, the focus has shifted to northern cities and efforts to integrate inner city schools through such techniques as bussing or redefinition of school districts to include both central city and suburban schools.

The racial integration of public schools is not a single issue, but a whole complex set of interrelated policy questions. Perhaps the most obvious of the many questions concerns public support for racial integration at least in principle. Several studies suggest that from the mid-1950s onward most Americans agreed with the general idea of racial integration of schools.[8] The data in Table 6-8 showing public endorsement of the Supreme Court's 1954 ruling declaring enforced segregation unconstitutional, reflect one important aspect of this support. More recent data (1970) from a Harris Poll, asking whether enforced segregation is right or wrong, confirms the minority status of prosegregation opinion.[9]

It is obvious, however, that opposition to the principle of segregation need not imply a demand for immediate integration (especially if one's own children are involved). One could favor racial integration, but only if it did not affect you personally, or if the amount of integration was numerically so small that it

Table 6-8   Public Support* for the Supreme Court's Ruling on
Legally Enforced Segregation

Date	Approve	Disapprove	No Opinion
1954 (July)	54	41	5
1955 (May)	56	38	6
1956 (Feb)	57	38	5
1957 (Jan)	63	31	6
1957 (Aug)	58	36	6
1957 (Sept.-pre Little Rock)	56	38	6
1957 (Oct.-post Little Rock)	59	35	6
1959 (July)	59	35	6
1961 (June)	62	33	5

*"The U.S. Supreme Court has ruled that racial segregation in the public schools is illegal. This means that all children, no matter what their race, must be allowed to go to the same schools. Do you approve or disapprove of this decision?"
SOURCE: Gallup Poll

[8] See, for example, Andrew M. Greely and Paul B. Sheatsley, "Attitudes Towards Racial Integration," *Scientific American* 225 (1971): 13-19. It should be noted, however, that at least during the 1950s, the existence of majorities favoring school integration frequently occurred due to overwhelming support by blacks for integration. Opinion polls of whites showed more moderate levels of support for racial integration. Other data on racial integration are reported in "The Polls: Race Relations," Hazel Gaudet Erskine, *Public Opinion Quarterly* 26 (1962): 138-48 and "The Polls: Speed of Racial Integration," compiled by Hazel Gaudet Erskine, *Public Opinion Quarterly* 32 (1968): 513-24.

[9] The Harris question asked in 1969 was: "Up to now in the South, segregated schools have resulted from the states and school districts providing that white children must go to white schools and black children go to black schools. This is called segregation by law. In general, do you think this system of separate white and black schools is right or wrong? Sixty-one percent said that this was wrong. However, virtually the identical proportion (60 percent) agreed that de facto segregation, i.e., segregation as a result of neighborhood residential patterns was permissible. *Harris Survey Yearbook of Public Opinion 1970*, pp. 225-26.

constituted tokenism. The impact of personal involvement and amount of integration on white peoples' attitudes is demonstrated by the data in Table 6-9. These data clearly show that between 1954 and 1969, whites became more accepting of their children attending school with blacks. Particularly among Southern whites, the extent of resistance to attending school with any blacks declined dramatically during this period. Nevertheless, these increases in acceptances of a few blacks should not obscure the continual opposition of majorities to integration where white children would be outnumbered by blacks.

A different issue involving the racial integration of schools focuses on enforcement. Especially in the 1960s and 1970s, when the principle of integration was no longer controversial, explosive battles occurred over the amount and types of coercion to be used in achieving desegregation. On the local level the enforcement question frequently became the dominant community issue as parents battled over school district lines, the "pairing" of black and white schools, and, of course, school bussing.[10] Despite all the commotions at the local level, however, it is clear that it is at the national level where the big decisions must be made. Indeed it is evident that the willingness or unwillingness of the federal government to push localities towards integration by use of court orders, federal money cut-offs, and the like, is perhaps the most crucial question in the whole issue. It is certainly true that if complete racial integration is to

Table 6-9   Support for School Integration among Whites, by Region and Degree of Integration, by Year.*

	Non-South			South		
	Percent Objecting When Blacks Constitute:			Percent Objecting When Blacks Constitute:		
Date	Few	Half	More than Half	Few	Half	More than Half
1954 (July)			45			82
1958 (Sept)	3	39	58	72	81	84
1959 (March)	7	34	58	72	83	86
1965 (April)	7	28	52	37	68	78
1966 (May)	6	32	60	24	49	62
1969 (Sept)	7	28	54	21	46	64

*Would you, yourself, have any objections to sending your children to a school where a few (half, more than half) of the children are colored?"
SOURCE: Gallup Poll

[10]Though integration tactics such as bussing only affect a small segment of the population, opposition to bussing, in particular, has been overwhelmingly negative. Three Gallup polls taken in 1970 and 1971 showed sentiment ranging from 86 to 76 percent in opposition. A 1965 Harris poll of blacks found only 35 percent endorsing bussing as a means to achieve racial integration.

occur, federal intervention is essential. For these reasons, our analysis of opinion-policy congruence in school integration will emphasize the role of the national government in enforcement.

Table 6-10 presents public opinion on the federal government's role in achieving integration. Perhaps the first point to be made about these data is that they tell us nothing about the precise nature of this intervention. Some people might interpret Washington's intervention as physical coercion to bring about instantaneous racial integration in every public school. At the other extreme, intervention could be construed merely as exhortation and encouragement. As is true of many opinion polls, the message conveyed is obscured by the absence of detailed, precise poll questions. A second aspect of Table 6-10 worth noting is the lack of a majority sentiment in any of the seven years. Hence, if one were to define "public opinion" as the majority preference of the public, these data would not show any predominate public opinion. Obviously, however, these data do portray public sentiment (albeit of imprecise meaning) and rather than create artificial majorities by eliminating the "no opinion", "not sure" responses, we shall speak in terms of pluralities instead of majorities.

What do these data say? One thing is clear—no obvious historical trend emerges during this period. Indeed, a slight change in the percentages in 1964 so that "oppose" sentiment outnumbered "intervene" sentiment would produce a situation where pluralities favoring government intervention alternated with pluralities endorsing the opposite position. Nor are the percentage differences in preference usually very large—only in two years (1966 and 1970) is the difference in preference greater than 10 percent and the very small differences for the years 1956, 1960, and 1964 may very well be due to sampling error or other sources of distortion than true differences in public opinion. Taken as a whole, these data can be construed almost as a tie in public sentiment—opinion is so evenly divided that while the results of individual polls are not split 50-50,

Table 6-10 Public Support for Federal Intervention in School Desegregation,* 1956-1972

Year	Favor Federal Intervention	Not Sure	Oppose Federal Intervention	Don't Know No Opinion
1956	39%	6%	43%	12%
1960	41	7	39	13
1964	41	7	39	13
1966	46	8	34	12
1968	38	7	44	11
1970	45	10	33	12
1972	37	7	45	12

*For all years the question was "Should the Government in Washington stay out of the question of whether White and Negro children go to the same school?" or a very close variant.
SOURCE: SRC, University of Michigan

the results of successive polls are very nearly split 50-50. On the other hand, it is also possible to claim that the thrust of public opinion is on the side of federal government intervention, though just barely (averaging all the results shows a 1.6 percent difference supporting intervention). Yet a third interpretation would ignore the lack of a clear pattern and simply view each poll result as a public mandate for a particular time period. Thus, between 1956 and 1960, the public said, "Don't intervene"; between 1960 and 1968 the message to the federal government was "Intervene"; and so on. Each of these interpretations has some degree of validity, but rather than settle the issue arbitrarily, we shall instead proceed to actual policy and leave the knotty question of the "meaning" of these data until the end of this section.

What do we examine when we look for the presence or absence of federal government intervention in school integration? Basically, there are two broad approaches to this question. The first is to examine government *efforts* at school desegregation. These would include, among other things, federal court rulings, Justice Department orders, use of federal funds to encourage compliance, legislation, and similar actions. Though such actions clearly constitute intervention, we must be aware of the difficulty of measuring the actual seriousness of these efforts. For example, the 1955 *Brown v. Board of Education of Topeka* decision called for the integration of public schools "with all deliberate speed," but yet many years passed before any substantial integration was attempted. Similarly, it is entirely possible for federal officials to sound as if they are moving full speed ahead on forcing desegregation while simultaneously granting delays or doing absolutely nothing of concrete significance.[11]

One way to get around this problem of separating words from deeds is to examine the actual progress in racial integration of public schools.[12] That is, we

[11] The difficulty of distinguishing genuine effort from a perfunctory effort cannot be overestimated. For example, the President and the heads of various departments have considerable discretionary power over staff composition, budgetary allocations, and legislative and judicial tactics. Thus, attempts at desegregation could be effectively sabotaged by appointing incompetents to important positions, providing inadequate resources, and pursuing unproductive lines of attack. Such an undermining would be far from evident to anyone but a knowledgeable, close observer of the situation.

[12] As is the case in measuring desegregation effort, the actual content of "desegregated" is far from unambiguous. On an explosive, emotional issue like racial integration great incentives sometimes exist for manipulating and distorting figures. For example, do we consider a school district "integrated" if schools, but not classrooms are racially mixed? At what precise point does a school become "integrated" (10 percent black, 20 percent, etc.). An excellent illustration of the distortions in desegregation data are the figures on the subject annually reported in the *U.S. Statistical Abstract,* showing the number of "desegregated" Southern school districts. These figures show that the vast majority of school districts were by 1966 "in compliance" with federal desegregation guide lines. However, most of these "in compliance" districts either have no Negro school children or merely *intend* to desegregate sometime in the future. The numbers game in school integration is discussed in "A Report of the United States Commission on Civil Rights," *Federal Enforcement of School Desegregation,* September 11, 1969, pp. 9-12.

can claim that the existence of widespread racial segregation, despite the Supreme Court's ruling to the contrary, indicates that whatever the appearance of federal intervention, actual intervention is negligible. In effect, this argument puts the final responsibility for desegregation on the national government by assuming that if the national government *really* wanted desegregation, it could have been achieved within a few years of the Supreme Court's decision. Hence, if we find that public schools are as segregated in 1974 as in 1954, we infer that the various interventions were really nothing more than a charade. Of course, there are reasonable counter arguments that the national government hardly possesses the power to enforce a law absolutely in the face of public opposition, but the argument for examining actual school integration outcomes is persuasive enough that we shall also include these data in our analysis.

Let us begin by examining various federal government efforts to enforce school desegregation. Table 6-11 depicts a chronology of federal court decisions on racial integration. It is clear that the initial *Brown* decision in 1954 has hardly settled the matter. It is also clear that the Supreme Court through the 1950s took a very un-militant stand on immediate integration.[13] In both *Brown* decisions, *Cooper v. Aaron,* and *Kelley v. Nashville,* the Court called for action, but avoided specific compliance dates and racial ratios. The Court's caution is roughly consistent with public opinion during this period depicted in Table 6-10. However, beginning in the early 1960s and continuing into the 1970s, the Supreme Court and lower federal courts adopted much tougher and more specific stances with regard to desegregation plans. Particularly after the *Alexander v. Holmes* (1969) decision, court policy was one of demanding immediate abolishment of racial segregation through bussing and numerical formuli. It is not the case, however, that judicial militancy has gathered increasing momentum in each succeeding year. Table 6-11 also shows that even in 1973 the Supreme Court is not willing to go as far as requiring the merging of school districts across political lines or deeming de facto school segregation unconstitutional.

The pattern followed by the courts is roughly paralleled by the activities of Congress and the executive branch (See Table 6-12). Except for the filing of court briefs supporting desegregation, federal action was just about minimal during the 1950s. With the election of John F. Kennedy, however, the national government began to take a more vigorous role in attacking segregation. The legislative high point of this more active role was reached with the enactment of the Civil Rights Act of 1964, which provided citizens and government officials with a variety of new weapons though it stopped short of granting *carte blanche* power of enforcement. Following the enactment of this legislation, the Department of Health, Education and Welfare (HEW), at first with limited

---

[13] For a more detailed analysis of the Brown decision, see Daniel M. Berman, *It Is So Ordered: The Supreme Court Rules on School Segregation* (New York: W.W. Norton and Co., 1966).

Table 6-11   Federal Court Rulings on School Integration, 1954-1973

Year	Decision
1954	Supreme Court in *Brown v. Board of Education of Topeka Kansas* rules that enforced racial segregation in public schools constituted denial of equal protection of the laws under the 14th Amendment. Declares that "separate but equal" educational facilities are inherently unequal.
1955	In a second *Brown v. Board of Education* case, Supreme Court holds local school boards responsible for implementing school integration and local courts responsible for deciding what action constituted compliance. Asked that lower courts start reasonable and prompt action towards compliance. Courts could grant delay for administrative purposes, but called for integration progress to be made "with all deliberate speed."
1958	Despite the existence of race related violence accompanying racial integration, Supreme Court rules in *Cooper v. Aaron* that Little Rock, Arkansas High School must make a prompt start on racial integration (prompt start is not, however, clearly defined). Court also upholds 1957 lower court ruling allowing Nashville, Tennessee to integrate under a "grade-a-year" plan (*Kelley v. Nashville Board of Education*).
1960	U.S. Third Circuit Court of Appeals over-rules Delaware's grade-a-year plan and orders complete racial integration by September 1961.
1963	In *Watson v. City of Memphis* Supreme Court expresses impatience with pace of school integration. Court notes that nine years have passed since *Brown* and it never contemplated that "all deliberate speed" would mean infinite delay.
1964	Supreme Court rules against closing of public schools in Prince Edward County, Virginia in order to avoid integration as well as state tuition payments so pupils can attend private schools (*Griffin v. County School Board of Prince Edward County*) Court also notes that in the area of school integration there has been "entirely too much deliberation and not enough speed."
1967	U.S. District Court in *Poindexter v. La. Financial Assistance Commission* invalidates Louisiana's plan of tuition grants to private schools so as to impede integration.
1968	Supreme Court in *Green v. County School Board of Kent County* rules against "freedom of choice" plans by which pupils can close any school in any district.
1969	In *Alexander v. Holmes* Supreme Court holds that standard of "all deliberate speed" for desegregation is no longer constitutionally permissable. Dual school systems must be terminated at once.
1971	In *Swann v. Charlotte-Mecklenburg County Board of Education* Supreme Court rules that bussing, racial balance ratios, and gerrymanded school districts are all permissible interim methods of eliminating state imposed segregation from Southern schools.
1972	Supreme Court rules in *U.S. v. Scotland Neck Board of Education* that Federal Courts can halt state or local action creating new school district designed to impede racial integration.
1973	Federal district court in Richmond, Virginia orders largely black inner city schools to be merged with white school districts in suburbs. This decision is overturned by U.S. Court of Appeals and, in 4-4 decision, Supreme Court upholds Court of Appeals. Supreme Court also considers 1970 Federal District Court decision that *de facto* segregation is unconstitutional. Court instructs District judge to re-examine case but does not rule on constitutionality of *de facto* segregation directly. Federal District judge orders HEW to begin cutting off federal funds to segregated schools in seventeen states despite declared Nixon policy of not employing fund cut-offs. Judge also issues strict timetable for desegregation.

TABLE 6-12 Legislation and Executive Action on School Integration

Year	Action
1955	Rep. Adam Clayton Powell of New York offers amendment to legislation banning segregation in schools. Amendment defeated and Powell criticised by President Eisenhower for offering "extraneous" antisegregation proposals.
1957	President Eisenhower federalizes Arkansas National Guard and sends in paratroopers to Little Rock, Arkansas to prevent antiblack violence and escort Negro students to school. Little Rock schools close for 1958-59 term to avoid integration.
1959	President Eisenhower proposes legislation making it a federal crime to interfere with school desegregation and offering federal assistance to desegregating schools. Various Congressmen sponser bills giving Federal government stronger power to enforce school desegregation. No action taken.
1954-1960	Attorney General files *amicus curae* (friends of the court) briefs in school desegregation cases in support of racial integration. However, no criminal prosecutions were brought against school officials who refused to allow Negro children to attend white schools.
1960	Civil Rights Act of 1960 passed which, among other things, provided criminal penalties for violent actions intended to prevent racial integration.
1962	President Kennedy takes a variety of executive actions to encourage school desegregation. Department of Health, Education and Welfare announces that only desegregated schools will receive federal aid to "impacted" school districts (school districts bearing extra burdens due to nearby federal installations). On-base desegregated schools are authorized where off-base schools are segregated. U.S. Office of Education sets up clearinghouse to help schools desegregate. Kennedy sends federal troops to University of Mississippi to prevent antiintegration violence.
1964	Civil Rights Act of 1964 required that (1) U.S. Office of Education report to Congress within two years on the status of school integration; (2) technical and financial aid be given to assist integration; (3) federal financial assistance could be terminated for noncompliance and; (4) the Attorney General be allowed to file suit for desegregation if a signed, meritorious complaint is received. Law explicitly stated that U.S. officials or courts were not thus authorized to transport pupils to schools for purposes of desegregation nor did legislation enlarge court's power of compliance.
1965	In accordance with Civil Rights Act of 1964, HEW issues compliance guidelines. Compliance was defined if district was under court order and assurances were given that compliance would occur or desegregation plan was approved by Commission of Education. By fall of 1965 almost all (90%) Southern school districts meet these compliance standards though actual amount of school integration is minuscule.
1966	HEW toughens up desegregation standards. School districts were made responsible for insuring that black children choosing to attend white schools would not be intimidated; dual school systems were to be eliminated as quickly as possible; and provisions were made for the possible use of numerical guides as measures of integration. These new guidelines excluded *de facto* school segregation.
1967	New HEW guidelines call for accelerated rate of integration in Southern schools. U.S. Commission on Civil Rights issue two reports highly critical of pace of desegregation.
1968	NEW guidelines for desegregation are made applicable to Northern schools.

Year	Action
	Civil Rights Act of 1968 provides criminal penalties for attempts to interfere with the exercise of various civil rights, one of which is the right to attend public schools. Legislation passed which forbids HEW from using power to withold funds to force schools to transfer pupil for purposes of correcting racial imbalance.
1969	Nixon administration moves on a number of fronts to delay full desegregation in Southern schools. HEW announces a switch from terminating federal funds to instituting lawsuits to enforce school integration. Litigations policy criticised by civil rights advocates in view of part relative ineffectiveness of lawsuits. Administration brings forty-three lawsuits against school districts, including non-Southern districts. HEW intervenes in a court decision to seek *delay* of integration (which was rejected by the Supreme Court).
1970	Nixon calls officially sanctioned school segregation unlawful and to be immediately eliminated. However, Nixon also reaffirms belief in neighborhood schools and animosity to bussing to overcome *de facto* segretion patterns. Commissioner of Education, James E. Allen, Jr., calls for the elimination of all types of segregation and is forced to resign. Officials from HEW and the Department of Justice threaten school district with lawsuits unless desegregation occur and numerous lawsuits are filed. Internal Revenue Service revokes tax exempt status of private schools which practice racial discrimination (however, proof of integration merely requires a written statement from the school). Legislation is passed requiring uniform application of desegregation standards in both the North and South.
1971	Strong antibussing to achieve racial integration sentiment is expressed in House vote on education appropriations bill. HEW begins procedures to terminate federal school funds in a number of Northern school districts. Nixon orders HEW and Department of Justice to minimize the use of bussing.
1972	Nixon calls on Congress to limit bussing designed to achieve desegregation, but no final action taken (though votes in House showed very strong support for measures). Senate rejects a number of bills designed to impede the desegregation of public schools.

pressure but gradually with greater vigor, began coercing Southern school districts to integrate.[14] These efforts were limited, however, by the lack of professional manpower available to HEW and the continual resistance of many deep South school districts.[15] The inauguration of Richard M. Nixon in 1969

[14] A more detailed description of this process is reported in Gary Orfield, *The Reconstruction of Southern Education* (New York: Wiley-Interscience, 1969), especially Chap. 3; and Thomas R. Dye, *The Politics of Equality* (Indianapolis: Bobbs-Merrill Company, 1971), Chap. 2. For an analysis of the desegregation effort in Northern cities, see Robert L. Crain, *The Politics of School Desegregation* (Chicago: Aldine, 1968) and Dye, *op. cit.* pp. 73-84.

[15] For example, in 1965 the Department of Justice's Civil Rights Division had authorization for only 105 attorneys (and only 86 were actually employed). In 1968 HEW had a mere 48 professional employees working on elementary and secondary school desegregation in Southern and Border states. When Congress required equal enforcement in both North and South, the number of professionals in the South dropped to 34. This manpower shortage is described more fully in United States Commission on Civil Rights, *Federal Enforcements of School Desegregation,* September 11, 1969, pp. 47-50.

complicated the thrust of executive policy on desegregation. On the one hand, both HEW and the Department of Justice continued their efforts to pressure school officials. Between 1968 and 1973 numerous lawsuits were filed and other actions were taken. Moreover, a much greater effort was made to integrate Northern as well as Southern schools. On the other hand, many of Nixon's policy pronouncements and changes in administrative techniques were widely viewed as retarding progress in desegregation. On several occasions both he and his aides spoke out against bussing and other similar tactics. Indeed, some of the Nixon administration's antisegregation actions were the result of Supreme Court pressures, not its own initiative.

A different dimension of public policy in school desegregation is presented in Figure 6-3 and Table 6-13, showing actual racial integration levels. Given the action of the courts, Congress and the executive in the 1950s, the miniscule rate of southern desegregation comes as no surprise. Beginning in 1963, a period in

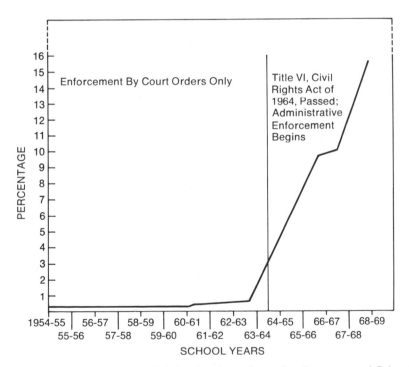

Figure 6-3 Percentage of Negro Students Attending Desegregated Schools in Seven Southern States*

*The states involved are Alabama, Georgia, Louisiana, Mississippi, North Carolina, South Carolina and Virginia. Save for North Carolina and Virginia, in none of these states did the percentage of Negro students attending desegregated schools, whether under court orders or under administrative enforcement, ever exceed 16 percent.

SOURCE: U.S. Commission on Civil Rights, Federal Enforcement of School Desegregation, Sept. 11, 1969, p. 36.

Table 6-13 Number and Percent of Negroes Attending Public Elementary and Secondary Schools, by Geographic Area and by Level of Isolation: Fall 1968 and Fall 1970

Level of Isolation	Continental United States[1]		32 Northern and Western States[2]		6 Border States and D.C.[3]		11 Southern States[4]	
	1968	1970	1968	1970	1968	1970	1968	1970
Total enrollment	43,353,568	44,877,547	28,579,766	29,451,976	3,730,317	3,855,221	11,043,485	11,570,351
Negro enrollment:								
Number	6,282,173	6,707,411	2,703,056	2,889,858	636,157	667,362	2,942,960	3,150,192
Percent of total	14.5	14.9	9.5	9.8	17.1	17.3	26.6	27.2
Negroes by level of isolation:								
Attending 0–49.9% minority schools:								
Number	1,467,291	2,223,506	746,030	793,979	180,569	198,659	540,692	1,230,868
Percent	23.4	33.1	27.6	27.5	28.4	29.8	18.4	39.1
Attending 50–100% minority schools:								
Number	4,814,881	4,483,905	1,957,025	2,095,879	455,588	468,703	2,402,268	1,919,323
Percent	76.6	66.9	72.4	72.5	71.6	70.2	81.6	60.9
Attending 80–100% minority schools:								
Number	4,274,461	3,311,372	1,550,440	1,665,926	406,171	404,396	2,317,850	1,241,050
Percent	68.0	49.4	57.4	57.6	63.8	60.6	78.8	39.4
Attending 90–100% minority schools:								
Number	4,041,593	2,907,084	1,369,965	1,475,689	383,059	380,185	2,288,570	1,051,210
Percent	64.3	43.3	50.7	51.1	60.2	57.0	77.8	33.4
Attending 95–100% minority schools:								
Number	3,832,843	2,563,327	1,198,052	1,288,221	368,149	355,512	2,788,642	919,594
Percent	61.0	38.2	44.3	44.6	57.9	53.3	77.0	29.2
Attending 99–100% minority schools:								
Number	3,331,404	1,876,767	834,898	878,357	294,844	294,104	2,201,662	704,306
Percent	53.0	28.0	30.9	30.4	46.3	44.1	74.8	22.4
Attending 100% minority schools:								
Number	2,493,398	941,111	322,408	343,629	160,504	154,409	2,000,486	443,073
Percent	39.7	14.0	12.3	11.9	25.2	23.1	68.0	14.1

[1] Includes 49 States and the District of Columbia. Excludes Hawaii.

[2] Includes Alaska, Arizona, California, Colorado, Connecticut, Idaho, Illinois, Indiana, Iowa, Kansas, Maine, Massachusetts, Michigan, Minnesota, Montana, Nebraska, Nevada, New Hampshire, New Jersey, New Mexico, New York, North Dakota, Ohio, Oregon, Pennsylvania, Rhode Island, South Dakota, Utah, Vermont, Washington, Wisconsin, and Wyoming.

[3] Includes Delaware, District of Columbia, Kentucky, Maryland, Missouri, Oklahoma, and West Virginia.

[4] Includes Alabama, Arkansas, Florida, Georgia, Louisiana, Mississippi, North Carolina, South Carolina, Tennessee, Texas, and Virginia.

NOTE.—Data are based on surveys of all school districts enrolling 3,000 or more students and a sample of smaller districts. Because of computer rounding, detail may not add to totals.

SOURCE: Kenneth A. Simon and W. Vance Grant, *Digest of Educational Statistics: 1971* (Washington, D.C., HEW, 1972), p. 136

which national public opinion favored greater federal government intervention, southern school integration accelerated rapidly. Of course, even by 1968-69, most southern black school children were still attending segregated schools. Table 6-13 further depicts the growing integration of southern schools but it also shows that in 1970 the vast majority of black school children were attending largely black schools regardless of region. Of particular note is that by 1970 the South had achieved a greater degree of desegregation than the North. Unfortunately, we lack comparable data through 1973, but various signs do not point to recent dramatic changes in racial integration of schools. Thus, if we make the assumption that the federal government could eliminate segregation if it *really* desired, the government's policy cannot be deemed strongly integrationist.

In the light of the complex public opinion data and the complicated character of our different policy indicators, ascertaining overall opinion-policy congruence is not simple. Prior to 1960, nationwide public opinion (as measured in 1956), government inaction, and lack of actual integration appear to all to be roughly consistent. At a minimum, no public majority endorsed a massive federal onslaught against school segregation, and none occurred. Opinions in 1960, 1964, and 1966 moved to the profederal government intervention side, and as we have seen, the pace of government action and results picked up considerably. Perhaps due to the lack of clarity of public support, however, even this increased government intervention was limited in both tactics and results.

The post 1968 opinion shifts are especially difficult to evaluate because the plurality switched sides from one survey to the next. Since the period between 1968 and 1972 was characterized by a relatively high degree of judicial and executive intervention, and on two of three polls pluralities opposed federal involvement, it could be said that substantial opinion-policy incongruity occurred. Nevertheless, in many policy areas—particularly the use of extensive bussing and vigorous elimination of de facto segregation—both the courts and executive refrained from going as far as they could. Despite various pressures, the national government continued the tradition of concentrating on eliminating blatantly dual school systems, while not requiring all black children to attend integrated schools. Federal intervention was thus consistent with the law, but the law was not interpreted to increase the scope and degree of federal action. In a sense, then, between 1968 and 1972 both the public and the government in Washington vacillated between greater intervention and retrenchment and thus it could be said that both the government and the public shared the same indecision.

RELIGION IN PUBLIC SCHOOLS, 1962-1975

Compared to many other countries the United States has not experienced extensive and divisive religious conflict. Nevertheless, as the issue of John F.

Kennedy's Catholicism in the 1960 presidential election demonstrated, religion does occasionally become an important political issue. One place in particular where religion and politics intersect is the public school. The First Amendment of the Constitution forbids Congress from making laws establishing or prohibiting religion, yet because public schools are widely considered as a place to inculcate traditional moral values, a long history exists of school-sponsored religious observances.[16] No doubt many parents have traditionally viewed such activities as school prayers, Bible readings, Christmas plays, and the like, not as state-sponsored establishment of religion, but as necessary nondenominational exercises designed to build character and virtue.

The potential conflict between the First Amendment prohibition against state religious involvement and common school practices came to a head in 1962 when the U.S. Supreme Court declared unconstitutional a New York town's regulation requiring that each school day commence with a nondenominational religious prayer. A year later the Court similarly banned school Bible reading. Given the long history of religion in American schools, as well as most peoples' strong feelings about teaching morality, public reaction to these decisions has

Table 6-14   Public Opinion on Religious Observances in Public Schools, 1962-75

Year	Favor Observances	Oppose Observances	Don't Know and No Opinion
1962[1]	79%	14%	7%
1963[2]	70	24	6
1964[3]	75	15	7
1965[3]	74	15	7
1966[3]	75	13	8
1968[3]	74	13	9
1975[4]	77	17	6

[1] Gallup Poll in which approval was asked of "religious observances."
[2] Gallup Poll in which respondents were told that the U.S. Supreme Court has ruled that the Lord's Prayer or Bible verses cannot be required in public schools. Respondents were then asked whether they approve or disapprove of this decision.
[3] In 1964 through 1968, the questions concerned whether schools should begin each day with a prayer. The 1965 data were collected by the Survey Research Center, University of Michigan, as part of the Student-Parent Socialization Study conducted by M. Kent Jennings. The remaining three results (1964, 1966, and 1968) were contained in national elections surveys.
[4] Gallup Poll in which respondents were asked whether they favored amending the Constitution to permit prayers in public schools.

[16] Richard D. Dierenfield, *Religion in American Public Schools* (Washington, D.C.: Public Affairs Press, 1962), especially Chap. 2.

been predictable and generally unambiguously negative.[17] In Table 6-14 we see that even after the Court's ruling, overwhelming majorities have consistently endorsed some form of religious exercises in public schools. Even six years after the Court decision, by which time most of the public outcry had substantially diminished, the proportion of "no opinion" and "don't know" responses has increased only very slightly. Examining public policy on religion in schools is complicated. If one accepts the argument that the Constitution is the highest law, and the Supreme Court is the final interpreter of this law, it is then clear that barring a repeal of the First Amendment or the passage of a new Constitutional amendment, prohibition of religious observances in schools is public policy. On the other hand, viewing public policy in terms of what actually occurs in the schools (and this ranges from no religious observances to silent prayers and hymn singing) could produce a radically different picture for it is well known that many Supreme Court decisions, e.g., forbidding segregation in schools, are ignored or circumvented in actual practice. Yet a third relevant indicator of public policy concerns attempts by policy makers to get around the Court's ruling by passing laws which, while allowing religious ceremonies in the schools, do not strictly violate the Court's interpretation of the First Amendment.

We begin our analysis of public policy by considering some of the actions taken by policy makers since the Supreme Court held school prayers to be unconstitutional. In Table 6-15 we see that the Supreme Court has specifically ruled against school prayers (1962) and the Lord's Prayer or Bible reading (1963). We should note, however, that Table 6-15, for brevity's sake, does not include the outcomes of numerous other cases on the subject that never reached the Supreme Court. Excluded, for example, is the *De Spain v. De Kalb County School District* (1967) case dealing with a situation where children were required to recite the following poem prior to their morning snack: "We thank you for the flowers so sweet; we thank you for the food we eat; we thank you for the birds that sing; we thank you for everything."[18] This poem was ruled not to be a religious prayer by the federal District Court, but the decision was overturned by the United States Court of Appeals. With very few exceptions, lower court rulings have taken a hard line against schools attempting to circumvent earlier Supreme Court decisions.

While the courts were busy trying to eliminate religious observances in schools, numerous legislators, aided by private organizations, were

---

[17] Especially in the South the outcry against the Supreme Court's antiprayer rulings has been very open and widely encouraged by high state officials. For example, in 1963, Governor George Wallace of Alabama threatened to stage a pray-in and personally read a Bible in a classroom. These and other defiant reactions to the Court's rulings are further described in William M. Beaney and Edward N. Beiser, "Prayer and Politics: The Impact of *Engel v. Schnepp* on the Political Process," *Journal of Public Law* 13 (1964): 486-91; and R.H. Birkby, "The Supreme Court and the Bible: Tennessee Reaction to the Schnepp Decision," *Midwest Journal of Political Science* 10 (1966): 304-19.

[18] Cited in *Congressional Digest*, January, 1974, p. 6.

Table 6-15   Chronology of Federal Action on School Prayer

June 1962	Supreme Court rules in *Engle v. Vitale* that New York school prayer is unconstitutional even if nondenominational and students not wishing to recite prayer are excused from the room.
June 1963	Supreme Court rules that Maryland and Pennsylvania were violating First Amendment by requiring public schools to start the day with either the Lord's Prayer or a Bible reading.
Early 1964	House Judiciary Committee holds hearings on proposed Constitutional Amendment allowing school prayers, but no action taken.
Mid 1965	Court of Appeals upholds action of New York school principal refusing request that school time be set aside for two prayers.
1966	Senator Dirksen proposes constitutional amendment allowing school prayer. In September, 1966, Senate fails by nine votes to provide two-thirds vote necessary to pass constitutional amendment.
1967-69	Dirksen amendment introduced in Senate twice, but no action taken.
1970	Senate by 50-20 vote adds school prayer amendment to pending constitutional amendment guaranteeing women equal rights. No final action taken.
1971	House considers school prayer constitutional amendment, but 240-162 vote in favor of amendment falls short of two-thirds requirement.
1973-75	A number of Senators introduce resolutions favoring a constitutional amendment allowing school prayer, but no conclusive action taken. Similar amendments introduced in House and here too, no action is taken.

SOURCE: Congressional Quarterly Weekly Report, Aug. 4, 1973, pp. 2141-2.

simultaneously working towards the passage of constitutional amendments designed to reverse the Court's 1962 and 1963 decisions. Beginning in 1964 and continuing into the early 1970s, Congressmen were offered innumerable opportunities to show their support for resolutions and constitutional amendments supporting religion in schools, and in those instances where votes were taken, the proreligion position was overwhelmingly endorsed.[19] Despite these lopsided votes and the sheer volume of agitation for a proprayer amendment, however, no concrete, federal legislation to establish school religious observances successfully came forth from Congress during this period.

A somewhat different picture of opinion-policy congruence emerges if we consider the actual policies on school prayers, Bible readings, etc. within classrooms. It is well known that the Supreme Court possesses little independent enforcement power and since stopping religious activities requires litigation on

---

[19] Congressmen were also busy winning points with proprayer forces by conducting various hearings on the issue and allowing a seemingly endless parade of proprayer (and some antiprayer) citizens to make their voices part of the official public record. See, for example, "Prayers in Public Schools and Other Matters," Hearings Before the Committee of the Judiciary, 87th Congress, Second Session (Washington, D.C.: U.S. Government Printing Office, 1963); and "School Prayer" Hearings Before the Subcommittee on Constitutional Amendments of the Committee of the Judiciary United States Senate, 89th Congress, Second Session (Washington, D.C.: U.S. Government Printing Office, 1966).

the part of the person objecting, or at least a complaint, it would come therefore as no shock to find widespread disregard of the Court's antireligious strictures.[20] As data from a number of studies presented in Table 6-16 suggests, there is indeed some lack of compliance with the Court's rulings. On the whole, all these studies indicate that schools have strongly moved towards eliminating various religious rituals, but by no means have school prayers and Bible readings vanished altogether. Thus, at least within some schools there was consistency between national opinion and public policy as defined by actual practices. Of course, we must realize that since we lack data on opinions within each school

Table 6-16 Compliance with Supreme Court Decisions on Religious Activities Within Public Schools

Morning Prayers and Bible Readings: before 1962 vs. 1964-65.[1]

	Prior to 1962	1964-65
Had morning prayers	61%	28%
Had Bible reading	48	22

School Prayers and Bible Reading: 1960 vs. 1966[2]

	1960	1966
Had Bible readings in district	41.7%	19.5%
Had prayers in district	50.2	14.0

Banning of School Prayers: 1960 vs 1967[3]

Had school prayers in 1960	61.3%
Had banned prayers by 1967	26.7%

[1] Data are based on figures reported in H. Frank Way, "Survey Research on Judicial Decisions: The Prayer and Bible Reading cases," *Western Political Quarterly* 21, (1968): 189-205. Data were from mailed questionnaires sent to five teachers in 464 schools.

[2] 1960 data reported in Richard B. Dierenfield, *Religion in American Public Schools* (Public Affairs Press: Washington, D.C., 1962), p. 51 and 56. Data collected by mailed questionnaires to 4000 school superintendents (response rate was 54.6%). 1966 data were also collected by Dierenfield and were cited by Kenneth M. Dolbeare and Phillip E. Hammond, *The School Prayer Decisions* (Chicago: The University of Chicago Press, 1971), p. 31. No information about the 1966 sample was given.

[3] Unpublished data collected by Kenneth M. Dolbeare.

[20] We must realize, of course, that since school prayers and Bible readings are violations of the law, it may be difficult to ascertain the extent of defiance. In addition, almost all measures of compliance are based on reports from school superintendents (not actual observations) and it may not be possible for an administration to know (or want to know) the practices of each teacher in all schools.

we cannot be sure that schools having religious exercises are in areas where opinions favor such activities.[21]

In sum, if we leave aside various congressional attempts to introduce Constitutional amendments (all of which have failed) and the minority of schools which have defied the Supreme Court rulings, it is obvious that a clear majority of the public is not getting what it wants in the way of religion in public schools. What is probably ironic about this lack of opinion-policy congruence is that most Americans undoubtedly support the doctrine of separation of Church and State as stated in the First Amendment. If confronted by this inconsistency, i.e., supporting both school prayers and the First Amendment prohibition against establishing religion, most citizens would probably respond by claiming that saying the Lord's Prayer, reading from the Bible, and the like, had nothing to do with establishing state-supported religion. Thus, if not for the Supreme Court, the public would have both the First Amendment and religion in public schools.

GUN CONTROL, 1959-1974

Like many crime related issues, the question of registration of firearms stirs vehement controversy. Particularly after the assassination of popular political leaders such as John F. Kennedy and Martin Luther King, there seemed to occur an outpouring of vocal opinion demanding that something be done about easily available firearms. The soaring homicide and armed robbery rates in large cities has also focused attention on the availability of cheap, unlicensed handguns (and during the 1960s the sale of handguns quadrupled, so that one-third of all civilian guns imported or produced in the United States since 1900 were sold during the 1960s).[22] Concurrent with these gun control sentiments have been the persistent efforts by certain organizations, particularly the National Rifle Association, to resist such regulation. Such organizations not only point to the Constitution's explicit guarantee of citizens' rights to bear arms, but go on to claim that firearms regulations could very well be the first step in the making of a defenseless, vulnerable citizenry at the mercy of governmental tyranny.[23]

---

[21] Our analysis is concerned with national policy, so our data are drawn from studies examining reasonably large numbers of school districts. However, a number of researchers have examined compliance with the Court's rulings on a smaller though more intensive scale. See, among others, Kenneth M. Dolbeare and Phillip E. Hammond, *The School Prayer Decisions* (Chicago: The University of Chicago Press, 1971); William K. Muir, Jr., *Prayer in the Public Schools* (Chicago: The University of Chicago Press, 1967); and Richard M. Johnson, *The Dynamics of Compliance* (Evanston, Ill.: Northwestern University Press, 1967).

[22] *Firearms and Violence in American Life,* a Staff Report submitted to the National Commission on the Causes and Prevention of Violence, George D. Newton, Jr., Director (Washington, D.C.: U.S. Government Printing Office, n.d.), Chap. 4 and Appendix C.

[23] A sampling of the various arguments is found in *Editorial Research Reports,* "Gun Control: Recurring Issue," July 19, 1972: 555-58.

Table 6-17 Public Opinion on Gun Registration*

Year	Favors Firearms Controls	Opposes Firearms Controls	No Opinion
1959	75%	21%	4%
1964	78	17	5
1965	73	23	4
1966	68	29	3
1967	73	24	3
1971	71	25	4
1972	71	25	4
1974	72	28	–

*"Would you favor or oppose a law which would require a person to obtain a police permit before he or she could buy a gun?"
SOURCE: Gallup Poll. Cited in "The Polls: Gun Control," compiled by Hazel Erskine, *Public Opinion Quarterly* 36 (1972): 460. 1974 data are from the *Gallup Opinion Index*, Nov. 1974 and respondents either agreed or disagreed with the statement: "Registration of all firearms should be required."

The entire issue of firearms regulation is complicated, involving everything from the manufacturing of cheap, concealable handguns (the so-called Saturday night specials) to the details of licensing. On one aspect of regulation—obtaining a police permit before purchasing a gun—public preferences for the period between 1959 and 1972 have been clear and consistent: overwhelming majorities in all eight surveys endorse a prior police permit.[24] Moreover, the data in Table 6-17 are also interesting for the low proportion of "No Opinion" responses. That less than five percent cannot offer a preference suggests that this issue is of more than passing concern for Americans.

Measuring the policy response to public demands for gun registration is deceptively difficult. The first major problem is that firearms controls are largely a state (or sometimes local) matter by tradition though the Federal government could (and occasionally does) intervene, expecially on matters relating to interstate shipment of arms. This means that unless the transportation of unregistered guns across state lines by individuals were completely prohibited (and this would be a difficult law to enforce), the existence of places where a purchase permit was not required would still allow the influx of unlicensed guns

[24] Earlier Gallup polls suggest that pro-gun control sentiment is a long-standing preference. For example, a 1938 Gallup Poll reported that 79 percent of the public endorsed mandatory registration of firearms with the government. Very similar results were reported in a 1940 Gallup Poll. Since we lack data from the 1940s and 1950s, however, our analysis examines only the period between 1959 and 1972. For other polls on firearms, see "The Polls: Gun Control," compiled by Hazel Erskine, *Public Opinion Quarterly* 36 (1972): 455-69.

into states having mandatory registration.[25] Thus, even if stringent control legislation existed in *most* states, a lack of national uniformity could allow for extensive unregistered possessions of firearms by citizens in *all* states.

A second problem in determining public policy relates to how firearms controls are handled at the state and local level. Obtaining a purchase permit can encompass everything from completing a perfunctory application which is automatically approved (as in obtaining a fishing license) to a rigorous set of requirements under which only relatively few applicants qualify for gun ownership. There is also the related question of the penalties for violation and how stringently they are enforced. Unfortunately, not only are these patterns difficult to determine for each and every locality,[26] but the opinion data in Table 6-17 fail to specify who should be given permits. Though it is probably safe to say that people endorsing gun permits want to prevent guns from falling into the hands of criminals and to help police in their work, any number of firearms control schemes appear to be consistent with these goals.[27]

There is also the problem of determining which of the many gun regulation laws satisfy public sentiment. Any review of state and local legislation reveals a wide variety of practices. In 1968 it was estimated that 20,000 laws existed to govern the sale, distribution, and use of firearms; and various attempts at standardization have been generally unsuccessful.[28] For example, some states (e.g., Alabama) regulate pistols only; others (e.g., Minnesota) cover all firearms. Similarly, are we to consider a law requiring a permit to *purchase* a gun roughly equal to a law requiring a permit to *possess* a gun? Though the question in Table 6-17 specifically mentions a permit in order to purchase a gun, it could very well be argued that "possession" and "purchase" invariably amount to the same thing. More difficult to handle are laws regarding licenses to carry a gun or mandatory firearm dealer records of purchase. Though such laws are obviously not the same as registration prior to purchase, they are nevertheless a good distance from no registration whatsoever. Clearly then, it is not simple to state

---

[25] For example, New York City has perhaps the toughest gun control system of any city, yet handguns have become widely available in recent years due to individuals who purchase guns in states with less severe laws and then bring these guns into New York City. This practice and its enormous scope is vividly described in Steven D. Brill, "How Guns Get to Town: Tracing the Southern Connection," *New York*, April 8, 1974, pp. 39-43. Brill reports that of the 1802 traceable handguns involved in crimes in the first six months of 1973, only 49 came from New York State.

[26] For a compilation of local firearms laws as of 1968, see: Department of the Treasury, Internal Revenue Service, *Published Ordinances Firearms* (Washington, D.C.: U.S. Government Printing Office, 1968), pp. 17003-17093. However, knowledge of the written statute does not necessarily tell one actual practices. For example, Texas law for years has banned carrying pistols except where an individual is a "traveler." The Texas courts for years have debated who is and is not a "traveler."

[27] Some of these alternatives are considered in American Bar Foundation, *Firearms and Legislative Regulations* (Chicago: American Bar Foundation, 1967), pp. 6-10.

[28] *Firearms and Violence in American Life,* p. 87.

Table 6-18 Number of States Possessing Gun Control Legislation by Type of Legislation, 1959-1973

Legislation	Year														
	59	60	61	62	63	64	65	66	67	68	69	70	71	72	73
Permit to purchase required	8[1]	8	8	8	8	8	8	8	10	10	10	10	10	10	10
Permit to possess required	2[2]	2	2	2	2	2	2	2	2	3	3	3	3	3	3
Permit to carry required	10	10	10	10	10	10	10	10	10	11	11	11	11	11	12
Dealer record kept	31[3]	31	31	31	31	31	31	31	31	31	31	31	31	31	33
Concealed weapons banned or required permit	38	38	38	38	38	38	38	38	38	38	38	38	38	38	39

[1] Excludes Virginia, where counties with population of less than 1000 per sq. mile are not required to have purchase permits.

[2] Does not include Louisiana which requires permits only for rifles with barrels less than 16″ and concealable firearms other than pistols and revolvers. Also excluded is Rhode Island which requires permits only for out-of-state purchases.

[3] Does not include Virginia where dealer records are county options.

precisely how much a particular set of laws is or is not consistent with the sentiments expressed in Table 6-17.[29]

Table 6-18 presents data on state legislation regulating the control of firearms. Before considering these data we must first emphasize the limited scope of this compilation of law. Though state laws are important, numerous localities possess their own laws and these can be far more stringent than the state law on the same subject.[30] As much as we might like to consider local ordinances in calculating opinion-policy congruence, such a task is too overwhelming to be attempted here. Moreover, Table 6-18 groups together a number of regulations that vary considerably in content and scope. For example, in some states dealer records of gun sales are automatically sent to the police or are maintained to provide quick access for law enforcement agencies; other states have no such procedure to centralize records of gun ownership, but we classify all dealer record laws under the same heading. Finally, we must reiterate our previous warnings that significant variation in enforcement exists among states having identical laws.

Nevertheless, even if we assume that the five types of legislation covered in Table 6-18 were tough, stringently enforced laws, the gap between the demands of public opinion and policy (as measured here) is enormous. Particularly in the area of laws controlling the ease of obtaining and using firearms, only a few states possessed such laws in 1959 and the existence of overwhelming public demand for such control was hardly reflected in the number of states adding new legislation. Even in what might be considered minimal attempts to control firearms—requiring dealer records or controlling the use of concealed weapons—only about two-thirds of the states in 1959 had such laws and, as in the case of tougher laws, no substantial spread of such legislation took place between 1959 and 1973. All in all, it is clear that while some change has occurred at the state level, gun control remains as loose in 1973 as in 1959.

This picture of very limited progress in controlling firearms at the state level is also found at the national level. As the chronology in Table 6-19 makes clear, not until 1968 did the federal government make a serious attempt to regulate firearms. Until then the only laws were the banning of sending pistols through the mail (they could, however, be shipped via common carrier) and the tax on machine guns and sawed-off shotguns. Even after the 1968 outpouring of gun control legislation, federal actions were still a far cry from the toughminded

[29] Another policy indicator that could be employed is the proportion of all guns registered with the police. Unfortunately, however, such data exist only in the form of very rough estimates and cannot be used in our analysis. For example, the National Commission on the Causes and Prevention of Violence estimated that in 1968 only 3-5 million of the approximately 24 million guns in circulation were covered by state records; and as we shall see, the nature of state record keeping varies considerably.

[30] In particular, large cities like New York, Chicago, and Philadelphia have very tough licensing laws and such cities typically comprise a large proportion of the state's population.

Table 6-19 Federal Regulation of Firearms

Date	Action
1927	Pistols and other concealable firearms disallowed from the mails.
1934	National Firearms Act of 1934 requires registration and taxation on manufacture, sale, or transfer of sawed-off shotguns, machine guns, and silencers. Bill sponsors originally intended to regulate handguns, but these sections were withdrawn. This legislation was declared unconstitutional in 1968 as a violation of the Fifth Amendment.
1938	Federal Firearms Act (1) requires manufactures and importers of firearms to be licensed by the Internal Revenue Service; (2) makes it illegal for licensed firearms dealer to ship firearms to unlicensed dealers in states requiring a license; and (3) made it a crime to ship guns to a criminal or someone under indictment.
1963-4	Senator Dodd introduces legislation controlling the selling of firearms, particularly to those under eighteen. Commerce Committee receives 20,000 telegrams opposing such regulation and two supporting further regulation. No Congressional action taken.
1965	President Johnson proposed legislation to ban mail order gun sales, prohibit over-the-counter sales to out of states, and in other ways control the flow of handguns. Extensive hearings are held but no action taken.
1966	Firearms control legislation considered by Congress, but no vote is taken.
1967	President Johnson again urges tougher gun controls and such legislation is introduced in Congress. President's Commission on Law Enforcement and the Administration of Justice issues report calling for state licensing of handguns and federal regulation where state takes no action. House and Senate Judiciary Committees approve Johnson endorsed legislation, but no final action taken.
1968	As part of Civil Rights Act of 1968 Congress makes it a federal crime to transport firearms across state lines to be used in civil disorder. The Omnibus Crime Control and Safe Streets Act of 1968 is passed, which, among other things, makes it a federal crime for felons, dishonorably discharged veterans, mental incompetents, illegal aliens and ex-citizens to own or sell firearms. Gun Control Act of 1968 becomes law which 1) requires a license for inter-state firearms shipment; 2) toughens licensing requirements; 3) prohibits sales to criminals, drug users, and those who cannot legally purchase guns in state of residence; 4) requires that guns be purchased personally unless sworn statement is made that purchase is legal (a copy of statement is sent to law enforcement officials in signers locality); and 5) importers and manufacturers are required to imprint serial numbers on all firearms.
1971	Senate Judiciary Sub-Committee on Juvenile Delinquency holds hearings in bill banning all handguns except those for sporting purposes. No final action taken.
1972	Senate passes legislation outlawing sale of cheap "Saturday night specials." Various amendments to bill that would register all guns and license all owners are overwhelmingly defeated. House Judiciary Committee does not report bill so legislation dies.
1973-5	Despite the shooting of Senator Stennis in a robbery attempt on a Washington street and various outcrys against rising rates of gun related homicides, attempts to institute federal gun registration fail.

public sentiment expressed in Table 6-17. Though better records were being kept of who bought guns and where, and mail order guns were more difficult to obtain, it was still possible for, say, a resident of Washington D.C., to take a Sunday drive to Virginia and return with a trunk full of weapons. Federal control is thus considerably less stringent than New York City's Sullivan law where a potential gun buyer must first apply to the local police for a permit (and many requests are denied). Finally, Table 6-19 also shows the lack of success of attempts by Congressmen to institute some form of national control. In almost every year since 1968, debate has occurred on the issue of increased firearms regulations but proponents of tougher laws have not even come close to success.[31]

It should be clear from our analysis that the issue of gun control is not an area characterized by a high degree of opinion-policy congruence. Though overwhelming majorities endorse police permits to purchase guns, such laws are an extreme rarity. And, given the ease with which guns can be purchased in states with lax requirements, the impact of stringent state or local law is seriously compromised. Moreover, despite a great continuity in the public's preferences, progress in meeting these demands has been sporadic and limited.

THE DEATH PENALTY FOR MURDER, 1936-1973

Compared to most public policies, the absence or presence of a death penalty for murder affects only a minuscule number of citizens. Indeed, in the thirty-six years between 1930 and 1966 only 3,859 executions took place, mostly for murder and largely of poor, nonwhites. Nevertheless, emotions on the death penalty have run higher on both sides of the issue and on occasion a well-publicized execution evokes a national debate on the subject. Most of this public debate revolves around the role of execution as a deterrent to crime. Some people see the death penalty as a distasteful though necessary check on those contemplating serious crimes; others reject state executions as an ineffectual, barbaric custom having no place in American justice.[32]

Public sentiment on the death penalty between 1936 and 1973 on the whole seems to support the pro-capital punishment posture. Table 6-20 shows that in each of the eleven polls save two (1957 and 1966) the pro-death penalty sentiment was more common than anti sentiment though in one instance (1965) only a plurality endorsed the death penalty. Our analysis is complicated somewhat by the lack of a clear historical trend in public opinion—support for capital punishment declined between the early 1950s and the mid-1960s, but in 1973 it reached a level virtually the same as the late 1930s. (Note, however, that we have data for only one year for the period between 1937 and 1957, so our inferences on public sentiment during this span must be treated cautiously.)

[31] For example, an amendment by Senator Edward Kennedy to a 1972 gun control bill that would require national registration of all firearms was defeated by an 11 to 78 margin.

[32] A sampling of these charges and counter charges can be found in the *Congressional Digest,* January, 1973, and "The Death Penalty," Hearings before the Subcommittee on Criminal Laws and Procedures of the Committee on the Judiciary, U.S. Senate, 90th Congress, 2nd Session (Washington, D.C., U.S. Govt. Printing Office, 1968).

Table 6-20 Public Attitudes Towards the Death Penalty *

Year	For Capital Punishment	Against	No Opinion
1936	62%	33%	5%
1937	60	33	7
1953	68	25	7
1960	47	50	3
1965	45	43	12
1966	42	47	11
1969	51	40	9
1970	50	41	9
1972	57	32	11
1973†	59	31	10

*"Are you in favor of the death penalty for murder?"
†The 1973 figure is from Harris Survey data. The Harris question was "Do you believe in capital punishment (death penalty) or are you opposed to it."
SOURCE: Gallup Poll, cited in "The Polls: Capital Punishment," compiled by Hazel Erskin, *Public Opinion Quarterly,* 34 (1970): 291.

The public policies relevant to these preferences are two in number. The first, and most obvious, are the laws governing capital punishment. While both the federal and state governments have statutes dealing with the death penalty, the questions asked in Table 6-20 are about the death penalty for murder, and this crime is handled almost entirely on the state level (federal crimes having death penalties deal with kidnapping, treason, etc., and of the 3859 executions between 1930 and 1967, only 33 were for violations of federal law). A second aspect of policy concerns the actual number of executions for murder, since it is entirely possible that states may choose not to employ all available punishments.[33] Data on legislation and executions are presented in Table 6-21 and Figure 6-4 respectively.

If we exclude the results of the 1957 poll in which anti-capital punishment sentiments predominated, we find that between 1936 and 1965 public sentiment and capital punishment policy were largely in agreement. That is, the death penalty was unchallenged by the courts, all but a few states allowed for executions, and numerous executions for homicide did occur, though the number of executions had steadily declined since the 1930s. In 1966, as in 1957, the majority of national opinion supported positions (opposed to capital punishment) inconsistent with the major thrust of public policy, but it could be argued that the very small number of executions in 1966 made for some degree of opinion-policy congruence. In 1969 and 1970, however, pro-capital punishment again came to dominate so opinion-policy consistency existed with respect

[33] A third possible indicator of public policy would be the number sentenced to execution though not necessarily executed. This is not an insignificant number of people (631 in mid 1972) and it could be argued that being sent to death row to await execution is not equivalent to life imprisonment.

Table 6-21   Chronology of Court Decisions and State Actions on Abolishing
Capital Punishment

	Court Decisions
Year	*Decision*
1946	In *Louisiana ex rel Francis v Resweber* Supreme Court held that the Eighth Amendment of the U.S. Constitution forbidding cruel and unusual punishment does not ban all capital punishment. Eighth Amendment is relevant only if cruelty is not inherent part of punishment.
1969	Supreme Court hears arguments in *Boykin v Alabama* that death penalty is unconstitutional and reverses death penalty conviction, but not on grounds of it being unconstitutional.
1970	United States Court of Appeals holds that death penalty for rape violates Eighth Amendment. This is first time that a high court has found a capital statute in violation of the "cruel and unusual punishment" provision.
1972 (Feb.)	California Supreme Court in *People against Anderson* holds that death penalty is "cruel and unusual punishment" under California Constitution but does not consider Eighth Amendment of U.S. Constitution.
1972 (June)	Supreme Court rules in *Furman v Georgia* that capital punishment is unconstitutional. This decision is interpreted to mean that capital punishment is permissable only where it is mandated, i.e., not left to judge's discretion, for specific offenses.

	State Actions
1846-1853	Michigan, Rhode Island, and Wisconsin abolish capital punishment.
1907-1919	Ten states abolish death penalty for murder but capital punishment reinstated in five by 1919.
1963	New York becomes last state to abolish mandatory death penalty for murder. Death sentence optional with jury.
1964-65	Oregon, West Virginia, Vermont, Iowa and New York abolish death penalty.
1969	New Mexico repeals death penalty.
1972	At time of *Furman v. Georgia* decision declaring capital punishment unconstitutional except where mandated, eleven states had no capital punishment whatsoever; five states retained death penalty for very special offenses, e.g., the killing of an on duty peace officer or prison guard; and sixteen states allowed capital punishment for murder.
1973 (Dec.)	In wake of *Furman v. Georgia* numerous states redraft laws governing capital punishment. By the end of 1973 twenty-three states have enacted legislation restoring the death penalty. However, a small number of these states have greatly restricted the death penalty to cover crimes like killing on duty police officers or the murder of prisoners by fellow prisoners doing life sentences.

to legal statutes, although not with respect to actual practices since no executions took place during this period (a significant number of prisoners were nevertheless awaiting execution).

The Supreme Court's 1972 ruling in *Furman v. Georgia,* which invalidated almost all capital punishment statutes, produced opinion-policy incongruity on both measures of policy. However, the Court's decision did not forever bar the death penalty and soon after the decision numerous states began to redraft their legislation on capital punishment so as to satisfy the latest requirements. Thus, as Table 6-21 indicates, by the end of 1973 a total of 23 states had successfully reinstated the death penalty (and a number of other states were seriously considering or discussing a reimplementation). Note, however, that measured against the popularity of the death penalty in 1971, this figure represents a reduction in the number of states possessing capital punishment statutes, so the Supreme Court's actions, at least for the period immediately subsequent to the *Furman* decision, contributed somewhat to opinion-policy incongruity.[34] Moreover, although this reinstitution of the death penalty has resulted in actual death sentences being handed down, actual executions have not occured since 1966.

Taken together, what do these data say about opinion-policy congruence in the abolition of the death penalty for murder? If we judge congruence in terms of years, it is clear that congruence existed for most of this thirty-six year period. Between 1936 and 1965 with the exception of one poll (1957) congruity existed: the public favored execution, almost all states allowed capital

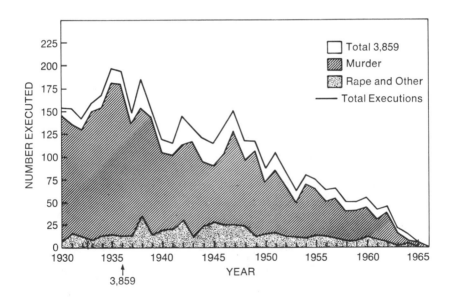

Figure 6-4 Executions 1930-1966

SOURCE: To abolish the Death Penalty Hearings before the Subcommittee on Criminal Laws and Procedures of the Committee on the Judiciary, U.S. Senate, 90th Congress, 2nd Session, p. 2.

[34] We should realize, however, that since the death penalty for murder is a state policy, and our opinion data are national data, it is theoretically possible for opinion-policy incongruity to exist in each state but not on a national basis. Recall from our discussions in Chapter 5 that the existence of a national majority favoring a particular policy does not imply a majority in every state.

punishment, and many states carried out executions. In subsequent years the picture becomes less clear. In 1969 and 1970 congruity existed with respect to most state laws but not with respect to the actual use of capital punishment. The *Furman* decision for a brief time produced complete incongruity, but this was partially overcome by states enacting new laws. However, as of the end of 1973, most states did not allow capital punishment, and executions have not occurred since 1966 despite popular majorities in four polls (1969, 1970, 1972 and 1973) endorsing the death penalty.

CONCLUSION

Several things are clear from our analysis of public opinion-public policy in these seven issue areas. Perhaps the most obvious conclusion is that the establishment of congruence is no easy matter. Many of the analytical problems described in Chapter 5 surfaced regularly in our discussions. A frequent problem was that in many instances both opinion and policy data were incomplete so numerous assumptions and guesses had to be made about data. Recall, for instance, the difficulties created by the lack of survey data on defense spending for the late 1960s or the lengthy gaps in public sentiment about capital punishment. Comparable difficulties emerged in our review of public policy, e.g., ascertaining the real government effort in enforcing school integration. If we assume that patterns of opinion-policy congruence should be clearly discernable, these inadequacies raise important questions about the polling priorities of survey organizations and citizen access to government information. While it is unlikely that both survey organizations and public officials are purposely trying to obscure relationships between opinion and policy, their respective policies are certainly not making analysis all that simple.

A similar problem repeatedly encountered concerns deciphering imprecise opinion and policy data. When we asked: "What do these poll results say?" our answer was frequently: "They could mean many things." Recall, for example, our difficulties in imputing clear policy preferences to poll questions on cutting defense expenditures, government subsidies to medical care, or controls of firearms. The data were obtained through conventional, relatively straight-forward poll questions, but they did not tell us very much about what citizens wanted. Without greater precision, judgments on opinion-policy relationships will necessarily be vague. At the same time, however, as the data in Chapter 3 suggest, most citizens may be incapable of anything more than a response to a diffuse proposition like "The federal government should help with the cost of medical care." Thus, to implore Gallup, Harris and others to ask more precise questions in the name of contributing to a better analysis of opinion-policy congruence may be a futile exercise. It could be the case that rigorous assertions about what citizens demand and what they get may therefore be an unreachable ideal.

A third, commonly-experienced difficulty relates to the juxtaposition of opinion and policy data. The most obvious aspect of this problem was the multiplicity of policy indicators for almost any expression of public preference. Even if public sentiment were perfectly clear and precise, this complexity would not disappear since many policy demands can be satisfied in several ways. For example, is it fair to say that in examining congruence between demands for reducing defense expenditures and policy, defense expenditure as a proportion of the total federal budget was a "better" policy measure than raw expenditure figures? Given limitations in our policy data, this difficulty is undoubtedly understated in our analyses. With perfect policy data we would almost invariably find ourselves faced with at least three or four appropriate policy indicators, and as if have repeatedly seen in this chapter, only rarely do these indicators follow similar patterns. Hence, even the possession of precise opinion and policy data does not completely eliminate the chance that the question of "Is there congruence" will be responded to by a vague "it depends."

Leaving aside these complexities, however, is there any general conclusion we can reach on the state of opinion-policy congruence for domestic issues? Perhaps the most salient conclusion is that considerable variation occurs by policy area in the degree of congruence. However, this range is not from perfect congruence to perfect incongruity, but rather from limited concordance to a completely negative relationship between opinion and policy. The best case for congruity can perhaps be found in the issue area of levels of defense spending, government subsidies of health care, government intervention in school integration, and the death penalty for murder. Even here, however, we frequently find as much incongruity as congruity. For example, in the area of federal support for medical care we found long periods of government inaction despite clear public demand for federal action. Similarly, on the question of defense spending, the amount of money committed to the military has steadily risen in the face of public resistance. Clearly then, the overall existence of opinion-policy congruence on these issues is far from self-evident.

There is, however, little ambiguity about the lack of opinion and policy concordance in other issue areas. Certainly in the case of religious observance in schools and police permits for guns, sharp disagreement exists between national opinion and policy. To be sure, an argument could be made that these matters are entirely local or state issues and hence national poll data are irrelevant, but such incongruity exists even if we consider only national policy (e.g., Supreme Court decisions on school prayers or the enactment of federal gun control laws). A third issue area displaying low opinion-policy congruence is income-tax policy. As we have seen, demands for tax reductions are long-standing and clear, yet the actual policy is one of no significant reduction in tax rates and sharp increases in actual tax payments. All in all, when we add these clear instances of incongruity to the mixed cases of congruity described above, it is evident that despite certain arguments about government closely heeding every popular whim, a lack of congruence is more the rule than the exception.

chapter seven

OPINION AND POLICY CONGRUENCE: FOREIGN POLICY

In dividing our analysis into separate chapters on domestic and foreign policy we are doing more than providing a convenient break between various policy questions. Although the validity of examining the relationship between domestic policy and mass opinion seems beyond question, a similar endeavor in the area of foreign affairs may, at least for some, appear to be less valuable. There are essentially two reasons why a search for public opinion-foreign policy congruence may be questionable—the first concerns the basic quality of public thinking about foreign affairs, while the second relates to the difference between domestic and international politics.

Regarding the quality of public thinking on foreign issues, study after study has demonstrated that the mass public possesses not only a paucity of factual knowledge about foreign relations, but generally low levels of concern as well.[1] This state of affairs is not difficult to understand. Except for a small part of the population, most of what goes on in Europe, Asia, or the international system has little direct bearing on peoples' lives. This perceived irrelevancy encourages unstable, superficial opinions easily swayed by recent events, stereotypes, and

---

[1] See, for example, Martin Kriesberg, "Dark Areas of Ignorance" in *Public Opinion and Foreign Policy*, Lester Markel, ed. (New York: Harper and Bros., 1949); Gabriel A. Almond, *The American People and Foreign Policy* (New York: Harcourt, Brace and Company, 1950), Chaps. 4 and 5; and Don D. Smith, " 'Dark Areas of Ignorance' Revisited: Current Knowledge about Asian Affairs," in *Political Attitudes and Public Opinion*, Dan D. Nimmo and Charles M. Bonjean (New York: David McKay Company, 1972). A more favorable picture of public thinking, at least with respect to the alleged gyrations of sentiment, is presented in William R. Caspary, "The 'Mood Theory': A Study of Public Opinion and Foreign Policy," *American Political Science Review* 64 (1970): 536-47.

various personality needs.[2] Hence, it could be argued that even if public leaders desired to heed public sentiment, the quality of mass thinking may well make this a hopeless task. Such limitations on the caliber of public thinking have even led advocates of popular influence in foreign policy to endorse a highly restricted role for citizen sentiment. As Gabriel Almond put it:

> The function of the public in a democratic policy-making process is to set certain policy criteria in the form of widely held values and expectations. It evaluates the results of policies from the point of view of their uniformity to their basic values and expectations. The policies themselves, however, are the product of leadership groups ("elites") who carry on the specific work of policy formulation and policy advocacy.[3]

Moreover, even if the public held coherent, stable foreign policy preferences and thus presented an intelligible mandate, the very nature of international politics may discourage popular influence. In the first place, much of foreign affairs is characterized by secret, intricate negotiations; and popular consultations on such matters might well be unwieldy and counterproductive to reaching agreements. It would be difficult to imagine, for example, American diplomats in the protracted Vietnam War settlement binding themselves to the results of opinion polls. Moreover, many of the issues of foreign policy are exceedingly complex and require so much expertise that it would be utopian to expect extensive citizen competency on these issues. Finally, it can be claimed that international events develop so rapidly, and are of such grave consequence to national survival, that quick action without popular consultation is often both desirable and virtually inevitable. Particularly, given the character of modern warfare, to wait until the public debated the issues and decided one way or the other could be disastrous.

At the same time, however, one might nevertheless maintain that both foreign policy and domestic issues are equally amenable to popular influence. Indeed, despite all the problems of public influence in international affairs, some statesmen and observers have claimed that the public does in fact control foreign policy. As Dean Rusk put it when he was Secretary of State:

> Throughout my long years in government, I have found that the American people expect their government to travel a broad highway of policy which responds to their own simple and decent purposes and when government wanders over toward the soft shoulder on either side of the road the people have a dozen ways to nudge the public vehicle back into the hard surface.[4]

---

[2] William A. Scott, "Rationality and Non-Rationality of International Attitudes," *Journal of Conflict Resolution* 2 (1958): 8-16.
[3] Almond, *The American People and Foreign Policy,* pp. 5-6.
[4] Quoted in Bernard C. Cohen, *The Public's Impact on Foreign Policy* (Boston: Little, Brown and Company, 1973), pp. 17-18.

Even if we could dismiss such utterances as mere reiterations of democratic myths, other reasons exist to suggest that foreign policy could be amenable to direct popular influence. Perhaps the most obvious one is that at least some questions of international policy, e.g., declarations of war, tariffs, disarmament, are as relevant to large groups of citizens as most domestic issues. Surely, American involvement in Vietnam has shown that issues of foreign policy can be as salient and explosive as any issue in domestic policy. Thus, at least on some international issues the public's preferences cannot automatically be dismissed as superficial, unstable, and politically irrelevant.

As for the argument that leaders will, by the very nature of situations, operate independently of popular constraints when dealing with foreign policy, the rejoinder is that only very rarely can officials have *complete* freedom to maneuver without any reference to citizen desires. To claim that leaders can and do operate with considerable leeway in foreign affairs does not necessarily imply that no publicly imposed restrictions apply. Though the public may care little for details of policy, it is scarcely indifferent to major successes and failures. At a minimum, since public officials must to some degree marshall public support, there is little to be gained by flaunting one's independence from the popular will.

Finally, the charge that policy in international affairs necessitates quick, decisive actions so popular consultation is precluded can be countered by the claim that even in some situations public opinion can be determining. To be sure, there may be instances requiring immediate government reaction, but any review of recent crises will show that many crises linger on for weeks if not months or years and public opinion has ample time to surface and make its presence felt. Furthermore, polls are quite capable of asking pertinent questions in advance of situations (e.g., "What should the U.S. do if . . . ?") and even where this information is lacking, public sentiment might be inferred from reactions to similar situations in the past.[5] In short, the frequency of situations demanding immediate reactions in international affairs does not constitute a *prima facie* case against the possibility of public opinion being politically relevant to decision-making.

These, then, are some of the arguments and counterarguments on the question of public opinion's influence on foreign policy. Whether or not any or all of them are correct is a moot point requiring an extensive historical analysis. Though we cannot settle these issues once and for all, we shall at least make a beginning by considering public opinion-public policy congruence in four relatively enduring issue areas. Specifically, following the format established in

---

[5] Actually, it is more than likely that in *extreme* situations like military confrontations, invasions, and the like, public sentiment would be known even without a poll. For example, President Roosevelt hardly needed a poll to fathom public feeling on entering war in the wake of Pearl Harbor. On the other hand, there are no doubt numerous situations, e.g., U.S. reaction to the Russian intervention in Czechoslovakia, in which citizen preferences probably are useless guides to officials.

the previous chapter we shall examine: (1) American military involvement in Vietnam; (2) appropriations for foreign aid; (3) the admission of Communist China to the United Nations; and (4) trade with Communist nations. Though no claim can be made that these four issues are either centrally important or typical of all other foreign policy issues, these case studies do range from the highly salient (e.g., Vietnam) to the highly removed from everyday life (e.g., Red China and the U.N.). This variation allows us, if only in a limited fashion, to see whether there is something about all foreign policy issue areas encouraging opinion-policy incongruity or whether such incongruity is limited to only the most personally distant types of issues.

AMERICAN INVOLVEMENT IN VIETNAM, 1964-1972

In recent history no other foreign policy issue has caused as much controversy, dissension and hostility as did American involvement in Vietnam. It was an issue that generated intense feelings and, perhaps more than any other issue in the last hundred years, it almost reduced American politics to violent chaos. A persistent, and frequently debated, theme during our involvement was the preference of the average citizen. Advocates of virtually all shades of opinion placed great stress on public opinion either as something to be won over or, if already won over, then as an indication of the virtues of one's cause. Recall, for example, the claims of high public officials, particularly Presidents Johnson and Nixon, that public acquiescence constituted a strong "silent majority" endorsing continued American intervention in Vietnam.[6] Counterpoint to such claims were unprecedented public protests, mass demonstrations, peace strikes, and even riots that suggested that vast numbers of citizens were deeply dissatisfied with events in Vietnam. Though neither side went as far as to claim that God was on its side, each asserted that the public was or would soon be on its side.

Differences of opinion on whom the public really supported were certainly not a consequence of a lack of information on public sentiment. Indeed, the very opposite was true: so many polls were conducted and so many different types of questions were posed that interpreting a completely unambiguous "true" public opinion was a difficult and sometimes hopeless task. If the advocates of, say, withdrawal did not like the results of one poll they could commission a different survey with "better" questions to get a more "truthful" result.[7] Even if people could agree to interpret the same questions, the strong

---

[6] For an analysis of this so-called "Silent Majority," see, among others, Milton J. Rosenberg, Sidney Verba, and Philip E. Converse, *Vietnam and the Silent Majority* (New York: Harper and Row, 1970), and Philip E. Converse and Howard Schuman, " 'Silent Majorities' and the Vietnam War," *Scientific America* (1970), pp. 17-25.

[7] Manipulation of public sentiment was not limited only to mere citizens. It has been suggested that many of President Johnson's actions were intended to change poll results. See, for example, Seymour Martin Lipset, "The President, the Polls and Vietnam," *Trans-Action* 3 (1966): 19-24.

personal convictions of many analysts, consciously or unconsciously, led to different interpretations of identical information.[8] As we saw in Chapter 3, it is difficult enough to make choices about including or excluding "don't knows," using more than two response categories, or what constitutes the predominant preference when one is indifferent about the results, but where analysts have a policy stake in these matters, consensus on such matters is probably impossible.

The confusion over the true meaning of public opinion during the war becomes even more comprehensible when we consider some of the typical poll questions employed during this period. Consider the message conveyed by responses to the question "Did the U.S. make a mistake in sending troops to South Vietnam?" This question was frequently asked throughout our involvement and was commonly interpreted as a rough index of public satisfaction with the war effort.[9] Though responses to this question undoubtedly express some form of public feeling on Vietnam, such a retrospective judgment conveys only the vaguest hint of a policy mandate for current government actions. It is entirely possible, and this was demonstrated in Chapter 3, that individuals giving the same response can differ completely in whether they favor withdrawal or further intervention. However, it is not beyond the realm of possibility that a leader lacking this additional information might construe answers to this "mistake" question as endorsing a particular line of action.

A second type of question frequently posed was of the "What should we do now?" variety. Though apparently a better means of eliciting a clear policy mandate, the bewildering variety of policy choices respondents were offered makes interpretation very complex. For example, some questions spoke of *gradual* troop withdrawals with no fixed deadlines as the military situation warranted it; on other questions the respondent was forced to choose between continued involvement and *immediate* troop withdrawal. Obviously the "get out" alternative in the first type of question is substantially different than the one offered in the second type of question. A second complication occurs when we stop to realize that the identical response can have different policy

---

[8] Nor was the use of loaded questions unknown. Perhaps the most common form of the biased question on Vietnam policy was the one where one of the alternatives—either withdrawal or further engagement—was described in unacceptable terms. For example, a February 1966 poll asked citizens: "If President Johnson were to announce tomorrow that we were going to withdraw from Vietnam and let the Communists take over, would you approve or disapprove?" Since few Americans approved of "letting the Communists take over," it is not surprising that 81 percent rejected withdrawal. On the other hand, another poll at the same time posed the alternatives in terms of gradual withdrawal ". . . and letting the South Vietnamese work out their own problems," and reported that 39 percent supported gradual disengagement. Both polls are reported in John E. Mueller, *War, Presidents and Public Opinion* (New York: John Wiley and Sons, 1973), p. 85.

[9] For an analysis of the correspondence between opinion as measured by the "Did the U.S. make a mistake" question and certain events and policies, see John E. Mueller, "Trends in Popular Support for the Wars in Korea and Vietnam," *American Political Science Review* 65 (1971): 358-75.

implications at different points in time. For example, in the early years of the war, e.g., 1965, "escalation" might mean a few thousand more troops, limited U.S. air strikes, etc.; at the height of the war a return to 1965 involvement could be considered as support for "withdrawal". The ideal solution, of course, would have been for every poll to offer the same set of several very concrete alternatives to respondents, but such a strategy would probably yield a highly fragmented picture of public opinion perhaps equally difficult to interpret.[10]

What is to be done? Given the sheer quantity of available poll data we must also avoid an oversimplification of public sentiment by using only those few identically worded questions asked over time. Our solution is to err on the side of richness of information and present a large array of poll questions that call for some type of government action, e.g., escalate or withdraw. We shall not consider judgments on the war that convey no policy message. Hopefully each of these separate and limited probes into public thinking will provide an overall composite picture of the emergence and development of what citizens "really" desired. Table 7-1 presents these survey data from 1964 to 1972.

When we examine polls taken in 1964 and the first half of 1965 the most salient fact that emerges is the relatively large proportion of people not interested in Vietnam. Among those offering a policy preference during this period, no single policy alternative even comes close to representing a majority viewpoint. Perhaps the strongest inference that could be made in these early figures is that if various alternatives are combined there is a slight edge to the escalate sentiment though it is far from a majority. However, beginning around the end of 1965 this pro-involvement sentiment becomes more pronounced though it stops considerably short of an overwhelming endorsement of an all-out military effort. For example, in December 1965 while escalation sentiment outnumbered withdrawal opinion four to one, a clear majority (65 percent) endorsed a policy of "holding the line," i.e., a policy of limited military intervention. Similarly, a little more than half the public (56 percent) in February of 1966 rejected gradual withdrawal and turning the war over to the South Vietnamese.

From 1965 to perhaps the middle of 1969 the overall "hawkish" disposition of the American public is clear though particular events, e.g., the Communist Tet offensive in 1968, and the particular policy alternatives offered on polls influence the general picture of opinion. Especially where the "dovish" policy choice indicated or strongly implied immediate military withdrawal, the preponderance of pro-intervention sentiment is evident (e.g., the polls of June, 1966, October 1966, July 1967, and October 1967). Observe that the greatest

---

[10] Recall, for instance, the problems of analysis encountered when we examined the seven point scale on Vietnam involvement in Chapter 3. No doubt the array of choices allowed a very sensitive reading of public opinion, yet interpreting the policy message was very difficult. Recall that by combining various combinations of adjacent categories it could be "demonstrated" that the public endorsed (a) withdrawal; (b) a "middle-of-the-road" policy; or (c) escalation.

Table 7-1 Public Opinion on American Intervention in South Vietnam, 1964-1972

Date	*Question*
May, 1964	Have you given any attention to developments in South Vietnam? What do you think should be done next in Vietnam? (Gallup)

Get out	43
Raise South Vietnamese standard of living	1
Send U.N. force	6
Maintain present policy	3
Get tougher, use more (non-military) pressure	5
Take definite military action	4
Either fight or get out	4
Other	3
Have given little or no attention to Vietnam	63

August, 1964
and Nov., 1964   What do you think should be done next in Vietnam? (Gallup)

	8/64	11/64
Get out	4	9
Avoid all war, talk	10	3
Keep troops there, don't be pushed around	27	5
Get tougher, put on more (non-military) pressure	12	10
Take definite military action	9	9
Either fight or get out	3	15
Other	9	19
Don't know	30	30

Oct., 1964   Have you been paying any attention to what is going on in Vietnam? Which of the following do you think we should do now in Vietnam? (SRC)

Pull out of Vietnam entirely	8
Keep our soldiers in Vietnam but try to end fighting	22
Take stronger stand even if it means invading North Vietnam	29
No opinion	15
No interest	18

April, May
and June, 1965   In your opinion what would you like to see the U.S. do next in Vietnam? (Gallup)

	4/65	5/65	6/65
Withdraw completely	17	12	13
Start negotiating, stop fighting	12	16	11
Continue present policy (continue military action but remain ready to negotiate)	14	20	16
Step up military activity	12	4	6
Go all out, declare war	19	17	17
Other	5 ⎫	33 ⎫	37
No opinion	28 ⎭		

(More than one response coded)

Date	Question
Sept. and Dec., 1965	All in all, what do you think we should do about Vietnam? We can follow one of three courses: carry the ground war into North Vietnam at the risk of bringing Red China into the fighting, withdraw our support and troops from South Vietnam or continue to try to hold the line there to prevent the Communists from taking over South Vietnam. Which do you favor? (Percentage of those with opinion) (Los Angeles Times)

	9/65	12/65
Withdraw	25	7
Hold the line, prevent Communist takeover	49	65
Carry war to North at risk of war with Red China	26	28

Date	Question
Feb., 1966	Would you approve or disapprove of the following action to end the fighting: Gradually withdrawing our troops and letting the South Vietnamese work out their own problems? (Stanford University release)

Approve gradual withdrawal	39
Disapprove	56
No opinion	5

Date	Question
June, 1966	Suppose you were asked to vote now on the question of continuing the war in Vietnam or withdrawing our troops during the next few months. How would you vote? (Gallup Poll)

Withdraw	35
Continue	48
No opinion	17

Date	Question
Oct., 1966	Have you been paying any attention to what is going on in Vietnam? Which of the following do you think we should do now in Vietnam? (SRC)

Pull out of Vietnam entirely	9
Keep our soldiers in Vietnam but try to end fighting	36
Take a stronger stand even if it means invading North Vietnam	36
No opinion	12
No interest	7

Date	Question
July, 1967	If you had to make a choice about the Vietnam War right now, which one would you favor: fighting to a total military victory, fighting until we achieved a negotiated peace, or try to end the war and get out as quickly as possible? (Washington Post)

Try to end war, get out quickly	37
Fight to negotiated peace	51
Fight to total military victory	21
No opinion	4

Date	Question
Oct., 1967	Just from what you have heard or read, which of the statements come closest to the way you, yourself, feel about the war in Vietnam? (Gallup)

The U.S. should begin to withdraw its troops	31

Date	Question		
	The U.S. should carry on its present level of fighting	10	
	The U.S. should increase the strength of its attacks on North Vietnam	53	
	No opinion	6	
Feb., and June, 1968	(No questions given) Cantril		
		2/68	6/68
	Discontinue the struggle and begin to pull out of Vietnam in the near future	24	42
	Continue the war but cut back the American military effort to a defense only of key areas in South Vietnam where most of the population is located	4	7
	Continue the war at the present level of military effort	10	8
	Gradually broaden and intensify our military operations	25	10
	Start an all-out crash effort in the hope of winning the war quickly even at the risk of China or Russia entering the war	28	25
	No opinion	9	8
Oct., 1968	Which of the following do you think we should do now in Vietnam? (SRC)		
	Pull out of Vietnam entirely	19	
	Keep our soldiers in Vietnam but try to end the fighting	37	
	Take a stronger stand even if it means invading North Vietnam	34	
	No opinion	10	
March, 1969	In your own opinion, what would you like to see the United States do next about Vietnam (New York Times)		
	Withdraw completely	26	
	Continue present policy	19	
	Go all out, escalate	32	
	End as soon as possible	19	
	No opinion	21	
July, 1969	Have you given any thought about what this country should do next in Vietnam? What, specifically, do you think the United States should do? (Gallup)		
	Stop fighting, withdraw immediately	12	

Date	Question			
	Give economic, but not military aid to S. Vietnam	2		
	Let South Vietnam take over	9		
	Gradual United States withdrawal	32		
	Stay in Vietnam as long as necessary; keep military pressure on; work for cease-fire at Paris	9		
	Step up military efforts	4		
	Bomb them, blow them up	3		
	Either go all out or get out	4		
	Other and no opinion	5		
	Have given no thought to what should be done	29		
Dec., 1969	Here are four different plans the United States could follow in dealing with the war in Vietnam. Which one do you prefer? (Gallup)			
	Withdraw all U.S. troops from Vietnam immediately	19		
	Withdraw all troops by the end of 1970	22		
	Withdraw troops but take as many years to do this as are needed to turn the war over to South Vietnam	39		
	Send more troops to Vietnam and step up the fighting	11		
	No opinion	9		
March, May, and July, 1970	Here are four different plans the United States could follow in dealing with the war in Vietnam. Which ONE do you prefer?			
		3/70	5/70	7/70
	Withdraw all troops from Vietnam immediately	21	23	22
	Withdraw all troops by end of 18 months (3/70)	25		
	Withdraw all troops by July, 1971 (5/70 and 7/70)		25	26
	Withdraw all troops but take as many years to do this as are needed to turn the war over to the South Vietnamese	38	31	34
	Send more troops to Vietnam and step up the fighting	7	13	10
	No opinion	9	8	8
Late 1970, early 1971	Which of the following do you think we should do now in Vietnam? (SRC)			
	Pull out of Vietnam entirely	32		
	Keep our soldiers in Vietnam but try to end the fighting	32		
	Take a stronger stand even if it means invading North Vietnam	24		

Date	Question
	No opinion 11
Jan, Feb. 1971	A proposal has been made in Congress to require the U.S. Government to bring home all U.S. troops from Vietnam before the end of the year. Would you like to have your Congressman vote for or against this proposal? (Gallup)

	Jan.	Feb.
Favor congressional requirement of withdrawal by end of 1971	72	66
Oppose	20	26
No opinion	8	8

Date	Question
June, 1971	Suppose one candidate for congress from your district said he favored getting the U.S. armed forces out of Vietnam by July 1. He is opposed by a candidate who says we must leave about 50,000 troops there to help the South Vietnamese. Other things being equal, which candidate would you prefer? (Gallup)

Withdraw all troops	61
Leave some troops	28
No opinion	11

Date	Question
Aug., 1972	Which of the two statements—A or B—would you vote for? (Gallup)
	A. The U.S. should withdraw all troops from Vietnam by the end of the year.
	B. The U.S. should not withdraw all troops from Vietnam by the end of the year.

A	B	Don't Know
62	34	4

support for deescalation during this 1966 to mid-1969 period comes on Cantril's June 1968 survey when withdrawal was to take place in the undefined "near future." Though pro-intervention sentiment clearly prevails here, it is not quite as clear overall how those with hawkish sentiment divide on the question of continued limited intervention versus further escalation. Where a choice exists between limited commitment or greater military action, e.g., July 1967, October 1967, February 1961, June 1968, and October 1968, the limited position prevails in some cases while the escalate stance prevails in others.

Beginning in March of 1969, we see the first sign of a possible shift in the balance of hawk and dove sentiment. It is still the case that the majority support involvement or escalation, but the proportion desiring to get out of Vietnam approaches the 50 percent level. By July of 1969 it is clear that the public's commitment to continued intervention has drastically weakened. Indeed, the July 1969 poll shows that those persisting in maintaining some form of Vietnam presence are outnumbered over three to one by those accepting withdrawal. To be sure, immediate withdrawal with no strings attached was still not widely endorsed in 1969, but the issue now had become one of how and when to get out of Vietnam, not whether to stay or leave. With the possible exception of the

1970 Survey Research Center poll, the main thrust of public opinion after late 1969 is for some form of graduated withdrawal with the possibility of continued military action gradually fading from the scene as a "non-issue."

Needless to say, the juxtaposition of American Vietnam policy against these trends in public opinion presents formidable obstacles if only due to the sheer number of relevant policies that must be considered. When people say "Let's get out of Vietnam" or "Let's step up the fighting" they could be demanding any number of government responses. For example, the most obvious meaning to "Decrease our involvement" would be to withdraw some number of U.S. troops. However, this preference could also entail other actions such as reducing the bombing of North Vietnam, a greater emphasis on defensive military action, and a curtailment of military and economic aid to South Vietnam. Though there may be some serious problems of obtaining accurate data on these indicators (recall the secret bombings of Cambodia and incursions into Laos as well as years of covert military operations conducted by the CIA), these measures are conceptually relatively straightforward.[11]

A much more difficult aspect of measuring policy concerns the actions of public officials (and conceivably, we might even include the behavior of foreign political leaders as well). How do we really know, for instance, whether a President's loudly proclaimed offer to meet the North Vietnamese to negotiate a peace settlement constitutes a pro-withdrawal policy? Similarly, a threat to step up the bombing if certain actions are not taken might under certain circumstances be interpreted as a "dovish" policy (e.g., if the demands are very modest and the threatened increases in bombing of slight military value). Moreover, how do we compare policy pronouncements that have no immediate impact, e.g., "I am willing to make great concessions to the enemy," with actual events, e.g., a troop reduction of 10,000 soldiers? The importance of this difficulty becomes clear when we recall that for several years American leaders appeared to say one thing about our Vietnam involvement while engaging in somewhat different behavior.[12]

---

[11] Though "American military effort" may be conceptually clear, the difficulty of knowing precisely what is and what is not such effort cannot be overestimated. As the so-called "Pentagon Papers" showed, the U.S. frequently armed, trained, and economically subsidized groups harrassing the communists. These operations were made to look like "spontaneous" independent anticommunist actions. Moreover, many ostensibly peaceful aid programs were actually designed for military purposes. For a fuller description of these activities see, Neil Sheehan et al., *The Pentagon Papers as Published by the N. Y. Times* (New York: Bantam Books, 1971).

[12] During President Johnson's administration, the alleged discrepancy between his overtures and pronouncements for peace, while increasing American military involved, became known as the "credibility gap." Of course, Johnson and his supporters saw no conflict between stronger military actions and holding out an occasional olive branch. Nor, for that matter, did many citizens see an inherent contradiction between escalation and searching for peace. Harris reports that in 1966 the public by a 60 to 25 percent margin, favored sending 500,000 U.S. troops to Vietnam, but "only if that would shorten the war." Cited in Louis Harris, *The Anguish of Change* (New York: W.W. Norton and Company, 1973), p. 59.

Table 7-2 Chronology of U.S. Actions in Vietnam, 1964-1972

Date	Action
1964	
Aug. 4	President Johnson orders retaliatory air action against military targets in North Vietnam in response to torpedo boat attacks against U.S. destroyers in Gulf of Tonkin.
Aug. 7	Congress approves Gulf of Tonkin Resolution giving support for "all necessary measures to repel any armed attack against the forces of the United States . . . to prevent further aggression . . . (and) to assist any member or protocol state of the Southeast Asia Collective Defense Treaty requesting assistance. . ."
1965	
Feb. 7	President Johnson announces joint U.S. and South Vietnamese air attacks against North Vietnamese staging areas.
May 12-18.	President Johnson raises possibility of moratorium of bombing of North to elicit peace feelers from Hanoi. No public response is offered by Hanoi.
June 8.	U.S. military commanders in Vietnam are given authority to use American troops in combat roles if so requested by South Vietnamese.
1966	
Jan. 31.	After thirty-seven day pause, U.S. airplanes resume bombing of North Vietnam.
March 1.	Senate attempt to revoke Gulf of Tonkin Resolution is defeated.
1967	
Feb. 2.	In a letter to North Vietnamese President Ho Chi Minh, President Johnson proposes direct talks to end the war.
Feb. 15.	Direct talks are rejected by Ho Chi Minh.
Sept. 29.	President Johnson says that U.S. bombing of North will cease "when this will lead promptly to productive discussions."
1968	
Jan. 30.	Communists launch Tet offensive which includes attacks on almost all provincial capitals of South Vietnam's forty-four provinces.
March 31.	In announcing that he will not seek reelection in 1968, President Johnson also says that he has halted bombing over about three quarters of North Vietnam.
May 13.	First substantive meeting occurs between U.S. and North Vietnam in Paris to discuss possible settlement of war.
Oct. 31.	U.S. completely halts all bombing of the North.
1969	
Jan. 18.	Paris peace talks open with representatives from U.S., North Vietnam, South Vietnam, and National Liberation Front (Viet Cong).
May 8.	Viet Cong presents ten point peace proposal calling for unilateral U.S. withdrawal and Communist participation in South Vietnam prior to elections. Offer rejected by U.S.
May 14.	Eight point program to end the war is announced by President Nixon. Program includes phased mutual troop withdrawal over year period, free elections as soon as possible and an internationally supervised cease-fire.
Nov. 3.	President Nixon says he plans withdrawal of all U.S. ground combat forces according to a secret timetable.

Date	Action
1970	
April 30.	U.S. and South Vietnamese troops invade Cambodia to destroy border area sanctuaries.
June 30.	U.S. troops leave Cambodia.
Sept. 17.	Viet Cong calls for U.S. troop withdrawal by June 30, 1971, and resignation of top South Vietnamese officials. Offer rejected by U.S.
Oct. 7.	U.S. proposes a standstill cease-fire for all of Indochina and general peace negotiations. Offer rejected by North Vietnam.
1971	
Jan. 31.	President Nixon signs bill repealing Gulf of Tonkin Resolution.
Feb. 8.	U.S. air and artillery support help South Vietnamese launch major attack on Ho Chi Minh trail in Laos.
1972	
Jan. 25.	President Nixon announces that an eight point proposal to end the war has been submitted to the communists through secret channels.
Jan. 26.	President Nixon's plan is denounced by Viet Cong and North Vietnamese.
March 24.	An indefinite suspension of Paris peace talks is called for by President Nixon.
March 30.	A major military offensive is launched by North Vietnamese.
April 16.	U.S. planes begin raids on North Vietnamese port of Haiphong, sixty miles south of Hanoi.
May 8.	North Vietnamese ports are mined by U.S. planes. President also announces that air strikes would continue against North.
July 13.	Paris peace talks resume.
July 19.	Henry Kissinger and Le Duc Tho, North Vietnamese politburo member, begin private meetings in Paris.
Sept. 2.	North Vietnam announces that it will release three American prisoners of war.
Oct.24.	A temporary halt of the bombing north of the 20th parallel in North Vietnam is ordered.

Let us begin our analysis of opinion-policy congruence by examining the actions of American public officials which are briefly summarized in Table 7-2. In general, an examination of American policy from 1964 to mid-1965 shows that leaders showed much the same ambivalence to military involvement as did the public taken as a whole. To be sure, President Johnson on several occasions took steps to increase American engagement, but each of these steps were specific and limited military ventures, not broad, all-encompassing declarations of warfare. Furthermore, in May of 1965, Johnson did make a public gesture to the North Vietnamese that the U.S. was willing to negotiate a settlement. Of course, it is unclear how serious this peace-making attempt was and it might even be argued it was merely a facade to hide greater interventionist intentions. Nor can we dismiss the contention that the pro-involvement that did exist was an after the fact result of dramatized incidents like the Gulf of Tonkin attack. All in all, however, during the 1964 to mid-1965 period, there appears to be a rough concordance between policy and opinion.

Recall from our analysis of public opinion that a discernible escalation sentiment began to grow stronger around mid-1965. The actions described in Table 7-2 and data on troop levels and military aid to South Vietnam (Table 7-3) closely parallel this change in opinion. Particularly between 1965 and 1967 our involvement as measured by number of troops and monetary commitment showed dramatic jumps. Again, however, the lack of clarity in public sentiment for a specific course of action is mirrored in the actions of the U.S. government. This is particularly evident in the indecision between waging all-out nonnuclear war and making gestures for peace. On the whole, both the government and the public in the aggregate during this period endorsed the policy of involvement though disagreements on how much involvement occurred repeatedly. Thus, if the entire question is reduced to the simple one of "stay or get out," opinion-policy congruence is evident between mid-1965 and the end of 1969.

Beginning in 1969 opinion polls begin to reflect significant increases in deescalation or withdrawal sentiment. This is especially evident in the July 1969 Gallup which shows a majority endorsing a policy alternative either directly or indirectly calling for disengagement. In the five surveys between December 1969 and early 1971, it has become clear that escalation preferences have become a distinct minority and overwhelming majorities accept the idea of withdrawal though the preponderance of opinion is for "eventual" not "immediate" disengagement. However, commencing with the Gallup polls conducted in January and February of 1971, considerable support emerges for a specific and relatively rapid rate of disengagement. Subsequent polls confirm that after 1970 the American public clearly wanted out with minimal time lag.

Policy during this period roughly reflects the shift in preferences though major discrepancies exist. For example, between 1969 and 1972 both troop levels and casualties declined substantially. Also, President Nixon during the same time span proposed several plans designed to end the American military presence in Vietnam and even signed a bill repealing the Gulf of Tonkin Resolution. Clearly then, the U.S. was making some effort to get out of Vietnam. At the same time, however, U.S. policy was far from completely

Table 7-3   American Military and Economic Involvement in Vietnam
1965-1972

Year	U.S. Troops Killed	Military Assistance (millions of dollars)	Number of Troops (as of Dec. 31 of each year)
1965	1,369	268.9	184,300
1966	5,008	861.8	385,300
1967	9,378	1,203.5	485,600
1968	14,592	1,054.4	536,100
1969	9,414	1,608.2	475,200
1970	4,221	1,689.4	334,600
1971	1,380	1,856.9	156,800
1972	300	1,849.4	24,100

SOURCE: Congressional Quarterly, January 27, 1973

dovish. Table 7-2 shows that several large U.S. military operations occurred during the period, e.g., raid on Haiphong, the invasion of Cambodia, and the figures in Table 7-3 reveal that military assistance to the Saigon government even increased between 1969 and 1972. Of course, from the perspective of President Nixon, there is no conflict between disengagement and military operations such as mining North Vietnam harbors. That is, Nixon would argue that peace would have been impossible unless the enemy wanted it, and these military ventures were designed to make the Communists want peace. Of course, the response to these assertions is that tactics such as "bombing for peace" are intended primarily to save face and not to speed up unilateral withdrawal.

On the whole, did substantial agreement exist between public opinion and public policy on the issue of American Vietnam involvement? Certainly at the most *general* level considerable though not complete congruence is evident. At the beginning of our engagement the public's feelings were fragmented with perhaps slight bias towards intervention and government actions were similarly characterized by a certain indecision leaning towards greater intervention. From 1965 to mid-1969 intervention sentiment and policy both clearly dominated though differences occurred on the issues of how much involvement. Between late 1969 and 1972 disengagement feelings predominated and much, but not all of governmental policy followed this preference. We must stress, however, that no degree of influence of public influence on policy making is suggested by our analysis. Much has been said about the impact of mass demonstrations on policy, but it is equally plausible to believe that the public feelings followed government action. In any case, the questions of influence and causality are beyond the scope of our analysis.

We must also stress that our analysis is concerned with *general* opinion and *general* governmental policy. It is entirely reasonable to conceive of the Vietnamese war as a succession of policy choices on separate though related issues. Thus, for example, we could ask whether opinion-policy congruence existed on such issues as passage of the Gulf of Tonkin Resolution, the commitment of U.S. troops to active combat roles, the bombing of Cambodia and so on. It is entirely possible that this approach to public opinion and the war might yield a picture showing a different pattern of congruence. Unfortunately, however, this approach suffers from several problems, not the least of which is that the Vietnam War probably consisted of thousands of separable decisions and opinion data exist only on a few of these actions. Perhaps, equally important, many—if not most—of these separate decisions lacked salience and popular opinion on these questions would probably be based on very limited information. That is, for every highly visible, straightforward question like whether to bomb North Vietnam, there were many more like aid to the government in Laos, the defoliation of forests, military aid to certain tribes, and the like, largely beyond the ken of the average citizen. For these reasons, then, we have emphasized support or opposition to American intervention in general, not each and every distinguishable aspect of involvement.

FOREIGN AID, 1952-1968

Like many foreign policy issues, the subject of economic assistance to other nations is not a question affecting people directly. Even momentous and visible changes in policy are unlikely to impinge on citizens as strongly as, say, major shifts in tax rates or racial integration policy. Nevertheless, the idea of giving away billions of dollars to foreign countries, some of which are hardly staunch U.S. allies, is fraught with potential controversy. This controversy was particularly salient in the years following World War II when the discrepancy between American wealth and worldwide poverty was starkest.[13] However, with the full economic recovery of other industrialized nations, through the Marshall Plan and the Point Four program, the issues have become more complex than simply feeding the millions in war-ravaged countries. The debate on foreign aid more recently involves a vast number of issues ranging from basic ones of whether the U.S. should have any program to differences over aid strategies and aims.

Any endeavor of annually dispensing billions of dollars contains a large array of policy choices that could be put to the public. For example, who will get how much? Should assistance be in cash, commodities, technical aid, or some mixture of these? Is economic help to be dispensed only to those who vow unswerving loyalty to American goals or is economic need to be the primary criteria? Should those receiving aid be expected to repay American help?[14] In the light of all these possible issues and changing international situations it is not surprising that opinion surveys tend not to focus on the same issues for long periods of time.[15] This presents problems for over-time analysis since it is reasonable to suppose, for instance, that a Korean War-era question stating that aid would be given to help fight communist influence is not equivalent to a question mentioning that aid would be given to all poor countries. Moreover, foreign aid opinions may not be held with deep conviction so the chance inclusion of emotionally laden terms like "our allies" can readily obscure genuine changes in public thinking.

[13] By no means, however, is foreign aid a new policy. In one form or another, the American government has been involved with overseas assistance programs from the very beginning of the Republic. Some of these activities and public feelings on these issues are described in Warren F. Ilchman, *Professional Diplomacy in the United States, 1779-1939* (Chicago: University of Chicago, 1961), and Frank R. Kingberg, "The Historical Alternation of Moods in American Foreign Policy," *World Politics* 4 (1952): 239-73. More recent and general analyses of the foreign aid program are found in Ernest B. Haas, *Tangle of Hopes* (Englewood Cliffs, N.J.: Prentice-Hall, Inc., 1969), pp. 144-63, and David A. Baldwin, *Foreign Aid and American Foreign Policy* (New York: Frederick A. Praeger, 1966).

[14] Indeed, in many instances it may be impossible to distinguish foreign aid from foreign trade. It is not unusual for the U.S. government to give special preferences on import quotas or financial credits to some countries and this in effect amounts to a subsidy though it never shows as a foreign assistance expenditure.

[15] For a fuller picture of the variety of poll questions having something to do with foreign assistance, see Michael Kent O'Leary, *The Politics of American Foreign Aid* (New York: Atherton Press, 1967), Chaps. 2 and 3.

Nevertheless, despite the diversity of poll questions, two types of basically similar questions can be analyzed that span a reasonably long time period. The first is a general one that essentially asks citizens whether they approve or disapprove of foreign aid. These poll questions make no mention of who is to receive aid or how much assistance is to be provided.[16] The second type of question is more specific insofar as it gives actual dollar amounts that could be spent and then asks approval or disapproval of these figures (again, however, no specific programs are spelled out). Since the two types of question are quite distinct, we shall treat each set of poll data separately both in interpreting popular sentiment and in analyzing the relevant public policy. We begin with the degree of public support for foreign aid in general.

Table 7-4 and Figure 7-1 depict public support for helping other nations and the actual extent of this assistance. In all eight years in which this question was asked, a majority of the public endorsed the principle of foreign aid, though in at least three instances the support figure is very close to 50 percent (however, at most, only 35 percent oppose the aid program).[17] The over-time trend in this opinion appears to be one of increasing support beginning around 1960 but reaching a plateau in the early 1960s, followed by a decline after 1965. When we compare this pattern of public opinion to the various indicators of aid described in Figure 7-1, no clear correspondence emerges. If opinion and aid covaried, we would expect a sizeable increase after 1960, followed by a five-year relatively level period and then a decline after 1965. Examination of the dollar amount data shows that foreign aid spending tended to stay within the 4 to 5 billion dollar amount during the entire period. Removing the purely military assistance part of the aid expenditures produces no greater degree of opinion-policy congruence—the gradual decline of money for military aid means that a progressively greater proportion of aid goes to civilian purposes, but this trend does not correspond to the opinion trend in Table 7-4.

---

[16] Since other poll data suggest a wide range of support for different types of aid programs, any question without such specific program details must be treated cautiously. For example, a 1966 Gallup Poll allowed respondents to choose among various programs, and while 61 percent supported programs in health care and education, programs in military assistance, road building and other capital projects drew an average support of only 24 percent. Similarly, in 1959 the idea of a "Great White Fleet" of surplus Navy ships made into hospitals, food ships, and training schools to be used to help poorer nations was approved by 73 percent of the public, probably a larger proportion than the percent approving foreign aid in general. Gallup poll data cited in O'Leary, *The Politics of American Foreign Aid*, pp. 13, 14, 20.

[17] The character of public opposition to foreign aid is interesting. In 1959, Gallup asked citizens what they would like to discuss in hypothetical letters to their Congressmen and opposition to foreign aid was volunteered by a mere 2 percent. On the other hand, when citizens in a different poll were asked whether government spending ought to be cut or taxes raised, among those favoring cuts in spending (72 percent), the largest single group (30 percent) thought spending cuts should be in the area of foreign aid. In other words, opposition to foreign assistance may be relatively extensive, but the matter is not of great concern to the vast majority of citizens. Data cited in O'Leary, *The Politics of American Foreign Aid*, pp. 23-24.

Table 7-4   Public Support for Foreign Aid, 1956-1968

Year	Favor Aid	Oppose Aid	Don't Know No Opinion
1956*	51%	30%	19%
1958†	51	33	16
1960*	61	25	14
1963†	58	30	12
1964††	64	23	13
1965†	57	33	10
1966†	53	35	12
1968††	50	35	16

*Data collected by the Survey Research Center, University of Michigan. The question was: "Should the U.S. give economic help to poorer countries of the world even if they can't pay for it?" The "depends" category has been omitted from calculations to provide greater comparability between SRC and Gallup data (Gallup offers no "depends" option).
†Gallup data. The question was: "In general, how do you feel about foreign aid—are you for it or against it?"
††SRC data with slightly different questions than in 1956 and 1960 surveys (questions referred to "countries needing help," as opposed to "poorer countries").

When we analyze aid expenditures not in absolute amounts, but in comparison to other federal programs and to the growth in the economy in general, the parallels between opinion and policy do not become any closer. The data in Figure 7-1 indicate that compared to other expenditures and the Gross

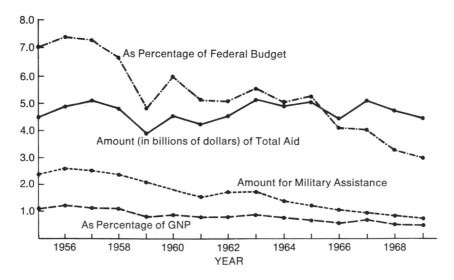

Figure 7-1   Government Spending on Foreign Aid, 1955-1969

National Product, foreign aid has steadily declined between 1955 and 1969. Perhaps the only evidence of opinion-policy congruence is the sharp post-1965 decline in foreign assistance as a proportion of all federal outlays, which occurred when opinion support also declined, but similar patterns of congruence in these data are not found in other years. All in all, using these measures of opinion and policy, congruence existed only at the most general level—a majority of the public desired some type of foreign assistance program and the government did consistently offer some form of assistance—but beyond such general agreement, little concordance between opinion change and policy change is evident.

A different and somewhat more precise test of opinion-policy concordance is presented in Table 7-5. In these six surveys the public was first offered a precise dollar figure to be spent on aid and then people were asked if this amount was too high, too low, or about right. In only two of the six instances do we find evidence of consistency between the course of action favored by the public and government action: in 1952, 60 percent thought that 8 billion in foreign aid was too much money and the subsequent amount spent was 2.96 billion below this figure; in 1952 a majority felt that 6 billion was about right and the actual sum spent approximated this figure. However, in four other instances public support was either on the side of cutting expenditures (1965 and 1967) or endorsed the *status quo* (1957), but subsequent expenditures were 1-2 billion more than the figures in the survey questions. In terms of percentage discrepancies, the gap

Table 7-5 Public Preferences on Foreign Aid Spending and Actual Expenditures, for Selected Years 1952-1967

	Date					
	3/52	5/53	4/54	4/57	2/65	4/67
Amount mentioned (billion)	8	6	3½	4	3.4	3.1
*Policy Preferences**						
Too Much	60%	20%	25%	37%	49%	51%
About Right	28%	57%	56%	48%	33%	30%
Too Little	2%	9%	8%	2%	6%	8%
Don't Know &						
No Opinion	10%	15%	11%	13%	12%	11%
Amount Spent (following yr)						
(billion)	5.04	6.41	8.77	5.08	5.04	5.14
Difference between amount in poll and amount appropriated (billions)	−2.96	+.41	+5.27	+1.08	+1.64	+2.04

*Questions varied from year to year. In some instances aid was to be sent to our allies; some questions merely mentioned "other countries." The 1957 question was the only one that said aid was to be both economic and military. In some instances the respondent was also told the amount of money currently then being spent on foreign aid.

SOURCES: 1952-1957 Opinion data were collected by the National Opinion Research Center; 1965 and 1967 are Gallup Poll data.

between public preferences and expenditures range between 25 to 67 percent—hardly trivial discrepancies.

All these opinion and policy data taken together suggest that foreign aid is not a policy area characterized by substantial congruence. As we already mentioned, only on the general idea of giving assistance to foreign nations can it be said that concordance occurs. Once we move beyond this broad area of agreement and consider fluctuations in public sentiment or actual dollar preferences, instances of opinion-policy congruence are overshadowed by instances to the contrary or lack of any parallel relationships.

THE ADMISSION OF RED CHINA TO THE
UNITED NATIONS, 1950-1970

The proper diplomatic and economic relationship between the United States and Communist China was a persistent issue during the 1950s and 1960s. Particularly during the 1950s, a significant number of leaders and citizen groups advocated a policy of isolating the People's Republic of China through such policies as nonrecognition, prohibitions against trade, and anticommunist military alliance. For these anticommunists, China should be treated as if it did not exist. A smaller number of leaders and citizens dissented from this position and advocated dealing with Communist China no differently than dealing with the Soviet Union.[18] One specific aspect of this controversy that continually surfaced between 1950 and 1971 was whether Red China should be admitted to the United Nations.

Though the Communist China and the U.N. issue never became a subject of intense public debate, it nevertheless received considerable attention from pollsters. In Table 7-6 we see that hardly a year passed between 1950 and 1971 in which public preferences were not ascertained. Compared to opinion mandates we have already examined (especially the question of Vietnam involvement), the public has consistently spoken clearly: between 1950 and 1970 the public preferred that Communist China not be admitted to the United Nations. Only in 1970 did the proportion opposing admission fall below a majority, but there is no question where the public's preference lay. However, the 1971 Harris poll showed a turnabout in public sentiment to favor admission, though the pro-admission sentiment constituted only a plurality, not a majority.

The relevant public policy, like the opinion mandate, is relatively unambiguous. Between 1950 and 1971 the question of admission of Communist China to the United Nations came up twenty-one times in a number of forms and in each

---

[18] Brief but incisive reviews of the various issues and debates are found in *China and U.S. Foreign Policy*, 2nd. ed. (Washington, D.C.: Congressional Quarterly, 1973); and A.T. Steele, *The American People and China* (New York: McGraw-Hill, 1966), especially Chap. 7.

instance but the last the United States opposed admission. However, while the U.S. vote in the General Assembly is the most important manifestation of our policy, it does not convey the complete picture of resistance to admission. Many other modes of opposition are available and it is not unreasonable to believe that merely voting against admission could be only perfunctory unless other actions, e.g., threatening retribution against other countries voting in favor of admission, were also taken. Indeed, an unwillingness to demonstrate opposition beyond just casting a "no" vote can frequently be construed as indicating indifference or nonopposition. Unfortunately, while we have good reason to believe that the United States engaged in arm twisting, economic threats, and various diplomatic maneuvers to block Red China's admission, this type of behavior is extremely difficult to observe so we cannot compare these actions with changes in public sentiment.[19] Nevertheless, some evidence of U.S. behavior in addition to voting

Table 7-6 Public Support for Admission of Communist China to the United Nations 1950-1970

Date	Favor Admission	Oppose Admission	Depends	No Opinion Don't Know
June 1950	11%	58%	—	31%
Nov-Dec 1953*	12	74	6	8
March 1954*	11	79	5	5
June 1954	7	78	—	15
July 1954	8	79	—	13
May 1955	10	67	—	23
Sept 1956*	17	73	5	5
Dec 1956	11	74	—	15
Feb 1957	13	70	—	17
Jan 1958	17	66	—	17
Aug 1958	20	63	—	17
March 1961	19	64	—	17
Sept 1961	16	64	—	20
Jan-Feb 1964	14	69	—	17
Feb 1965	22	64	—	14
March 1966	25	55	—	20
Sept 1966	25	56	—	19
Jan 1969	33	54	—	13
Sept 1970	35	49	—	16
May 1971†	48	27	—	25

*The question was "Would you approve or disapprove of letting Communist China become a member of the United Nations?" All other questions were "Do you think Communist China should be admitted as a member of the United Nations?"
†Harris Poll
SOURCE: 1950-1966 data are Gallup and NORC polls reported in Alfred O. Hero Jr., "The American Public and the UN, 1954-1966," *Journal of Conflict Resolution* 19: 441. Other data are from the *Gallup Opinion Index.*

[19] For a more general description of UN politics involving the admission of Communist China, see Lung-Chu Chen and Harold D. Lasswell, *Formosa, China and the United Nations* (New York: St. Martins Press, 1967).

record is available and a brief chronological array of this evidence is presented in Table 7-7.

The action described in Table 7-7 supports the contention that United States opposition to Red China's admission was more than a perfunctory vote. The strength of this opposition is especially revealed in the United States' action in 1961 making the questions of China's admission an "important question" and thereby necessitating a two-thirds majority for admission. Given the growing number of newly admitted nations, many of whom were sympathetic to admitting Communist China, it had become clear that a simple majority (50%+) would soon favor admission. By changing the issue from a substantive one to a procedural one (albeit with major substantive consequences), the United States succeeded in delaying China's admission ten years until 1971.

Though one might assume that little congruence between opinion and policy would exist in issues as far removed from daily life as seating Red China at the United Nations, our data unambiguously shows this not to be the case. Without a single exception in each year between 1950 and 1971, government action is in accord with public sentiment. It is also interesting to observe that the opinion shift to favoring admission *preceded* not only the admission decision, but the actual change in U.S. policy (including President Nixon's announcement of his trip to China). Thus, at least in this instance, opinion-policy concordance cannot be attributed simply to the public accpeting a *fait accompli.* To be sure, there is nothing in our analysis that even hints that the public caused or influenced government opposition to admitting Red China to the U.N. (or that the

Table 7-7   Chronology of United States Actions on the Admission of Communist China to the United Nations, 1950-1971

Date	Action
1950-1970	Congress expresses opposition to the admission of Red China to U.N. through resolutions usually attached to foreign aid appropriations bills.
1951-1960	U.S. uses influence in UN General Assembly to have questions of voting on seating Red China delayed for a year, in effect defeating admission.
1961	In the face of declining opposition in General Assembly to delaying vote on admitting Communist China, U.S. gets General Assembly to make admission question an "important question" requiring a two-thirds vote. Thus, pro-admission nations need a two-thirds majority for Communist China to gain admission.
1971	On August 2, the United States endorses the seating of Communist China at the UN, but opposes expulsion of Nationalist China (the official Chinese People's Republic position is that Formosa must be expelled before they will accept membership in the UN). On October 25, U.S. sponsored resolution on making Red China admission an "important question" loses by 59 to 55 margin. Seating of Communist China and expulsion of Nationalist China overwhelmingly approved by General Assembly.

government manipulated public opinion to prepare Americans for the change). All we can say is that congruence existed.

TRADING WITH THE COMMUNISTS, 1953-1972

Since the end of World War II and the emergence of the so called Cold War a major issue in American foreign policy has been our economic relationship to communist nations. Two basic positions can be identified. On the one hand, a number of militant anticommunists argue that any commercial interchanges with the Soviet Union or Red China only help those committed to the destruction of the United States. It is argued that trade between the technology-rich U.S. and the more backward communist economies would considerably strengthen Soviet and Chinese war capacity while merely providing limited financial advantage to certain American businessmen. The counter argument frequently offered is that economic transactions between capitalist and communist nations will provide: a) greater interdependence of economies; b) raised standards of living for all participants and; c) opportunities for personal contacts. These developments, it is asserted, will thus reduce mutual hostility and lessen the chances of war.[20]

The issue of trade with Communist nations has been analyzed by pollsters since the late 1940s. Unfortunately, however, as the particulars of this issue shifted so did the poll questions; consequently, while considerable data are available, much of it relates to one or two issues for a very limited time span.[21] There were, however, two questions asked on a number of separate occasions during the post World War II period. The first concerns whether the United States and Russia should work out a business arrangement to facilitate trade, while the second speaks of communist countries in general and specifically excludes trade in goods that might be used for military purposes. These data are presented in Tables 7-8 and 7-9. Since the questions are different, we shall consider each set of questions separately.

Tables 7-8 and 7-9 both display reasonably clear trends in their respective time periods. On the question of a U.S.-Russia trade arrangement, public support switched from negative to positive in 1955 and remained that way in all subsequent surveys (though in November of 1957 support was only a plurality). A similar pattern is found in Table 7-9—support for trade with communists is

[20] For a sampling of these arguments, see Samuel F. Clabaugh and Edwin J. Feulner, Jr., *Trading with the Communists* (Washington, D.C.: The Center for Strategic Studies, 1968), pp. 17-22.

[21] For example, between 1947 and 1953 the Gallup Poll and National Opinion Research Center asked a number of questions on U.S.-Russia trade. Some of these questions specifically mentioned trade in machinery; others added oil or automobiles. In some instances respondents were told that the United States would receive valuable minerals in return for our machinery. Finally, questions varied as to whether "war materials" would be excluded from such trade. If we had reason to believe that preferences on U.S.-Soviet trade were deeply rooted and not susceptible to details of questions wording, these diverse data could be used, but as we shall see below, this assumption is unwarranted.

Table 7-8 Public Opinion on United States and Russian
Trade, 1953-1963*

Date	Should	Should Not	No Opinion
1953 (Aug.)	40%	48%	12%
1954 (Jan.)	42	44	14
(Korean War ends)			
1955 (June)	55	29	16
1957 (June)	50	33	17
1957 (Nov.)	46	33	21
1959 (Feb.)	55	27	18
1963 (Oct.)	55	33	12

*"Should the United States and Russia work out a business
arrangement to buy and sell goods to each other?"
SOURCE: Gallup Poll

low in 1964, increases somewhat by 1968, and becomes a majority by 1972. As
for the puzzling question of why a majority endorsed a trade arrangement with
the Russians in 1963 (Table 7-8), yet only 28 percent accepted nonmilitary
trade with communist nations in general in 1964 (Table 7-9), no ready answer
exists. It is unlikely, however, that citizens were distinguishing between U.S.
trade with Russia only versus trade with Russia and Red China, since a 1961
Gallup Poll found a clear plurality (47 percent vs. 35 percent) supporting a
U.S.-Red China trade agreement.[22] It is also worth noting that these polls
display a fairly large "don't know" and "no opinion" response. This fact, plus
the distant character of foreign trade for most citizens, suggests that this may
not be one of the central public issues in the minds of the average person.

Our indicators of relevant public policy for both sets of questions are of two

Table 7-9 Public Opinion on Doing Business with Communist
Nations, 1964-1972

Date	Allowed To Trade	Depends	Forbidden	Don't Know and No Interest
1964	28%	5%	43%	24%
1968	31	4	38	26
1972	62	3	33	2

SOURCE: SRC, University of Michigan. The question in all surveys was:
"Some people say that our farmers and businessmen should be able to
go ahead and do business with communist countries as long as the goods
are not used for military purposes; others say that our government
should not allow Americans to trade with Communist countries.

[22] Another (though unverifiable) explanation would be the use of "Russia" as opposed
to "Communist". It could be argued that since many Americans have a "knee-jerk"
anticommunist reaction, any question mentioning communists will elicit an anticommunist response regardless of specific content. This explanation would not, however,
account for the 1972 data in Table 7-9.

types. First, there are the various laws and trade agreements governing who can import or export what type of goods and to whom. Because the opinion questions do not spell out the particulars of trade policy, we shall consider all such policies regulating commerce between U.S. and communist nations. Moreover, since the true impact of formal trade regulations is not self-evident from their intent, a second measure of policy will be the actual quantity of trade. This second indicator will be measured in both actual dollar amounts and trade with communist nations as a proportion of total U.S. foreign trade.

The chronology of legislation and executive action described in Table 7-10 clearly show that extensive trade with the Soviet Union was discouraged during the 1953-1963 period. Particularly during the Korean War a number of official actions made it virtually impossible for American businessmen to export goods to Russia, or for Russia to sell goods to the United States. Such U.S. Government policy was consistent with the 1953 and 1954 opinion data presented in Table 7-8, but when opinion shifted in 1955 to a pro-trade position, changes in regulations were not immediately forthcoming. To be sure, in the late 1950s, trade restrictions to Eastern European Communist nations, particularly Poland, were relaxed, but these benefits were extended to the Soviet Union only much later. Even in 1962, when public support for liberalized trade laws was of relatively long duration, Congress reiterated its anti-Soviet trade position by requiring the revocation of most favored nation status for all Communist bloc nations.

The second aspect of U.S.-Communist trade concerns economic interchanges with Communist nations in general, not just Russia. Beginning about the mid-1960s, the U.S. Government began slowly moving in the direction of more liberal U.S.-communist bloc (excluding Red China, Cuba and North Korea) trade arrangements. By the end of the 1960s, American businessmen achieved a substantial amount of freedom and financial backing for Eastern European ventures through the Export-Import Bank. This government action was not, however, paralleled by shifts in public sentiment. The data in Table 7-9 imply that such policy changes were made in the face of public opposition, though the relatively high proportion of "don't know" and "no interest" responses suggests a lack of conviction in this subject.[23] With the change in public opinion in the early 1970s, and the further de-regulation of U.S.-communist bloc trade during the same period, public opinion and public policy moved towards greater congruence.

Analyses of actual trade figures in Tables 7-11 and 7-12 provide a somewhat different version of public opinion-public policy congruence. Perhaps the first

---

[23] However, data collected in 1970 by Harris indicate that such policy responses were perfectly consistent with public opinion on trading with Russia. Harris found that 74 percent of the public favored expanding trade with the Soviet Union, 14 percent opposed, and 12 percent were not sure. *The Harris Survey Yearbook of Public Opinion 1970* (New York: Louis Harris and Associates, Inc., 1971), p. 104.

Table 7-10   Legislation and Executive Action Regulating Trade with Communist Nations

Year	Action
1917	Trading with the Enemy Act of 1917 gave the President virtually unlimited power to regulate trade when the United States is at war or the President declares a state of national emergency. This authority invoked in 1950 at outbreak of Korean War to prohibit trade with Red China and North Korea. Invoked again in Vietnam War to ban trade with North Vietnam in 1964.
1934	Johnson Act of 1934 makes it a crime for private persons to purchase bonds, securities, or other obligations of countries in default on obligations to the U.S. Government. Though the Soviet Union has continually been in default to the U.S. Government, the Attorney General ruled in 1963 that deferred Soviet payment for U.S. wheat does not violate this Act.
1949	Export Control Act of 1949 gives authority to the Department of Commerce to list goods that cannot be exported to Communist nations. Over a thousand items were on the prohibited list as of 1968 and Congress has extended this Act virtually unchanged through 1969.
1951	Mutual Defense Assistance Control Act of 1951 tightened controls of exports of strategic goods to communist nations. Besides prohibiting the sale of arms, Act also included specified forms of metalworking machinery, various electronic equipment, petroleum products and equipment, and certain metals. President is given some power to make exceptions, but attempts by Eisenhower and Kennedy to broaden discretionary power were unsuccessful.
1952	President Truman withdrew most favored nation trade status from all communist nations except Yugoslavia due to Korean War.
1953	U. S. Treasury Department prohibited U.S. firms from using their foreign subsidiaries to sell strategic goods to Soviet bloc nations.
1954	Public Law 480 provided for sale or distribution of surplus agricultural products. Communist nations were excluded from participation.
1956	Trade restrictions with European Communist nations were relaxed somewhat by the removal of certain items from the restricted list.
1957	Controls on exports to Poland were further relaxed.
1961	Agriculture Act of 1961 prohibited export of subsidized agricultural products to communist bloc nations.
1962	Trading with the Enemy Act invoked to bar Cuban goods from import. Also, Cuba's most favored nation status was revoked. Trade Expansion Act of 1962 required mandatory revocation of most favored nation status for all communist nations.
1963	Foreign Aid bill for 1964 included section prohibiting U.S. Government from guaranteeing credit to communist nations through the Export-Import Bank. However, provision was made for the President to waive this rule if it serves the best interests of the United States.
1964	Most favored nation status extended to Poland and Yugoslavia. Regulations governing trade with Rumania were liberalized.
1966	President Johnson ordered 400 items removed from the list of strategic commodities that were not allowed to be exported to European communist nations (East Germany and Soviet Union were excluded). Johnson also extended Export-Import Bank credit to

Year	Action
	Poland, Hungary, Bulgaria, and Czechoslovakia, but his attempt to extend favorable tariff treatment to Eastern European nations was ignored by Congress. Legislation designed to further U.S.-Communist trade was introduced but died in committee.
1969	Export Administration Act of 1969 passed. Like the Export Control Act of 1949 which it replaced, this Act provided for the close regulation of sales and strategic goods to communist nations. However, it allowed the sale of items to communist nations which were readily available from Western European and Japanese producers. President retained power to restrict trade for reasons of national security. Foreign subsidiaries of U.S. companies allowed to trade in non-strategic goods with Red China.
1971	Ban on Export-Import Bank giving credit to nations at war with U.S. was lifted, thus allowing guaranteed loans for trading with communist nations. The list of goods that could be exported to Red China was increased substantially.
1972	Congress passes legislation removing unilateral export controls except where such removal would endanger national security.

thing to be noted is that U.S.-Communist trade from the 1950s to the 1970s constitutes only a very small part of total U.S. imports and exports. Moreover, some of the enormous jumps in trade figures are due to one-shot agricultural sales made under duress and therefore may not be indicative of real policy changes. In any case, even though the changes in U.S.-Russian trade are small by comparison, the trend depicted in Table 7-11 roughly parallels opinion shifts previously described in Table 7-8. That is, prior to 1955 when the public

Table 7-11   U.S.-Russia Trade, in Dollars, 1952-1964

Year	Exports		Imports	
	Value (in thousands of dollars)	As Percent of All Exports	Value (in thousands of dollars)	As Percent of All Imports
1952	20	*	16,818	.16
1953	19	*	10,791	.10
1954	219	*	11,809	.11
1955	252	*	17,134	.15
1956	3,823	.02	24,468	.19
1957	3,504	.02	16,503	.13
1958	3,415	.02	17,462	.14
1959	7,398	.04	28,304	.19
1960	38,440	.19	22,629	.15
1961	41,650	.19	23,228	.16
1962	15,297	.07	16,298	.10
1963	20,239	.08	20,330	.12
1964	144,553	.55	20,238	.11

*less than .01%
SOURCES: U.S. Bureau of the Census, *Statistical Abstract of the U.S.* (Washington, D.C.), 1955, 1960, 1962, 1965.

Table 7-12   U.S.-Communist* Nations Trade, 1963-1973

Year	Exports		Imports	
	Value (in millions of dollars)	As percent of all exports	Value (in millions of dollars)	As percent of all imports
1963	328	1.4	141	.8
1964	483	1.8	170	.9
1965	288	1.0	218	1.0
1966	371	1.2	270	1.1
1967	291	.9	275	1.0
1968	305	.9	302	.9
1969	335	.9	300	.8
1970	521	1.2	323	.8
1971	558	1.3	325	.7
1972	1048	2.1	504	.9
1973	2487	3.5	585	.8

*Communist nations are the Soviet Union, Eastern European nations including Yugoslavia, Red China, and North Korea.
SOURCES: U.S. Bureau of the Census, *Statistical Abstracts of the U.S.* (Washington, D.C.) 1967, 1968, 1971, 1973, 1974

opposed U.S.-Russian trade arrangements, total trade (exports and imports) was substantially less than in the post-1955 period when the public endorsed such arrangements. However, by no means did U.S.-Russia trade skyrocket after 1955 and almost all of this change resulted in increased exports since pre-1955, while post-1955 import figures show little systematic variation.

On the question of trading with the communists in general, the trade data in Table 7-12 shows a mixed relationship with public opinion. On the one hand, the actual dollar amounts of U.S.-Communist trade did generally increase between 1963 and 1973 and this could be construed as being consistent with opinion changes. Nevertheless, though U.S. trade with the Communist bloc increased in dollars between 1963 and 1973, the percentage trends in Table 7-12 do not correspond to opinion shifts. For example, in 1964 when a plurality opposed trading with Communists, the U.S. did almost as much business with the Communists (proportionately) as in 1972 when a clear majority favored trade. Table 7-12 also shows that despite wide fluctuation in opinion on the subject, the figures on imports from Communist bloc nations remained quite stable. All in all, the percentage figures suggest that our increased trading with Communist bloc nations is perhaps more due to general increases in U.S. trade (and inflation) than to shifts in whom U.S. businessmen do business with.

On the whole, there exists no clearcut answer as to whether policy on U.S.-communist bloc trade is in accordance with popular preferences. During some periods and using certain measures of policy there is evidence of congruence; the opposite is true for other periods and when different methods are employed. Perhaps the best way to describe this relationship is to say that opinion and policy are roughly independent of each other. That is, knowing what the public's preferences were would provide little if any clue as to the nature of U.S.-communist trade. In the light of the sometimes contradictory character of mass opinions, this conclusion should come as no surprise. Even if public officials were devoted to adhering to every public whim, such slavish adherence would be impossible where the opinion messages were casually held and conveyed different orders (e.g., favoring U.S.-Russia trade while opposing trading with communists) depending on the details of specific questions.

CONCLUSION

At the beginning of this chapter we suggested the possibility that little, if any congruence would exist between public opinion and policy on issues related to foreign affairs. That is, because such questions are typically remote from the daily lives of most citizens, and since leaders can rarely follow public instructions, we would not expect a one to one relationship between opinion and government action. Our expectations are to a large extent confirmed on the subjects of foreign aid and trade with communist nations. In both cases we saw that some data indicated opinion-policy congruence; other data suggested incongruity so our overall judgment was that opinion and policy were generally independent of each other. However, on the issue of American intervention in Vietnam we saw that considerable concordance existed on broad patterns of action, and in the case of the admission of Communist China to the United Nations, citizen sentiment and government behavior were in agreement 100 percent of the time. Certainly the existence of congruence on the Chinese admission to the U.N. raises serious doubts about the contention that personally remote issues will necessarily be uncorrelated with mass opinion.

It is also clear from our analyses that little evidence exists for the claim that opinion-policy congruence is more likely to occur in domestic rather than foreign policy issues. Indeed, the best instance of a close relationship between opinion and policy in all eleven issues we considered is in the question of communist admission to the U.N. More generally, while a good case for congruence can be made in half (two of four) of our foreign policy subjects, the percentage for domestic policy would certainly appear to be lower. Of course, since the seven domestic and four foreign affairs issue areas we have analyzed are but a small sampling of the multitude of salient issues in the last thirty years, our comparison of opinion-policy congruity must be highly tentative. Nevertheless, we certainly can say that opinion-policy agreement appears to be no greater on subjects of direct personal relevance, e.g., income tax rates, than where government action is far removed from daily life, e.g., foreign aid expenditure.

It is crucial to realize, of course, that when we compare the amount of opinion-policy congruence across issue area we are *not* making assertions about the relative amount of popular influence in these policy areas. The presence or absence of opinion-policy congruences says nothing about popular influence. It is entirely possible that the government does precisely what a majority of citizens want without the slightest coercion from these citizens. Similarly, public pressure may be very important on some policy questions where the end product may have only the faintest relationship to what is desired by the public. For example, it is quite likely that decision-makers are aware of public hostility towards higher income tax rates and are reluctant to incur this hostility, but the tax rate has nevertheless risen in response to demands for various government services. Thus, public preferences have not been heeded, but no doubt they would have been heeded even less if not for public influence. It is this important question of popular influence that our analysis considers next.

chapter eight

SOURCES OF CONGRUENCE: ELECTIONS

The preceding analyses have shown a wide variation in the amount of congruence between public opinion and public policy. In some instances, e.g., the admission of Communist China to the U.N., government and public are in nearly complete accord; on other issues, e.g., income tax rates, considerable incongruity occurs; in still other issues the pattern either varies over time or is ambiguous. The interesting question, of course, is why do we find congruence for some issues but not others? Are there particular types of policies where congruence is more likely to occur? Unfortunately, however, a policy by policy analysis is beyond our reach. Not only would such an endeavor require an enormous quantity of very specific data, much of which do not exist, but even if the information were available, we do not possess a sufficiently complete theory of opinion and policy to organize these facts and thus offer a coherent explanation for each and every opinion-policy relationship.

Instead we shall approach the problem of accounting for opinion-policy congruence from a broad perspective. The basic question is: what factors help or hinder a close relationship between popular preferences and government policy in *general*. Our analytic strategy will be to pose three different, though complementary, processes that could bring about opinion-policy congruence. Then, in this and subsequent chapters we shall examine the validity of each alternative. Briefly, the three possibilities are: 1) through the election process citizens select officials who enact popular preferences; 2) citizens and leaders essentially prefer the same things so people get pretty much what they want without expressly demanding it; 3) the government manipulates public opinion to support its actions. Each of these alternatives is a plausible way of creating harmony between opinion and policy and each may be correct or incorrect. By no means are these the only conceivable mechanisms to achieve congruence, but these three mechanisms are certainly among the most plausible ones to account for the relationship between popular preference and public policy.[1] Let us begin by considering whether or not elections contribute to greater congruity.

ELECTIONS AS MEANS OF POPULAR CONTROL OF POLICY

For most people no doubt, elections are seen as *the* primary mechanism through which common citizens control their government. Elections are, supposedly, the means by which leaders gone astray are replaced by ones more attuned to popular desires. Indeed, even more than public opinion polls, the vote is often depicted as the ultimate and authoritative "voice of the people." This imagery is well supported by testimonials from public officials proclaiming their fear of public retribution if their constituents are not satisfied.[2] Perhaps only the lunatic fringe openly challenges the utility of the electoral process as the mechanism giving political power to the people.

Recent research, however, has at least partially challenged these claims. In particular, several studies report widespread voter ignorance on both candidates and issues; voting choices made on traditional partisan, not policy grounds; and a tendency to distort and selectively perceive political information.[3] These studies in turn have been challenged and other pieces of evidence offered to show that voters are not incompetents unable to choose what they want.[4] Both schools of thought, however, focus largely on the capacity of individual voters, not the electoral system in its entirety. To be sure, the decisions made by individual voters are one of the most important elements in the electoral system, but a

[1] Several additional linkage mechanisms are suggested in Norman R. Luttbeg, ed., *Public Opinion and Public Policy,* rev. ed. (Homewood, Ill.: The Dorsey Press, 1974), pp. 1-10. Also see John L. Sullivan, "Linkage Models of the Political System," in *Public Opinion and Political Attitudes* ed., Allen R. Wilcox (New York: John Wiley and Sons, 1974), pp. 637-59.

[2] For example, see John W. Kingdon, "Politicians' Beliefs about Voters," *American Political Science Review* 61 (1967): 137-45.

[3] Among others, see Angus Campbell, Philip E. Converse, Warren E. Miller and Donald E. Stokes, *The American Voter* (New York: John Wiley and Sons, 1960), especially chap. 20; Donald E. Stokes and Warren E. Miller, "Party Government and the Saliency of Congress," *Public Opinion Quarterly* 26 (1962): 531-46; Bernard R. Berelson, Paul F. Lazarsfeld, and William N. McPhee, *Voting* (Chicago: University of Chicago Press, 1954).

[4] For example, V.O. Key, Jr., *The Responsible Electorate: Rationality in Presidential Voting, 1936-1960* (Cambridge, Mass.: The Belknap Press, 1966); David E. RePass, "Issue Salience and Party Choice," *American Political Science Review* 65 (1971): 389-400; Richard W. Boyd, "Popular Control of Public Policy: A Normal Vote Analysis of the 1968 Election," *American Political Science Review* 66 (1972): 429-49; John Osgood Field and Ronald E. Anderson, "Ideology in the Public's Conceptualization of the 1964 Election," *Public Opinion Quarterly* 33 (1969): 380-98, among others.

complete analysis also requires examination of leadership behavior and institutions. As we shall see, it is conceivable that the election system could give voters what they want even if individual voters behave incompetently. And, by the same token, even if everyone chooses the candidate closest to his own preferences, it is not guaranteed that subsequent policy will be consistent with the majority's preferences.

To make clear what we mean when we speak of citizen *control* of policy through elections, consider the following highly simplified situation. Let us imagine an electorate with 100 voters, an election with a single issue, a 60-40 split on this issue and two candidates who differ on this issue. Control—as opposed to mere opinion-policy congruence—would occur if (1) voters correctly perceived each candidate's issue stand; (2) citizens voted in accordance with their own policy preferences; (3) the candidate receiving a majority won; and (4) the winner implemented the position originally advocated. It should be obvious that opinion-policy agreement can occur despite the violation of these conditions. For example, if some of the 60 percent majority misperceive a candidate's issue position, the "wrong" candidate could be elected. But if this winning candidate reverses his stand upon taking office, the majority's wishes are satisfied. Alternatively, everyone could vote on the basis of a coin flip and the candidate whose program was supported by the 60 percent wins by chance alone. Other breakdowns in control can be imagined, but the point to be stressed is that many conditions must exist for *control* to operate, and mere agreement between voters and officials is not *prima facie* proof of control.

More generally, in order for us to say that citizens control policy through the electoral process, the following conditions must be met:

1. Citizens possess policy preferences.
2. Candidates offer choices on the policies of concern to citizens. For example, if citizens think that inflation is *the* issue, prospective office holders must state their future policies on inflation. Should candidates instead decide to debate the merits of Apple Pie and Motherhood, voters cannot express their preferences on inflation.
3. Citizens correctly associate policy preferences with candidates. Thus, if one candidate proposes wage and price controls as the best means of controlling inflation, citizens know the fact.
4. Citizens vote for the candidate who best approximates their own policy preferences. This gives each candidate a clear policy mandate.
5. The candidate with the most votes wins (for simplicity's sake, we assume only two candidates, so a simple majority wins). The victorious candidate implements his/her policy. If implementation does not occur, the official is defeated at the subsequent election.

This set of requirements constitutes an idealized version of the electoral process. The probability of its being perfectly realized is very remote. Nevertheless, it provides a useful standard to compare the existing system's capacity to provide a popular control of policy. By using this ideal standard in conjunction with empirical data, we can say where popular control breaks down and by how much, as well as make suggestions on when changes are to be made if we desired to increase popular control. It should also be noted that these requirements pertain to voters, candidates, and the rules of the political system and *all* conditions must be satisfied for control to exist.

Are all these conditions satisfied in American elections? Considering all the elections at various levels of government, to conduct a thorough analysis of a single election year would be impossible. To be sure, elections have been the subject of considerable research, but the existing data are incomplete and piecemeal. We shall focus on data largely, but not entirely, from recent national, particularly congressional and presidential, contests. It is clear that if citizens cannot greatly influence public policy in national elections, the amount of political power lost is substantial. Moreover, since these elections are the most visible contests, we suspect that if control does not occur here, it is even less likely to occur in lesser contexts.

THE EXISTENCE OF CITIZEN PREFERENCE

At first glance, the requirement that citizens possess policy preferences may appear very easy to satisfy. As we have previously seen, most citizens will readily respond to pollsters even when questions are nonsensical. Certainly, on major controversial issues few people can resist offering a "yes" or "no" to broad questions. If we use more demanding criteria for determining a genuine preference, however, increasingly larger numbers of citizens can be categorized as lacking "real" policy demands. For example, the Survey Research Center's questions typically allow respondents the option of expressing "no interest" or "don't know" in an issue and particularly on questions far removed from everyday life, e.g., diplomatic recognition of Communist China, "no interest" or "don't know" responses can comprise a third of all responses. Even on issues with a more direct personal impact, e.g., federal income tax rates, small though significant numbers of citizens have nothing to say.

A different, and perhaps more fruitful way of approaching this requirement of possessing preferences is not to ask whether citizens can express a preference if confronted with a concrete alternative, but instead to simply ask citizens "What do you want the government to do?" This approach to ascertaining preferences assumes implicitly that unless citizens can demand a policy spontaneously, the underlying motivation is so low that the demand is peripheral at best. Moreover, by relying on spontaneous calls for government action (or inaction) we avoid the problem of having people demand every conceivable policy of any merit without having to think about what is possible or most important. In both its 1968 and 1972 election surveys, the Survey Research Center did pose the open-ended question "What do you personally feel are the most important problems the government in Washington should try to take care of?" Up to three responses were coded by the interviewer.

The data in Table 8-1 indicate the extent to which citizens expressed policy demands prior to the 1968 elections.[5] It is clear that most people could think of something that ought to be done by Washington. It is also true, however, that a significant number of individuals in each instance were at a loss on what the government should do. For example, a person might say that "race relations" were a big problem but be totally unable to say whether leaders should take more or less action, or what kind of action. Such expressions of "something ought to be done but I don't know what" are of limited value in holding leaders accountable to public sentiment. Table 8-1 also shows that most citizens can express no more than two important concerns. This extensive inability to articulate numerous policy demands stands in stark contrast to the image conveyed by more structured surveys where citizens can easily say "yes" or "no" to an almost endless series of policy alternatives.

More important, however, than the relative paucity of citizen demands is their enormous diversity. Individual responses were coded into categories by the Survey Research Center and we have further combined similar responses, but Table 8-2 nevertheless still reflects considerable variation in what constitutes the key political issues. Moreover, this agenda of concerns is further fragmented by the fact that those specifying the same issue probably disagree on what ought to be done about it. Indeed, in those instances where only a handful of citizens mention a particular issue, probably as many different preferences exist as

Table 8-1   Public Demand* for Government Action, 1968

	Problem		
	First Problem	Second Problem	Third Problem
Some type of action	67.4	65.5	43.2
Satisfied with present policy	.1	.2	–
Don't know or not clear about what should be done	29.9	19.4	9.7
No important problem	2.6	14.9	47.1
	100.0%	100.0%	100.0%
N =	1557	1557	1557

*The question was: "As you well know, the government faces many serious problems in the country and in other parts of the world. What do you personally feel are the most important problems the government in Washington should try to take care of?
SOURCE: Survey Research Center, University of Michigan

[5] Although both the 1968 and 1972 SRC (Survey Research Center) studies ask about the most important problem facing the country, coding procedures for the 1972 study do not allow us to ascertain the number of people without political concern. There is no reason, however, to suppose that 1972 data would differ substantially from 1968 data.

Table 8-2 Perceived Major Political Problems the Government in Washington Should Do Something About, 1968 and 1972

Problem	1968		1972	
	Percent Mentioning*	Number of Responses	Percent Mentioning	Number of Responses
Population increase/ birth control	.3	4	2.2	23
Unemployment and economic conditions	4.4	69	12.4	129
Improving educatonal quality	4.0	63	2.3	24
Medical problem of the aged	2.8	43	1.7	17
Medical care in general	.4	6	2.2	22
Other social welfare problems	.9	14	—	—
Agricultural problems	1.1	18	4.1	43
Resource conservation/ pollution	1.3	20	8.5	89
Developing natural resources	.1	1	.2	2
Other agricultural and resource problems	.1	1	.3	3
Regulation of labor unions	1.0	16	.1	1
Wage guidelines and pay raises	.3	5	—	—
Change in minimum wage	.5	8	.1	1
Other labor problems	.1	2	.2	2
Black civil rights	6.7	105	1.1	11
Economic assistance to blacks	3.5	55	—	—
Civil rights of other minorities	.4	6	.6	6
Economic assistance to other minorities	.5	8	—	—
Protection of white majority	2.6	41	1.3	13
Racial problems generally	14.7	230	17.9	186
Protection of civil liberties	.6	10	1.2	12
Black riots	.6	10	—	—
Riots and public disturbances	—	—	1.7	18
Law and order	29.9	466	28.7	298
Gun control	.5	8	.2	2
Anti-Vietnam war demonstrators	1.9	29	—	—
Controlling left-wing extremists	1.9	30	1.3	13
Moral, religious decay	.8	13	4.7	49
School prayers	.1	1	.1	1
Problems of young people	2.2	35	4.1	41
Revolutionary ideas	—	—	.3	3
Other racial and public order problems	.4	7	1.3	13
Hijacking	—	—	.6	6
Inflation and higher prices	4.8	74	26.1	271
Taxes	7.8	121	8.7	90
Government economic policy	4.8	74	4.4	46
State of national economy	.8	13	7.8	81
Foreign trade	.4	6	1.3	13

174

Table 8.2 (cont.)

Problem	1968		1972	
	Percent Mentioning*	Number of Responses	Percent Mentioning	Number of Responses
Interest rates	.1	2	.3	3
Immigration policies	.1	2	.2	2
Consumer protection and safety	.3	7	.3	3
Mass transportation	.1	2	.1	1
Other economic problems	.1	2	.5	5
Vietnam	68.4	1065	44.9	466
Relations with Communist nations	1.6	25	1.3	13
Relations with Western Europe	.3	5	–	–
German unification	.1	1	–	–
Czechoslovakia	.4	6	–	–
Korea	1.7	26	–	–
Middle East	.8	12	–	–
Nigerian civil war	.1	2	–	–
Foreign involvement generally	3.6	56	5.9	61
Foreign aid	7.1	110	.8	8
U.N. relations	.3	4	.2	2
Relations with Third World nations	–	–	.1	1
Solving domestic problems before foreign problems	4.2	66	1.0	10
Foreign relations in general	2.2	34	2.2	23
Other specific foreign affairs problems	.3	5	.3	3
Disarmament	.5	8	.1	1
Military policy	1.2	18	.6	6
Influence of the military	.1	2	.1	1
Weapons development	.3	4	–	–
Space race	.8	13	.3	3
Veterans benefits	.1	1	.1	1
Patriotism and national spirit	.3	4	1.1	11
National defense generally	.1	2	.3	3
Morality and competence of public officials	2.4	38	4.9	51
Government control over private citizens	.1	1	1.6	17
Power of government	2.4	37	1.5	16
Salaries of public officials	–	–	.1	1
Other problems relating to government functioning	–	–	1.6	17

*The percentages refer to the proportion of the total sample giving at least one response. Since up to three responses were coded, percentages add to more than 100 percent. This procedure also means that citizens giving three responses are more heavily weighted in these calculations.
SOURCE: Survey Research Center, University of Michigan

respondents. To be sure, since these data are drawn from a sample, even an issue receiving only slight concern is considered important by many thousands. Nevertheless, these data do not convey a picture of focused concern that would allow leaders to appeal to majorities on the basis of only a handful of issue stands. The American public can thus be characterized as a collection of "issue publics," not a monolithic entity concerned with one or two policies.

Whether the requirement that citizens possess policy preferences is reasonably well satisfied (at least at the presidential level) obviously very much depends on what one is willing to accept as a genuine preference. If a response to a question of peripheral personal concern like "Do you favor or oppose military assistance to Outer Mongolia?" is judged a valid indicator of a policy demand, then the requirement is generally well satisfied. On the other hand, if one emphasizes the need for policy demands to be characterized by high salience, then the picture is less clear. Certainly, citizens possess policy concerns, but the immense diversity of these spontaneously expressed concerns prevents a potential leader from appealing to more than a collection of relatively small issue publics. Hence, if leaders did everything asked of them once elected, we would have government policy directed at those few who really cared about the particular issue, not a majority.

POLICY CHOICES

Since requirements two and three both stress the policy alternatives offered citizens, we shall consider both together. Regarding the first of these demands—that candidates offer choices on issues of concern to citizens—it is possible to claim that virtually all candidates at least nominally satisfy this demand. That is, particularly beyond local elections, it is almost customary for candidates to formulate "issue position" statements on almost every conceivably relevant topic. This custom is most conspicuous at presidential nominating conventions where elaborate platforms on virtually every current subject are formulated (and in principle the approved platform planks extend to all candidates of the party). Even where issue stands are not concretely spelled out item by item, an incumbent's (or party's) record can readily serve as a good predictor of future behavior, so at least one has the opportunity to vote for or against a position. Finally, American electoral campaigns tend to be lengthy and replete with numerous statements of policy that are commonly widely disseminated by the mass media.

Nevertheless, though most candidates may spew forth their positions on a variety of matters, such behavior may only *appear* to meet the requirement of offering citizens a policy alternative. It is entirely possible that policy positions may be so vague as to be meaningless. Thus, for example, one can safely call for changes in the federal income tax that make it "fair and just" (whatever that means). Or, one can offer contradictory proposals giving something to everyone, e.g., reduce military spending while keeping America the strongest nation. One could even take all sides of all positions and hope that people impressed with, say, your opposition to policy X, do not discover that in front of another audience you came out in favor of policy X. Hence, it is not enough that candidates technically offer citizens politically relevant policy choices; if choices are to be meaningful, they must be specific and accurately perceived by citizens.

Some data on this question for two presidential elections are presented in Figures 8-1 through 8-4. For each election we have selected two issues that were salient controversies of some duration on which most people were likely to have some interest. In each instance respondents were asked to place candidates on a one to seven scale with one and seven representing the extreme policy preferences. Turning first to the 1968 election, on both the urban unrest and Vietnam questions, one observes considerable variations in perceptions of where Humphrey and Nixon stood on these questions. To be sure, by combining these seven point scales into, say, three (or even two) point scales, it is possible to see that a majority of perceptions did cluster near some point, but this procedure would produce consensus under any conditions and is thus beside the point. On

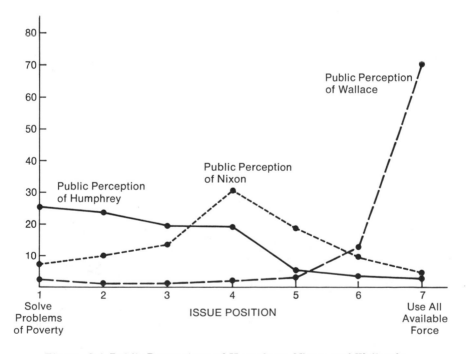

Figure 8-1 Public Perceptions of Humphrey, Nixon, and Wallace's Position in Urban Unrest 1968

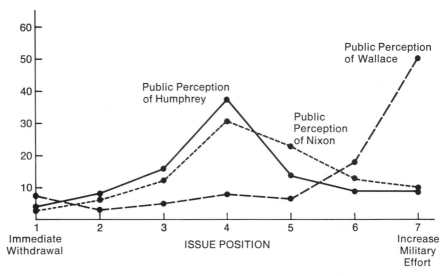

Figure 8-2   Public Perceptions of Humphrey, Nixon, and Wallace's Position on Vietnam, 1968

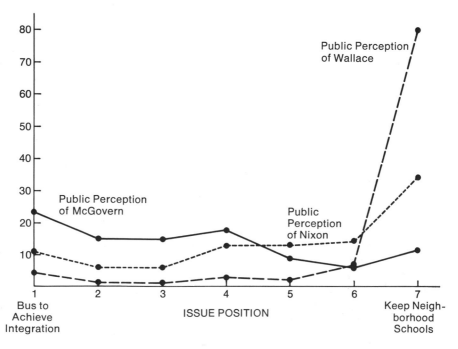

Figure 8-3   Public Perceptions of McGovern, Nixon, and Wallace's Position on the Use of Bussing to Achieve Racial Integration, 1972

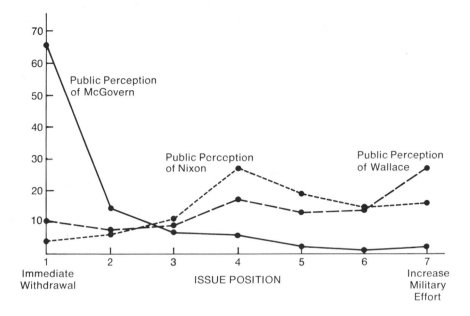

Figure 8-4   Public Perceptions of McGovern, Nixon, and Wallace's
Position on Vietnam, 1972

the other hand, perceptions of Wallace's position on both issues show
considerably less dispersion. Only a relatively small handful of citizens saw
Wallace as standing for less force in dealing with urban unrest or withdrawal
from Vietnam.

The 1972 election data in Figures 8-3 and 8-4 show a similar mixture of
dispersed and highly clustered perceptions. In the case of Vietnam policy, only
on McGovern's policy is there a high degree of consensus. Though most citizens
place Nixon and Wallace toward the "hawk" end of the scale, this perception is
not shared by sizeable numbers (e.g., over a quarter put Wallace towards the
"dove" position). When it comes to bussing to achieve racial integration in
public schools, however, it is Wallace who becomes the most consensually
viewed candidate while Nixon and McGovern are seen in widely differing ways.
It is particularly interesting that although McGovern was consistently placed on
the extreme "liberal" end of the scale on several other issues, such categorization
was not generalized to the school bussing issue.

Of course, it could be argued that it is unreasonable to expect every citizen to
know each candidate's position on every issue. For example, a farmer deeply
concerned with agricultural subsidies is far more motivated to follow a
candidate's position on agricultural price supports than the candidate's stance
on, say, urban redevelopment. To see whether having a strong interest in a
particular policy area produces less dispersion in perceptions of issue positions,

Table 8-3   Perceptions of Candidates' Urban Unrest Positions Among Those Considering Urban Unrest A Very Important Problem,* 1968

Perceptions of:	*Position on Urban Unrest*								
	1 Solve Economic Problems	2	3	4	5	6	7 Use All Available Force		N
Humphrey	26.1	29.5	19.3	14.8	5.7	3.4	1.1	99.9%	88
Nixon	10.5	12.8	12.8	30.2	15.1	15.1	3.5	100.0%	86
Wallace	3.4	3.4	1.1	3.4	5.7	9.1	73.9	100.0%	85

*Respondents were asked what they considered the most important problems the government in Washington should try to take care of. Three problems were recorded and those mentioning any problem closely related to urban unrest were included in this analysis.
SOURCE: Survey Research Center, University of Michigan

we shall examine the relationship between perceptions of candidates and perceptions of what is the most important issue facing the government. If the argument that specialized interest leads to more accurate perceptions is correct, these data should show less dispersion than previous data on perceptions.

Comparisons between the data in Figures 8-1, 8-2 and Tables 8-3 through 8-6 on the whole show only slight differences. Particularly in 1968, even those citizens especially attuned to an issue diverge substantially on exactly where Humphrey and Nixon stand. We again find a clear consensus in some instances, e.g., Wallace's stand on urban unrest, but it is no clearer a consensus than among the general citizenry. Furthermore, even those having a high interest in the presidential campaign display no sharper an image of where the candidates stood on these important issues.[6] No doubt a similar analysis of perceptions of

Table 8-4   Perceptions of Candidates' Vietnam Positions Among Those Considering Vietnam a Very Important Problem,* 1968

Perceptions of:	*Positions on Vietnam*								
	1 Immediate Withdrawal	2	3	4	5	6	7 Complete Military Victory		N
Humphrey	4.3	8.2	16.1	37.0	14.7	10.7	9.1	100.0%	981
Nixon	3.5	6.3	12.4	30.5	25.1	13.9	8.3	100.0%	953
Wallace	6.6	3.4	5.2	8.5	7.1	18.5	50.4	100.0%	940

*See Footnote in Table 8-3 for explanation of handling of "most important problem."
SOURCE: Survey Research Center, University of Michigan

[6] With very few exceptions, those who claim to follow campaigns very closely are almost identical to those who pay hardly any attention in their perception of candidates. The differences that do exist are small (less than 5 percent) and are unsystematic.

Table 8-5 Perceptions of Candidates' School Bussing Positions Among Those Considering Racial Integration A Very Important Problem,* 1972

Perceptions of:	*Position on Bussing to Achieve Racial Integration*								
	1 Bus to Achieve Integration	2	3	4	5	6	7 Keep Neigh- borhood Schools		N
McGovern	22.9	7.1	15.7	18.6	11.4	7.1	17.1	100.0%	70
Nixon	8.8	4.4	6.6	13.2	13.2	13.2	40.7	100.1%	91

*See Footnote Table 8-3.
SOURCE: Survey Research Center, University of Michigan

candidates less in the public limelight (e.g., Ronald Reagan) would show even greater dispersion of perceptions of issue positions.

Do these data show that the public has failed in its civic duty to associate correctly each candidate with a policy preference? If we could say precisely where each candidate stood on the issue, the public's capacity to accurately perceive candidates could be measured. As any astute followers of electoral campaigns have observed, however, few candidates for the presidency (or other offices) go much out of their way to make all of their policy stands crystal clear (except, of course, to come out strongly against sin, etc.). Typically, candidates will offer policy alternatives sufficiently vague and encompassing to attract many people, some of whom will disagree over the specifics. Not surprisingly, then, even thorough analyses of speeches and documents may at best provide only a diffuse "feel" of where a candidate stands.[7] Only when an office seeker

Table 8-6 Perceptions of Candidates' Vietnam Positions Among Those Considering Vietnam A Very Important Problem,* 1972

Perceptions of:	*Position on U.S. Involvement in Vietnam*								
	1 Immediate Withdrawal	2	3	4	5	6	7 Complete Military Victory	Total	N
McGovern	64.4	13.8	6.9	8.1	1.4	2.9	2.6	100.0%	421
Nixon	4.0	5.6	12.8	26.7	18.9	15.7	16.2	100.0%	445

*See Footnote, Table 8-3.
SOURCE: Survey Research Center, University of Michigan

[7] A sampling of some of the problems involved in ascertaining candidates "true" issue positions is provided by Page and Brody's analysis of Humphrey and Nixon's Vietnam positions. Extensive examination of public statements shows that both candidates made little effort to state precisely where they stood and both avoided extremist positions. See Benjamin I. Page and Richard A. Brody, "Policy Voting and the Electoral Process: The Vietnam War Issue," *American Political Science Review* 66 (1972): 979-95.

makes a strenuous and continuous effort to articulate an issue position (e.g., Wallace's opposition to racial integration or McGovern's desire for Vietnam withdrawal) do citizens clearly link candidates to policies; but such consensus is the exception, not the rule.[8]

Are the requirements that (1) candidates offer relevant policy choices and (2) that citizens correctly see these choices, reasonably well satisfied? The answer must be: only to a limited extent. It is entirely possible, for instance, for two citizens in 1968 who both strongly want immediate U.S. withdrawal from Vietnam to disagree on who advocates such a position.[9] In 1972 two such citizens would be more fortunate since at least one candidate (McGovern) made his position clear, but it was still not clear what the other candidate (Nixon) advocated. Similarly, if we exclude George Wallace, it is entirely reasonable for two citizens with identical preferences on the race question to disagree about the best candidate. Of course the data frequently show that general differences between candidates are accurately perceived, so at least some policy messages are getting through to citizens. Nevertheless, to paraphrase a slogan used by Barry Goldwater in decrying the lack of "true" alternatives in elections, Americans are (usually) faced with echoes, not choices.

VOTING AND CREATING ISSUE MANDATES

Whether the average citizen votes rationally or wisely evokes substantial disagreement. Since the advent of mass political participation philosophers and statesmen have offered assertions ranging from "citizens choose foolishly" to "the people are geniuses." The advent of modern survey analysis has helped to continue the debate but with little change in the range of answers. Indeed, the sheer availability of empirical data has led to such a plethora of definitions of "issue-voting" (and variants such as "rational voting") and tests for such voting

[8] For a variety of reasons we would expect even less agreement on where candidates for lesser offices stood. Not only are citizens frequently unaware of candidates' names, but even those aware of the personalities can offer little in the way of issue related characterization. Moreover, the media play given to lesser officers is overshadowed by national campaigns and many citizens are less engrossed in more local contests. Data for issue perceptions for congressional races in 1958 are reported in Donald E. Stokes and Warren E. Miller, "Party Government and the Saliency of Congress," *Public Opinion Quarterly* 26 (1962): 531-46. Similar data on 1970 elections are analyzed in Stanley R. Freedman, "The Salience of Party and Candidate in Congressional Elections: A Comparison of 1958 and 1970," in *Public Opinion and Public Policy,* rev. ed., ed., Norman R. Luttbeg (Homewood, Ill.: The Dorsey Press, 1974), pp. 126-31.

[9] Differences of opinion over where candidates stand on an issue can occur even where the candidates are viewed as substantially different from one another. For example, Page and Brody report that even among those perceiving a major difference between Humphrey and Nixon on Vietnam, sharp differences occurred over who was seen as the "hawk" and who constituted the "dove." See Page and Brody, "Policy Voting and the Electoral Process," p. 986.

Table 8-7   Importance of Urban Unrest in Vote Perception of Candidates and Vote, 1968

	Importance Attributed to Urban Unrest Issue								
	Most important or very important issue in vote			Somewhat important in vote			Not very important in vote		
	Candidate perceived closest to own issue position*			Candidate perceived closest to own issue position*			Candidate Perceived Closest to Own Issue Position		
VOTE	H	N	W	H	N	W	II	N	W
H	90.3	11.9	10.7	67.7	25.0	22.2	58.0	21.9	35.0
N	7.6	78.3	26.7	29.9	71.2	51.9	40.0	75.6	50.0
W	2.1	9.8	62.6	3.4	3.8	25.9	2.0	2.4	25.0
	100.0%	100.0%	100.0%	100.0%	100.0%	100.0%	100.0%	99.9%	100.0%
N =	145	143	75	87	104	27	50	41	12

*Respondents gave own position and perceptions of candidates' positions on seven point scale where solutions ranged from solving problems of poverty and unemployment to using all available force. A respondent was considered closer to, say, Humphrey where the distance between his and Humphrey's positions was less than the distance between his and the other two candidates' perceived positions. Only respondents who differentiated among the three candidates are included in this analysis.

SOURCE: Survey Research Center, University of Michigan

that we are perhaps no closer to a final answer than before the days of opinion polls.[10]

Nevertheless, the basic question is too important to be dismissed. We shall approach the problem as follows. First, let us simply define "issue voting" as choosing the candidate who best represents one's own position on a particular issue. The emphasis is on selecting the *closest* candidate, so one may vote for someone who differs somewhat from one's own precise preferences if all other candidates differ even more. Second, we assume that if such issue voting occurs it will be on personally salient issues. That is, if one is very agitated about school bussing and cares little about Vietnam, issue voting will occur in the bussing question. Third, we assume that choosing the best candidate is a subjective, not objective process.[11] Consequently, if a voter is most interested in furthering

[10] Some of the principal issues in this debate as well as an extensive bibliography on the subject can be found in John H. Kessel, "Comment: The Issues in Issue Voting," *American Political Science Review* 66 (1972): 459-67.

[11] We are assuming, of course, that candidate choice follows issue choice, not vice versa. It is not unreasonable to suppose, however, that particularly on issues of low personal relevance citizens choose their candidate first and then rationalize this support in terms of issues. Precisely how much rationalization occurs may be impossible to determine but undoubtedly it is fairly common on many issues. Nevertheless, for our purposes the existence of such rationalization is inconsequential; what matters most is the overall consistency between issue stand, candidate perception, and vote. Some evidence on issue rationalization is discussed in Richard A. Brody and Benjamin I. Page, "Comment: The Assessment of Policy Voting," *American Political Science Review* 66 (1972): 450-58.

racial integration and votes for George Wallace out of the mistaken belief that Wallace is best suited to further integration, this constitutes "issue voting." Let us consider whether citizens issue vote; following this analysis we shall examine whether issue votes add up to a policy mandate for the victorious candidate.

Tables 8-7 and 8-8 show the relationship between the 1968 vote, perceptions of which candidate is closer to one's own position on urban unrest and Vietnam, and the claimed importance of these issues in a person's vote. The data clearly show extensive issue-oriented voting among those attributing importance to the two issues in their vote. For example, in Table 8-7 we see that among those saying urban unrest was important, 90.3 percent of those believing that Humphrey's stance was closest to their own did indeed vote for Humphrey. Similarly, 78.3 percent of those who judged Nixon closer to themselves selected Nixon. With the exception of those seeing Wallace as closest to their Vietnam positions, the existence of extensive policy voting is also evident in Table 8-8 (Vietnam). Other analyses of this data show clear evidence of policy voting even among those not attributing enormous relevance to the urban unrest and Vietnam issues.[12] With the exception of those believing that Wallace is closer to their own position, in every instance for both issues those perceiving Humphrey as closer to themselves are more likely to vote for Humphrey than Nixon. Comparable voting behavior is shown by those judging Nixon closer to their own policy preferences.

Table 8-8   Importance of Vietnam in Vote, Perception of Candidates and Vote, 1968

	Importance Attributed to Vietnam*								
	Most important or very important issue in vote			Somewhat important in vote			Not very important in vote		
	Candidate perceived closest to own issue position			Candidate perceived closest to own issue position			Candidate perceived closest to own issue position		
VOTE	H	N	W	H	N	W	H	N	W
H	80.3	8.9	21.2	62.5	32.9	43.8	66.7	15.0	37.5
N	19.0	86.7	67.3	31.3	58.9	37.5	30.0	75.0	56.3
W	.7	4.4	11.5	6.3	8.2	18.7	3.3	10.0	6.2
	100.0%	100.0%	100.0%	100.1%	100.0%	100.0%	100.0%	100.0%	100.0%
N =	142	135	52	80	73	32	30	20	16

*Method of computing distance between respondent and candidate's position is described in Table 8-7. Position on Vietnam was measured by seven point scale ranging from immediate withdrawal to complete military victory.
SOURCE: Survey Research Center, University of Michigan

[12] Page and Brody report that among those who were able to distinguish Nixon and Humphrey on Vietnam, a fair degree of consistency existed between perception and vote. This consistency is, however, interpreted as projection, not policy voting. Page and Brody, "Policy Voting and the Electoral Process," pp. 986-87.

Table 8-9   Preferences on Vietnam and Presidential
Vote Among Those Considering Vietnam
a Very Important Problem, *1972

	Candidate Perceived Closest to Own Policy Position on Vietnam	
Vote:	McGovern	Nixon
McGovern	66.0	13.2
Nixon	34.0	86.8
	100.0%	100.0%
N =	100	189

*See Footnote, Table 8-8
SOURCE: Survey Research Center, University of Michigan

The 1972 data presented in Tables 8-9 and 8-10 make use of the "What are the important problems" question since the "How important was issue X in your vote" question was not asked in 1972. Nevertheless, both questions obviously reflect the relevance of the issue to the voter. These data again show strong evidence of policy-oriented voting. Thus, about two-thirds of those judging Vietnam a very important issue and seeing McGovern as closer to their stand on Vietnam chose McGovern over Nixon. The exception to the pattern of policy voting occurs among those viewing McGovern as closer to their own preferences on bussing to achieve racial integration. In sharp contrast to those viewing Nixon as closer to themselves, the group divides its vote evenly between the two candidates. On the whole, however, a good case that policy is a strong component of voting can still be made.

Does this evidence of issue-oriented voting allow one to conclude that leaders receive a policy mandate from the electorate? Given what we already know about the diversity in perceptions of candidates' issue positions, it is impossible to infer the existence of a policy mandate even if perfect issue-oriented voting

Table 8-10   Preferences on Bussing and Presidential Vote
Among Those Considering Bussing a Very
Important Problem, *1972

	Candidate Perceived Closer to Own Policy Position on Bussing	
Vote	McGovern	Nixon
McGovern	50.0	17.9
Nixon	50.0	82.1
	100.0%	100.0%
N =	18	39

*See Footnote, Table 8-8
SOURCE: Survey Research Center, University of Michigan

Table 8-11   Position on Urban Unrest and Presidential Vote, 1968

	Position on Urban Unrest								
	1 Solve Economic Problems	2	3	4	5	6	7 Use All Available Force		
VOTED FOR:									N
Humphrey	29.0	14.8	15.5	25.0	5.5	4.0	6.3	100.1%	400
Nixon	11.6	11.4	8.7	35.8	14.8	9.0	8.7	100.0%	458
Wallace	5.9	3.0	5.0	19.8	13.9	15.8	36.6	100.0%	100

SOURCE: Survey Research Center, University of Michigan

were universal. To understand why issue-based choices at the *individual* level do not necessarily produce issue mandates at the *collective* level, consider the following possibility. Let us suppose that in a campaign there is only a single issue with a "liberal," "moderate," and "conservative" position. Let us further assume that there are only three voters, and each takes a different stand on the single issue. Finally, one clever candidate successfully convinces all three voters that he "really" best represents their preferences. Obviously, an issue-oriented vote by each voter will produce a victor whose "mandate" calls for the adoption of all three positions. Such a "mandate" is patently meaningless since it cannot be followed.

To what extent have recent presidential elections conveyed such a meaningless mandate? The data in Tables 8-11 and 8-12 show the urban unrest and Vietnam policy preferences of Nixon's 1968 supporters. Though perhaps all victorious candidates interpret their election as a mandate for the policies they advocated, for our purposes a mandate can be said to exist only when a candidate's voters show a high degree of consensus on issue positions. In terms of this criterion for a mandate, it is clear from the data in Tables 8-11 and 8-12 that Nixon received no policy message from his voters. Indeed, almost as many

Table 8-12   Position on Vietnam and Presidential Vote, 1968

	Position on Vietnam								
	1 Immediate Withdrawal	2	3	4	5	6	7 Complete Military Victory		
VOTED FOR:									N
Humphrey	16.1	9.2	9.5	33.2	10.7	6.6	14.6	99.9%	391
Nixon	10.2	8.4	8.6	30.8	13.3	10.2	18.4	99.9%	451
Wallace	9.0	3.0	0	23.0	5.0	21.0	39.0	100.0%	100

SOURCE: Survey Research Center, University of Michigan

Table 8-13 Position on Vietnam and Presidential Vote, 1972

	Position on Vietnam								
	1 Immediate Withdrawal	2	3	4	5	6	7 Complete Military Victory		
VOTED FOR:									N
McGovern	38.4	16.6	14.2	18.5	5.5	2.3	4.5	100.0%	529
Nixon	9.2	6.2	13.5	28.5	18.4	9.6	14.6	100.0%	960

SOURCE: Survey Research Center, University of Michigan

Nixon voters wanted to use force to solve problems of urban unrest as wanted to solve problems of unemployment. In view of the distribution of Nixon voters, particularly the clustering in the "4" category, it is evident that this figure could be juggled so that regardless of Nixon's method of solving urban unrest, his actions would coincide with the preferences of a majority of his voters. Nixon's "mandate" on Vietnam shows less dispersion than his "mandate" on urban unrest, but again a clear policy thrust is not evident. Moreover, considering the relatively small differences in Vietnam preferences between Nixon and Humphrey voters, neither candidate could validly assert that his victory or defeat was an unambiguous message on Vietnam from the electorate.

The data for the 1972 presidential election present a clearer relationship between voting and policy preferences, but a straight-forward mandate is not readily discernible. McGovern voters, for example, were overwhelmingly disposed to getting out of Vietnam immediately; and had he won the election, he could have claimed a mandate on this issue (see Table 8-13). However, Nixon won in 1972 and the distribution of preferences among Nixon's supporters once again is relatively dispersed so almost any broad policy message can be created by manipulating the data. The data on school bussing (Table 8-14) presents an interesting situation: Nixon can legitimately assert that since he drew most of his

Table 8-14 Position on School Bussing and Presidential Vote, 1972

	Position on Bussing to Achieve Racial Integration								
	1 Bus to Achieve Integration	2	3	4	5	6	7 Keep Neighborhood Schools		
VOTED FOR:									N
McGovern	10.1	6.4	5.8	8.2	5.2	9.1	55.1	99.9%	515
Nixon	.9	.5	1.1	4.1	3.2	7.7	82.5	100.0%	982

SOURCE: Survey Research Center, University of Michigan

votes from those opposing bussing, he has a mandate to stop such bussing, but McGovern can make the identical statement. Obviously, given the vast opposition to bussing, it is clear that any victorious candidate would get a mandate on this issue regardless of the policy advocated.

A NOTE ON NONVOTING

Thus far our analysis has examined the preferences of citizens who vote for one of the major presidential candidates. However, when we speak of citizens controlling public policy through elections we implicitly mean *all* citizens, not merely some portion of the citizenry. Since even in presidential elections one finds sizeable amounts of nonparticipation, the question emerges whether nonvoting weakens the extent of citizen policy control. Put somewhat differently, if we instituted a system in which all citizens were forced to vote for a presidential candidate, would the victor possess a clearer mandate? Or, on the other hand, does the addition of still more voices merely add more confusion to an already confused situation?[13] We assume that the existence of a clear policy mandate, though not sufficient in itself to assure public control of policy, is nevertheless a prerequisite for such control.

To assess whether "compulsory" voting would provide sharper policy mandates, let us consider Nixon's 1968 "mandate" on what to do about urban unrest and Vietnam when nonvoters are "forced" to vote. We shall "coerce" nonvoters into voting in the following way. First, if the person did not vote, but indicated a preference for Nixon (or the Republican candidate), this person was added to Nixon voters. If no such candidate preference was expressed, citizens were assigned to one or the other voting groups on the basis of partisan identification.[14] A very small group of nonvoters still remained after these operations, but in view of their number and political indifference, they were excluded from further analysis. Also, our analysis of 1968 is further simplified by not attempting to deal with Wallace voters who might have voted for Nixon had Wallace not competed. The two mandates in the two issue areas are presented in Figures 8-5 and 8-6.

[13] One aspect of the impact of voting abstentions beyond our consideration is whether a complete turnout would change the outcome of an election. It is undoubtedly true that many elections at all levels of government would have different outcomes if every citizen participated, but which elections in particular is difficult to say since any estimate of likely voting among non-voters involves considerable guessing. More important, however, merely because total participation would produce electoral *changes* does not mean that this would increase the amount of citizen policy *control* exercised through elections.

[14] Our decision to assign people to one or the other candidate on the basis of partisan identification is based upon the well documented close association between political party affiliation and voting. For a further analysis of this association, see in particular Philip E. Converse, "The Concept of the Normal Vote," in Angus Campbell *et al., Elections and the Political Order* (New York: John Wiley, 1966).

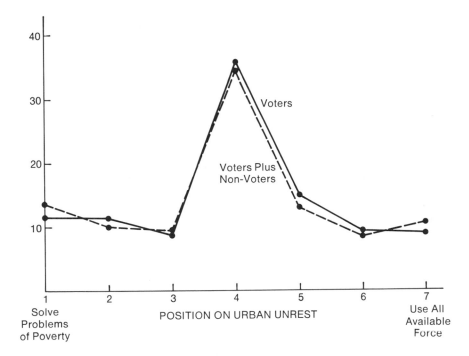

Figure 8-5 Comparison of Urban Unrest Policy Mandate Given Nixon by Voter and Votes Plus Nonvoters, 1968

The data in both figures reveal that Nixon's mandate on dealing with urban unrest and Vietnam would have been only slightly different if nonvoters had been forced to participate in the election. Indeed, the largest difference in the mandate given by voters versus the one given by nonvoters is two percentage points. Thus, the fuzziness of the electoral message on these two policies remains. It would probably be the case, however, that had victory come with almost complete citizen participation (i.e., a turnout of 95 percent), Nixon would have been even more emphatic that his victory represented a call for specific policy action. Of course, our analysis here concerns only two issues in two presidential elections. Nevertheless, though nonvoting may be deplorable to many advocates of greater democracy, it is unlikely that total citizen involvement would further contribute to greater citizen control.

In sum, this fourth condition for elections as a means of policy control is not well satisfied. To be sure, at least citizens interested in a particular policy demonstrate some capacity to vote consistently with their preferences, but the net result of such individual behavior is not the creation of policy mandates. The primary reasons for the disjuncture between individual choices and aggregate results are: (1) a certain proportion of citizens vote against their policy

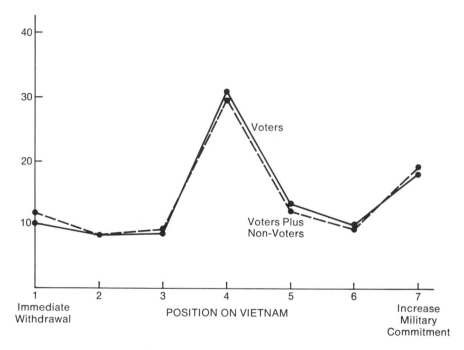

Figure 8-6   Comparison Vietnam Policy Mandate by Nixon by Voters and Votes Plus Nonvoters, 1968

preferences and (2) the policy stands of candidates are interpreted so diversely that even citizens voting on the basis of issues and showing the identical preferences may choose different candidates. A winning majority is therefore more of a *pot pourri* of policy demands than a call for specific action. Even if a majority of one's supporters favors a single position, it might well be the case that any winning candidate would receive the same mandate.

IMPLEMENTING THE PUBLIC MANDATE

The final requirement to achieve opinion-policy congruence through elections is that popularly elected officials are the willing conduits of the "voice of the people" as expressed at the ballot box. There are really two parts to this requirement: (1) winning candidates are the choices of a majority of voters[15] and (2) public officials follow the desires of those electing them. Regarding the first part, the evidence is relatively clear: though exceptions do occur on

[15]Though statements about the relationship between leaders and citizens commonly do not distinguish between "the people" and "a *majority* of the people," it is apparent that a representational relationship can only involve some portion of the entire population. If we required leaders to represent *all* the people they would necessarily represent contradictory sides of the same issue, an impossible task.

occasion, public officials are elected by majorities. Perhaps the most conspicuous exception to the general tendency has been at the presidential level where the presence of minor party candidates has prevented majorities from emerging in the 1948, 1960 and 1968 elections.[16] We must note the obvious fact, however, that a majority of the voters in any given election almost never coincides with a majority of "the people." Not only are sizeable numbers of people prohibited from voting, e.g., minors, transients, and institutionalized criminals, but turnout among those eligible to vote rarely exceeds 60 percent (especially at state and local levels).[17] Thus, in many instances the choice of leaders is made by 20 to 40 percent of the adult population (and frequently by far fewer where the primary rather than the general election is the "real" election). Nevertheless, the first part of this requirement is reasonably well satisfied.

But do public officials heed public sentiment? As we shall discuss later in greater detail, on many broad, highly consensual issues, public officials undoubtedly give citizens what they want. For example, virtually all Americans want general economic prosperity and few—if any—leaders would consciously advocate policies designed to cause depressions. Furthermore, on much of the minutiae governments must deal with, e.g., resolutions in support of national family day, most citizens are so indifferent that it is inappropriate to speak of leaders representing or misrepresenting popular preferences. What about leaders heeding popular preferences on controversial issues such as federal government intervention in school integration?

Though the question of leaders implementing citizen preference is obviously important, research directly examining the linkage has been limited. The most comprehensive examination of this question was conducted in 1958 by Warren E. Miller and Donald E. Stokes and dealt with the relationship between U.S. Congressmen and their constituents. Miller and Stokes collected data on the attitudes and roll-call voting behavior of a sample of Congressmen; attitudes of citizens from these Congressmen's districts; and attitudinal data on those challenging the incumbent in the 1958 elections. Three broad issue areas were studied: (1) social welfare policies (government's responsibility to provide jobs, medical care, and educational facilities); (2) civil rights (federal action against employment discrimination, intervention to integrate public schools); and (3) foreign involvement (foreign aid, stationing of soldiers overseas, isolationism).[18]

---

[16] At other levels the incidence of pluralities, though small, is not totally insignificant. For example, in 1968, 3 of 34 Senators and 6 of 435 Representatives received less than a majority of all votes cast. In 1972, 1 of 33 Senators, 3 of 18 Governors, and 6 of 435 Representatives owed their victories to pluralities.

[17] Due to a variety of suffrage requirements, the right to vote is not nearly as universal as might be assumed. The number of Americans legally prohibited from participation runs into the millions. See William G. Andrews, "American Voting Participation," *Western Political Quarterly* 19 (1966): 639-52.

[18] A further description of this study appears in Warren E. Miller and Donald E. Stokes, "Constituency Influence in Congress," *American Political Science Review* 57 (1963): 45-56.

The emphasis was on issues affecting many citizens, not issues that may be of special salience to some citizens and a few Congressmen, e.g., import duties on foreign bicycles, or higher government subsidies for soybeans. Whether or not Congressmen represent their constituents' opinions on these local issues may be very important, but given the vast number of such issues, they cannot be systematically examined here.[19]

Table 8-15 represents the correlation between the Congressman's roll-call vote and the opinion of his constituents who identify with the Congressman's political party for each of the three issue areas.[20] In the case of social welfare and civil rights district sentiment and Congressmen's roll call votes are positively related so the more liberal the district is, the more liberal a Congressman's vote is likely to be. However, though in the right direction, correlations of .36 and .57 still show considerable disagreement between leaders and supporters. In addition, on questions of foreign involvement there is a *negative* association between a Congressman's vote and the preferences of his partisans in his district.

Table 8-15   Correlation between Representative's Roll Call Votes and Attitudes of Constituents of Same Party, by Issue, 1958

Issue Domain	*Correlation (Pearson r)*
Social Welfare	.36
Civil Rights	.57
Foreign Affairs	−.10

SOURCE: Survey Research Center, University of Michigan

[19] Exclusion from analysis of highly localized issues should not be construed as a rejection of the importance of such issues in the electoral process. Indeed, for many citizens the health of, say, the local ship building industry, not civil rights or social welfare, may be the only thing leaders are held accountable for. For a general discussion of this question, see John W. Kingdon, *Congressman's Voting Decision* (New York: Harper and Row, 1973), pp. 36-38. For an illustration of a very close association between leader behavior and constituency opinion on a local issue, see Wilder W. Crane, Jr., "Do Legislators Represent?" *Journal of Politics* 22 (1960): 295-99. Crane examines the issue of having daylight saving time and reports that legislators both knew constituency opinion and claimed to vote on the basis of this opinion.

[20] Though the most relevant correlation would be between preferences of Congressmen's *voters* and legislative behavior, we substitute the preferences of partisan identifiers for those of voters. Our reason is practical—attitudes of voters were not available in the data set. However, since we know that partisan affiliation and voting are highly correlated in off-year congressional elections, the discrepancy between the two variables is probably small. In addition, it could even be argued that preferences of partisans are more relevant than those of voters since (a) a Congressman does not know precisely who voted for him and (b) under such uncertainty the Congressman's best guess of who his supporters are would be fellow party identifiers in the district. The association between party identification and vote in the 1958 congressional election is discussed in Donald E. Stokes and Warren E. Miller, "Party Government and the Saliency of Government."

All in all, perhaps only in the case of civil rights can we claim that Congressmen are in step with those electing them.[21]

It could be argued, of course, that a lack of close agreement between supporters and Congressmen might be due in part to Congressmen's lack of complete freedom to follow constituency preferences. A Congressman's vote might be influenced by such nonconstituency factors as pressure from party leaders, agreements with colleagues to trade votes, agreements made in committee, or presidential exhortation.[22] Thus a better test for linkages between Congressmen and constituents would be under conditions where Congressmen were unconstrained by nonconstituency factors. To test this possibility, we have recalculated the correlations in Table 8-15 according to whether or not the Congressman asserted that his roll-call vote behavior was free of any nonconstituency coercion. These data, which are presented in Table 8-16, do not provide evidence for the contention that where a House vote is a "free" choice, a closer alignment occurs between Representative and supporters. In the case of both social welfare and civil rights the closest association between a Representative's vote and the preferences of his supporters did not occur when

Table 8-16   Correlation Between Representative's Roll Call Votes and Attitudes of Constituents of Same Party, by Issue, by Constraints on Congressman's Vote, 1958

Issue Domain	Extent to Which Vote Represents Own Opinion		
	Well	50-50	Not Well†
Social Welfare	.34	.57	.24
Civil Rights	.50	*	.71
Foreign Affairs	.03	*	−.44

*Too few cases for analysis
†This last column excludes Congressmen who said their vote did not represent their real opinion because they followed constituency opinion
SOURCE: Survey Research Center, University of Michigan

[21]There are, of course, other ways of considering these issue domains. For example, Segal and Smith argue that the more general notion of the scope of government power is more appropriate to linkages between Congressmen and constituents. Using three questions from these three scales and roll call votes regarding federal spending, Segal and Smith report a correlation of .18 between constituents' attitudes and roll call vote. See David R. Segal and Thomas S. Smith, "Congressional Responsibility and the Organization of Constituency Attitudes," in *Political Attitudes and Public Opinion,* ed., Dan D. Nimmo and Charles M. Bonjean (New York: David McKay, 1972), pp. 562-68.
[22]For a general overview of nonconstituency pressure on legislators, see Malcolm E. Jewell and Samuel C. Patterson, *The Legislative Process in the United States,* 2nd ed. (New York: Random House, 1973), especially chaps. 7 and 12.

the Congressman was unconstrained in his behavior. Indeed, the data suggest that at least in the case of civil rights, such factors as legislative party pressure, presidential influence, and the like may increase agreement between Representative and constituents despite legislators' contrary preferences. Perhaps the best case for greater agreement occurring when Congressmen are free to vote as they please can be found in the area of foreign policy, but the correlation of .03 as opposed to −.44 indicates that even then, the situation is one of zero representation versus a moderately negative relationship.

Another way of considering the behavior of Congressmen is in the context of whether they *want* to follow constituent opinion in these issue areas. At least some leaders may have no desire whatsoever to heed their supporters' preferences and thus to include this group in our analysis exaggerates the overall results toward misrepresentation.[23] In Tables 8-17 and 8-18 we have divided Congressmen according to two indicators of their relationship to their supporters. If the above reasoning is correct, we should find that Congressmen who want to represent opinion do in fact better implement their supporters' desires. On the whole, the data do not support the reasoning. The strongest evidence for this argument is the increase in the correlation on civil rights issues as a Congressman's role orientation changes from "vote own opinion" to "vote district opinion." At the same time, however, not only is this change not consistent (note a correlation of −.17 for civil rights in the "depends" category), but there is no comparable change in the other two issue areas. Moreover, the data in Table 8-17 show a *weaker* association between legislative behavior and

Table 8-17   Correlation Between Representative's
Roll Call Votes and Attitudes of
Constituents of Own Party, by Issue,
by Effort to Ascertain District
Opinion, 1958

Issue Domain	Effort to Ascertain District Opinion		
	Much	Some	Little
Social Welfare	.35	.56	*
Civil Rights	.55	.70	*
Foreign Affairs	−.04	−.54	*

*Too few cases for analysis
SOURCE: Survey Research Center, University of Michigan

[23]On occasion we shall use the term "representation" to mean the degree to which an official implements the preferences of those who put him in office. This is, of course, only one of several means to "representation." For a more complete analysis of this concept, see Hanna Fenichel Pitkin, *The Concept of Representation* (Berkeley & Los Angeles: University of California Press, 1967).

Table 8-18 Correlation Between Representative's
Roll Call Votes and Attitudes of
Constituents of Own Party, by Issue,
by Congressman's General Attitudes
Towards Following Constituency
Opinion, 1958

Issue Domain	*Perceptions of Legislative Role*		
	Vote Own Opinion	Depends	Vote for District
Social Welfare	.35	.48	.40
Civil Rights	.56	−.17	.72
Foreign Affairs	−.09	−.87	.02

SOURCE: Survey Research Center, University of
Michigan

supporters' preferences for civil rights and social welfare among those Congressmen claiming to spend considerable effort to ascertain the opinions of their constituents. Only in foreign policy does disagreement between leaders and followers decline as effort to gather information declines, but a correlation of −0.4 is certainly not an indicator of close agreement. In short, other factors besides personal unwillingness to heed constituent opinion are at work here.

It may be that the generally low to moderate relationships between Congressmen's roll call votes and their constituents' opinions in these three issue areas are largely due to lack of Congressmen's fear of electoral reprisal. That is, leaders may have little motivation to heed popular opinion because most of them are regularly reelected by lopsided margins.[24] This argument implies that if districts were made more competitive the chances of misrepresentation being punished by electoral defeat would be increased. To test this reasoning we have subdivided the data on Representative-Constituency according to the degree of electoral competition for the district's Congressional seat. (Competitiveness is based on Congressmen's perceptions). These data are presented in Table 8-19.

If the likelihood of electoral defeat encourages a close subservience to the preferences of voters, the correlations between roll call votes and constituency opinion should increase the more competitive the district. In the case of social welfare and civil rights, precisely the opposite occurs. Especially in the domain of civil rights, where Congressmen are not safe from defeat they do a much

[24]This argument is from the perspective of an outsider who would evaluate a Congressman's chances of reelection based on previous elections. However, a Congressman may nevertheless feel electorally in danger regardless of the magnitude of past victories. In fact, such fear for one's electoral life seems to be quite prevalent and thus undermines the reasoning underlying this hypothesis. For an analysis of this fear of electoral defeat, see John W. Kingdon, *Congressman's Voting Decisions* (New York: Harper and Row, 1973), pp. 59-64.

Table 8-19   Correlation Between Representative's Roll
Call Votes and Attitudes of Constituents
of Own Party by Issue Area, by Safeness
of Congressional Seat, 1958

Issue Domain	Safeness of District		
	Very Safe	Moderately Safe	Competitive
Social Welfare	.40	.30	.17
Civil Rights	.57	.53	−.57
Foreign Affairs	−.09	−.28	−.07

SOURCE: Survey Research Center, University of Michigan

worse job of voting their supporters' preferences than where incumbency is unchallenged. For foreign affairs no sizeable difference in representation exists between very safe and competitive districts (misrepresentation is greatest in moderately safe districts). What might account for this pattern so contrary to our expectations about fear of electoral reprisal and following citizen sentiment? One possibility is that Congressmen who represent well are rewarded for their efforts by overwhelming victories. Thus, extent of representation determines degree of electoral competition and not *vice versa.*[25] A second explanation would be that in an evenly divided district a successful candidate has to appeal to at least some followers of the other party, and if this appeal takes the form of legislative voting, the Congressman's agreement with members of his own party is therefore muddied. A third possibility is that district homogeneity is all important: if everyone is pretty much alike we are more likely to find both safe congressional seats and closer representation without the one causing the other. Whatever the reasons for the patterns depicted in Table 8-19, it is clear that we cannot claim that electoral competition leads Congressmen to heed the wishes of their supporters.

Our analysis has thus far focused on the relationship between the individual Congressman and his or her supporters in the district. We have assumed implicitly that if leaders heeded the public, this public would be those who elected them. There is, however, another way of viewing the relationship between Congressmen and constituents. It is conceivable that while each Congressman does not represent those electing them, the House of Representa-

---

[25]A variation in this argument is that the best electoral strategy for Congressmen is to move towards the center of every issue distribution. Thus, an attempt by a legislator to represent "extreme" views, even if these views are shared by a sizeable number of constituents, will result in reduced electoral support. This reasoning receives strong confirmation in Erikson's study of Representatives' roll call votes and electoral margins. Erikson finds that extremely conservative Republicans (and to a lesser extent, extremely liberal Democrats) fare worse at the polls than their less extreme colleagues. Robert S. Erikson, "The Electoral Impact of Congressional Roll Call Voting," *American Political Science Review* 65 (1971): 1018-32.

tives *in the aggregate* may follow the preferences of the public *in the aggregate* even though each Congressman does a poor job of reflecting his own constituents' preferences.[26] Such a mode of representation, however, is inconsistent with the idea of public control of leaders since a particular citizen can only vote for his or her Congressman, not for all 435 Representatives. Nevertheless, this mode of representation could be of considerable political significance. To see how such representation in the aggregate can occur, consider the hypothetical data depicted in Table 8-20.

Table 8-20(a) shows that while close agreement between constituents and leaders occurs in only one of three districts, the *average* preference of citizens and legislators is identical. On the other hand, in Table 8-20(b), the same scores rearranged somewhat differently yield perfect representation both within the separate districts and between the population and the legislature as a whole. To see whether the House of Representatives on the whole reflects citizens' preferences, we have computed these various differences for our 1958 data. Not unexpectedly, these data (see Table 8-21) show that the discrepancy between citizens and their elected Representatives is less in the aggregate than when

Table 8-20 Hypothetical Relationships Among Legislators and Citizens in Three Districts

(A) Poor District-by-District Agreement, Perfect Aggregate Agreement

Opinion/Roll Call Scores for:	District			
	1	2	3	Mean for all Districts
Constituents preferences (Mean)	1	2	3	2
Representatives preferences	3	2	1	2
Differences in preferences	−2	0	2	

(B) Perfect Agreement at Both District by District Level and at Aggregate Level

Opinion/Roll Call Scores for:	District			
	1	2	3	Mean for all Districts
Constituents preferences (Mean)	1	2	3	2
Representatives preferences	1	2	3	2
Differences in preferences	0	0	0	

[26]This concept of Representation is further discussed in Pitkin, *The Concept of Representation*, pp. 216-25.

Table 8-21   District by District Versus Aggregate Representation,*
By Issue Domain, 1958

Issue Domain	(1) Average Difference Between Congressman and Supporter on District by District Basis	(2) Difference Between Representatives and Constituents in the Aggregate	Ratio of (1) to (2)
Social Welfare	3.26	2.45	.75
Civil Rights	2.92	2.41	.82
Foreign Affairs	4.34	2.62	.60

*Since the absolute value of these scores is purely a function of the numerical range of the various attitudes and roll call scales, we must emphasize that it is only the ratio between 1 and 2 that is significant. The size of the figures themselves say nothing about whether malrepresentation is big or small.
SOURCE: Survey Research Center, University of Michigan

measured on a district by district basis. For example, while an average gap of 3.26 exists between each legislator and his supporters on social welfare policy, this discrepancy is cut substantially when we look at attitudes of citizens more generally. However, we must reiterate our remarks about such representation being unrelated to citizen control of public policy although "aggregate representation" may be very important politically.[27]

The last aspect of our analysis of these 1958 data concerns electoral retribution and poor representation. Specifically, are Congressmen who are particularly bad at representing their constituents more likely to be thrown out of office? The evidence on this question is inconclusive. In the first place, though our preceding data suggest that particularly in foreign policy, and to a lesser extent social welfare, considerable constituent-Congressman disagreement exists, the amount of House turnover is surprisingly low. The 1958 election saw eighty-one new members in the House, but of these only half (forty-one) did not return because of electoral defeat. The remaining forty either retired, died, or ran for a different office. Moreover, this low turnout due to voter actions in 1958 is not at all atypical of House elections in recent years.[28]

On the other hand, if we examine the representativeness of successful and

[27]This improved "aggregate representation" statistically speaking is a result of district-representative discrepancies cancelling each other out when scores are summed across districts and representatives. For example, a deviation of −3 and 3 yield 0 when added and divided by the number of districts.

[28]For example, in the 1972 House elections the figures were very similar to those in 1958: Seven incumbents were defeated in primaries, thirty-one were displaced in the general election, and three were defeated because they were redistricted into districts with another incumbent. Thirty-four incumbents did not return due to retirement or running for another office. Additional data on the subject are reported in Charles O. Jones, "Intra-Party Competition for Congressional Seats," *Western Political Quarterly* 17 (1964): 461-76.

Table 8-22 Correlation Between Representative's
Roll Call Vote and Attitudes of
Constituents of Own Party, by Issue
Area, by Outcome of Election, 1958

Issue Domain	*Electoral Outcome*	
	Incumbent Reelected	Incumbent Defeated
Social Welfare	.41	−.27
Civil Rights	.58	−.02
Foreign Affairs	−.12	.15

SOURCE: Survey Research Center, University of Michigan

unsuccessful Congressmen, we see that poor representation and electoral defeat are associated. Table 8-22 shows that in two of the three issue domains—social welfare and civil rights—defeated Congressmen did a worse job of representation than did reelected Congressmen. Only on foreign policy were successful Congressmen worse representatives than unsuccessful ones, but the differences are comparatively small. But, these data do not necessarily prove that "bad" (i.e., misrepresenting) officials are replaced with "good" (i.e., representing) leaders. First, Table 8-22 also shows that many Congressmen who do not perfectly reflect their supporters' attitudes in their votes still manage to get elected.[29] Second, there is no guarantee that officials doing a poor job of representing their supporters will be replaced by officials who will do a better job. Indeed, in view of our previous discussion of the relationship between safeness of congressional districts and the degree of leader-supporter agreement (disagreement increased as safeness declined), high turnover and poor representation may be closely related without the latter being the cause of the former. This argument is strongly borne out if we examine the relationship between supporters' attitudes prior to the 1958 elections and the roll call behavior of newly elected Congressmen. If elections are to be means of improving representation, these new leaders should be more in tune with their supporters than leaders they replaced. The data in Table 8-23 clearly show in both civil rights and foreign affairs the *defeated* Congressman represented relatively better. On social welfare issues the association, though in the predicted direction, still shows considerable misrepresentation. In short, electoral retribution does not

[29]Part of the reason for many Congressmen's success despite a poor job of representation is that voters are not offered any better alternatives. Sullivan and O'Connor in their study of the 1966 House elections find that only 73 of 435 districts are characterized by both electoral competition and significant policy differences between candidates. Hence, "throwing the rascals out" is either difficult or ineffective in changing policy. John L. Sullivan and Robert E. O'Connor, "Electorical Choice and Popular Control of Public Policy: The Case of the 1966 House Elections," *American Political Science Review* 66 (1972): 1256-68.

necessarily produce new leaders who are more attuned to the electorate. In fact, those who live in the least fear of such retribution seem to do a better overall job of translating opinion into policy.

Though our analysis has considered whether leaders follow the desires of those selecting them, all our data are from a single set of leaders at one point in time. It is essential, therefore, that we at least consider whether our findings are more general than Congressmen and their supporters in 1958. We cannot, of course, repeat our analyses for the tens of thousands of state and local officials who have held office at one time or another. Nevertheless, bits and pieces of data exist that are broadly relevant to the question. And, as we shall see, though such a review cannot be absolutely conclusive, the overall thrust is consistent with the conclusions drawn from the 1958 congressional study.

One well researched piece of information relevant to analysis concerns the desires of public officials to do what their constituents want them to do. Several studies have examined the attitudes of public officials towards acting in strict accordance with popular desires. Almost without exception, regardless of level of government, the vast majority of officials reject the role of mere instructed delegates.[30] Moreover, this rejection of the delegate role is probably not inconsistent with public attitudes toward leadership. No doubt many citizens are willing to tolerate leaders who justify their independence from constituency pressure by "following their own conscience" or using their own best

Table 8-23 Incumbency Changes and Changes in Representation, by Issue Area, 1958

| | *Correlation of Attitudes of Congressmen's Supporters with Roll Call Votes:* | | |
Issue Domain	*Before Incumbent was Defeated (85th Congress)*	*For New Incumbent (86th Congress)*	*Improvement Due to Election*
Social Welfare	−.27	−.11	.16
Civil Rights	−.02	−.30	−.28
Foreign Affairs	.15	−.46	−.61

SOURCE: **Survey Research Center, University of Michigan**

[30]For data at the state level see: John C. Wahlke, et al., *The Legislative System* (New York: John Wiley and Sons, 1962); John W. Soule, "Future Political Ambitions and the Behavior of Incumbent State Legislators," *Midwest Journal of Political Science* 13 (1969): 439-54; Frank J. Sorauf, *Party and Representation* (New York: Atherton Press, 1963). Data on the House of Representatives are reported in Roger H. Davidson, *The Role of the Congressman* (New York: Pegasus, 1969). We should note, of course, that merely because officials say they will not religiously follow constituency opinion is no guarantee that they do as they say.

judgment.[31] The prevalence of these leadership orientations and public tolerance of them does not, of course prove that most leaders systematically represent the public, but it does make close adherence to popular sentiment unlikely.

A second type of evidence supporting the generality of our findings concerns both public political knowledge and leaders' awareness of the policy preferences of their supporters. As we saw in Chapter 3, the general public has only limited knowledge of such elementary facts as officials' names, the behavior of leaders, existing public policy, and the choices offered by challengers. Hence, even if citizens were willing to coerce leaders and leaders were willing to submit to public pressure, the paucity of political knowledge among citizens would make such coercion inefficient.[32] It is also true that except on those issues highly salient in a particular area, e.g., civil rights in a largely black city, leaders will frequently misperceive what citizens want or not even concern themselves with citizen opinion.[33] Moreover, the various mechanisms by which leaders can ascertain popular sentiment, i.e., leader-sponsored opinion polls, the mail, personal contacts, and the like, rarely provide accurate pictures of overall sentiment. The common result of this mutual ignorance is that if agreement

[31] This public endorsement of leaders following their own, not constituents' opinions is well illustrated in a study where citizens were asked whether a President could commit U.S. troops overseas if he believed it should be done even if a majority of the public opposed such troop commitment. Three quarters of the public approved such defiance. Though impressionistic, the evidence suggests that many Americans admire a public leader defying public demands if such defiance appears as a call to "higher reason" or "inner voices" as opposed to "crude insensitivity." See Roberta S. Siegel, "Image of the American Presidency: Part II of an Exploration into Popular Vision of Presidential Power," *Midwest Journal of Political Science* 10 (1966): 123-37. Concurring data are presented in Carl D. McMurray and Malcolm B. Parsons, "Public Attitudes towards the Representational Roles of Legislators and Judges," *Midwest Journal of Political Science* 9 (1965): 167-85.

[32] See, in particular, Donald E. Stokes and Warren E. Miller, "Party Government and the Saliency of Congress."

[33] The evidence from the 1958 representation study suggests that Congressmen are reasonably accurate at perceiving district sentiment on civil rights but relatively poor at perceiving the remaining two issue areas. Studies of the accuracy of judgments made by state and local leaders have produced mixed results. On the one hand, Hedlund and Freisema in the study of Iowa legislators' ability to predict constituency votes on four state referenda found very high accuracy on some issues and some legislators who were accurate on all four issues. See Ronald D. Hedlund and H. Paul Friesema, "Representatives' Perceptions of Constituency Opinion," *Journal of Politics* 34 (1972): 730-52. Similarly, a study of Florida legislators reports accurate perceptions on how their constituents would vote on three referenda dealing with school racial integration and school prayers. See Robert S. Erikson, Norman R. Luttbeg, and William V. Holloway, "Knowing One's District: How Legislators Predict Referendum Voting," *American Journal of Political Science*, forthcoming. However, Roberta S. Sigel's study of local leaders finds vast misinformation about popular opinion. See Roberta S. Sigel and H. Paul Friesema, "Urban Community Leaders' Knowledge of Public Opinion," *Western Political Quaterly* 18 (1965): 881-95.

occurs between leaders and followers such representation is not likely due to any conscious knowledge of either party.

A third set of relevant factors are the institutional arrangements holding public officials at all levels accountable to citizens. As indicated in Chapter 4, the American constitutional system is not designed to allow close citizen control of officials. Leaders are chosen for fixed terms and once in office are very difficult to remove (even the availability of recall procedures has not substantially affected removability). Moreover, even if particular officials were removed, our fragmented, decentralized government makes it virtually impossible to replace entire administrations as opposed to particular people in that administration.[34] The existence of large numbers of non-elected officials in important positions, e.g., federal judges, also frustrates the public's ability to "throw the rascals out." Finally, incumbent officials at all levels of government possess a variety of advantages, e.g., free publicity, visibility, that help insulate them against opposition.[35] What all these factors add up to is that even if citizens were upset over their leaders' behavior and were capable of choosing better leaders to replace existing ones, such desires would be thwarted by existing political mechanisms.

In sum, then, the last requirement of our model of citizen control of policy via elections—that leaders do what their supporters want—is not very well satisfied. Our analysis of the relationship between opinion and leadership behavior in Congress in 1958 indicates that in only one of three broad issue areas (civil rights) can it be said that officials carry out reasonably well the wishes of those electing them. This translation is less pronounced in the domain of social welfare and entirely absent in foreign policy. Analyses of the relationship between Congressmen and their supporters according to other variables such as absence of nonconstituency pressure or degree of electoral competition does not change our overall conclusion. Perhaps the best case for leadership adherence to popular preferences occurs when we consider Congress and citizens in the aggregate, but this improvement has nothing to do with electoral control. Finally, although we cannot be perfectly sure, data drawn from several other studies suggest that our general conclusions are the rule, not the exception, in American politics.

[34]Sullivan and O'Connor's analysis of ideological differences between incumbents and challengers in the 1966 House elections suggests that even getting rid of every challenged Representative would have only a limited overall impact on policy. Sullivan and O'Connor, "Electoral Choice and Popular Control of Public Policy," p. 1259.

[35]It is also true, particularly at the local level, that many leaders possess little or no desire to continue in office or the threat of retribution is meaningless. Prewitt's study of city councilmen in eighty-two California cities not only shows the infrequency of electoral councilmen, but also suggests that without retribution, popular influence in government is less important. See Kenneth Prewitt, "Political Ambition, Volunteerism, and Electoral Accountability," *American Political Science Review* 67 (1970): 5-17.

CONCLUSION: ELECTIONS AS INSTRUMENTS
OF POPULAR CONTROL

From the foregoing analysis one may conclude that if elections ought to be the means by which the public can translate its preferences into public policy, such control is not demonstrated in the data we considered. None of the five criteria necessary for public control to exist were very well satisfied. Moreover, the "failure" of elections as a conduit for public demands results from numerous aspects of the political process: Citizens, candidates, and institutional arrangements are all at fault. Of course, these "faults" are defects only from the perspective of elections as means of popular control. As suggested in Chapter 4, the American electoral system is not designed to be a neutral, highly efficient conveyor belt for public opinion, and if it were, certainly the Founding Fathers would judge the Constitution a failure.

At the same time, however, our analysis does not completely settle the issue. Two arguments can be offered in support of American elections as instruments of popular control. The first emphasizes that not *every* election at *all* levels of government need be an example of popular control for elections to serve as a control mechanism. It is reasonable to suppose that only in special circumstances does the public get an opportunity to exercise control, and such opportunities did not occur in the particular data we examined. Proponents of this view maintain that some elections can be characterized as critical elections that offer basic choices to voters and the resulting decision affects policy for years to come.[36] For example, in 1932 and 1936 Americans overwhelmingly chose Roosevelt and the New Deal over conservative Republican policies, and this decision enormously affected a vast array of policies for the subsequent forty years. Similarly, the crushing defeats suffered by the Democrats in 1892 and 1896 cleared the way for decades of Republican domination and attendant policies favoring private enterprise and the wealthy.

That certain elections have profoundly affected subsequent public policy is undeniable. Clearly, the selection of Roosevelt over Hoover in 1932 was not trivial. However, it is one thing to acknowledge the impact of elections on policy but quite another to assert that voters actually *controlled* these consequences. The New Deal may not have come into existence without an election, but it is far from obvious that voters *caused* the particular policies associated with the New Deal. A more reasonable interpretation is that Roosevelt voters were dissatisfied with Hoover's behavior and wanted *something* to be done, yet probably differed among themselves on what should be done (if they had any coherent preferences at all). Hence, Roosevelt was "ordered" to improve upon the job done by Hoover, and while such an "order" is not politically

---

[36] See, among others, Walter Dean Burnham, *Critical Elections and the Mainsprings of American Politics* (New York: W.W. Norton, 1970).

meaningless, it is nevertheless a far cry from our conception of policy control via elections. In short, the existence of critical elections is not necessarily the same thing as the existence of elections in which the public controls policy.

A second defense of elections maintains that while the vote does now allow precise citizen control, it is still an effective mechanism for popular influence. If only because measuring "influence" is difficult and since the quantity of popular influence claimed for citizens by elections is usually left unspecified, this argument is difficult to prove or disprove. Nevertheless, several features of the electoral process appear to give citizens at least some degree of political say in government. For example, as long as elections are open and competitive, and as long as candidates can be found, voters can always throw out an incumbent. "Throwing the rascal out" may merely result in the selection of a new rascal, but there is always the *possibility* of making an improvement. In effect, elections allow citizens to say collectively: "We may not be able to get what we want, but we can at least get rid of what we don't want."

Similarly, by requiring leaders to pass public review there is an opportunity to eliminate grossly objectionable types. As an alternative consider leadership selection in a monarchy—short of revolution or assassination, there is no way of preventing the patently incompetent, morally objectionable or politically unacceptable leader from taking office. To use an extreme case, that we vote for president means that most Americans need not worry that by some biological or psychological accident our next leader will be a lesbian Maoist slowly going insane due to an advanced case of syphillis. This is not to argue that elections somehow produce "better," more qualified leaders, but rather elections encourage leaders to be selected from a pool of types more or less acceptable to significant numbers of citizens.

It has also been suggested that elections offer citizens the opportunity to demonstrate a retrospective approval or disapproval of policies already enacted. For example, V.O. Key, Jr. suggests that the congressional election of 1934 and the presidential election of 1936 are best interpreted not as calls for particular policies but as mass approvals of newly instituted policies.[37] In a similar vein it was probably true that many voters greatly concerned with American involvement in Vietnam chose Nixon not because he offered a more popular Vietnam policy, but rather because the Johnson-Humphrey policies had proved so disastrous. Of course, such retrospective judgments (if indeed they do occur), while greatly influencing particular political careers, do not automatically lead to opinion-policy congruence. We could readily imagine citizens rejecting official after official as each tries unsuccessfully to satisfy popular demands (which might in fact be unmeetable). Perhaps only after several rejecting elections would a majority of voters finally give their approval to certain policies.

[37]V.O. Key, Jr., *Public Opinion and American Democracy* (New York: Alfred A. Knopf, 1963), p. 474. The retrospective judgment argument is also advanced in Gerald M. Pomper, *Elections in America: Control and Influence in Democratic Politics* (New York: Dodd, Mead, 1970), pp. 255-57.

Finally, and most speculatively, one may argue that as long as public officials believe that voters are watching them and will punish them for their transgressions, elections keep officials within certain bounds.[38] To appreciate this mode of influence, consider a political system in which leaders could not be removed from office regardless of their actions. It is certainly not true that American leaders slavishly attempt to follow popular desires, but without elections there would probably be even less motivation to adhere to popular demands. This form of influence is particularly well illustrated by the issue stands of officials that sometimes run completely contrary to their personal beliefs yet are taken because to do otherwise would mean almost certain electoral defeat (e.g., Senator Fulbright's anti-civil rights votes despite his own liberal sentiments). Put another way, elections may not create perfect opinion-policy congruence, but they can eliminate leadership behavior contributing to gross incongruity.

On the whole, these arguments in support of citizen influence through the electoral process does not weaken our assertion that close opinion-policy congruence cannot be attributed to elections. As we have seen, the influence provided by elections is the opportunity to reject or approve leaders, not the opportunity to pick and choose what policies become law. The voter can also wreak havoc with political careers, the fortunes of political parties, and major public policies, but again this capacity to wreak havoc is not the same thing as policy control. By no means are we suggesting that such influences are politically trivial; indeed it could be claimed that given these broad controls the precise determination of public policy is not all that important. Nevertheless, it remains clear that when we speak about policies such as defense spending, income tax levels, gun controls, and foreign aid, it is misleading to claim that the public caused these policies via the ballot box.

[38]This is suggested in Kingdon, "Politicians' Beliefs about Voters," p. 145.

chapter nine

SOURCES OF CONGRUENCE: SHARED PREFERENCE

Popular elections are one mechanism potentially capable of bringing about a close relationship between public opinion and public policy. Alternatively, citizen opinions may be translated into government decisions through the efforts of well-organized interest groups, or because leaders attempt to satisfy public demands out of a sense of civic duty or *noblesse oblige*. There are, moreover, two other plausible linkage mechanisms that deserve our serious attention. The first is what we shall call the "shared preferences" model: citizens and leaders hold more or less the same fundamental policy preferences so congruence occurs even if leaders only follow their own preference. The second linkage model may be called the opinion manipulation model: opinion-policy congruence results from government manipulation of public opinion; i.e., the public demands policies that the government wants them to demand. These two models are hypothetical linkages; whether they can or cannot account for patterns of congruence remains to be proved. Moreover, like elections, these mechanisms are more akin to general descriptions of the relationship between opinion and policy than they are explanations of why some specific policies show more (or less) opinion-policy concordance than others. This chapter considers the contribution of consensually held opinions to the opinion-policy relationship; Chapter 10 will analyze government manipulation of public opinion.

SHARED PREFERENCES AND OPINION-POLICY CONGRUENCE

Our analysis of voting and elections assumed that when leaders give the public what it wants, such responsiveness would result from citizen coercion. Officials

206

represented the popular will because the public via the vote *made* them follow opinion. It is, of course, entirely possible that leaders could heed public sentiment without citizens ever exercising any coercion. The use of coercion is necessary only where leaders and citizens *disagree* on issues; if the two were in basic agreement, such control mechanisms as issue voting, forcing officials to adhere to previous positions, and so on, would be redundant. Indeed, it is clear that the most efficient way of achieving perfect opinion-policy congruence would be to have every citizen (including leaders) hold identical preferences. Under such conditions of unanimity there would be almost no chance whatsoever of leaders distorting popular desires.

In its extreme form the argument that all opinion-policy congruence is attributable to policy homogeniety is clearly untenable. We have seen that even when opinion-policy congruence occurs, sizable division of opinion exists among citizens, so at least on many issues it is impossible to argue that congruence exists because "everyone holds the same preference." At the same time, however, the opposite conclusion—a lack of congruence is a consequence of the absence of widely shared preference—is perhaps as equally unrealistic. Certainly there are issues, e.g., the value of economic prosperity or the virtues of democracy, on which virtually everyone is on the same side and opinion-policy congruence is thus assumed. What is important, then, is to determine under what circumstances does homogeneity of policy preferences contribute to opinion-policy congruence. We shall approach this question in two steps. First, we shall consider which policy choices are so widely accepted that virtually all leaders and citizens share essentially the same positions.[1] Because such consensually held preferences are rarely the subject of opinion polls, our analysis will in part make use of evidence drawn from political learning occurring in childhood. As we shall see, it is prior to adulthood that future leaders and common citizens acquire many of their shared preferences. Second, several studies of elite and mass differences on various policy questions will be examined. Our basic question in analyzing these differences is: if leaders did what they themselves wanted, how different would policy be than if they followed citizen preferences? Let us begin by analyzing common ground between leaders and citizens.

---

[1] Throughout our analysis the concept "leader" denotes political leaders, particularly those occupying high elective office. We implicitly assume that these officials are the actual political decision-makers. However, it is sometimes asserted that public office holders are not the real power wielders; rather, members of a corporate and military elite possess ultimate control over important decisions. If this were true, most of our data would be irrelevant. Nevertheless, the major thrust of our conclusion would remain the same. As we shall see, political leaders differ from nonleaders in many ways, and it is likely that members of the corporate-military elite are likewise different from the average citizen. For a further discussion of the role of military and corporate officials in government decision-making, see C. Wright Mills, *The Power Elite* (New York: Oxford University Press, 1959), especially pp. 269-97.

THE ACQUISITION OF SHARED PREFERENCES

Though a review of recent American political history would reveal the emergence of an enormous number of important policy questions, many important issues have almost always remained beyond the realm of controversy or public attention. Nor are many of these issues likely to be raised in the future. The principal reason why these questions remain dormant is that since everybody takes the same side, there is never any need to raise the question. For example, there is no debate over whether the U.S. should have aristocratic titles. And the major reason why citizens share these preferences is the pervasiveness and uniformity of the political socialization process. Long before a citizen reaches adulthood he or she learns certain things about politics and once acquired, such learning is unlikely to be substantially undone.[2] Indeed, because most of what is acquired through political socialization is so widely shared and left unchallenged in day to day politics, few citizens may be consciously aware of this unanimity of opinion. These preferences are taken for granted perhaps much in the same way that people unquestioningly accept many cultural truisms.

Consider, for example, the pervasiveness of deeply ingrained identity with the American political community. Very few citizens reject "America" as the object of their primary political loyalty. If one were to step back and consider all the possibilities, or examine the perspectives of citizens in many other political systems, it would be clear that giving primary political loyalty to a geographically defined entity such as the United States of America is only one of many reasonable alternatives. For example, Catholics in Northern Ireland identify politically much more closely with fellow Catholics in the Republic of Ireland than with Protestants living in the same area and under the same government. Similarly, many white residents of African nations consider themselves to be Englishmen or Frenchmen due to their race and language, although their families have lived in Africa for generations. With the possible exception of the Black Muslims and some small religious sects, disagreements over what constitutes the basic political unit are virtually unknown.[3] This is not to say that differences in nationalistic sentiment do not exist among religious, ethnic and regional groups.

---

[2] The persistence of early political learning into adulthood has not been exhaustively documented. Most researchers assume however that much learning does persist though it can undergo substantial change with age. The various arguments on this issue are presented in Robert Weissberg, *Political Learning, Political Choice, and Democratic Citizenship,* (Englewood Cliffs: Prentice-Hall Inc., 1974), pp. 23-30.

[3] For example, a 1968 CBS news poll reported that only 5 percent of the blacks who were interviewed favored a separate black nation (cited in Gary T. Marx, *Protest and Prejudice,* revised edition (New York: Harper and Row, 1969), Reprinted in Calvin J. Larson and Philo C. Washburn, *Power, Participation and Ideology* (New York: David McKay, 1969), p. 446. A similar figure (6 percent) is repeated in a 1968 study of black attitudes in fifteen major cities. See Angus Campbell and Howard Schuman, *Racial Attitudes in Fifteen American Cities* (Ann Arbor: Survey Research Center, 1968), p. 16. More recently, the 1972 Survey Research Center poll found that 6.4 percent of blacks believed that there should be a separate black nation within the U.S.

However, even, say, the most militant Italian-Americans or racially conscious blacks place the United States ahead of their respective ethnic or racial loyalties.

To understand the political importance of the consensual nature of this loyalty one only has to recall the Civil War. Any review of recent conflicts over the nature of the political community (e.g., the abortive secession of Biafra from Nigeria or the successful secession of Bangladesh from Pakistan) suggests that this policy question may be the most important one in a political system. Imagine what politics in the U.S. would be like if, say, New Englanders were French-speaking Catholics desiring to unite with their brethren in Quebec or if Texas was populated only by Spanish-speaking people who really considered themselves as Mexicans. Under such circumstances leaders would be faced with several explosive policy choices not unlike present-day Canadian officials who must consider many issues against the backdrop of separatist demands in Quebec. The situation never arises in American politics however since all citizens (including leaders) basically accept the primacy of national loyalty and unity. Thus, with not much thought or coercion public officials will behave consistently with the nationalistic sentiments of citizens.

In a similar vein, there is virtually universal acceptance of the basic constitutional order. As any reading of the debates of the Constitutional convention makes clear, our basic political institutions, e.g., the Presidency, a two-house legislature, a federal system, were not preordained choices, but one of many viable alternatives. Nevertheless, the choices of institutional arrangements and many of the basic rules embodied in the Constitution are now among the eternal verities of American politics.[4] Not many leaders or citizens are likely to consider abolishing the Supreme Court, the Senate, the federal system of government, a Presidency elected independently of the legislature, and all the other essential constitutional structures. Movements to reconstitute basic political structures are commonly viewed as crackpot schemes not meriting serious consideration. Even "reasonable" changes such as a parliamentary system (which, after all, is quite common in other nations) are perhaps given only slightly more attention than more radical proposals such as anarchism.

This is not to suggest that every aspect of the constitutional order is forever fixed in the people's minds and no debate occurs on important issues. For one, many important changes have occurred in recent history (e.g., limiting the President to two terms) and many more have been suggested by responsible leaders (e.g., electing the president to one six-year term). Furthermore, because

---

[4] One indication of this feeling comes from a 1959 five nation survey asking citizens what aspects of their nation they took pride in. Eighty-five percent of the Americans mentioned their form of government; this compares with 46 percent of the English, 7 percent of the Germans, 3 percent of the Italians, and 30 percent of the Mexicans. Gabriel A. Almond and Sidney Verba, *The Civic Culture* (Princeton: Princeton University Press, 1963), p. 102. Another interesting piece of data on this question is a 1937 Gallup poll that asked if people wanted a dictatorship established in America. Only 3 percent wanted a dictatorship. Cited in Hadley Cantril, *Public Opinion, 1935-46* (Princeton: Princeton University Press, 1951), p. 869.

conflict over the relationships between different institutions is virtually endemic, demands for change have been common. Thus, for example, when Chief Justice Earl Warren's Supreme Court pushed hard on civil rights, proposals were made to limit drastically the Court's powers; more recently, in the wake of Watergate, arguments have been advanced to constrain the President's power. Finally, the courts and other officials are continually affecting the basic structures as they interpret the law. Nevertheless, when we review the last 100 years (or even 150 years) it is clear that enormous continuity is the rule. Despite occasional fears of presidents becoming monarchs and courts running roughshod over elected representatives, the basic features remain intact and unchallenged and this persistence is preferred by almost all citizens.

A third collection of policies that is almost universally accepted pertain to the role of government in society. With the possible exception of some extreme conservatives, consensus exists that government is a positive force ultimately responsible for dealing with a wide range of problems. The doctrine of laissez faire is no longer taken seriously except among a handful of economists.[5] This consensus on the idea of an active government is frequently obscured by what appears to be sharp conflicts over so-called big vs. small government. We are all familiar, for example, with debates over whether government should meddle in medical care, housing, transportation, and several other policy areas. However, closer inspection of such conflicts typically shows that the issue of government intervention itself is not at the controversy's center. Frequently the debate is over whether intervention should largely be at the national or local level; whether intervention should be direct (e.g., government administered housing) or indirect (e.g., government guarantees of mortgages); or whether intervention will be closely monitored by government officials. This debate over the form of intervention is well illustrated in the long-standing controversy over "socialized medicine" (i.e., government subsidized health care). Recall from our discussion of health care policy in Chapter 6 that while the American Medical Association bitterly opposed direct payments for personal health care, government expenditures of hundreds of millions of dollars on medical research and hospital construction were not deemed "socialistic." Clearly, then, the inclination to involve government in the solution of social problems comes easily to most Americans though divisions are rife on the specific details.

Coexisting with these sentiments, however, are other consensually shared values about the *limits* on government power. It is difficult to draw a precise picture of areas widely believed to be beyond the state's reach, but such

---

[5] This is the conclusion reached by Lane from extensive in-depth interviewing of a small sample of New Haven, Connecticut men. See Robert E. Lane, *Political Ideology* (New York: The Free Press of Glencoe, 1962), Chap. 12. This is supported by Easton and Dennis' nation-wide study of children in grades 3-8 conducted in 1959. At all ages very few children thought that government was getting too big for America and about three-quarters agreed that the government should give money and food to the unemployed. David Easton and Jack Dennis, *Children in the Political System* (New York: McGraw-Hill, 1969), p. 130.

forbidden areas obviously exist.[6] For example, it is difficult to imagine any citizens or leaders seriously advocating government programs to determine people's occupations, their places of residence, their marriage partners, or the number of their children. Nor could we conceive of government intervention in the area of group related identities by, for example, assigning people their religious preferences or making it illegal to think of oneself as, say, a German-American. Obviously, the government does interfere with personal liberty to a great extent (e.g., by prohibiting the use of certain drugs, enacting public dress codes, and even legally regulating sex relations) so we are not claiming that all strictly personal matters are beyond the government's reach. Nevertheless, in many such matters both citizens and leaders agree that government involvement is too "ridiculous" to be taken seriously.

A fourth policy area in which widespread agreement exists concerns some of the general rules of political conflict. Innumerable criteria exist for settling political disputes, but among these a few possess a deep and widespread appeal to most Americans. The use of voting and regular elections are perhaps the most prominent of these mechanisms. As studies of early political learning show, most Americans even as children accept voting as the legitimate way to choose among leaders or policies.[7] Implicitly rejected are such alternatives as chance (e.g., choosing leaders by lot), appeal to mystical sources (e.g., consulting oracles), holding physical contests, or deferring to expertise derived from age, character or training. At the systems level the emphasis on voting translates into the use of elections, as opposed to revolutions or palace coups, as a means for changing leadership. Closely associated with voting is the notion of majority rule. To appreciate how deeply ingrained these mechanisms are, consider what public reaction would be if a leader announced that from now on the U.S. were to be ruled by a council of elders chosen by lot who would decide all issues using the unanimity rule after due consultation with the spirits.

At first glance these policies that virtually all Americans unthinkingly take for granted might not appear important. Questions regarding the basic constitutional order, the political community, and so on certainly do not generate the intense reaction associated with crucial and controversial political topics. Nevertheless, in many respects the policies we have described here overshadow more specific,

---

[6] For example, a 1939 Gallup poll asked whether the government should supervise all religious observances by establishing a national church. Four percent endorsed this idea. Cantril, *Public Opinion, 1935-46*, p. 104. Of course, if questions are formulated so that favoring government intervention in highly personal matters means endorsing some sacred principle, e.g., should government fight sin, then support for intervention will probably appear high.

[7] The symbolic importance attributed to voting is shown by the fact that many young children perceive the voting act as representative of government itself. Moreover, the belief about the importance of voting grows with age and political sophistication. See Robert D. Hess and Judith V. Torney, *The Development of Political Attitudes in Children* (Garden City: Doubleday Anchor Books, 1968), especially pp. 86-88. Data on adult support for the electoral process are presented in Jack Dennis, "Support of the Institution of Elections by the Mass Public," *American Political Science Review* 64 (1970): 819-35.

day-to-day issues. The virtually universal acceptance of these policies sets major boundaries on what is reasonable and permissible on day-to-day policy-making and are thus of fundamental political importance despite their low salience. The constraints placed upon policy choices can be graphically depicted as follows:

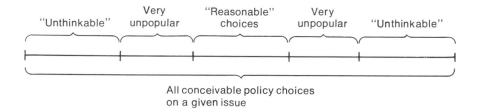

All conceivable policy choices
on a given issue

Let us illustrate the importance of consensus on an acceptable range of alternatives by imagining that the American public were confronted with the problem of severe economic depression. What are the possible responses by citizens and leaders? Several options are obviously beyond the pale of even public mention (i.e., are "unthinkable"). Hardly anyone would suggest that the United States politically and economically merge with other nations to achieve better economic conditions. Strictly from the perspective of increased economic efficiency this choice is not bizarre, but it is clearly politically impossible and thus not even raised. What about dismantling existing political structures and replacing them with a small council of all-powerful leaders instructed to make whatever changes necessary to bring about prosperity? Such policy changes might include forced migration, involuntary salary cuts, and drastically reduced production of consumer commodities. Needless to say, since this council would be all-powerful, citizens would not be given the opportunity to raise objections or to remove leaders. Like the possibility of surrendering national sovereignty, this all-powerful council is equally inconceivable.

Other policy alterantives in dealing with a depression are perhaps a little less bizarre, but they, too, are "unreasonable." Imagine public reaction to proposals to cut down on public spending by, say, raising gasoline prices to $5.00 a gallon, rationing meat to one pound per person per week, or sharply curtailing the number of professional sporting events. Policies like these have been instituted as wartime emergency measures so they are not implausible, but it is obvious that under more normal conditions they would be widely viewed by both citizens and leaders as unacceptable. At best, extreme choices such as these will only be considered very privately and, if advanced at all, will appear as anonymous "trial balloons" or in reports issued by research organizations. They will not, however, be part of the general public debate over policy.

The policy alternatives considered reasonable will, obviously, constitute only a sample of the possible choices. We would expect to find more discussion of, for example, government make-work programs, adjustments in tax rates, modifications of import-export controls, and so on, than of the extreme measures mentioned above. It is quite likely that virtually all the alternatives actually considered will be at least *tolerable* though not necessarily preferred by the vast majority. Thus, although the precise preferences of 50 percent plus one may not be satisfied by the policy outcome, the losers would not regard the results as completely unacceptable. Put another way, the underlying broad consensus on the range of permissible choices probably guarantees that almost everyone will get no lower than, say, their third or fourth choices (as opposed to, say, their twenty-fifth choice).

By no means are we implying that citizens and leaders agree on each and every policy choice. On occasion, differences of opinions have been so deep that citizens were even willing to forsake the basic political community and institutional structures (e.g., Black Panther demands for separate black communities). Differences over, say, greater government involvement in school integration are not squabbles over mere detail to those involved in this controversy. But imagine public reaction if the government decided that mandatory miscegenation would immediately be instituted to "solve" the race problem. Compared to this alternative, differences over whether bussing to achieve integration should be increased or decreased appear minor. Our discussion merely points out that even people who vehemently disagree on certain issues nevertheless share numerous basic assumptions about acceptable political solutions.

This situation is not inherent in every political system. Politics in many nations displays a range of alternatives that covers almost the whole spectrum of possible choices. Consider, for example, the ideological diversity among Italian political parties. At one end of the scale are monarchists and fascists; at the other end are communists. Between the two extremes are several parties whose policy differences far exceed differences between Democrats and Republicans. Under such circumstances it is unlikely that almost any policy suggested by almost any leader will be tolerable to most people. Nor are circumstances like those in Italy relatively unique. Particularly among the developing nations in Africa and Asia, the range of publically considered alternatives runs from the extreme right to the extreme left.

CITIZEN AND LEADER AGREEMENT ON SPECIFIC ISSUES

Our argument thus far suggests that no matter what the policy outcome, as long as certain basic preferences (e.g., holding elections to choose leaders) are not violated few citizens will be completely outraged. Thus a certain degree of broad opinion-policy congruence is assured. How far can we push this argument of citizen-leader consensus on crucial issues? In view of all the poll data examined in Chapters 6 and 7, which showed sizeable divisions on many issues, the argument that all leaders and all citizens share the same preferences is obviously untenable. At least some leaders must disagree with at least some nonleaders. On the other hand, it is improbable that opinions on more specific policy questions are distributed so that citizens almost unanimously support one side and all leaders support the other. Clearly, then, the question is one of the amount of overlap between leaders and citizens preferences. To answer this question on the degree of overlap, let us consider (1) data on various social and demographic characteristics of leaders and (2) several opinion surveys of leaders and nonleaders.

SOCIAL BACKGROUND DIFFERENCES
AMONG LEADERS AND NONLEADERS

Though surveys of citizen preferences and leadership opinions abound, simultaneous analysis of both groups are surprisingly rare. Although such data are obviously important, we are not completely limited to such evidence. Specifically, we know a great deal about the social and economic characteristics of leaders and nonleaders. Even though the inferences one can draw from personal background data must be treated carefully, such information is valuable.[8] In examining such background characteristics as social status, occupation, education, and the like, we are assuming that such personal characteristics are systematically related to policy preferences among both the general population and political leaders. We expect, for example, that if among the general population Jews are more liberal on social welfare policy than non-Jews, then Jewish leaders would on the whole support more liberal policies than the general population. Of course, this approach only approximates the use of mass-leader opinion polls, but particularly where differences in both opinions and social characteristics are large and consistent, this strategy is a good second best solution.

Perhaps the most salient differences between leaders and nonleaders in American politics are the differences in the socioeconomic status of the two groups. Regardless of the particular measure of social standing we employ, or of the level of government or point in time, status differences are very apparent. Consider differences in educational attainment. In his study of U.S. Senators between 1947-1957 Donald Matthews reports that 84 percent of the Senators had attended college compared to 14 percent of the nonwhite male population over twenty-five. Even this gap underestimates leader-nonleader educational differences since a disproportionately large number of Senators have graduated

---

[8] For a general discussion of some of the methodological and theoretical problems associated with inferring attitudes from background characteristics, see Lewis J. Edinger and Donald D. Searing, "Social Background in Elite Analysis: A Methodological Inquiry," *American Political Science Review* 61 (1967): 428-45.

from prestigious elite schools such as Harvard or Yale.[9] Among Presidents and Supreme Court Justices a college education is the rule.[10] Analyses of the background of less prominent officials do not significantly alter this picture. Prewitt, for example, in his study of city councilmen in small cities in the San Francisco Bay area, finds that almost every councilman attended college (95 percent) in contrast with a little more than half (57 percent) of the general population in these cities.[11]

Not surprisingly, leaders also consistently differ from the people who choose them in terms of previous occupation. The folksy notion that anyone—regardless of how humble one's origins—can aspire to positions of leadership is not borne out by the data. For example, though about a third of the U.S. labor force in 1960 was employed in some form of unskilled manual labor, U.S. Senators in Matthew's study (1947-1957) with this occupational background were extremely rare.[12] Moreover, though local and regional variations certainly exist, the exclusion of the working class from political leadership roles is pervasive. This contrast is made even sharper when we realize that among leaders there are a disproportionate number of lawyers, independent businessmen, and other professionals whose occupational status is upper middle class. Nor does the "from humble origins to political leader" story receive much confirmation if we look at the social status of leaders' parents. While almost every leader could claim one or more ancestors of impoverished origins, most leaders probably began with most of the middle-class advantages.[13]

This picture of the advantaged social origins of political leaders should not be interpreted as showing that a type of economic aristocracy monopolizes political power. For we are describing general trends and numerous exceptions can and do occur (e.g., President Truman was of relatively humble origins). More important, the well-educated, upper-middle-class citizens holding political power

---

[9] Donald R. Matthews, *U.S. Senators and their World* (New York: Vintage Books, 1960), pp. 25-30. Similar educational data are reported in Andrew Hacker, "The Elected and the Anointed: Two American Elites," *American Political Science Review* 55 (1961): 541-42. Hacker finds that presidents of corporations are even more likely than Senators to have graduated from elite Ivy League colleges. At the state level, educational differences are still sharp though perhaps not as extreme as they are at the national level. For data on state legislators in California, New Jersey, Ohio and Tennessee, see John C. Wahlke, Heinz Eulau, William Buchanan and LeRoy C. Ferguson, *The Legislative System* (New York: John Wiley & Sons, 1962), p. 489.

[10] Supreme Court justices in particular seem to have an affinity for prestige colleges and law schools. Additional data on the "elitist" character of the Supreme Court is presented in John R. Schmidhauser, "Justices of the Supreme Court: A Collective Portrait," *Midwest Journal of Political Science* 3 (1959): 1-49.

[11] Kenneth Prewitt, *The Recruitment of Political Leaders: A Study of Citizen-Politicians* (Indianapolis: The Bobbs-Merrill Company, 1970), p. 26.

[12] Matthews, *U.S. Senators and their World*, pp. 30-33.

[13] Matthews, *U.S. Senators and their World*, pp. 19-20. Occupational data on state legislators as well as occupations of their parents are presented in Wahlke et al., *The Legislative System*, pp. 489-90.

are usually not all that removed from the average citizen. To appreciate this fact one must realize that prior to the democratization of American politics during the nineteenth century, top political leaders were much more likely to come from long established and frequently aristocratic families much more socially and economically distant from the average citizen than are contemporary politicians.[14] It is now far more common for a manual worker to be represented by a middle-class lawyer whose own family was comfortable though not affluent than to be represented by the multi-millionaire son of a socially prestigious family (though exceptions such as Henry Cabot Lodge and the Rockefellers do exist).

Leaders differ from nonleaders in several other ways as well. One of the most obvious differences is age. In the first place, many political offices have minimum age requirements. Perhaps even more important, with few exceptions it takes time to achieve a position of political authority and thus, especially at higher levels, leaders tend to be middle-aged or older. For example, in 1970 the average age of all U.S. citizens was 28.1 years; while in 1972 the average age of U.S. Representatives was 51.9 years and of U.S. Senators 53.0 years. Chairmen of important Congressional committees, Supreme Court Justices, and many other political influentials are frequently in their seventies or even eighties.[15] This tendency for politics to be dominated by older people occured even in the 1972 Democratic presidential convention—while the proportion of those under thirty at the convention increased substantially between 1968 and 1972, young people were still underrepresented despite explicit attempts to give an equal voice to youth.[16] In short, due to their ages the average political leader has experienced a very different set of events than the average citizen and thus is also likely to take a different perspective on many policy questions.

Another equally obvious difference is sex. Though women constitute slightly more than half the general population, they are almost completely absent from important positions of political power. There has never been a woman president or Supreme Court Justice; and very few women have occupied high administrative or cabinet posts. Recently, a vocal and conspicuous movement of "women in politics has emerged" and some women have won offices, e.g., governorships, not normally considered women's positions, but they still constitute, for example, less than 5 percent of all Congressmen, one of fifty governors, and 0

[14] See, for example, Robert A. Dahl, *Who Governs?* (New Haven: Yale University Press, 1961), chaps. 2-5 and Donald S. Bradley and Meyer N. Zald, "From Commercial Elite to Political Administrator: The Recruitment of Mayors of Chicago," *American Journal of Sociology* 71 (1965): 153-67.

[15] Additional data on these differences are presented in Herbert Jacob and Robert Weissberg, *Elementary Political Analysis*, 2nd. ed. (New York: McGraw-Hill, 1975), p. 256.

[16] Dennis G. Sullivan, Jeffrey L. Pressman, Benjamin I. Page, *The Politics of Representation: The Democratic Convention 1972* (New York: St. Martins Press, 1974), p. 23.

percent of mayors of large cities.[17] Males dominate even in nonelected civil service positions where being female would not, ostensibly, be a political liability.[18]

Differences between leaders and nonleaders are also quite apparent in race and ethnicity. Like women, blacks have long been largely absent from prominent national offices. Also like women, blacks have made dramatic political gains recently, but they still remain underrepresented in Congress, top jobs in administration, federal judgeships, state legislatures, and almost every other arena where important political decisions are made.[19] Moreover, not only can politics be described as white-dominated, but even among white leaders foreign-born citizens or those whose parents trace their origins back to countries not in northwestern Europe still appear to be at a competitive disadvantage despite their numbers.[20] To be sure, particularly in certain northeastern cities (e.g., Boston) being of white, Anglo-Saxon decent may sometimes be a major political handicap, but such handicaps are exceptional.

In describing these characteristics we do not wish to imply that certain groups are purposely excluded from political power. Such exclusion certainly has occurred on occasion, e.g., the disenfranchisement of Southern blacks, and it may be more common than many would admit, but the mere existence of social, economic, educational, and sex differences between leaders and nonleaders is

[17] In the 1974 elections the sudden increase in women running for office (about 1300) gave a somewhat misleading impression of new-found political equality. Women at all levels remained a distinct minority, and despite some well publicized successes, most female candidates met defeat. Moreover, many successful female candidates had begun their careers by following their husbands into office. See *U.S. News and World Report,* September 16, 1974 for a fuller analysis of recent female political successes.

[18] Between October 1970 and October 1972 the proportion of higher servants (GS-18 and higher) who were female virtually doubled. However, such progress was deceptive since even in 1972, only 4.8 percent of very high white collar positions in the federal government were occupied by females. See U.S. Civil Service Commission, *Study of Employment of Women in the Federal Government 1972,* Washington, D.C., p. 163. On the social backgrounds of higher civil servants more generally, see W. Lloyd Warner, *et al., The American Federal Executive* (New Haven: Yale University Press, 1963), especially chapters 2-9; and David T. Stanley, *et al., Men Who Govern* (Washington, D.C.: The Brookings Institution, 1967), chaps. 2-3.

[19] For example, between 1970 and 1974 the number of black elected officials (including education officials) increased from 1,472 to 2,991. Three thousand officials is no small number, but this compares to over half a million elected officials within the entire United States. Data on elected officials are presented in U.S. Bureau of the Census, *Statistical Abstract of the United States: 1974,* Washington, D.C., 1974. A similar situation occurs in holding top positions in the higher civil service. Despite dramatic percentage increases, blacks still remain greatly underrepresented. For example, in 1971 only 2.7 percent of top civil service jobs (GS 16-18) were occupied by blacks. U.S. Civil Service Commission, *Minority Group Employment in the Federal Government, May 31, 1971,* Washington, D.C., especially pp. 8-10.

[20] See, for example, Matthews, *U.S. Senators and their World,* pp. 22-23. In recent years only one Supreme Court Justice (Felix Frankfurter) was foreign born and the Constitution prohibits the foreign born from the presidency.

not hard proof of political discrimination. Nor do these data demonstrate the existence of an upper status, white, older, male ruling class that runs government for its own interests at the expense of the less well-educated, nonwhite, young, and female. Conclusions about whose interest government works for cannot, obviously, be inferred solely from socioeconomic attributes, though these characteristics are suggestive.[21]

What these differences do imply is that on the whole, leaders are likely to have different political perspectives than the general population. We expect, for example, elderly white male Congressmen who graduate from prestigious colleges to see things differently than, say, youthful, black ghetto dwellers. Moreover, the very process of rising to leadership positions can change one's viewpoint. Even if a young ghetto resident were to become a Congressman, the very experience of being a Congressman, e.g., earning $42,000 a year, having a staff to arrange one's schedule, being treated with great respect, and having one's opinion asked on important issues may contribute to losing touch with one's earlier and less exalted background. Indeed, the very process of becoming a leader provides a variety of experiences, e.g., raising vast sums for a campaign, that differentiates one from the average citizen. In short, on the basis of these background differences it is unlikely—though not impossible—that if leaders followed their own preferences, these actions would be perfectly consistent with citizen demands.

That leaders and nonleaders on the whole have different preferences is generally confirmed by survey analysis. One such study, conducted by McClosky and his associates, compares Democrat and Republican party leaders attending the 1956 presidential conventions with the general populations. One major area of investigation was support for democratic values. McClosky finds that except for the most general expressions of support for free speech, leaders were consistently more likely to be tolerant than nonleaders. For example, while 13.3 percent of the leaders agreed that "Almost any unfairness or brutality may have to be justified when some great purpose is being carried out," 32.8 percent of the nonleaders agreed.[22] Similar differences occur on questions of free speech for unpopular ideas, the maintenance of procedural rights for criminals and political deviants, and support for the principles of political equality (e.g., the capacity of citizens to choose their leaders wisely).[23]

---

[21] However, such an analysis can readily be done. As an illustration see G. William Domhoff, *The Higher Circles: The Governing Class in America* (New York: Vintage Books, 1971).

[22] Herbert McCloskey, "Consensus and Ideology in American Politics," *American Political Science Review* 58 (1964): 365.

[23] McClosky, "Consensus and Ideology in American Politics," pp. 366-67. The pattern of greater leader support for democratic principles is also reported in Samuel Stouffer, *Communism, Conformity, and Civil Liberties* (New York: John Wiley, 1955). It should be noted, however, that Stouffer's sample of leaders is comprised of prominent local citizens, e.g., newspaper publishers, as well as political decision-makers.

On questions relating to social equality, however, McClosky finds that non-leaders are the more "liberal" of the two groups. For instance, more than twice as many citizens as leaders (20.8 *vs.* 44.8 percent) endorse the proposition that labor does not get a fair share of what it produces. Citizens were also considerably more favorable towards government involvement in housing and guarantees of a decent standard of living.[24] Moreover, when leaders are divided according to partisan affiliation, it appears that Republican leaders in particular are more conservative than nonleaders on economic issues such as public ownership of resources or the regulation of business (in fact, on some issues Republican followers were closer to Democratic than to Republican leaders).[25]

A second analysis of leader vs. nonleaders differences in preferences is the Miller-Stokes study of Congressmen and their constituents. In Chapter 8 we focused on the relationship between Congressional roll call votes and the preferences of the Congressman's constituents of the same party. Here, however, our interest is on Congressmen's *attitudes* and we focus on the opinions of all constituents not just partisan supporters. The correlations between Congressman's attitude and citizen attitude on the issues of civil rights, social welfare, and foreign policy are presented in Table 9-1. On the whole, these correlations suggest that citizens and their representatives have similar opinions, but except for civil rights, the relationship is not strong. Constituencies characterized by liberal sentiment on these issues are more likely to have liberal rather than conservative representatives, but there are numerous exceptions. Of course, even in districts where Congressmen and most constituents disagree, it is probably true that at least some citizens and leaders see eye to eye on these issues.

The third, and final, piece of information treats Congress and the general public as a whole instead of district by district. Table 9-2 presents the results of a 1970 CBS poll of the general public, all U.S. Representatives, and all U.S. Senators. Comparisons of the percentages show that the liberal positions in the five issues surveyed is more likely to be taken by leaders in both houses of

Table 9-1 Relationship Between Congressman's Opinion and Constituency Opinion, by Issue Area, 1958

Issue Area	*Correlation between Congressman's Attitude and Constituency Attitude*
Civil Rights	.50
Social Welfare	.26
Foreign Policy	.32

SOURCE: Survey Research Center, University of Michigan

[24] McClosky, "Consensus and Ideology in American Politics," p. 369.
[25] Herbert McClosky, Paul J. Hoffman and Rosemary O'Hara, "Issue Conflict and Consensus among Party Leaders and Followers," *American Political Science Review* 64 (1960): 411-12.

Table 9-2   Congressional and Public Opinion on Five Policy Issues, 1970

	Public	U.S. House Members	U.S. Senators
Percent favoring speeding up our withdrawal from Vietnam	27	30	45
Percent wanting to place less emphasis on military weapons programs	30	37	45
Percent approving at least 1600 dollars for a family of four or more	48	65	76
Percent saying government should go further to improve black conditions	53	58	76
Percent denying that Supreme Court gives too much consideration to rights of people suspected of crimes	29	36	56

SOURCE: "Candidates, Congress, and Constituents," CBS News Poll, Series 70, No. 7, Report 5. Questions for Congressmen and public were similar but not identical.

Congress (particularly in the Senate) than by the general population. Further analyses of these figures show, however, that it is only on the question of a guaranteed income of $1600 for a family of four that Congress and the general public are on different sides of the issue (on the Supreme Court question, the House and Senate differ, with the House being closer to the public). Thus, while Congressmen and the general public sometimes differ substantially, a public referendum on these issues would probably approximate Congressional decisions on these topics more than half the time.

BELIEF SHARING: SUMMARY AND CONCLUSION

Though the data on leader-citizen policy consensus are not as precise or extensive as we might like, a number of broad conclusions are warranted. First, due largely to the political socialization process virtually all citizens (including future leaders) acquire certain preferences and expectations. The pervasiveness and thoroughness of this learning effectively places numerous policy choices into the "unthinkable" category. Yet other policy choices are made to appear very "unrealistic" (though perhaps not inconceivable) through the socialization process. Thus, it is highly unlikely that leaders will ever seriously consider policies that would completely outrage most citizens. Such a lack of consideration by leaders is perhaps based on the knowledge that the public will never "buy" certain alternatives, but more likely, these alternatives do not even occur to leaders. In a sense, this common political socialization is more important for preventing the adoption of completely unacceptable policies than guaranteeing choices preferred by a majority.

The analysis of leaders' background characteristics as well as survey data indicate, however, that there are limits to this shared preferences model. Leaders as a group are not a microcosm of the general population though it is probably true that almost every policy preference found in the general population can find expression among at least some leaders. Thus, if leaders did whatever they themselves wanted, policy outcomes would not be the same as if, say, 5,000 citizens were randomly selected to fill positions of political authority. At the same time, however, the lack of overlap between leaders and nonleaders should not be exaggerated. Rarely are both groups on different sides of an issue. In short, shared preferences among leaders and nonleaders is a linkage mechanism more suited to eliminating gross inconsistencies between policy and opinion. It is likely that leaders acting on their own will give the public neither precisely what it demands nor the exact opposite.

chapter ten

SOURCES OF CONGRUENCE: GOVERNMENT MANIPULATION

Implicit in most analyses of the relationship between public opinion and public policy is that if influence is exerted, it is exerted by citizens on political leaders. That is, by such means as voting, letter writing, financial contributions and the like citizens attempt to make officials follow their preferences. Even analysts who deny the existence of strong citizen influence, nevertheless frequently assume that citizens *ought* to control leaders, and thus focus their attention on the upward flow of communication between masses and elites. Perhaps because of our early learning about the efficacy of voting and the importance of the individual citizen in the political process, we are reluctant to imagine any other flow of influence except from citizen to leader.

Nevertheless, opinion-policy congruence can also be achieved through the reverse process: government influencing mass opinion. Indeed, given the resources of modern government and leaders' easy access to mass communications channels, this policy-determines-opinion conception is as plausible as the more customary opinion-affects-policy version. In raising the possibility we are not necessarily implying that such influence on opinion is evil, undemocratic, or part of a conspiracy to exploit the American public. Government manipulations can be benign, e.g., media campaigns for automobile safety, or even unintended, e.g., normal military maneuvers that may inspire greater patriotism and support for leaders.

The existence of government manipulation of popular preferences is a complicated question that cannot be approached on an issue-by-issue basis. Instead we shall consider the question more generally. Our analysis is divided into four sections. First, we shall review certain aspects of the political socialization process that affect the probability of citizens being susceptible to

222

manipulation. As we shall see, this early learning at once provides a high potential for manipulation and constitutes a powerful bulwark against it. Second, we shall examine some attempts of government to change mass opinion. Of particular interest are attempts by the government to "sell" policies to both the general public and community leaders. Third, using public opinion polls we shall examine the capacity of government to influence shifts in opinion merely by taking certain actions even when no conscious propaganda effort is made. What happens, for example, when leaders take dramatic actions that fly in the face of overwhelming public sentiment? Fourth and finally, is there anything in addition to beliefs acquired in childhood that prevents leaders from readily creating majorities to support their actions? Obviously, if the government could easily create a supportive majority on any issue, this would raise serious problems about how to interpret the mere existence of opinion-policy congruence.

POLITICAL SOCIALIZATION AND THE POTENTIAL FOR MANIPULATION

Though many adults view politicians and the political process with skepticism, considerable evidence indicates that earlier in life Americans typically acquire very different images. Several studies have characterized children's view of political authority (especially the President) as highly benevolent. Politicians are seen as honest, virtuous people who do good deeds and protect citizens.[1] In a sense, the President and other authorities are powerful, protective, father-like figures. The notion that, say, the President would do something for personal gain that might harm America is virtually inconceivable to young children. To be sure, these highly positive images decline with age and more recent evidence suggests that the Vietnam War and the Nixon Presidency may have increased cynicism levels, but it is true nevertheless that the benevolent image of political authority, especially for the President, but for lesser officials as well, is the dominant view throughout early childhood.[2]

A second element in children's conception of political authority is a

---

[1] Among others, see Fred I. Greenstein, "The Benevolent Leader: Children's Images of Political Authority," *American Political Science Review* 54 (1960): 934-43; and David Easton and Jack Dennis, "The Child's Image of Government," *The Annals of the American Academy of Political and Social Sciences* 361 (1965): 40-57.

[2] For example, Tolley's 1969 study of children aged seven to fifteen found that only 29 percent believed that Nixon always told the truth about Vietnam and less than a third believed he did the right thing in Vietnam. Howard Tolley, Jr., *Children and War* (New York: Teachers College Press, 1973), p. 65. Data on the impact of Watergate on children's perceptions are reported in Fred I. Greenstein, "The Benevolent Leader Revisited: Children's Images of Political Leaders in Three Democracies," *American Political Science Review*, forthcoming. However, it is quite likely that events like Watergate will have their greatest impact on older children (who are more attuned to current events) and these children are also more likely to be able to separate the particular incumbent from the presidency.

widespread belief in its personal responsiveness. Leaders are not only good and protective, but they are believed to be keenly interested in responding to citizen opinion. For example, in their eight-city study Easton and Dennis report that only a small handful of children in grades 4 through 8 reject the belief that the government would help them if they needed assistance.[3] This responsiveness is further reinforced by children's infatuation with the concept "democracy" and their association of the existing American political system with democracy. Even at a young age children know that "democracy" is good and America is a democracy. With age, however, democracy is increasingly associated with "where the people rule" and thus by association the political system is endowed with an aura of popular responsiveness.[4] Of course, adulthood may weaken such idealistic perceptions, but like benevolence, the image of responsiveness dominates for many early years.

A third, and perhaps most significant, childhood acquired set of beliefs concerns the competence of political leaders and the correctness of their decisions. Logically, there is no reason why goodness and responsiveness need be associated with competence, but all three attributes nevertheless seem to be associated in children's belief systems. For example, Easton and Dennis find that the vast majority of children in their study believe that the government "almost never" or "rarely" makes mistakes. Even by eighth grade, when children supposedly are better able to analyze government action, only 38 percent acknowledge that the government "sometimes" or "very often" makes mistakes.[5] A similar pattern is displayed in beliefs about presidential competence. The President is perceived to be right virtually every time, knows a great deal more than other people, and works very hard at his job.[6] Other political authorities such as the Supreme Court and Senators likewise strike children as exceptionally competent and knowledgeable.[7]

Although even adolescents hold highly positive images of political authority, we obviously cannot claim that these rosy beliefs completely survive maturity. However, the growth of negative sentiment does not make this early learning irrelevant. What appears to occur is that these positive images of political authority are separated from the particular people who happen to occupy an authority position and are transferred to the institutional structures.[8] While a very young child might have thought of Johnson when judging the president's qualities, by about eighth grade the individual is able to separate the *presidency* from *a president*. This substitution of a political role for a political personality means that later on in life we are able to express doubts about the performance

---

[3] David Easton and Jack Dennis, *Children in the Political System* (New York: McGraw-Hill, 1969), p. 133.

[4] Robert D. Hess and Judith V. Torney, *The Development of Political Attitudes in Children* (Garden City: Doubleday Anchor Books, 1968), pp. 75, 86.

[5] Easton and Dennis, *Children in the Political System,* p. 133.

[6] Easton and Dennis, *Children in the Political System,* pp. 180-182.

[7] Easton and Dennis, *Children in the Political System,* pp. 251, 263.

[8] Easton and Dennis, *Children in the Political System,* p. 246.

of an incumbent Senator or Supreme Court Justice, but these doubts are limited to specific people and probably even specific actions, not institutional roles. This separation of role and person no doubt accounted for the capacity of many citizens during the late 1960s to be highly critical of the President's handling of Vietnam yet simultaneously argue that the President's authority should be respected.

What is important about these childhood acquired evaluations of political authority for our analysis is that they automatically provide leaders with an enormous reservoir of credibility, competency, and good will. In effect, merely becoming the incumbent mobilizes positive bias since he or she is now associated with highly esteemed institutional roles.[9] Whereas pronouncements made by an average citizen are not treated with special attention, the identical utterance coming from a high political leader is usually imputed to be based on some greater understanding and compassion for the public interest. Even if leaders should be challenged by those claiming special competence in an area, e.g., technical experts, it is likely that citizens will give political authority the benefit of the doubt. In short, thanks to the early inculcation of positive images of leaders, when the government speaks it is likely to speak with convincing authority.

At the same time, however, we should also realize that the very same political socialization process that mobilizes this positive bias also greatly inhibits what leaders can advocate. We have already seen that certain political values such as the primacy of loyalty to America, are so deeply ingrained that no political leader would dare oppose them. Imagine public reaction, for example, if the President publicly endorsed a state religion or the dismantling of the Supreme Court. Particular political personalities are not viewed as god-like figures more important than "mere" institutions or the rule of law. Not unlike the Japanese Emperor, American leaders are prisoners of the structures and roles providing them with their power and prestige.

Moreover, thanks to our early learning, we expect leaders to behave in certain "statesman-like" ways. While a certain amount of "politics" is permissible even for the President, e.g., helping elect members of his own party to Congress, publicly playing "power politics" may generate an adverse reaction. Surely, even the most power-oriented leader would think twice before announcing that all those resisting his efforts to help America would find themselves in serious trouble with the government.[10] Finally, our political socialization also leads us

[9] See, for example, L. R. Anderson and A. R. Bass, "Some Effects of Victory or Defeat upon Perceptions of Political Candidates," *Journal of Social Psychology* 73 (1967): 227-40 and I. H. Paul, "Impressions of Personality, Authoritarianism and the *Fait Accompli* Effect," *Journal of Abnormal and Social Psychology* 53 (1956): 338-44.

[10] This aversion to having an exalted leader like the President playing "dirty politics" perhaps accounts for some of the vast public indignation with Nixon's Watergate related behavior. Though many citizens could probably imagine Nixon's allowing his subordinates to engage in "dirty tricks," the idea of the President himself engaging in such activities (and using such lurid language in the process), went well beyond established limits of overt presidential action.

to expect political authority to at least appear to be responsive to "the people" as a whole. This does not mean, of course, that Governors, Congressmen or Presidents are prohibited from giving special attention to particular groups or points of view. Leaders must be careful, however, to avoid appearing as if they were paid lobbyists for special interests. Hence, while a presidential call for economic optimism during a recession is perfectly acceptable, to call for buying more Chevrolets would completely overstep acceptable boundaries.

GOVERNMENT PROPAGANDA

Does the government try to "sell" its policies to the American public? Though many people are probably only vaguely aware of such efforts, and most citizens would in the abstract disapprove of "government propaganda," the answer to this question is an emphatic "yes." Indeed, the government communications effort directed at its own citizens equals the efforts of commercial advertisers selling soap and automobiles. However, unlike television commercials for consumer products, the selling of government policy is considerably more subtle and far less obtrusive. Let us examine three different aspects of this communications effort: (1) indoctrination in the formal educational system; (2) government public relations activities; and (3) the use of the media by public figures to generate support for their policies.

Since the advent of compulsory public education, virtually every American citizen has had a lengthy exposure to state-prescribed political messages. "Classroom indoctrination" may be a term reserved for the Soviet or Chinese Communist educational system, but the United States spends as much educational time and money on achieving the "correct" political values as do the Soviets.[11] The most obvious manifestation of this effort is the state-required history and "civics" courses offered in primary and secondary schools. As critics of these courses have long noted, these offerings provide far from a straight, unbiased picture of American history and politics. Typically, the United States, its political institutions, and people are glorified; and government mistakes, incompetence, greed and other unvirtuous characteristics are treated superficially or ignored altogether.[12] Even in courses not dealing with explicitly political matters, e.g., geography, music, art, and English, as well as in ritualistic exercises such as pledging allegiance to the flag, political values are conveyed though the process is frequently subtle.

Does this vast educational effort result in the uniform "brainwashing" of citizens to prefer only those choices offered by the government? Not exactly. In

[11]George Z. F. Bereday and Bonnie B. Stretch, "Political Education in the U.S.A. and the Soviet Union," *Comparative Education Review* 7 (1963): 9-16.
[12]Among others, see John R. Palmer, "American History," and Bryan B. Marsialas, "American Government: We are the Greatest," in *Social Studies in the United States: A Critical Appraisal,* eds., C. Benjamin Cox and Bryan G. Marsialas (New York: Harcourt, Brace, Jovanovich Inc., 1967).

the first place, this "indoctrination" is neither completely uniform nor completely efficient. Education in the United States is not centrally directed by a Ministry of Education in Washington that controls textbook content, curriculum, and classroom structure in every school. Regional and local autonomy lead to a variation in the political messages that are communicated.[13] Moreover, despite the best efforts of teachers, not every attempt at political instruction succeeds. Several recent studies on the impact of civics courses have shown, for example, that instruction has only a slight impact on political knowledge, opinions and ideological sophistication. These studies do not assert that civics courses are without any impact; rather, the courses' impact is not uniformly great in every area of political learning.[14]

In the second place, the political content of formal education is typically not at odds with either parental political values or the existing predispositions of school children. "Brainwashing" might be an appropriate description of such education if the schools were used by government to "reeducate" children away from parental preferences, but such redirection is rare. Instead, the school, by and large, reinforces consensually held political values. Young children learn about the benefits of being American, the virtues of the existing constitutional system, the fine qualities of national leaders past and present, the benefits of "freedom" and "democracy" enjoyed by U.S. citizens, and the importance of voting and elections. Few people would argue that the inculcating of these beliefs constitutes "brainwashing." When political preferences are controversial or significant differences of opinion occur, such subjects are not usually part of the school's political message, e.g., high school students are not taught that tax rates should be changed or that Social Security ought to be abolished.

It is probably fair to say that many of the demands made by citizens for specific policies, e.g., stricter gun control legislation, do not result from government controlled early education. At the same time, however, the government, through the educational system, does play a crucial role in deeply instilling support for basic features of the political system as well as fostering certain attitudes that can encourage leadership influence on more day-to-day political opinions. Hence, long before individuals are old enough to vote and present their demands "officially" they have acquired many beliefs and attitudes that will contribute to a close relationship between their preferences and public policies. For example, thanks in part to their schooling most citizens want elections as the method of selecting leaders and public officials (who also learned these preferences in school) readily go along with this demand. Similarly, thanks in part to their schooling many citizens assume that leaders know what they are doing and are thus more likely to agree with their decisions. The government

[13] For example, see Edgar Litt, "Civic Education, Community Norms and Political Indoctrination," *American Sociological Review* 28 (1968): 69-75.
[14] These studies are reviewed in Robert Weissberg, *Political Learning, Political Choice and Democratic Citizenship* (Englewood Cliffs: Prentice-Hall, Inc., 1974), pp. 157-68.

contributes to opinion-policy congruence then, not only by enacting policies desired by citizens, but also by shaping these demands through the educational system.

The use of the educational system is not, however, the only way the government can affect opinion-policy congruence by influencing opinion. In addition to the vast governmental expenditures on education, an enormous effort is also made in government public relations. Though one may associate "public relations" with the activities of big businesses concerned about their public image, the United States government wages perhaps the largest PR program in the world. Due to ambiguities of job classification, it is not precisely clear how much governments at all levels spend on public relations, but even the most conservative estimates show that hundreds of millions of dollars each year are spent publicizing the activities and accomplishments of government to its own citizens.[15] Such efforts have long worried both citizens and leaders, but all attempts to abolish or reduce government self-publicity have failed.[16]

We are not suggesting that the mere existence of well financed public relations bureaucracies constitutes proof of government manipulation of public opinion. Most public relations work is purely informational and done with little or no attempt to change opinions. This includes such activities as daily distribution of weather reports, publication of the monthly Consumer Price Index, and dispensing of a vast quantity of technical information to consumers, farmers, businessmen, and others (e.g., every year the Department of Agriculture distributes 13 million copies of the *Home and Garden Bulletin*).[17] Many public relations workers spend their time answering questions about various government programs, publicizing new programs, and the like, and if their actions have an ulterior political motive, it is more than likely to be increasing the bureaucratic importance of their own positions than swaying general public opinion.

Nevertheless, along with such innocuous activities are overt efforts to

[15] In 1967 the Associated Press estimated that the Executive Branch spent 400 million a year on public relations and public information. This estimate, like similar estimates of government public relations, must be treated cautiously since many PR people are not classified as such and various activities with high PR value, e.g., televised space launchings, are not included. The amount of government money spent on public relations is further discussed in J. William Fulbright, *The Pentagon Propaganda Machine* (New York: Vintage Books, 1971), pp. 17-29; and David Wise, *The Politics of Lying: Government Deception, Secrecy and Power* (New York: Vintage Books, 1973), pp. 291-95.

[16] Fears of government propaganda probably go back to the founding of the Republic. In 1913 Congress enacted a law forbidding the hiring of "publicity experts" unless explicitly authorized by Congress. This restriction merely led to the use of titles such as "Director of Publications." These anti-public relations attempts and a history of early PR programs is described in James L. McCamey, *Government Publicity: Its Practice in Federal Administration* (Chicago: University of Chicago Press, 1939), especially pp. 6-20.

[17] Cited in Fulbright, *The Pentagon Propaganda Machine*, p. 19.

manipulate public opinion. Much of this manipulation effort is not aimed directly at the mass public, but instead at the mass media which then in turn (hopefully) will pass along the messages. Newspaper reporters, radio and TV stations, magazine editors and almost everyone else in a position to influence the public receives news releases, canned speeches and films, even complete news "stories" designed to put the activities of various government agencies in the best possible light. In recent years this process of image-building has even become automated—nine of eleven cabinet departments in 1972 had installed Spotmaster machines so that radio stations around the country could call in to hear prerecorded speeches that were "news."[18] On occasion the communications effort is far more direct. When the Department of Transportation in 1969 was advocating the Supersonic Transport, for example, it distributed 50,000 copies of the seventy-three page *Teacher's Guide for SST* which attempted to rally support for the SST by providing children with favorable stories about the SST involving such characters as "Supersonic Pussycat."[19] The result of these varying efforts is that the average citizen frequently receives news whose main purpose is to convince him or her of the government's accomplishments. News about the "wonder grains," the enormous benefits of the space program, the successes of conservation programs, the gratitude of starving people for gifts of U.S. wheat, and the like, are educational, to be sure, but such news also helps mold favorable dispositions toward existing policies.

One of the clearest, and perhaps also the most important, manifestation of government propaganda occurs in the area of military policy. Not only does the American military spend large amounts of money and time selling its virtues to the public, but the policy aims of this sales pitch are frequently very ambitious. The military's organizational investment and effort alone is most impressive. For example, the Defense Department runs something called the Defense Information School that has a ninety-three man faculty and graduates about 2,000 information specialists a year.[20] There is also the National Security Seminar conducted by the Industrial College of the Armed Forces that since 1948 has conducted two-week seminars for the general public on topics usually related to foreign affairs.[21] Each service also maintains a "home town news center," which reports information about the activities and accomplishments of local servicemen to hometown newspapers.[22] Within the Pentagon there is the Office of the Assistant Secretary for Public Affairs which, among other things maintains its own TV crews to cover events for commercial TV stations; offers high-ranking military officers and civilians as free speakers to groups (492 such speakers in fiscal year 1969); and maintains a magazine and book branch that serves as a

[18] Wise, *The Politics of Lying,* p. 305.
[19] Ibid., p. 306.
[20] Ibid., p. 266.
[21] Fulbright, *The Pentagon Propaganda Machine,* p. 40.
[22] Ibid., p. 28.

literary agent to find commercial outlets for material authored by military personnel.[23]

The output of these various organizations is prodigious. In 1969, for example, the Washington public relations office of the Navy distributed 1,136 news releases and 39,000 photographs to the news media, produced 49 news films and 51 one-minute TV news "featurettes," and assisted in 12 commercial films.[24] Not to be outdone, the U.S. Army in 1969 produced a series of thirty-minute color films about Army life and accomplishments called "The Big Picture," at a cost of $900,000. Though ostensibly produced for its own troops, these films were shown on 313 commercial and 53 educational TV stations (more than half of all U.S. TV stations). Ironically, these freely distributed films were used to fulfill the "public affairs" time required of the TV station by the Federal Communications Commission.[25] The U.S. Air Force, in addition to the usual barrage of news releases and films, also employed a "soft sell" with its weekly "Serenade in Blue" distributed to two-thirds of all AM and FM radio stations as well as a thirty-minute TV program with a Christmas theme sent to 204 stations.[26]

\The Armed Forces also attempts to influence public opinion through direct contact with citizens. This effort frequently entails "open houses" at military installations, marching bands in parades, travelling exhibits, and a variety of other programs⌋ The number of people exposed to these displays is considerable. For example, in fiscal year 1968, 770,000 people visited Navy ships as part of the Navy's "Open House" program; and over 6 million people saw the Blue Angels (the Navy's flying acrobatics team).[27] In the first six months of 1968, 13.5 million people viewed twenty-two Army exhibits at state fairs, military bases, shopping centers, and the like.[28] The greatest public relations effort is directed not at the average citizen, however, but at community leaders who can be more influential in the shaping of opinion. Typically, such efforts involve "VIP tours" of military installations (frequently in resort areas such as Hawaii), displays of weaponry, talks by military dignitaries, and wining and dining.[29] Needless to say, few citizens can avoid being impressed by the military after they have been flown 3,000 miles, given a guided tour of a gigantic aircraft carrier, witnessed a deafening display of fire-power, and treated like visiting royalty.

As an illustration of how the military establishment will sometimes use its vast resources to influence policy preferences, consider the Defense Department's attempt in 1968 to sell the Anti-Ballistic Missile (ABM) system to the

[23] Ibid., p. 33.
[24] Ibid., p. 55.
[25] Ibid., p. 70.
[26] Ibid., p. 26.
[27] Ibid., p. 56.
[28] Ibid., p. 77.
[29] Ibid., pp. 34-37.

public. According to Pentagon documents, this selling involved the following features. Newspapers and magazines would receive pictures of Sentinal missiles and previously unpublicized test-firings. Films of these tests would be distributed to TV stations. Editors, reporters and broadcasters would be invited to test sites to observe firings and would be given information useful for countering criticisms of the ABM. A complex, expensive scale model ABM installation would be put on display in communities selected as missile sites (local leaders, however, would receive direct visits from military personnel). All Senators and Representatives from affected areas would be given classified briefings on the ABM; and important, prestigious scientists would be recruited to support ABM. The Army would also assist in whatever way possible (including financial aid) the public relations of defense contractors involved in ABM. Finally, "Operation Understanding" would fly civic leaders to impressive military installations such as the underground headquarters of the North American Air Defense Command.[30] Though the ABM eventually was approved only on a very restricted scale, this failure cannot be attributed to a lack of public relations effort by the military.

The military also took an aggressive approach in portraying our involvement in Vietnam. During the height of the war, for example, the Pentagon maintained five TV news crews in Southeast Asia to cover events that were eventually shown over commercial television. These TV crews stressed the "other side" of the conflict, e.g., the Army's role in building hospitals and roads, as opposed to the belligerent images conveyed by network news crews.[31] When Vietnamization of the war became official U.S. policy, films were produced showing the newly developed skills of South Vietnamese in actual combat situations (at least some of these situations were completely faked). Meanwhile, according to an Army community relations report, in 1967 and estimated 1,000 speakers per month were giving talks to U.S. citizens about Vietnam. Many of these talks were standard speeches prepared by the Army for extensive use by numerous different speakers.[32] The Army in 1968 even had two traveling exhibits about Vietnam, which among other things, displayed captured weapons, gave a brief history of the war, and told about the Army's civic projects in the midst of the conflict.[33]

A third way besides the educational system and public relations by which government can shape public preferences is the use of the mass media, particularly television. Though we usually associate media usage with election campaigns, many national political leaders make extensive use of radio and television almost continuously. Indeed, Congress, the White House, and other governmental agencies maintain their own studies to facilitate such communica-

---

[30] Ibid., Chap. 1.
[31] Ibid., pp. 71-72.
[32] Ibid., pp. 79-84.
[33] Ibid., p. 77.

tions efforts. For example, between April and June of 1971 (a nonelection period), House members, through their own production facilities, made 1700 hours of radio recordings, 172 hours of videotape, and 12 hours of films.[34] These totals do not include the numerous appearances of Congressmen on TV news shows such as "Face the Nation" or appearances on evening news programs and the like. Moreover, on rare occasions Congress can virtually dominate radio and television when it allows live coverage of controversial investigations such as the McCarthy Army hearings or, more recently, the Senate Watergate Committee investigation and the subsequent impeachment hearings.

Far more prominent than Congressional efforts, however, is the President's use of the mass media. Although the total number of hours of congressional broadcasts and TV programs may equal presidential exposure, presidential appearances not only attract a vast national audience, but there is something about a presidential message—even if it is merely Season's Greetings from the White House—that makes it newsworthy and interesting. The President is also uniquely able to request and receive enormous quantities of free prime time radio and television coverage simultaneously on all three major networks. On several occasions in recent years Presidents have suddenly decided that they have something important to say to their fellow Americans and have been able to make their pitch for free to evening audiences of up to 70 million people. Network executives and viewers alike might prefer to see "All in the Family" instead, but neither group has any real choice in the matter.

The President can reach the average citizen through TV in quite diverse ways and each President devises yet new methods. For example, Eisenhower allowed television coverage of a rehearsed Cabinet meeting. Kennedy held news conferences on live TV and allowed an hour-long tour of the White House conducted by Jacqueline Kennedy. President Johnson initiated the practice of signing bills into law on camera while President Nixon sought public attention by appearing during the half-time of a college football game, making a telephone call to Neil Armstrong on the moon, and his traveling to Communist China. Such "special events" are in addition to the usual parade of formal speeches, interviews, and broadcast appearances with visiting dignitaries or war heroes.

Far more important than the quantity of contact with the public, however, is the President's control over his messages. Merely by appearing on radio or TV is no guarantee that a political leader will win over his or her listeners. Under certain circumstances, e.g., when interviewed by a hostile reporter or confronted by hecklers, leaders can be made to look foolish. Although public embarrassment might occur to the President occasionally, numerous ways exist to increase the likelihood of the media being used to increase the President's influence. In the first place, the President can pick the format that best suits his abilities. For

---

[34] Newton N. Minow, John Bartlow Martin and Lee M. Mitchell, *Presidential Television* (New York: Basic Books, Inc., 1973), p. 114.

example, Kennedy favored live news conferences which put his articulateness, vigor, intellectual alertness and wit on display (and this was helped by planting questions among newsmen). On the other hand, Nixon placed greater reliance on formal speeches or highly staged question and answer sessions.[35] In short, unlike other public officials, the President can usually show himself to the best advantage.

In addition, by virtue of his visibility and capacity to raise issues, the President's speeches can shape subsequent discussions of public issues. During the war in Vietnam the terms of the debate over our involvement were greatly influenced by the facts and arguments presented in Johnson's and Nixon's televised appearances. Recall, for instance, how Johnson's Gulf of Tonkin speech emphasized that American warships were attacked without provocation or warning and we must, therefore, respond militarily. Even Senators who viewed Vietnam from a very different perspective were overwhelmed in their attempt to reverse this "the-attack-has-begun-rally-around-the-flag" atmosphere. Particularly when information is scarce and opposing versions of the truth are not presented simultaneously, the President's reporting of facts can put his opponents at a serious disadvantage.[36]

The President's advantage due to his access to the mass media is reinforced by the inability of those disagreeing with him to respond equally. Though the Federal Communications Commission requires "equal time" to opponents where news media provide only one side of an issue, this doctrine has not been interpreted to give those opposing the President equal access to free radio and television time. Specifically, the "equal time" provision has been construed as giving equal time to ideas, not groups, so as long as arguments against the President's position are offered in some form or shape, "equal time" is satisfied. This allows the President's pronouncements to go largely unchallenged. This situation is well illustrated by other public officials' inability to challenge the President's televised proclamations on Vietnam. For example, a day after Senators McGovern and Hatfield introduced legislation to end U.S. involvement, Nixon gave a three-network, prime-time address in favor of continued involvement. The next day McGovern asked the networks either to give him free time or to sell him time to offer counter proposals. Two networks refused altogether and the third (NBC) offered a half an hour for $60,000 cash in advance. McGovern took the offer and for his money reached 9.1 percent of the television audience compared with 50 percent usually reached by the President.[37]

The frustration of McGovern is by no means an isolated example. During the antiwar demonstrations of late 1969 and early 1970, Nixon preempted

[35] Ibid., pp. 40,54.
[36] Ibid., p. 61.
[37] Ibid., p. 118.

prime-time television seven times to defend his policies (in one of his speeches Nixon reached 72 million people).[38] Despite complaints, threats of lawsuits, and the like, efforts to offer well-publicized alternatives to presidential pronouncements on "silent majorities," "light at the end of the tunnel," and the dubious patriotism of those opposing the war came to little. Similar frustrations occurred when Nixon on several occasions used television to criticize Congress for its inaction or for the passage of inflationary legislation. Neither a specially created program called "The Loyal Opposition" nor appearances on regular news programs could provide Nixon's opponents with opportunities comparable in audience to a "special message from the President of the United States" during prime time.[39] In short, thanks to his position and access to TV and radio the President occupies what has been described as the "Bully Pulpit."

GOVERNMENT-INFLUENCED OPINION CHANGE

Our preceding analysis highlights some of the government's massive efforts to affect public opinion. While it is probably true that at least some of this effort has had the desired impact, it is very difficult to show precisely how much any *particular* public relations program or presidential speech influences public opinion. If, for example, the Pentagon were prohibited from engaging in propaganda programs such as "Operation Understanding," would a public clamor arise to cut defense spending by 50 percent? Do televised presidential addresses really persuade or do they merely reach persons already convinced? To evaluate the government's success in influencing opinion change, we shall examine two types of data. First, we shall consider the changes in public opinion brought about by televised Presidential endorsements of certain policies. Is it true that the President can mobilize instant majorities merely by taking his message directly to the people? Second, we shall consider whether the President can change people's policy preferences merely by associating his name with certain positions.

Table 10-1 presents before and after opinion polls on subjects that were discussed on television by the President. Examining the differences in opinion before and after televised speeches is only an approximate measure of presidential influence. At least some citizens surveyed after the presidential address may have changed their minds independently of presidential prompting. These poll results also suffer from the problem of not distinguishing among those who saw the program (or heard about it) from those oblivious to the presidential message. Since many—if not most—Americans did not actually see the address, an analysis of opinion shifts among the entire population probably

[38] Ibid., p. 60.
[39] Ibid., p. 118.

Table 10-1 Public Opinion on Policy Before and After Presidential
Pronouncements on Television

Date	Presidential Action	Poll Results	
July 26, 1963	Kennedy announces nuclear test ban treaty	Before:	73 percent favored
		After:	81 percent favored
Aug., 18, 1963	Kennedy appeals for tax cut from Congress	Before:	62 percent favored
		After:	66 percent favored
May 2, 1965	Johnson tells of Gulf of Tonkin incident and explains his Vietnam policy	Before:	42 percent positive on LBJ Vietnam policy
		After:	72 percent positive on LBJ Vietnam policy
Jan. 31, 1966	Johnson announces resumption of bombing of N. Vietnam	Before:	61 percent favored bombing resumption
		After:	73 percent favored bombing resumption
March, 1968	Johnson announces end to bombing of N. Vietnam	Before:	40 percent favored
		After:	64 percent favored
June 7, 1968	Johnson endorses stronger gun control legislation	Before:	71 percent favored
		After:	81 percent favored
May 14, 1969	Nixon announces phased troop withdrawals from Vietnam	Before:	49 percent favored phased withdrawals
		After:	67 percent favored phased withdrawals
April 30, 1970	Nixon announces invasion of Cambodia	Before:	7 percent favored invasion of Cambodia
		After:	50 percent favored invasion of Cambodia
June 1971	Nixon announces 90 day price and wages freeze	Before:	50 percent approved of "freeze"
		After:	68 percent approved of "freeze"

SOURCE: "Public Service Time for the Legislative Branch," Hearings Before the Communications Subcommittee of the Committee on Commerce, 91st Congress, second session, pp. 20-21. June 1971 data are reported in *Gallup Opinion Index,* August, 1971.

minimizes the importance of TV addresses. Many of these shifts would undoubtedly have been larger if everyone had watched.

Second, the "before-after" approach does not register the longterm presidential efforts to make very unpopular policies more "reasonable" by letting it be known that he is "considering" such policies as one of a number of possible alternatives. This is well illustrated by President Ford's handling of the amnesty issue. Since amnesty for those refusing induction into the army was first broached by antiwar activists, it was overwhelmingly rejected by the public. However, in August and September of 1974 the fact that Ford was seriously considering some form of conditional amnesty was widely publicized. Public opinions on some form of amnesty also became more supportive—from 45 percent in favor during January to 56 percent in favor during September of 1974.[40] Ford's subsequent announcement of conditional amnesty was thus

[40] Louis Harris news release reported in the *Ithaca Journal,* September 17, 1974.

consistent with a majority of public opinion, a majority created in part by Ford himself. No doubt many other similar incidents could be found where presidents "softened up" public opposition to unpopular policies by letting it be known that such policies were "possible."

Even with these reservations in mind, the data in Table 10-1 suggest a considerable net impact on public opinion by presidential addresses. In none of the nine cases did the President lose support by taking his case directly to the people. More important, in five instances the President's advocacy of a minority position helped to convert that position into the majority position. This shift is perhaps most dramatic in Nixon's announcement of the U.S. invasion of Cambodia, where support jumped 43 percentage points, but increases of 15 percentage points or more also occur in the other four majority creation cases. We are thus faced with the perplexing situation that in five policy areas the President acted without initial majority support, but thanks to TV broadcasts, it could not be said that these policies conflicted with public opinion. Observe that the "failures" at creating a majority on other issues all occur because of the prior existence of a majority favoring the President's position. Hence, we can say that at least on these issues whenever a minority could be transformed into a majority, it occurred.

The importance of a presidential endorsement, even where the message is not conveyed by radio or television, is confirmed by other studies. In 1941, for example, the Gallup Poll asked several questions about U.S. involvement in World War II and in some instances President Roosevelt's name was associated with a proposal and in other cases just the "United States" was used. When asked whether President Roosevelt had gone too far in helping Britain, 57 percent said that his behavior was "about right"; when the "United States" was substituted for President Roosevelt, approval dropped to 46 percent. Similarly, a Roosevelt proposal to keep the Germans out of Africa received greater support than the same proposal without the President's name.[41] More recently, Corey Rosen reports that when citizens were asked their opinion on a hypothetical Family Assistance Plan, 48 percent favored it, 40 percent opposed it, and 12 percent did not know. However, when President Nixon's name was associated with this plan, support increased by two percentage points and opposition declined by 14 percentage points. However, among the minority actually familiar with the Family Assistance Plan, the linking of Nixon to this proposal produced a 12 percent drop in support. This suggests that the President can sometimes serve as a negative cue.[42]

Though we have occasionally employed the term "manipulation" to describe opinion change due to presidential communications, it is clear that such communications need not be a result of "evil" motives. Indeed, in a large

[41]Reported in Hadley Cantril, *Gauging Public Opinion* (Princeton: Princeton University Press, 1944), pp. 39-40.

[42] Corey M. Rosen, "A Test of Presidential Leadership of Public Opinion: The Split-Ballot Technique," *Polity* 6 (1973): 282-90.

proportion of these instances the president communicates directly with citizens because he wants people to better understand his actions and policies. If the President did *not* publicly associate himself with administration policy, he would undoubtedly be accused of shrouding himself in secrecy and shirking his responsibilities as a national leader. Hence, a certain degree of public opinion "manipulation" is probably inherent in the office regardless of the intentions of a particular office holder. Since the alternative would be a virtual silencing of the President, perhaps a certain degree of "manipulation" is tolerable.

LIMITS IN GOVERNMENT'S INFLUENCE
ON PUBLIC OPINION

The preceding analyses might give the impression that the United States government can readily create the opinion it wants. If, for example, the United States and the Soviet Union should agree to carve up the rest of the world, the schools, government agencies, and the presidency would all be mobilized to convince the public of this decision. School children would suddenly find themselves learning about "nice Ivan, the good communist"; television and radio programs would spontaneously appear showing the benefits of U.S.-Soviet agricultural exchanges; and prime-time television would carry an "historic first"—direct line satellite transmission of the President of the United States personally addressing the Central Committee of the Communist Party (and the speech receiving wild applause). Does the government possess such manipulative capacity? Would such efforts be effective?

In the first place, our previous analysis of early political socialization suggests that certain basic features of American politics are deeply ingrained among citizens. Thus, attempts to convince Americans of, say, the virtues of monarchy are unlikely to be very successful regardless of the amount of effort expended. True, citizen preferences for existing political arrangements are reinforced at government expense, but not every government political educational effort would be equally successful. Unfortunately, because leaders share most (if not all) these basic political attachments, examples of government attempts to manipulate public opinion on basic issues are rare. Perhaps the closest attempt at such influence was President Roosevelt's well publicized attempt to increase the size of the Supreme Court in order to weaken its conservative majority. Despite Roosevelt's public relations effort, public support for this "constitutional tinkering" could not be mobilized and in fact declined in the face of presidential appeals.[43]

---

[43] See Frank V. Cantwell, "Public Opinion and Legislative Power," *American Political Science Review* 40 (1946): 924-35. Actually, public support in favor of enlarging the Court rose after two nationally carried Roosevelt speeches, but the President was never able to turn this support into a clear majority. Cantwell suggests that part of the reason for this was the willingness of the Court to give in to Roosevelt as well as vocal opposition in the Senate.

A second reason why the government's capacity to influence public opinion is limited concerns divisions within government itself. To be sure, the flow of government public relations by no means gives equal weight to all policy alternatives, but rarely does the government speak with a completely unified voice. Such diversity in part results from competition within government for particular programs. For example, though all three branches of the Armed Forces work towards creating promilitary sentiments, competition for defense dollars sometimes leads one branch to direct its public relations apparatus against the other branches. During the debate over the building of additional aircraft carriers, the Navy's VIP tours of carriers, seapower seminars and the like were countered by the Air Force's well-publicized "demonstrations" of how bombers could neutralize "enemy" naval strikes. A similar intraservice public relations battle occurred in the mid-1950s over the merits of Army and Air Force missile systems.

This type of rivalry is also found in Presidential-Congressional relations. As we have previously seen, Congress is rarely an equal match for a Presidential public relations effort, but on occasion it can destroy a President's attempt to speak solely for the "government." Recall that as the Vietnam War became increasingly unpopular, the outspoken antiwar activities of Senators Fulbright, Morse, McGovern, Hatfield, Church and others at least legitimized opposition to Presidents Johnson and Nixon. Bureaucrats in competing agencies can provide information to friendly reporters and newscasters that can undermine the public credibility of top officials. No doubt any President who entertains the thought of hoodwinking the American public with contrived information must consider the very real possibility that unsympathetic subordinates will "leak" contrary information. In short, the existence of decentralized political power, fragmented decision-making, and an absence of complete executive control over subordinates hinders a thoroughly concerted propaganda effort.

Closely related to the lack of government unanimity is the existence of various "watchdogs" who can be counted upon to hinder government public relations efforts. Perhaps the most conspicuous of these is the press, but various private foundations, research organizations, lobbyist groups and even a few individuals, e.g., Ralph Nader, devote considerable time and energy unmasking what they consider to be government attempts to fool the public. The work of such people can occasionally be devastating to the government's public image. For example, much of the government's rhetoric about peaceful motives and efforts to end our involvement in Vietnam was undermined by newspaper publications of the so-called Pentagon Papers. Even more damaging was the exposé of government corruption and abuse of power that came out of the Watergate incident. Less spectacular, but still quite important, have been other revealing and well publicized analyses of enormous cost overruns on military hardware, mismanaged conservation programs, and covert U.S. involvement in the overthrow of foreign governments, and many more political embarrassments.

Such exposés do not, of course, completely inhibit public officials from trying to shape public opinion, but they undoubtedly help minimize such efforts and provide some antidote to the image of government infallibility.

A fourth factor limiting government's manipulative capacity is that on some occasions the public standing of leaders may be quite low. Our analysis of political socialization showed that citizens early in life acquire a deep respect for political authority and this learning provides leaders with a reservoir of positive popular support. However, as we have seen, with age these positive feelings are transferred from the individual who happens to occupy the office (e.g., President X, Senator Y) to the office itself (e.g., the presidency, the Senate). The significance of this change is that a citizen can have very negative feelings towards a political leader while still maintaining an enduring respect for the institutional position. And as the history of Gallup poll ratings of political leaders has demonstrated, Americans frequently give their leaders' performance poor marks.[44]

That leaders are sometimes viewed negatively is important for, as considerable communications research has demonstrated, one of the major factors affecting opinion change is the credibility of the message sender.[45]   Thus, if leaders habitually make mistakes, are involved in scandals, appear to be unable to cope with various problems, or just project a poor public image, their capacity to bring about opinion change will be curtailed. Indeed, if their image becomes very bad, their support for a policy or even mere statement of fact might generate a negative reaction. Recall that at one point President Johnson's popularity and credibility were so low that had he publicly announced that the earth is round, at least some citizens would have assumed that it must be flat. By the same token, President Nixon's repeated denials of guilt in the Watergate coverup reduced his overall believability to the point where almost anything he said was suspect.

A fifth general limiting factor on government manipulation of public opinion is political apathy. It is customary to decry citizen apathy and to assert that such indifference is dangerous to "democracy." Nevertheless, it is clear that avoiding political communications makes it difficult—though not impossible—to be seduced by presidential addresses, contrived news events and the like.[46]   In a

---

[44] These figures are described and analyzed in John E. Mueller, "Presidential Popularity from Truman to Johnson," *American Political Science Review* 64 (1970): 18-34.

[45] See, for example, Carl I. Hovland and Walter Weiss, "The Influence of Source Credibility on Communications Effectiveness," *Public Opinion Quarterly* 15 (1952): 635-50.

[46] Some evidence on this point is offered in Philip E. Converse, "Information Flow and the Stability of Partisan Attitudes," *Public Opinion Quarterly* 26 (1962): 578-99. However, it is plausible that even those insulated from the effects of the media may be affected "second-hand" though friends and family members who have been exposed to media. See Elihu Katz, "The Two-Step Flow of Communications: An Up-to-Date Report on Hypothesis," *Public Opinion Quarterly* 21 (1957): 62-78.

sense, the availability and attractiveness of "I Love Lucy" re-runs, sports news, and pulp romance magazines insulate at least part of the American public from being won over by official propaganda. Perhaps for this reason support for continued American involvement in Vietnam was stronger among those citizens most in touch with "current events" as transmitted by the media.[47] While the well-informed who were busy reading about "the light at the end of the tunnel," "the President's secret plan," and so forth, tended to support our involvement; the less well educated (perhaps more concerned with the exploits of Joe Namath than General Westmoreland), were far more dubious about our involvement.

A sixth bulwark against manipulation is the extent to which some preferences are very important to citizens. Recall that many of the instances of presidentially induced opinion shifts depicted in Table 10-1 were on matters of little personal relevance for most citizens, e.g., the invasion of Cambodia, bombing halts, or in the case of the wage and price freeze, a policy whose impact was still unknown. Numerous studies of opinion change indicate that these sort of issues, i.e., issues that are personally irrelevant or ambiguous, are where opinion change is most likely.[48] Where individuals have a considerable personal stake in an issue, e.g., one's income or neighborhood racial composition, opinions are less susceptible to change. To be sure, as indicated in Chapter 3, most policies are not perceived as being highly relevant personally, so the opportunities for manipulation are extensive. Nevertheless, the minority of policy areas in which opinions tend to be deeply rooted are among the most important politically, including policies with a clear economic or personal impact on people's lives, e.g., tax rates, racial integration, and religious affiliation.

An excellent illustration of the limits of massive government public relations efforts when confronted with deeply held preferences is provided by recent government efforts to cut energy consumption. Scarcely a tool in the government PR arsenal was left unemployed: the President gave impassioned public speeches; films and pamphlets were widely distributed; and various conservation programs were publicized. However, despite some limited initial success, few Americans were convinced by the government's message that changes in lifestyle were essential. Not that Americans by and large found this government effort unbelievable; rather it was insufficiently convincing given strong opposing preferences.

---

[47] Sidney Verba et al., "Public Opinion and the War in Vietnam," *American Political Science Review* 61 (1967): 326-27. Similar evidence is presented in William A. Gamson and Andre Modigliani, "Knowledge and Foreign Policy Opinion," *Public Opinion Quarterly* 30 (1966): 187-99.

[48] Among others, see Carl I. Hovland, O.J. Harvey, and Muzafer Sharif, "Assimilation and Contrast Effects in Reactions to Communications and Attitude Changes," *Journal of Abnormal and Social Psychology* 55 (1957): 244-52; and more generally, Joseph T. Klapper, *The Effects of Mass Communications* (New York: The Free Press, 1960), pp. 45-47.

The last factor that we shall consider that inhibits government manipulation is the distortion of messages. It is well known from the study of communications that only rarely are messages perfectly comprehended.[49] A variety of processes can conspire to garble a message—listeners can selectively perceive a message, communications can be distorted by "reading in" unintended meanings, and one's memory of the message may be very selective. Equally important, people tend to seek out messages they already agree with, so it may be very difficult to reach citizens who "need" to be convinced (and even if these citizens are reached, their resistance has to be overcome). Thus, even if a communicator does produce attitude change, there is no guarantee that the results will be the intended ones.

The consequence of these research findings are clear. Even the most carefully planned TV speech by the President may be unsuccessful unless the message is so simple and unambiguous that even a half-asleep ten year old can comprehend it. Even then, opinion changes will be fewer than hoped for since many potential converts will avoid the broadcast entirely. The same kinds of problems exist for less prominent government influence attempts. To appreciate how garbled political messages can become we only have to recall George McGovern's ill-fated 1972 election proposal guaranteeing everyone a $1,000 annual income. Despite McGovern's repeated attempts to explain what he meant, widespread distortion of this proposal was very common. Such communications problems force communicators to keep their messages simple and limited to unambiguous topics. Thus, even if no distortion occurs, the possibility of selective perception and distortion places limits on potential manipulative efforts.

GOVERNMENT MANIPULATION EFFORTS:
A CONCLUSION

Though we have seen that the government's attempt to create certain policy preferences involves an enormous allocation of resources, and that under certain conditions the government appears to be successful in these efforts, we still cannot say precisely how much opinion-policy congruity is caused by communications flowing from government to citizen. Certainly at least *some* congruence, particularly on basic political preferences acquired early in life, is a result of government action, though such action generally serves to reinforce, not change preferences. It is also probably true that all the highly positive

---

[49] Research on the distortion of communication is discussed in further detail in Klapper, *The Effects of Mass Communications,* pp. 18-26. An interesting illustration of how well-known presidential messages get interpreted: consider the meaning of John F. Kennedy's "Ask Not What Your Country Can Do For You, But What You Can Do For Your Country." This slogan has been widely interpreted as an idealistic commitment to public life. However, if someone like George Wallace had said the same thing, many of Wallace's liberal critics would have this as a fascistic slogan putting the needs of the state ahead of individual values.

government public relations activities contribute to a citizenry willing to "go along" with many existing policies, e.g., continued investment in expensive military hardware. Furthermore, we have already seen that Presidential addresses on television can generate instant support for certain policies. Nevertheless, it is equally obvious that citizen opinions are not completely malleable in the hands of manipulative leaders. Many factors ranging from early political learning to apathy insulate citizens from government propaganda. Government propaganda increases opinion-policy congruity but is far from successful in bringing about a complete harmony between citizen demands and government action.

OPINION-POLICY LINKAGES: A CONCLUSION

In light of our analyses of elections, belief sharing among leaders and nonleaders, and government manipulation of public opinion, what can we say about the opinion-policy relationships depicted in Chapters 6 and 7? One such conclusion is perfectly clear—no one of these three mechanisms is capable of promoting close opinion-policy congruence on a wide variety of issues over long periods of time. Elections, common socialization, and government public relations programs are limited and sometimes unreliable tools for precisely aligning mass public opinion with government policy. It is not that these mechanisms are useless—in fact we shall argue just the opposite—rather, on fairly specific questions such as government involvement in medical care, the death penalty, and trading with communist nations, these mechanisms are usually too clumsy. Recall from our analysis of elections, for example, that elections are better suited to barring grossly objectionable types from public office than selecting candidates who will implement a public mandate. Thus, it should not be too surprising that on so many of these specific issues, opinion and policy appear to be largely independent of each other.

Nevertheless, by no means are these mechanisms politically unimportant. On several occasions we have argued that while these mechanisms are inappropriate for achieving congruence on detailed issues, they are crucial for establishing the range of opinion-policy relationships. Take as an illustration policy on government intervention in school desegregation. It is unlikely that any of the three mechanisms we have considered could bring about precise opinion-policy congruence (assuming, of course, that a coherent and feasible public preference existed). However, all these linkage mechanisms probably narrow down both public demands and government responses to a point where almost any publicly considered policy will be at least tolerable (though not preferred) for most people. Thanks to the electoral process, shared preferences and government propaganda, most citizens do not have to worry about waking up one morning to discover that their government has undertaken to, say, physically force blacks to act more like whites or equally bizarre actions. And, by the same token, government officials can rest assured that the slightest violation of public demands will not result in an outraged mob calling for an overthrow of the government. Such might not be the case if, for example, leaders were imported from a radically different culture, did not have to pass any form of public scrutiny, and had no opportunity to marshall public support for their programs before such programs were announced.

Of course, the rejoinder to this reasoning is that linkages this broad are really not mechanisms that *control* the relationship between opinion and policy. They are much closer to the broad political and cultural context in which linkages can operate, but cannot themselves be viewed as part of the normal political process. In a sense, so long as people respect their leaders, and leaders come from the same general environment as nonleaders, and leaders must pass a minimum of public scrutiny, and so on, such broad linkages cannot help but exist. Therefore, to demonstrate their existence is not to show very much. It is probably true that every political system—from the most democratic to the most totalitarian—exhibits a high level of very general opinion-policy congruence due to these mechanisms.

This rejoinder is plausible, obviously, but it is an attack on the use of the word "linkage" to describe certain situations, not a denial of the previous arguments. Thus, whether or not we use terms like "linkage," the fact remains that when we talk about mechanisms affecting the relationship between opinion and policy, we are talking about mechanisms that affect *ranges* of relationships, not specific instances of congruity or incongruity. Because extremely objectionable alternatives are rarely part of the debate over public policy, this narrowing down of choices may appear unimportant, but without the linkages we have described, politics would probably be chaotic, violent, and highly divisive. Just imagine a discussion of racial integration were the range of viable alternatives to include genocide, mass deportation, forced intermarriage, and other choices completely intolerable to large numbers of citizens.

chapter eleven

CONCLUSION: PUBLIC OPINION AND PUBLIC POLICY CONGRUENCE

This book began by observing that the role of public opinion in government is both much praised and damned, yet relatively little is known about this relationship. To be sure, thanks to modern survey analysis, the opinions of average citizens have been regularly reported, and at the same time there has rarely been a dearth of information on what leaders are up to (though there is still much that is unknown), but the connection between the two has rarely been self-evident. In the space of over two hundred pages of clarifications, distinctions, and a plethora of opinion and policy data, have we come any closer to making an informed statement about the relationship between opinion and policy in the United States? Or are we still no better off than the analysts issuing pronouncements and speculations in the days before scientific opinion polls?

A perfectly safe and reasonable answer to this basic question is: Depending on the topic and the time period, opinion-policy congruence does occur; however, widespread instances of incongruity can also be found. For instance, on the subject of Communist China's admission to the United Nations the preferences of a majority were in accord with government action for a period of twenty years. On the other hand, perfect *in*congruity is displayed in the area of religious observances in public schools. Between these two extremes we find almost every conceivable type of relationship. In some policies, e.g., capital punishment for murder, opinion-policy congruence occurs in some years, but not in others. A more complex situation prevails for policies such as defense spending where according to one policy indicator congruence exists but another indicator gives a different picture. If we recall from our discussion in Chapter 5 that what we mean when we say "policy is in accord with public opinion" is far from obvious, judgments on the extent of congruence become further complicated.

It is certainly fair to ask whether this imprecise (though reasonable) answer is the best we can do. Probably yes. In the first place, it is unlikely that consideration of still more policies, or the same policies in different time periods, will provide a sharper picture of the overall pattern of opinion-policy congruence. Even if complete opinion and policy data were available for every major issue in the last fifty years, most cases would probably follow the common pattern of some degree of congruity, some evidence of incongruity, and much that remains ambiguous. Moreover, merely laying out all the data hardly solves some of the important conceptual problems whose solution must precede an answer to the question of how much congruence exists. Thus, two reasonable people can examine the identical data and reach opposite conclusions if they differ on what they mean precisely by "public," "opinion," "policy," and so on. Should terms be agreed upon, disagreement would no doubt arise over issues like just how closely policy has to follow opinion to constitute "close" agreement.

This "sometimes yes, sometimes no, largely mixed" type of response is not, of course, the only answer we can offer. The whole problem can be approached quite differently. For example, if we focus only on very broad policies that are usually not part of the daily political struggle (e.g., the constitutional order, national sovereignty, capitalism, the social status hierarchy) and also conceive of public opinion as mass acquiescence to standing decisions about the political and social order, then clearly opinion-policy congruence is the rule. Such an argument claims that so long as citizens get what they want on the "basic" issues, disagreement with some of the specific details of policies within these limits are largely trivial. Furthermore, the verification of this argument hardly needs much data; that few Americans demand substantial changes in these "basic" policies is all the evidence needed to reach the conclusion of extensive congruence. From this perspective, our entire analysis could be characterized as an exercise in political nit picking.

At the same time, it is equally plausible to maintain that given the state of mass political thinking and the paucity of mechanisms for precisely controlling leaders, any evidence of opinion-policy concordance is probably a result of accidental factors. That is, given enough polls and policy outcomes, by chance alone the government would sometimes do what the people prefer, so the results described in Chapters 6 and 7 could very well be obtained by randomly picking poll results and policies from a hat. Thus, analysis should have ceased with Chapter 3 since it was clearly shown that much of "the voice of the people" was barely (if at all) intelligible on most issues. The use of such data in conjunction with policy, then, is a meaningless exercise. Indeed, such a conclusion hardly needs the vast quantity of survey data presented in Chapter 3; opinion analysts like Walter Lippmann have reached similar conclusions based only on their personal observations and conversations.[1]

---

[1] Walter Lippmann, *Essays in the Public Philosophy* (Boston: Little, Brown and Company, 1955), Chap. 1.

The question of "how much opinion-policy congruence exists" can be approached from yet other perspectives. Recall from our discussion in Chapter 2 that it is possible to speak of different issue publics, not a single public. Conceivably, congruence might exist on an issue public by issue public basis without necessarily existing at a general level. Perhaps the most forceful version of this argument is that there exists a small, well-informed segment of the public that follows policy and if congruence exists, it is congruence with the preference of this group. This "attentive public," as it is usually called, not only possesses well formulated preferences, but also occupies visible and important positions in society and is thus more likely to count among political decision-makers.[2]

What evidence exists that congruence occurs between policy and the opinions of the attentive public and not the opinions of the general public? The most systematic analysis of the question was conducted by Donald Devine who examined attentive and nonattentive policy preferences over time in seven issue areas.[3] In some policy areas Devine finds that no positive government action occurred until at least a majority of the attentive public supported the policy.[4] In other policy areas the preferences of the attentive public more closely corresponds to policy than the preferences of the general public though by no means does the nonattentive public completely lose on these issues.[5] However, on the whole the evidence presented by Devine does not clearly support the contention that the attentive public consistently gets the policies it wants and prevents the enactment of policies it opposes. Only on one or two of the seven policy areas can it be said that the attentive public does noticeably better than the general public; much more common are patterns that clearly resemble our own results of mixed, ambiguous opinion-policy congruence.

[2] Various versions of the "attentive public" formulation appear in Gabriel Almond, *The American People and Foreign Policy* (New York: Frederick A. Praeger, 1960), Chap. 7; James N. Rosenau, *Public Opinion and Foreign Policy* (New York: Random House, 1961), Chap. 4; and V. O. Key, Jr., *Public Opinion and American Democracy* (New York: Alfred A. Knopf, 1961), Chap. 21.

[3] Donald J. Devine, *The Attentive Public: Polyarchial Democracy* (Chicago: Rand McNally and Company, 1970), Chap. 5. The seven policy areas were: foreign aid, government subsidized medical care, federal care, federal aid to education, federal enforcement of black civil rights, federal government involvement in school racial integration, "toughness" of American foreign policy, and allocation of resources to private vs. public sectors of the economy.

[4] These are the issue areas of government involvement in medical care and federal intervention in school racial integration. It should be noted, however, that Devine's policy indicators in both these areas consist solely of Congressional votes, and thus his analysis and conclusions are not comparable to ours.

[5] These were: foreign aid, black civil rights, and foreign policy. Though Devine makes some strong claims (pp. 91-92) for the argument that policy more closely follows attentive, rather than nonattentive preferences, close inspection of the data shows these claims to be weaker than implied. For example, in the case of foreign aid expenditures (pp. 78-79), Devine concludes that the opinion patterns of the attentive public gives a better "fit" with policy data, yet the differences between the attentive and non-attentive opinion patterns derives from a difference of about 10 percentage points in one of four time points. In the area of black civil rights the average difference between the two publics is 2.6 percent and this is for five time periods (the largest difference is 4.5 percent).

A different focus on the possibility of opinion-policy congruence also making use of the "issue public" concept emphasizes discrete issue publics. That is, while the argument advanced by Devine conceived of two "publics" (attentive and nonattentive), it is also plausible that since not everyone is equally interested in all issues, the relevant unit of analysis in considering congruence is those people interested in a particular policy. For example, if some people are interested in environmental pollution but not tax reform, the lack of congruity on tax policy for such people might be irrelevant so long as antipollution preferences were satisfied. On the other hand, those interested in the tax issue might find the same set of policies intolerable. Hence, given the likelihood of issue publics being less than a majority of all citizens, it is possible for a majority of each public to be satisfied while incongruity exists more generally.

A satisfactory test of the possibility would mean subdividing surveys into discrete groups of people sharing the same major concerns. However, as we clearly saw in Chapter 8 when we considered whether citizens possessed policy preferences, many "issue publics" are too small to be considered in the average sample survey. This means that only a few of the many issue publics can be considered. Thus, our analysis must be more of an illustration than an adequate test. Nevertheless, we shall consider two issues that were among the most important politically in 1968—civil rights and the war in Vietnam. If this version of the issue public argument is correct, we should find greater opinion-policy congruence among those interested in these issues compared to those not interested.

Table 11-1 compares those considering black civil rights an important national problem with those who do not according to their "successes" in having their preferences on civil rights issues enacted into policy. On the whole, the rate of policy success varies only slightly and unsystematically according to interest in civil rights. While the civil rights issue public is slightly more likely to show

Table 11-1 Interest in Civil Rights Issues and "Success" on Civil Rights Issues,* 1968

Agreement Between Own Opinion and Policy		Considers Civil Rights Very Important Problem	Does Not Consider Civil Rights Important Problem
Low	1	29.6%	36.2
	2	13.9	11.8
	3	8.3	6.0
	4	11.3	12.4
High	5	36.8	33.6
		99.9%	100.0%
	N =	503	1054

*Three issues were used to construct the agreement scale: federal government intervention in school desegregation, federal intervention for blacks in public accomodation, and federal government action to combat racial discrimination in employment. Support for each of these policies was scored on a "success" and individual position on this "success" scale, based on the proportion of "successes."
SOURCE: Survey Research Center, University of Michigan.

the most congruence (a score of "5"), this segment of the general public is probably as satisfied (or dissatisfied) with policy as the noninterested public. A similar conclusion can be reached when examining Table 11-2 which depicts preferences on Vietnam according to interest in this policy. Majorities of neither group endorsed the then current Vietnam policy of keeping soldiers in Vietnam while trying to reduce the fighting. If there is a difference between the concerned and the unconcerned public, it is that the Vietnam issue public was slightly more dovish and in 1968 the "complete withdrawal" was far from a public policy.

In short, though our analyses of both these versions of the "issue public" approach to opinion-policy congruence has been limited, they do not suggest that our conclusion on "how much congruence" will be substantially altered if we focused on smaller segments of the general public. This is not to say that the attentive public or specialized issue publics are no more important politically than the general population. Clearly, the opinions of at least some portions of the public are better satisfied than others (though it is difficult to say precisely which portions). However, acknowledging this differential amount of influence is not equivalent to saying that there are readily discernible patterns of opinion-policy congruence at the issue public level.

It is obvious that in terms of "hard," scientifically verified knowledge we are perhaps no closer to a definitive answer on opinion-policy congruence than we were at the beginning. This is not to say that we have not expanded our understanding of opinion and public policy. Certainly our knowledge about the state of American opinion, governmental activities, methods of controlling public policy, and various meanings of terms has increased substantially. Perhaps we can characterize our present state of knowledge as "well-informed ignorance." Whereas previously an answer to the question of "How much congruence" would have received a brief and probably vague response, now we can wax eloquently at length on the subject though in the end our answer is probably no more final than before. Perhaps our answer to the question of "How much congruence" should be—It's all very complicated and confused, so don't bother asking.

Table 11-2   Interest in Vietnam and "Success" on Vietnam Issue, 1968

Position on Vietnam	Considers Vietnam Important	Does Not Consider Vietnam Important
Pull out entirely	23.8%	17.0%
Keep soldiers there but try to stop fighting	40.6	41.5
Stronger military effort	35.6	41.5
	100.0%	100.0%
N =	1063	494

SOURCE: Survey Research Center, University of Michigan.

If our answer to the question of "How much congruence" is inconclusive, can we at least offer meaningful answers to other important questions relating to opinion and policy? One such question that we have touched on in a variety of contexts is the problem of making policy more in accord with popular desires. Leaving the knotty, conceptual problems aside for the moment, can we offer some informed advice to those interested in furthering opinion-policy congruence? Our answer is "yes," but none of the suggestions we can offer will be readily implemented. Indeed, much of our advice consists merely of identifying the problem areas since existing solutions appear to be of only slight help.

Consider, for example, the political capabilities of most American citizens. The average citizen is far from a bumbling political buffoon, but as we have demonstrated on numerous occasions, a substantial gap exists between present levels of political sophistication and the capacity necessary to offer intelligible preferences and hold leaders to these choices. Even officials who seek to follow the public will are frequently perplexed at what to do, and those who ignore it (at least on some issues) do not suffer at the hands of irate citizens. Increasing opinion-policy congruence would certainly entail changes in citizen political capacity, yet attempts to "improve" citizenship through education, public information campaigns, "educational" public broadcasting, and various other schemes has yielded sparse results.[6] Moreover, given almost universal literacy and mass media saturation, the likelihood of some type of breakthrough in citizen political competence is small. It is quite reasonable to suppose that if congruence is to be increased, it must be done with only limited changes in the quality of public thinking.

If people cannot be remolded, what about the institutional structures that affect the formulation and content of policy? Here we encounter an interesting paradox. We argued in Chapter 4 that the American constitutional system can be characterized as a "stacked deck" against the accurate translation of popular preferences into policy. Both constitutional history and present institutional structures strongly suggest that governing in accord with pressing mass desires has been a relatively low political priority for leaders. But it is also fair to say that the existing political order enjoys considerable popular support. Though no precise poll data exist on the subject, few citizens would want, for instance, to abolish a bicameral legislature because it potentially impedes the popular will.[7]

[6] Perhaps the most systematic analysis of the difficulty of "enlightening" citizens in political matters is presented in Kenneth P. Langton and M. Kent Jennings, "Political Socialization and the High School Civics Curriculum in the United States," *American Political Science Review* 62 (1968): 852-67.

[7] As we have already seen in the previous chapter, recent research on the early political learning of American children clearly shows that existing institutional arrangements, e.g., the Presidency, and basic political processes, e.g., voting, are deeply ingrained. Though dissatisfaction with particular leaders and policies does occasionally arise, most Americans are probably hard put to conceive of significant political alternatives to existing structures. The deeply rooted quality of most political attachments is described in greater detail in Robert Weissberg, *Political Learning, Political Choice and Democratic Citizenship* (Englewood Cliffs: Prentice-Hall, Inc., 1974), especially Chaps. 3 and 4.

Hence in order to organize the political system so as to increase the likelihood of opinion-policy congruence, we would have to violate mass preferences. Barring some unforeseen political catastrophe, however, it is utopian to expect most Americans to part with their Constitutional order for purposes of a possible greater opinion-policy concordance.

Even if this Herculean job of convincing could successfully be accomplished, Chapter 4 also suggested that mechanisms to enhance the relationship between opinion and policy do not always perform as intended. In reviewing the discrepancies between intended consequences and actual consequences of devices such as the initiative, referenda, and the MINERVA system, we reached an overall conclusion akin to Murphy's First Law: If anything can possibly go wrong, it will (and at the worst possible moment). Our analysis did not, of course, settle the issue forever. Perhaps political systems in some other nations are better at translating opinion into policy; perhaps new mechanisms are waiting to be discovered that will yield dramatic results. The important point, however, is that offering drastic institutional solutions to improving opinion-policy congruence is no easy matter and can scarcely be viewed as panaceas.

What about "improving" existing translation mechanisms as a compromise between no change and instituting an entirely new system? Can we make elections into a more accurate device to transmit preferences into policy? Though changes in electoral politics may appear more modest than some of the other possibilities we have broached, such an impression is misleading. In the first place, once again we face the formidable problem of upgrading citizen political competence. And even if this were accomplished, it is not obvious exactly what institutional controls could be used to force elected leaders to heed public preferences. As we saw in Chapter 8, elections are at best approximate instruments of popular control and it is not clear that this can be changed unless government by continuous plebiscite were adopted (and this in turn would require major institutional modifications). This is not to claim that American elections are not worth "reforming"; rather, almost all suggested reforms, e.g., controlling campaign contributions, are unlikely to make elections a more sensitive and efficient conduit for popular sentiment.

Another possibility for relatively nondrastic reform of existing translation mechanisms emphasizes the role of political parties as conduits of popular influence. In particular, several political scientists have argued that American political parties should be made more ideologically distinctive and given greater power so that they could better implement their policies.[8] Advocates of this position, which is commonly referred to as the "responsible party" position,

---

[8] One of the clearest formulations of this position is found in The American Political Science Association Committee on Political Parties, "Towards a more Responsible Two-Party System," *The American Political Science Review* 44 (1950): Supplement. More generally, see Austin Ranney, *The Doctrine of Responsible Party Government* (Urbana, Ill.: The University of Illinois Press, 1962).

disagree over some details, but the essential characteristics would be as follows. First, two (or more) political parties would offer voters broad, coherent "packages" of policies. Typically, one package would be "liberal" and the other "conservative." Second, voters would select one party over the other and the victorious party would then systematically implement its program. Individualistic officials who deviated from their party's position would not be tolerated. Finally, institutional checks thwarting complete party domination of policy-making, e.g., separation of powers, judicial review, are eliminated so that the winning party has a free hand to implement its mandate.

Clearly on the face of it this "responsible party" solution has considerable appeal. Nevertheless, several objections can be raised. The most obvious one concerns the actual, as opposed to theoretical capacity to perform as an efficient mechanism translating opinion into policy. The British political system provides a good opportunity for the operation of the responsible party ideal but judging from their experience, several things can undermine the opinion-policy translation process. For example, intraparty factors can sometimes greatly constrain a party's ability to appeal to the general public. Moreover there are no real mechanisms for forcing political parties to take alternative positions on salient issues. In British politics this possibility is well illustrated by the unwillingness of either party to take a clear stand on the race issue despite its public salience.[9] More generally, once elected the only mechanism that exists to force the party to follow its program is the possibility of electoral defeat after several years of ruling. And, as we have seen from our analysis of U.S. Representatives, the possibility of electoral retribution is by itself not always sufficient to make leaders heed public sentiment.

The responsible parties solution is also vulnerable to the criticism that it too requires a level of citizen competence that is presently unrealistic. To be sure, the existence of two distinctive parties as opposed to a multitude of individualistic candidates does simplify voting, but the voter is still required to pick out the "best" candidate and punish leaders making the wrong decisions.[10] Perhaps even more damaging to the possibility of responsible party government is the fact that most citizens presently do not want such a system. Certainly few Americans would be willing to part with such constitutional features as separation of powers, checks and balances, an independent judicial system and a presidential form of government. Nor does the idea of filling

---

[9] For a more encompassing picture of how British politics deviates from the responsible party ideal despite opportunities for fulfillment, see David E. Butler, "American Myths about British Parties," *Virginia Quarterly Review* 31 (1955): 45-56.

[10] Data on British elections similarly show a picture of limited citizen political competence even though in principle politics is simplified by the existence of disciplined, ideologically oriented political parties. See, for example, David E. Butler and Anthony King, *The British General Election of 1965* (London: The Macmillan Co., 1965); and David Butler and Donald E. Stokes, *Political Change in Britain: Forces Shaping Electoral Choice* (New York: St. Martin's Press, 1969).

important positions on the basis of partisan considerations as opposed to civil service type criteria appeal to many citizens. Finally, as Dennis' study of attitudes towards political parties shows, there is little public support for a party system composed of sharply differentiated parties able to enforce its preferences on individual candidates.[11] Americans may not be completely satisfied with present parties, but Dennis' data clearly show that responsible parties are not the desired alternative.[12] In sum, then, changes in the party system, like changes in the electoral system, do not hold out much realistic promise for increasing opinion-policy congruence.

Changing patterns of political recruitment to make the elite a microcosm of the general population similarly involves difficult changes. As was true in other changes involving at least some modifications of the basic constitutional order, the greatest obstacle to such "reform" is that most citizens probably do not want this type of change. Recent controversies over so-called biological quotas, i.e., if blacks are 11 percent of the population they should therefore receive 11 percent of the jobs, make it clear while Americans probably want leaders to be *something* like the people they represent, *precise* correspondence is not desired. Moreover, even if the public did accept the principle of leaders perfectly reflecting nonleaders, the means to accomplish this goal are not self-evident. Which categories should be the basis of representation? Does a black female from the South represent blacks? females? or Southerners? The obvious solution to getting the best possible microcosm is selection by lottery, but even though this method is well supported by probability theory and was practised in ancient Athens, the idea of voting for leaders is too deeply ingrained in the public's values to be easily altered.

A final possible means for increasing opinion-policy congruence we shall consider concerns improving techniques for ascertaining true public preferences. To be sure, congruence demands more than merely knowing public preferences, but it is also true that (1) compared to other problems, the difficulties associated with improved survey accuracy appear minor and merely technical and (2) almost every change previously suggested requires an accurate expression of opinion so improving survey techniques, while not the answer, will be a step in the right direction. Would better polls encourage greater congruence? Probably not. Given the state of public thinking, it is more than likely that survey instruments sensitive to every nuance of thought would yield *less,* not more intelligible messages. Such a sensitive polling instrument would undoubtedly yield a highly confused portrait of public thinking. It would be as if an old

[11] Jack Dennis, "Support for the Party System by the Mass Public," *American Political Science Review,* 60 (1966): 600-615. Dennis' data are limited to residents of Wisconsin, but his conclusions are probably valid nationally.

[12] For example, only 31 percent agreed that things would be better if parties more frequently took opposing issue stands; 23 percent supported the idea of party leaders being able to coerce other office holders, and 53 percent agreed that our system of government would work much better if partisan conflict were eliminated. Dennis, "Support for the Party System by the Mass Public," p. 605.

phonograph record were placed on a modern high fidelity machine—in addition to the music we would also get an enormous quantity of extraneous noise faithfully reproduced. The simple Gallup type "yes" or "no" question on general issues, with minimal effort to weed out uninformed respondents, at least has the advantage of distorting the message to make it *appear* intelligible.

In view of all these costs in improving the relationship between opinion and policy we might as well ask: Is it worth it? What reasons exist for making the effort? One possible justification is that greater opinion-policy congruence would make the political system more democratic, and few would argue that democracy should not be promoted. In the first place, the assertion that more and more democracy is desirable is hardly an obvious truism. Not only would many people argue that democracy cannot be infinitely extended, but many people also believe that the existing political system—despite all the opinion-policy incongruity—is nevertheless sufficiently democratic. Moreover, this argument implicitly associates "democracy" with close congruence between mass preferences and public policy and this opinion-policy congruence is only rarely considered a unique or obligatory aspect of "democracy."[13] Definitions of democracy probably run into the thousands, but most of these emphasize the people as the source of ultimate political authority not the arbiter of day to day policy choices. Even those theories giving citizens some role in policy formation stop considerably short of saying that officials should be neutral conduits for citizen demands. In short, maximizing opinion-policy congruence is only loosely related to the amount or quality of democracy in the United States. Democracy and opinion-policy congruence are related, but this is not a one to one association and increased congruence does not automatically increase democracy.

Can a greater opinion-policy correspondence be justified in terms of making for better public policy? After all, defenders of the public's role in policy-making have occasionally claimed that "the public ultimately knows best." Unfortunately, this reasoning is very difficult to test, since reasonable people will differ over what are "good" or "bad," or "effective" policies. Furthermore, even if we could decide these complex issues, we rarely have cases where the expressed public will was unambiguously either flaunted or followed. Nevertheless, for the sake of argument let us consider the "goodness" or "badness" of two policy areas showing extremes of congruity—religion in public schools (perfect incongruity) and admission of Communist China to the United Nations (perfect congruity). If "the people know best" argument were true, the former policy should have produced "bad" results while the latter would yield "good" results.

Did court rulings against religious observances in schools prove disastrous while just the opposite occurred with the Communist China issue? Perhaps a full answer on the religion in public schools issue will not be known until the

---

[13] It would be impossible to review the many thousands of definitions of "democracy." A sampling of such conceptions can be found in M. Rejai, *Democracy: The Contemporary Theories* (New York: Atherton Press, 1967), Chaps. 1 and 2.

generation without such religious exposure reaches adulthood, but impressions thus far suggest that the courts' rulings have made little perceptible difference. It seems unlikely that the banning of Bible reading, the Lord's Prayer, and the like can be held accountable for sudden upsurges in juvenile immorality. As for the Communist China admission issue, there is a body of expert opinion claiming that U.S. resistance to U.N. membership was counterproductive to national interests.[14] Even if not a "bad" decision, resistance to admission did not appear to have the desired effect of isolating the Chinese or appreciably undermining communism. Of course, such brief analysis of only two policies (and certainly not two crucial policies) hardly constitute a full test of "the people know best" argument. However, this analysis does suggest that claims of collective competence cannot automatically be accepted as self-evident truths.

What about an argument that the existence of opinion-policy congruence is, in some sense, beneficial for the political system? That is, even if the electoral fortunes of leaders did not depend on heeding public sentiment, something could be gained by following this sentiment. One way of approaching this difficult and complex problem is to ask whether incongruity is associated with citizen attitudes not conducive to the effective functioning of government. Specifically, is it true that leaders' failure to satisfy popular preferences will lead to a decline in citizen respect for government, greater questioning of authority, and increased political estrangement? We shall approach these questions as follows. First we want to assess the extent to which perceptions about government responsiveness are rooted in actual policy outcomes. If citizen beliefs about government responsiveness are independent of real decisions, then even if these beliefs were important, leaders would be powerless to effect them one way or the other. Second, we shall consider the association between individuals' "successes" on policies and their beliefs about the honesty and competence of government and leaders. We shall assume it is beneficial to leaders if they are perceived positively and thus factors such as congruence which affect these perceptions are politically relevant.

To determine the extent to which beliefs about government responsiveness were associated with holding enacted policy preferences, we scored respondents on the 1968 SRC study according to whether or not their preferences were policy on twelve different issues.[15] Table 11-3 compares people's scores on this

---

[14] See for example, Lung-Chu Chen and Harold D. Lasswell, *Formosa, China and the United Nations* (New York: St. Martin's Press, 1967), Chap. 1; Foster Rhea Dulles, *American Policy Towards Communist China 1949-1969* (New York: Thomas Y. Crowell Co, 1972); and *A New China Policy*, a report prepared for the Americans Friends Service Committee (New Haven: Yale University Press, 1965), especially Chap. 4.

[15] The twelve issues were government aid to education, government involvement in medical care, government guarantees of employment, federal efforts to guarantee blacks fair treatment in employment, federal intervention in school integration, government action in public accomodations for blacks, support for foreign aid, the admission of Communist China to the U.N., trading with Communists, Vietnam involvement, and progress in public schools. Except for the admission of Communist China to the UN, and progress in public schools, support for these policies was scored as a policy "success."

Table 11-3 Beliefs About Whether Public Officials Care About Citizens and Successes on Public Policy, 1968

	Extent of Policy Successes				
Beliefs About Public Officials*	Low 1	2	3	High 4	Total
Officials Care	50.3%	62.9%	56.4%	66.7%	59.7%
Officials Don't Care	49.7	37.1	43.6	33.3	40.3
	100.0%	100.0%	100.0%	100.0%	100.0%
N =	429	334	195	517	1475

*The question was "Would you say that most public officials care quite a lot about what people like you think, or that they don't care much at all?"
SOURCE: Survey Research Center, University of Michigan.

indicator according to their beliefs about whether politicians care about citizens. Analysis of these data show some degree of association between beliefs and actual successes. This is especially true if we compare the least with the most successful—while about half of those with "low" success rates think officials care, two-thirds of very successful respondents believe that officials care. A similar conclusion can be drawn from the data in Table 11-4 which makes use of the question on people's beliefs about the attention given people's opinions by government. Observe that as the rate of policy successes increases, so does the likelihood of believing that government is attentive to citizen desires. Also note,

Table 11-4 Beliefs About Responsiveness of Public Officials and Success in Public Policy, 1968

	Extent of Policy Successes				
Beliefs About Public Officials' Attention To Public*	Low 1	2	3	High 4	Total
Officials very attentive	16.8%	22.8%	27.2%	30.8%	24.6%
Somewhat attentive	39.8	45.3	46.7	47.0	44.5
Not very attentive	43.4	31.9	26.0	22.2	30.9
	100.0%	100.0%	100.0%	100.0%	100.0%
N =	357	285	169	451	1262

*The question was: "Over the years, how much attention do you feel the government pays to what people think when it decides what to do: a good deal, some, or not much?"
SOURCE: Survey Research Center, University of Michigan.

however, that even among the most successful citizens, less than a majority believe government to be very attentive. Nevertheless, the data in Tables 11-3 and 11-4 do suggest some feedback between policy outcomes and political beliefs.

What about being "successful" on policy and evaluations of government? Does opinion-policy incongruity lead to hostile views of political authority? Tables 11-5 and 11-6 consider the question by examining levels of trust in national government and judgments in the competence of government. In both instances the relationship between policy success and evaluation is in the expected direction, but as in our previous findings, the association is very moderate. The strongest associations occur when we compare extremely unsuccessful respondents with the most successful group. It is important to realize, however, that these two extreme groups are not all that different in terms of the distribution of beliefs. For example, majorities in both groups agree that public officials are usually competent and neither group shows much support for the "always" or "none of the time" positions on the trust in government question (See Table 11-5).

On the whole, these data do not suggest that government failure to meet public preference on issues such as the national government's role in racial job discrimination, foreign aid, or subsidized medical care will have dramatic repercussions on citizen feelings toward the political system.[16] The consequences of incongruity are by no means trivial, but the size of these relationships

Table 11-5   Trusting the National Government and Successes on Public Policy, 1968

How Frequently Can One Trust Government*	*Extent of Policy Successes*				
	Low 1	2	3	High 4	Total
Always	4.5%	5.9%	7.6%	10.9%	7.5%
Most of time	44.1	55.9	65.9	60.0	55.3
Some of time	50.8	38.2	26.5	29.1	37.1
None of time	.5	.0	.0	.0	.2
	99.9%	100.0%	100.0%	100.0%	100.1%
N =	374	302	170	460	1310

*The question was: "How much of the time do you think you can trust the government in Washington to do what is right?"
SOURCE: Survey Research Center, University of Michigan.

[16] For an analysis of a similar set of relationships employing the 1970 SRC election data, see Arthur H. Miller, "Political Issues and Trust in Government, 1964-70," *American Political Science Review* 68 (1974): 951-72. Also see Jack Citrin, "Comment: The Political Relevance of Trust in Government," in the same issue of the *American Political Science Review*: 973-88.

Table 11-6 Beliefs in Competence of Government Officials and
Successes on Public Policy, 1968

Belief in Govt.'s Competency*	Extent of Policy Successes				
	Low 1	2	3	High 4	Total
Public officials					
usually competent	51.9%	55.5%	66.1%	66.4%	59.7%
Usually incompetent	46.5	43.1	31.6	31.4	38.5
Depends	1.6	1.3	2.3	2.2	1.8
	100.0%	99.9%	100.0%	100.0%	100.0%
N =	376	299	171	458	1304

*The question was: "Do you feel that almost all of the people running
the government are smart people who usually know what they are doing,
or do you think that quite a lot of them don't seem to know what they
are doing?"
SOURCE: Survey Research Center, University of Michigan.

does not suggest a picture of extreme popular disenchantment when people lose
on these sorts of issues. Given what we know of the early political socialization
of most citizens, that beliefs about government honesty, responsiveness, or
competence are relatively impervious to many subsequent events should come as
no surprise. Of course, this does not mean that leaders can do anything they
want without generating hostile attitudes. Our analysis does not address the
violation of deeply held preferences, e.g., support for the constitutional order,
and it is more more than likely that should leaders oppose these types of
policies, public reaction would be intense and widespread.

What about greater opinion-policy congruence contributing to individual
happiness? It is not unreasonable to suppose that regardless of whether
popularly supported policies are "good" or "bad" for the nation as a whole, or
even whether they affect attitudes towards politics, citizens will be happier when
they get the policies they prefer. One way of testing this assertion is to see
whether the amount of policy success one has is associated with personal
satisfaction with life. These data are presented in Table 11-7. Unlike our
previous analyses of successes on public policy, even comparisons of the most
and least successful categories shows no relationship (the figures in both columns
are virtually identical). In short, most citizens are reasonably well satisfied (at
least in 1968) and being a big policy winner or loser makes little apparent
difference.

When we stop and recall some of the data we reviewed in Chapter 3 on the
relevance of politics for most people, this lack of an association is no surprise.
Most political issues are not salient to most citizens, and it is probably true that
many of the policy questions in our index are not the type that excite large

Table 11-7   Personal Satisfaction with Life and Success on Public
Policy, 1968.

Satisfaction With Life*	*Extent of Policy Successes*				
	Low 1	2	3	High 4	Total
Completely satisfying	23.6%	22.4%	27.4%	23.9%	24.0%
Pretty satisfying	64.8	69.6	61.1	65.9	65.8
Not very satisfying	11.5	8.0	11.4	10.2	10.2
	99.9%	100.0%	99.9%	100.0%	100.0%
N =	381	312	175	472	1340

*The question was: "In general, how satisfying do you find the way
you're spending your life these days?"
SOURCE: Survey Research Center, University of Michigan.

numbers of citizens. Under such conditions of low centrality, we obviously
cannot expect differing outcomes to make a significant difference in one's
overall personal satisfaction. Clearly, it is unreasonable to suppose that a
favorably perceived Supreme Court decision on religious observances in public
schools would be as satisfying as, say, a salary increase, the purchase of a new
home, or similar personal accomplishments. Perhaps such policy victories are
personally meaningful to those devoting their lives to politics, but this group is
only a small minority in the United States.

What about concrete benefits of opinion-policy congruence in policy areas
likely to have considerable personal meaning? Imagine, for example, the personal
impact on blacks if the federal government suddenly agreed to all black policy
demands. Consider what the joyful reaction among those strongly opposing the
Vietnam war would have been if in 1968 President Johnson had suddenly
announced total and immediate troop withdrawal. That some citizens will be
enormously satisfied by certain political outcomes is self-evident, but it is
essential to realize that such intense individual satisfaction may or may not be
associated with *overall* opinion-policy congruence. As we saw in Chapter 8,
citizens exhibit considerable diversity in what deeply concerns them, so even a
policy satisfying those most concerned with an issue may only satisfy only a
very small portion of the general public. In 1968, for example, a decision to
withdraw from Vietnam, while vastly increasing *some* people's policy satisfaction, would nevertheless result in incongruity at the *overall* level. Hence, unless
we were willing to redefine "majority" to give special weight to issue publics
with intense preferences, the argument that opinion-policy congruence at the
general level necessarily furthers satisfaction in areas of deep personal concern,
must be rejected. Put somewhat differently, in giving everyone their most
important demand, leaders could very well *decrease* the overall opinion-policy

relationship. Personal satisfaction with salient public policy can equally occur under conditions of congruence and incongruence.

Do all of our preceding analyses suggest that efforts to achieve opinion-policy congruence are so difficult and costly compared to possible benefits that efforts in this direction ought to be abandoned? Of course not. On several occasions we have stressed the importance of maintaining opinion-policy congruence on policies considered the "givens" of American politics. These are the almost unthinkingly accepted institutional structures and roles that narrow the day to day controversies to a range of policy choices tolerable to virtually all citizens. Thus, instead of arguing about, say, whether there should be an independent United States, citizens debate whether the defense budget should be cut or increased by 5 billion dollars. Needless to say, because these broad policy choices are so deeply and so universally accepted, it takes little (if any) conscious leadership effort to maintain this opinion-policy congruence despite its overwhelming importance.

It is also important to realize that even if leaders' efforts to achieve opinion-policy congruence on day to day issues shows mixed results, it may nevertheless be essential that leaders *appear* to make vast efforts to improve congruence. Most citizens probably do not want public officials to heed slavishly every popular whim, but by the same token no official is above making symbolic, somewhat ritualistic homage to following popular desires. Even when officials publicly proclaim that they are heeding their own instincts and not popular clamor, most citizens would like to be reassured that at least in the long run, or in some way not immediately obvious, their desires are being taken into account. This situation is perhaps not unlike public veneration of "democracy"—citizens possess only a vague understanding of "democracy" and are willing to accept violations of democratic principles in practice, but it would be intolerable for a leader to denounce "democracy."

What is clear from our preceding analyses is that the real question is not one of opinion-policy congruity versus incongruity, but of how much congruity and on what policy choices. What the answer to this question is, we cannot say. Probably no two people agree precisely on what issues and to what extent opinions and policy ought to be in accordance. What we can say, however, is that *perfect* congruity is not part of this debate. Even if such perfection were possible, and we have time and again suggested otherwise, it is unlikely that perfect opinion-policy congruence occupies the highest position in people's political priorities. No doubt some citizens are genuinely afraid of a government automatically translating every popular sentiment into policy. For such people, constitutional barriers to popular rule, the "failure" of direct legislation mechanisms, imperfection in polling technology, ambiguities in messages conveyed by surveys, the ability of elections to control public officials, and the like are virtues, not defects of the present political system. Other citizens may base their opposition to perfect congruence on mass incompetency. If men were all-knowing angels, government in strict accordance with public opinion would be desirable, these people would argue, but given what we know about the average citizen's capabilities, such government would be disastrous. Yet others would reject perfect congruence on personal grounds—being asked to make choices on all policy questions would interfere too much with more pressing nonpolitical matters, In short, while we must acknowledge the importance of some opinion-policy congruity, the glorification of perfection is unnecessary and likely to be an exercise in futility.

INDEX